A Practitioner's Guide to Correcting Mistakes in Pension Schemes

Paul Newman QC
Wilberforce Chambers

Bloomsbury Professional

LONDON • DUBLIN • EDINBURGH • NEW YORK • NEW DELHI • SYDNEY

BLOOMSBURY PROFESSIONAL

Bloomsbury Publishing Plc
50 Bedford Square, London, WC1B 3DP, UK
1385 Broadway, New York, NY 10018, USA
29 Earlsfort Terrace, Dublin 2, Ireland

British Library Cataloguing-in-Publication Data

A catalogue record for this book is available from the British Library.

ISBN: PB: 978 152652 270 2
Epub: 978 152652 271 9
Epdf: 978 152652 272 6

Typeset by Evolution Design & Digital Ltd (Kent)
Printed and bound by CPI Group (UK) Ltd, Croydon, CR0 4YY

Foreword

Mistakes in pension scheme documentation and administration are all too common. There is no wonder given the complexity of scheme documentation which has often built up incrementally over many decades, and the interaction of the provisions themselves with complex primary and secondary legislation in relation to both pensions and tax.

Those mistakes can have a profound effect on pensioners and active members alike. Mistakes can also be extremely serious and very costly for employers and may threaten the continuation of the business itself.

The Office for National Statistics estimated that as at 31 December 2020, the total membership of both defined benefit and defined contribution funded occupational pension schemes was in the region of 41 million. Apart from inheritance, pensions are perhaps one of the chief ways in which the law intersects with people's lives, and in just the same way, it may do so at a time when they are at their most vulnerable.

With all this in mind, I very much welcome this comprehensive, clear and authoritative book which will be an essential resource for all pension practitioners and trustees.

It brings together a wide variety of possibilities which may be open to trustees, employers, members and practitioners once mistakes and their accompanying issues are discovered, and contains valuable practical guidance about how those possibilities can be best pursued. It will assist both in the avoidance of mistakes and in their correction.

It also provides the practitioner with a clear guide to the essential law and practice in an area which is often a morass of detail and which is fraught with complexity and uncertainty. It also maintains a careful balance between the legal and the practical which will be welcome to all.

Dame Sarah Asplin
Sussex

Preface

Well, nobody's perfect!

Osgood Fielding III

Mistakes in the administration of pension schemes are as widespread as they are potentially serious for trustees, employers and members. The complexity of schemes, their interaction with legislation and tax practice, and their long-term operation provide fertile ground for the making of mistakes. Moreover, pension scheme documents were historically prepared by insurers and benefits consultants who were not legally trained, and who often relied on precedents which were out of date or otherwise not wholly fit for purpose.

Changes in pensions law and practice over the years have led to many schemes undertaking comprehensive document reviews, which have disclosed drafting and other administration errors. Such reviews have also taken place during the process of buying in and buying out benefits with insurers, who require clarity on the liabilities they are being asked to undertake.

As a result, the past 25 years have seen a significant increase in the number of court and Pensions Ombudsman decisions on the correction of pension scheme mistakes, most notably in the fields of rectification and construction. This reflects the number and cost of such mistakes, which have led to attempts to find imaginative legal solutions to these problems.

The discovery of mistakes can have serious consequences beyond the scheme itself, where the error was the responsibility of the advisers to the trustees or the employer, perhaps the same advisers who initially discovered the error. The importance of dealing effectively with mistakes is therefore heightened by underlying issues of liability which may arise if the mistakes cannot be put right.

The purpose of this book is to provide those involved in making decisions and giving advice in relation to pension schemes with the material for considering how pension scheme mistakes may be corrected and – if possible – avoided in the future. It is intended to be both a legal and a practical guide, and most of the chapters contain specific sections discussing practical considerations which arise in the context of such mistakes.

The structure of the book is as follows. **Chapter 1** introduces the types of mistake which arise in pension schemes. **Chapters 2** to **9** discuss various legal techniques used to correct mistakes in changes made by scheme documents. **Chapters 10** to **12** discuss how to deal with mistakes made in the payment of benefits to members, leading to overpayments, underpayments or incorrectly calculated transfer payments. **Chapter 13** deals with mistakes in the decision-making process leading to the exercise of pension scheme powers. **Chapter 14** gives an overview of the principal tribunals in which pensions mistakes may be corrected: the Pensions Ombudsman and the courts. **Chapter 15** deals with compromises of claims, which is a popular method for correcting mistakes. **Chapter 16** considers the scope for recovering losses caused by mistakes from the professional advisers involved in their commission. The book concludes with a consideration in **Chapter 17** of the tax issues that commonly arise in the course of correcting mistakes.

The book is specifically aimed at trust-based occupational pension schemes, although many of the principles are equally applicable to private trusts. Contract-based personal pensions and public sector pensions give rise to their own issues which are outside the scope of this book. Unless the context requires otherwise, all references in this book to scheme members include their contingent beneficiaries.

I would like to thank Mark Atkinson, Mark Blyth, Rosalind Connor, Emma Game, David Pollard and Dan Schaffer, who very kindly read draft chapters of this book and whose comments have considerably improved it. My thanks also to Mark Jenkins, and particularly to Dame Sarah Asplin for writing the foreword.

All remaining errors are, of course, my own. Should anyone have comments or suggestions as to how future editions of this book may be improved, please contact me at pnewman@wilberforce.co.uk.

I would finally like to thank my wife, Emily Campbell, for her wisdom and her forbearance, but most of all for the fun and chats.

The law is stated as at 1 December 2021.

Paul Newman QC
Wilberforce Chambers
December 2021

Contents

Abbreviations

Legislation

AJA 1985	Administration of Justice Act 1985
FA 2004	Finance Act 2004
ITEPA 2003	Income Tax (Earnings and Pensions) Act 2003
LA 1980	Limitation Act 1980
PSA 1993	Pension Schemes Act 1993
PA 1995	Pensions Act 1995
PA 2004	Pensions Act 2004
Contracting-out Regulations	The Occupational Pension Schemes (Contacting-out) Regulations 1996 (SI 1996/1172)

Other legal material

Chancery Guide	HM Courts & Tribunals Service, Chancery Guide 2016 (as amended)
CPR	Civil Procedure Rules
PD	Practice Direction
PTM	HMRC Pensions Tax Manual

Textbooks

Goff & Jones	Charles Mitchell, Paul Mitchell and Stephen Watterson (eds), *Goff & Jones: The Law of Unjust Enrichment* (9th edn, Sweet & Maxwell, 2016)
Jackson & Powell	John L Powell QC and Roger Stewart QC (eds), *Jackson & Powell on Professional Liability* (8th edn, Sweet & Maxwell, 2017)
Lewin	Lynton Tucker, Nicholas le Poidevin QC and James Brightwell (eds), *Lewin on Trusts* (20th edn, Sweet & Maxwell, 2020)
Lewison	Sir Kim Lewison, *The Interpretation of Contracts* (7th edn, Sweet & Maxwell, 2020)
Phipson	Hodge Malek QC (ed), *Phipson on Evidence* (19th edn, Sweet & Maxwell, 2018)

Other abbreviations

CARE	Career Average Revalued Earnings
DB	Defined Benefits

DC	Defined Contribution
GMP	Guaranteed Minimum Pension
HMRC	Her Majesty's Revenue and Customs
IDRP	Internal Dispute Resolution Procedure
PASA	Pension Administration Standards Association
PPF	Pension Protection Fund

Table of Statutes

Table of Statutory Instruments

Table of European Legislation

Table of Cases

B

D

I

J

K

L

M

P

Table of Pensions Ombudsman Determinations

Y

1 Types of Mistake

A taxonomy of pensions mistakes

1.1

This book focuses on three broad types of mistake which commonly arise in pension schemes: mistakes in documents making changes to the terms of the scheme (document errors); administrative mistakes leading to the payment of wrong benefits to members (administration errors); and mistakes in the trustees' or employer's decision-making process (decision errors).

1.2

Each of these involve errors in the exercise by the trustees and/or the employer of powers conferred by the scheme rules or by legislation. There are a number of ways in which mistakes in the exercise of such powers can be categorised,[1] but the most fundamental distinction is between acts which are outside the scope of the power and acts which are within the scope of the power but which constitute a breach of duty: the former renders the exercise of the power ineffective (void), whereas the latter causes the exercise of the power to be capable of being nullified by the court (voidable).[2]

1 Dr Jessica Hudson and Professor Charles Mitchell have identified ten different reasons for the defective exercise of pension scheme powers: Hudson and Mitchell 'Legal Consequences of the Flawed Exercise of Scheme Powers' in Agnew, Davies and Mitchell (eds), *Pensions: Law, Policy and Practice* (Hart, 2020), ch 7. See also *Lewin on Trusts* (20th edn, Sweet & Maxwell, 2020) (*Lewin*), para 30-101.

2 *Sieff v Fox* [2005] EWHC 1312 (Ch), [2005] 1 WLR 3811 at [38] per Lloyd LJ; *Pitt v Holt* [2011] EWCA Civ 197, [2012] Ch 132 at [96] per Lloyd LJ and [2013] UKSC 26, [2013] AC 108 at [93] per Lord Walker of Gestingthorpe.

1.3

Before these are considered in detail, mention should be made of another type of mistake which commonly occurs in pension scheme documents, arising by reason of a failure to reflect UK or EU legislation which affects scheme benefits in a way that overrides the terms of the scheme. However, there is generally little or no scope for the correction of such mistakes: all that can be done is to ascertain the consequences of the error on the validity of the document and on the liabilities of the scheme; and these can give rise to issues of statutory construction. One such provision which is of particular relevance to pension schemes, however, is the restriction on amendments imposed by s 37 of the Pension Schemes Act 1993 (PSA 1993): this is considered in **Chapter 3**.

Document errors

1.4

Where a document error has led to the underprovision of benefits, the correction of that error by the exercise of the amendment power is unlikely to be legally problematic, if care is taken not to infringe any prohibition on the retrospective exercise of the power. However, increases to past and future benefits may well have tax implications.[1]

1 See **17.11–17.64**.

1.5

The principal challenges arise where the document error has led to the conferral of an unintended entitlement to benefits, as both legislation and scheme provisions make it very difficult to correct such errors by amendment.[1]

1 See **Chapter 3**.

1.6

Document errors requiring correction most commonly arise because of the following:

(a) a failure to comply with the requisite formalities for valid amendments;

(b) a failure to comply with restrictions on amendments contained in the amendment power; and

(c) a failure to reflect the intentions of the parties to the document.

Failure to comply with the formalities for valid amendments

1.7

Most amendment powers in occupational pension schemes require changes to comply with certain formalities,[1] for example, that the changes be recorded in a formal document such as a deed or a resolution signed by all the trustees, or that the employer must consent to any amendment made by the trustees.[2]

1 Other scheme powers may also contain similar requirements, such as for the appointment or removal of trustees (which is dealt with at **1.41–1.42**) or for the augmentation of benefits (the correction of which, by a fresh exercise of the same power, will generally not be problematic).

2 Another example relates to certain very old schemes which were registered under the Superannuation and other Trust Funds (Validation) Act 1927, as any amendment of such a scheme is required by s 3(3) of that Act to be registered with the Financial Conduct Authority. Examples of exercises of powers invalidated by a failure to obtain the consent of a non-party include *Re Forster's Settlement* [1942] Ch 199 and *Ritchie v Blakeley* [1985] 1 NZLR 630.

1.8

Prior to the turn of this century, there was a view within the pensions industry that changes, such as those which needed to be made in order to comply with the EU requirement to equalise male and female benefits,[1] could be validly effected by informal means such as announcements or explanatory booklets, without regard to any requirement in the amendment power for the change to be made more formally. That view was often justified on the basis that members who had been notified of the changes would be estopped from denying their validity.[2] However, that view was firmly rejected in 2001 in *Bestrustees plc v Stuart*,[3] in which Neuberger J required strict compliance with the formalities of the amendment power, explaining his decision in the following terms:

> 'I bear in mind that a pension scheme is likely to continue for a substantial period of time and that those most affected by them and entitled to protection from the trustees, the employer and indeed the Court, will be people who are comparatively poor, who will not have easy access to expert legal advice, and who will not know what has been going on in relation to the management of the Scheme. In those circumstances, it seems to me that protection of the beneficiaries requires the Court to be very careful before it permits a departure from the plain wording and plain requirements of the trust deed.'

1 See **1.34**.
2 Reliance may also have been placed on Knox J's comment in *LRT Pension Fund Trustee Co v Hatt* [1993] Pens LR 227 at [112], set out at **1.42**.
3 [2001] EWHC 549 (Ch), [2001] Pens LR 283 at [34].

1.9

This was the first in a long line of cases which have adopted the same uncompromising attitude to amendment powers.[1] This approach was most graphically explained by Peter Smith J in *Walker Morris Trustees Ltd v Masterson*,[2] when rejecting an argument that strict adherence to the formalities involved an overly-technical construction of the power:

> 'This is to misunderstand the problem. It is not the clause and its construction that is the difficulty; it is the failure of the Trustees to consider the clause and its impact. … I accept that the consequences are unfortunate. However, one cannot bend the construction and try and find an ambiguity or difficulty so as to re-draft the clause to dispense with what was considered to be a fundamental requirement by the draftsman.'

1 *Capital Cranfield Trust Corp v Sagar* [2002] OPLR 151; *Trustee Solutions Ltd v Dubery* [2006] EWHC 1426 (Ch), [2007] ICR 412; *Sovereign Trustees Ltd v Glover* [2007] EWHC 1750 (Ch), [2007] Pens LR 277; *Independent Trustee Services Ltd v Knell* [2010] EWHC 650 (Ch), [2010] Pens LR 195; *Capita ATL Pension Trustees Ltd v Gellately* [2011] EWHC 485 (Ch), [2011] Pens LR 153; *Safeway Ltd v Newton* [2017] EWCA Civ 1482, [2018] Pens LR 2.
2 [2009] EWHC 1955 (Ch), [2009] Pens LR 307 at [48].

1.10

Consequently, it is now generally accepted – at least as far as English law is concerned[1] – that the courts will be inclined to require changes to pension schemes to adhere to the formal requirements of the amendment power.

1 Scottish law tends to adopt a more relaxed attitude in such cases: *Low & Bonar plc v Mercer Ltd* [2010] CSOH 47; *Scottish Solicitors Staff Pension Fund v Pattison & Sim* 2016 SC 284; *Bett Homes Ltd v Wood* [2016] CSIH 26.

1.11

Such an attitude is not, of course, the same as the court striving to construe exercises of amendment powers as invalid. On the contrary, when faced with competing constructions one of which does, and one of which does not, result in invalidity the court will prefer the one which does not, in the absence of compelling reasons to the contrary. Thus, in *Premier Foods Group Services Ltd v RHM Pension Trust Ltd*,[1] Warren J adopted a purposive construction of a 'deed of intention', holding that it had been effective in amending the scheme, rather than merely expressing an intention to amend later, notwithstanding that a subsequent deed had been executed which repeated the terms of the amendment.

1 [2012] EWHC 447 (Ch), [2012] Pens LR 151.

Effect of non-compliance

1.12

A failure to comply with the formalities of the amendment power is outside the scope of the power, so that the exercise of the power is void and the amendment is invalid.[1]

1 See, for example, *Bestrustees plc v Stuart* [2001] EWHC 549 (Ch), [2001] Pens LR 283 at [50] per Neuberger J.

Failure to comply with restrictions on amendments

1.13

Many amendment powers contain restrictions which prohibit certain types of amendments. The range of prohibitions can vary considerably, but typical restrictions are those which provide that the amendment power cannot be exercised to:

(a) alter the objects or main purposes of the scheme;

(b) provide for the payment of any scheme assets to the employer, save on the winding-up of the scheme;

(c) prejudice the favourable tax status of the scheme; or

(d) detrimentally affect members' benefits.

1.14

For the purposes of this book, by far the most important of these is the final restriction, which has not only been the cause of many document errors but has also operated as a significant obstacle to the correction of those errors. This restriction, and the different forms which it may take in practice, are discussed in **Chapter 3**. Many schemes established after the coming into force of s 67 of the Pensions Act 1995 (PA 1995)[1] will limit this type of restriction to the protection covered by that provision; however, many other restrictions operate to protect members' benefits in ways which exceed the scope of that provision.

1 See **3.34-3.37**.

1.15

At one time, the restriction on the payment of scheme assets to the employer, which derived from old Inland Revenue requirements for approval of occupational pension schemes,[1] was an important restriction, and a number of early pensions cases involved attempts by employers to circumvent it.[2] However, the importance of such restrictions had diminished by the late 1990s, following the introduction of statutory conditions on the return of surplus to the employer[3] and the general disappearance of surpluses in occupational pension schemes.

1 See *Mettoy Pension Trustees Ltd v Evans* [1990] 1 WLR 1587, 1630 per Warner J.
2 For example, *Taylor v Lucas Pensions Trust Ltd* [1994] Pens LR 9; *Hillsdown Holdings plc v The Pensions Ombudsman* [1997] 1 All ER 862; *Harwood-Smart v Caws* [2000] Pens LR 101.
3 Sections 37 and 76 of PA 1995.

1.16

Another potential restriction on the use of the amendment power arises on the winding-up of the scheme. The general rule is that an amendment power cannot be exercised during that period, because the winding-up provision usually obliges the trustees to administer the scheme in mandatory terms, which is inconsistent with the existence of a right to change the scheme's provisions.[1] However, this rule can be overridden by an express term in the amendment power,[2] and there is no reason in principle why such a term cannot be inserted into the amendment power prior to the commencement of the winding-up.[3] The general rule also does not apply while the scheme is closed to new members and accruals,[4] or (probably) during the period of notice given by the employer to terminate its liability for contributions.[5]

1 *Jones v Williams* [1989] Pens LR 17 at [21] per Knox J; *Thrells v Lomas* [1993] 1 WLR 456, 462 per Sir Donald Nicholls V-C; *Leadenhall Independent Trustees Ltd v Welham* [2004] OPLR 115 at [11] per Park J. Cf. *Air Jamaica Ltd v Charlton* [1999] 1 WLR 1399, 1411 in which Lord Millett stated that it was difficult to see how the scheme could lawfully be amended '*in any significant respect*' once it had actually been discontinued; however, in *Scully v Coley* [2009] UKPC 29 at [49], Lord Collins of Mapesbury agreed with Lord Millett's statement, but without reference to that qualification.
2 As was the case in *Capital Cranfield Trust Corp v Sagar* [2002] OPLR 151.
3 See **3.53–3.57**.
4 *Re Edward Jones Benevolent Fund* (8 March 1985, unreported), Deputy Judge Chadwick QC.
5 *Municipal Mutual Insurance Ltd v Harrop* [1998] Pens LR 149 at [55] per Rimer J.

Effect of non-compliance

1.17

The consequences of a failure to comply with the restrictions on amendments will depend upon the nature of the restriction and the scope of the amendment.

1.18

If the restriction operates as a precondition of the validity of the amendment, and the amendment in question wholly fails to comply with the restriction, the exercise of the power is void and the amendment is invalid.[1]

1 See, for example, *Walker Morris Trustees Ltd v Masterson* [2009] EWHC 1955 (Ch), [2009] Pens LR 307 at [46], where the trustees failed to comply with the requirement in the restriction that the actuary advise them that the amendment did not prejudice the protected rights.

1.19

If the restriction operates as a precondition of the validity of the amendment, and the amendment complies with the restriction to some extent but also operates beyond its constraints, that is an example of an excessive execution of a power. Whilst that part of the exercise which is not compliant will be void, the question then arises as to whether the whole exercise is vitiated or whether it is possible to allow the compliant part of the exercise to take effect.[1] A classic example of such an amendment is one which reduces members' benefits in respect of both past and future service, in contravention of a restriction which protects benefits referable to the former period of service but not benefits referable to the latter. The (not wholly satisfactory) legal treatment of such amendments is considered in **Chapter 4**. That chapter also deals with the application of statutory restrictions on the amendment of pension schemes, most notably s 67 of PA 1995, the current version of which renders the amendment in question voidable rather than void.

1 *Lewin*, paras 30-106–30-107.

1.20

Finally, the restriction may not operate as a precondition of the validity of the amendment at all, so that a failure to comply with it will not affect the amendment. Thus, in *Betafence Ltd v Veys*,[1] the amendment power required the trustees to notify each affected member of the amendment, but did not expressly make the validity of the amendment conditional upon compliance with that requirement. Lightman J held that the accident of a failure of notification did not prejudice the legal effect of the amendment, and did no more than give a possible basis for a claim for compensation against the trustees to a member who was able to show prejudice by reason of the failure.

1 [2006] EWHC 999 (Ch), [2006] Pens LR 137 at [67]. See also *HR Trustees Ltd v Wembley plc* [2011] EWHC 2974 (Ch) at [69] per Vos J.

1.21

Whether the restriction operates in that way will depend on its proper construction. In *Briggs v Gleeds (Head Office)*,[1] the relevant amendment power provided as follows:

> 'The Principal Employer and the Trustees may from time to time without the concurrence of the Members by deed alter or add to the terms and provisions of the Rules and the trusts, powers and provisions of this Deed

whether retrospectively or otherwise. The Principal Employer and the Trustees shall forthwith declare such alteration or addition in writing and the Deed and/or Rules shall stand amended accordingly.'

1 [2014] EWHC 1178 (Ch), [2015] Ch 212 at [84]–[85].

1.22

It was contended on behalf of the members that a particular amendment was invalid because it had not been declared in writing by the employer and the trustees, and that the rules were to '*stand amended*' only when an appropriate declaration had been made. Newey J rejected that contention – albeit with some hesitation – on the basis that it would create a good deal of scope for argument as to whether an amendment had been sufficiently declared: how much detail had to be given? Was it good enough to post information on a website? Was it adequate to say something in a newsletter? What would the position have been if letters sent to some members had gone astray? Would an amendment have taken effect when letters were posted or on some later date? The judge therefore construed the declaration requirement as not being a pre-condition of an effective amendment, relying on the principle that a pension scheme should be construed so as to give a reasonable and practical effect to the scheme, and that it was necessary to test competing permissible constructions of a pension scheme against the consequences they produce in practice.[1]

1 See **5.6–5.12**.

Failure to reflect the intentions of the parties

1.23

The final type of error differs from the other two types, in that it does not result in the actual or potential invalidity of the act recorded in a formal document: the document operates according to its terms, but not in the way that the parties to it intended.

1.24

Mistakes which fall into this category include simple clerical errors such as missing words or wrongly transposed terms, and more complex drafting errors, arising from a lack of appreciation of how provisions interact with each other or from a misunderstanding by the drafter of what the parties intended the document to achieve.

Methods of correcting document errors

1.25

Chapters 2 to **9** consider the various methods by which document errors may be corrected. What these demonstrate is that there is relatively limited scope for correcting errors caused by the failure to comply with either the formalities required by, or the restrictions contained in, the amendment power:

(a) as to the failure to comply with formalities, there are legal techniques for dealing with missing evidence of compliance (**Chapter 2**) as well as the equitable concepts of relief for defective execution and 'equity treating as done that which ought to be done' (**Chapter 8**), the latter of which may be used to strengthen the possibility of correcting such errors without the need for an application to court;

(b) as to the failure to comply with restrictions, unless the amendment power itself can be used to correct the failure to comply with the restriction (**Chapter 3**), all that is likely to be left is to try to salvage part of the amendment which is not affected by the restriction (**Chapter 4**).[1]

1 However, **Chapter 9** (at **9.5**) refers to the possible use of contract to avoid falling into the error of making a substantive amendment which would infringe a restriction in the amendment power.

1.26

By contrast, there are several effective methods for correcting document errors caused by the failure to reflect the intentions of the parties: corrective construction (**Chapter 5**), rectification (**Chapter 6**), and setting aside for mistake (**Chapter 7**).

1.27

This book recognises that trustees, employers and their advisers will, if at all possible, wish to avoid a remedy that involves an application to court, given the costs, delays and attendant publicity. These chapters accordingly include practical suggestions for self-help remedies to increase the prospects of managing the risks on the discovery of document errors.

1.28

Finally, for all document errors, it may be argued that the parties should be bound by contract or estoppel to accept the changes which were intended to be made, notwithstanding the error (**Chapter 9**).

Administration errors

1.29

Mistakes in the general administration of the scheme can lead to the payment of incorrect benefits without the occurrence of any document error or decision error. The issue of whether the mistake renders the exercise of the power void or voidable is irrelevant, as the trustees will in any event be under an obligation to make good any underpayments (subject to any valid defences they may have) and to at least consider whether to recover any overpayments.

1.30

Overpayments of benefits raise practical issues of how to handle their recovery fairly and sensitively. Where benefits have been underpaid in error, the trustees will usually be obliged to make a catch-up payment, together with interest, unless the provisions of the scheme relieve them from that obligation. These issues, together with the particular problems associated with compensating or recovering from members who have transferred their benefits to other arrangements, are dealt with in **Chapters 10** to **12**.

Decision errors

1.31

For decision errors, unlike the other two types of error, the focus is not on mistakes in the implementation of the decision, but on mistakes in the decision-making process which led to the exercise of the power. Whilst a number of the methods of correcting errors identified above are also relevant to decision errors – most notably setting aside for mistake – the particular characteristics of decision errors merit separate treatment, and are dealt with in **Chapter 13**.

Practice point 1: amendments to look out for when reviewing scheme documents

1.32

Pensions mistakes often lay undetected for years, with the scheme being administered in the meantime in ignorance of those errors. Mistakes tend to surface on the review of scheme documents on the change of legal adviser, and now more frequently during a buy-out of scheme benefits, where the trustees' and insurer's advisers conduct a root and branch review of the benefits specification in the scheme. In that latter situation, there is often a lack of time and appetite to correct any discovered errors, and the risk of a claim from members for increased benefits due to the mistake is often apportioned between the insurer and the employer (with an appropriate indemnity for the trustees) on the winding-up of the scheme.

1.33

When reviewing pension scheme documents to determine whether they are consistent and correct, practitioners should be particularly aware of the following types of amendments, which commonly give rise to mistakes and which, if not corrected, will lead to increases in liabilities or difficulties for the administration of the scheme.

Equalisation of retirement ages

1.34

A very common type of document error in the 1990s and 2000s involved attempts to comply with the EU law requirement to remove sex discrimination in the provision of pension benefits, by adopting a common normal retirement age for male and female members. As a result of a series of cases in the European Court of Justice,[1] the requirements for the equal treatment of male and female benefits were established as follows:[2]

(a) for benefits relating to pensionable service prior to 17 May 1990,[3] it was not contrary to EU law for male and female pension benefits to be provided at different ages, such as 65 for men and 60 for women;

(b) a scheme could be amended to equalise benefits up or down, for example, to set both male and female members' retirement ages at 60 or 65;

(c) however, for pensionable service between 17 May 1990 and the date of any such amendment (known as the '*Barber* window'), male members were entitled to be treated as if their retirement date age was 60 if that was the female members' retirement age.

Thus, to terminate the favourable treatment of male members during the *Barber* window, it was necessary to equalise retirement ages by way of a valid amendment to the scheme.

1 In particular, *Barber v Guardian Royal Exchange* [1991] 1 QB 344 and *Coloroll Pension Trustees Ltd v Russell* [1994] OPLR 179.
2 See, for example, *ICM Computer Group Ltd v Stribley* [2013] EWHC 2995 (Ch), [2013] Pens LR 409 at [7] per Asplin J.
3 The date of the *Barber* decision.

1.35

Attempts to comply with this requirement often led to two types of document error:

(a) a failure to comply with the formalities in the amendment powers, caused by a widespread but often mistaken belief amongst benefits consultants that the requisite changes could be made by informal means such as announcements and explanatory booklets;[1] and

(b) a failure to comply with the restrictions in amendment powers which protected members' accrued rights, caused by the implementation of the equalisation requirement which adversely affected female members' accrued benefits, such as increasing their retirement age to align with that of male members, without giving them a right to retire on an unreduced pension at their previous retirement age in respect of already-accrued service.

1 See **1.8**.

1.36

Although the publicity generated by the widespread commission of these errors means that the equalisation status of many schemes has already been investigated, there are likely still to be many schemes whose benefits have not yet been properly equalised by reason of document errors.

Reductions to benefits

1.37

Another common type of document error requiring correction arises from steps taken by employers to reduce members' benefits, particularly after the cost of funding defined benefits (DB) schemes began to increase considerably in the late 1990s. Such changes have given rise to all three types of document error and consequent increases in pension liabilities.

1.38

Such reductions take numerous forms, including:

(a) reducing the rate of benefit accrual;

(b) reducing the rate of increases to pensions in payment and the rate of revaluation of deferred members' benefits;

(c) changing the definition of pensionable earnings or pensionable service;

(d) closing the scheme to future accruals, and changing the calculation of the salary-related element of the benefit from the member's salary at retirement to their salary at the date of closure – known as 'breaking the final salary link';[1] and

(e) changing the entitlement or formula for death benefits, life cover, early retirement benefits or incapacity benefits.

These reductions could be expressed only to apply to benefits for future service, or to benefits referable to all service.

1 See **3.17**.

Increases to member contributions

1.39

In seeking to make DB schemes more affordable, reductions to benefits would often be accompanied by increases to member contributions. If those increases related to members' already-accrued service, they may bring into play a restriction in the amendment power. Thus, if the restriction protects members' accrued '*interests*' or '*rights*', it is arguable that the restriction included not only the benefits, but also the right to pay only those contributions charged while the benefits were accruing. Such an argument is more difficult, however, if the protection relates to members' '*benefits*', particularly if those benefits are themselves defined by reference to past contributions.

Changes to amendment powers

1.40

These are considered at **3.53–3.57**.

Appointment/removal of trustees and employers

1.41

A category of documents which may be overlooked on review are those relating to the removal or appointment of trustees, changes in principal employers and the admission of employers to participate in the scheme. The powers in issue are often subject to formal requirements, but those changes are often simply assumed to be valid. However, if the changes are found to be invalid, that can cause havoc in the administration of the scheme, as subsequent amendments may be invalidated because they are executed by the wrong trustees or principal employer, or doubts may arise as to whether the employees of employers who were not validly admitted into the scheme should be treated as members at all.

1.42

In this respect, there may be greater scope for the adoption of a more liberal attitude to compliance with the formalities, given that the following comments of Knox J in *LRT Pension Fund Trustee Co Ltd v Hatt*[1] were made in the context of a trustee appointment power:

> 'The court will be legitimately averse to the frustration of bona fide transactions by technical points which passed unperceived by all concerned at the time of the transaction in question.'[2]

1 [1993] Pens LR 227 at [112].

2 Although the judge went on to say that '*However there are limits to the extent to which rules of law, whether or not properly described as technicalities or even merest technicalities, can be circumvented.*' See also *Shannan v Viavi Solutions UK Ltd* [2016] EWHC 1530 (Ch), [2016] Pens LR 193 at [52]–[62] per Deputy Judge Fancourt QC.

Practice point 2: building in protection to prevent a document error becoming operative

1.43

This book demonstrates that the court can offer only limited assistance in the correction of pensions mistakes. This fact, combined with the desirability of avoiding litigation if at all possible, makes it attractive to include within the document itself a provision which may assist in curing any document error. It is suggested that the inclusion of the following provision in a deed introducing changes to pension benefits may enable a document error to be corrected by a process of construction, without the need for a court application:[1]

1.1 The Trustee and the Principal Employer amend the Rules of the Scheme as set out in the Appendix to this Deed.

*1.2 It is not the Trustee's and the Principal Employer's intention to increase or diminish any legal rights (including in respect of benefits for past or future service) of any Member immediately before the date of this Deed [except so as to achieve [**describe**] and in so far as any provision in the Appendix would have such effect it shall be null and avoid ab initio and the Rules shall be construed accordingly.*

*1.3 In so far as the provisions in the Appendix do not achieve [**describe**] such omission shall be treated as corrected to achieve [**describe**] by operation of this clause as included in the Appendix and the Appendix shall be construed accordingly.*

1.4 Any proposed amendment in the Appendix that is inconsistent with the above intention is automatically corrected. The detail and express wording to reflect that automatic correction on the face of the Rules shall, for housekeeping, be applied through a subsequent deed of amendment with effect from the date of this Deed, without the need for court direction, rectification or approval or other legal proceedings.

1 This provision is a suggestion only, and does not constitute legal advice or involve any representation that it will have any particular legal effect.

2 Proving Compliance

2.1

One of the most common formalities found in pension scheme amendment powers is the need for formal evidence of a step in the process, such as a record of the amendment, the written consent of the employer or the signatures of the trustees. In addition, certain relevant legislative provisions may also require evidence, such as the need for written actuarial confirmation for the purposes of s 37 of PSA 1993.[1]

1 See **3.40–3.42**.

2.2

The absence of such evidence is not necessarily because the step had not been complied with: it may be that the evidence has been lost due to the passage of time. This chapter considers when such evidence is necessary, and the extent to which it can be argued that the formal requirements have been complied with, notwithstanding the lack of such evidence.

When evidence of a formal record is necessary

2.3

Whether evidence of a formal record is necessary will turn on the construction of the scheme or statutory provision. In principle, if the provision is silent as to the need for a formal record of a decision or action, there no requirement for it to be formally recorded. Whilst amendment powers usually require a formal record of an amendment, it is not unknown for such powers simply to provide for the employer or trustees to consent, without requiring that such consent be documented. In those cases, consent can, if necessary, be proved by oral evidence[1] or by inference from other facts.[2]

1 *Entrust Pension Ltd v Prospect Hospice Ltd (No 2)* [2013] EWHC 3640 (Ch), [2013] Pens LR 73 at [35] per Henderson J.
2 *Briggs v Gleeds (Home Office)* [2014] EWHC 1178 (Ch), [2015] Ch 212 at [98]–[102] per Newey J.

2.4

If the power in question requires a formal record of the decision or action, the nature of the record may be such as to require strict compliance with certain formalities. Thus, where the power requires a deed, it is necessary to prove that the legal requirements for the execution of deeds have been satisfied;[1] and where a power provides for the trustees to amend the scheme '*by writing effected under hand*', it is necessary for all the trustees to have signed the relevant document.[2]

1 See, for example, *Briggs v Gleeds (Home Office)* [2014] EWHC 1178 (Ch), [2015] Ch 212.
2 *Trustee Solutions Ltd v Dubery* [2006] EWHC 1426 (Ch), [2007] ICR 412.

Resolution

2.5

A resolution means an opinion or decision arrived at by vote at a meeting.[1] If the resolution was required to be made by a corporate body, it will be necessary to comply with any provision in that body's constitution which sets out the requirements for a valid resolution to be made.

1 Mick Woodley (ed), *Osborn's Concise Law Dictionary* (12th edn, Sweet & Maxwell, 2013) 276.

2.6

A requirement for an amendment to be made '*by resolution (in writing) of the Trustees*' was considered in *Burgess v BIC UK Ltd*.[1] In that case the members argued that that requirement was satisfied by the minutes of a trustee meeting which, after describing the proposed changes, concluded as follows: '*It was RESOLVED that the proposed action be carried out as soon as possible.*' The employer argued that the minute was not sufficient and that what was required was a resolution setting out the text of the amendments.

1 [2018] EWHC 785 (Ch), [2018] Pens LR 380 (Arnold J); [2019] EWCA Civ 806, [2019] ICR 1386 (CA).

2.7

At first instance,[1] Arnold J agreed with the members and held that, provided that the resolution was sufficiently clear in its effect, the text of the amendment did not need to be set out, and the resolution in question was sufficiently clear. In the Court of Appeal,[2] the judge's decision was overturned on a different basis, but Henderson LJ went on to say (obiter) that he was inclined to disagree with the judge on this issue too: he considered that the minute did no more than record a resolution on future policy, leaving the implementation of that policy to '*be carried out as soon as possible*'. Henderson LJ said that, if the intention of the minute had been to effect an immediate alteration of the rules, one would have expected to find the text of the necessary amendments set out in a written document signed by the trustees and employer, and a formal reference in the amending document to the consent of the employer.

1 [2018] Pens LR 380 at [130]–[131].
2 [2019] ICR 1386 at [87]–[88].

2.8

It is arguable that Henderson LJ went too far in requiring both the text of the amendment and the employer's consent to be included in the minute: it may be sufficient if the minute included sufficient reference to the changes being made to understand what those changes were and from when they were to take effect. However, the reference in the minute to the change being '*carried out as soon as possible*' is arguably inconsistent with an intention to vary the scheme by that document, and suggests an intention to amend by a different document, which should preclude the minute from constituting the relevant amendment.

2.9

In *Municipal Mutual Insurance Ltd v Harrop*,[1] an amendment power required a resolution of the board of directors of the employer, and the employer's articles provided that a resolution could be passed at a duly convened board meeting or by a written resolution signed by all the directors. A memorandum setting out a resolution to amend the scheme was circulated amongst the seven directors: five of them gave their oral agreement and the other two abstained. At the next board meeting the minutes of the previous meeting recorded that the board had approved the resolution. Rimer J held that the resolution did not comply with the articles and was not ratified by the directors at the time of the memorandum as they did not act unanimously. However, the judge held that the subsequent approval of the minutes of the board meeting which recorded the resolution was a ratification of a previous informal decision, which converted it into a valid resolution.

1 [1998] Pens LR 149.

Memorandum in writing

2.10

An amendment power may require the decision or action to be recorded in '*a memorandum in writing*'. Whilst there is no case law on this requirement in a pensions context, there is a considerable body of authority on its meaning in legislation requiring certain contracts to be evidenced by such a document.[1] These cases show that the form of the document is immaterial,[2] and almost any properly-signed document will suffice.[3]

1 Such as s 4 of the Sale of Goods Act 1893 or s 40 of the Law of Property Act 1925.
2 *Welford v Beazley* (1747) 3 Atk 503.
3 Even a telegram: *Godwin v Francis* (1869-70) LR 5 CP 295. Presumably, an email will also be sufficient.

Declaration

2.11

The requirement for an amendment to be made by a declaration does not require any formality: the Pensions Ombudsman has determined that an announcement notifying members that the trustees had adopted the changes was a sufficient declaration.[1]

1 *Mr K* (PO-22082, 15 October 2020) at [48].

Proof of the formal record

2.12

A requirement to prove the requisite formal record of the decision or action does not necessarily require the original of the document, or even a copy of the original, to be produced. There is no requirement for the original document to be put in evidence, provided that a reasonable explanation can be given for its non-production.[1] Secondary evidence, such as oral testimony, is admissible to prove the contents of the document, and the probative weight of such evidence is a matter for the court to determine in each case.[2] This principle applies even to documents which are required to be in writing.[3]

1 *Springsteen v Masquerade Music Ltd* [2001] EWCA Civ 563, [2001] EMLR 25 at [87] per Jonathan Parker LJ.

2 *Promontoria (Oak) Ltd v Emanuel* [2020] EWHC 563 (Ch) at [46] per Marcus Smith J. (This point was not challenged on appeal: [2021] EWCA Civ 1682 at [80].)

3 *Read v Price* [1909] 2 KB 724.

2.13

Thus, if the amendment power requires the change to be made by a written resolution but the document cannot be found, secondary evidence may be adduced to prove its contents, provided that there is also evidence explaining why the document cannot be produced and the steps taken to locate it.[1] For example, in *Hodgson v Toray Textiles Europe Ltd*,[2] Lewison J said that, in a case where an interim deed referred to an announcement annexed to the deed but no such announcement could be located, if it could be established that a copy of the deed with the annexed announcement had been destroyed in a fire which had broken out in the employer's factory, the contents of the document could be proved by secondary evidence.

1 In this latter respect, it is stated in *Phipson on Evidence* (19th edn, Sweet & Maxwell, 2018) (*Phipson*), para 41-28, that it is enough if the party has in good faith exhausted all the sources and means which the nature of the case suggested, and which were reasonably accessible to them. However, the case cited by *Phipson* in support (*R v Saffron Hill* (1852) 22 LJ MC 22) is not authority for that proposition.

2 [2006] EWHC 2612 (Ch), [2006] Pens LR 253 at [52].

2.14

As to the nature of the secondary evidence, this will usually be oral testimony from a witness who had read the document, but the court may be prepared to rely on circumstantial evidence, such as the fact that the parties had acted on its supposed terms.[1]

1 *R v Fordingbridge* (1858) 27 LJ MC 290.

2.15

If the missing document in question was required to be executed in a particular manner (such as a deed or a resolution signed by all the trustees), and oral evidence can only be adduced as to the contents of the document but not as to its due execution, it would appear that the court can infer that the formal requirements for the valid execution of the document had been satisfied. In *Entrust Pension Ltd v Prospect Hospice Ltd (No 2)*,[1] Henderson J had to determine whether a trustee had in the past adopted a particular policy when exercising a power to apply a share of surplus to the deferred benefits of members when they left the service of the employer. The judge said that, if it was established that such a policy had been adopted, there was scope to infer, on the balance of probabilities, that the decision to adopt the policy had been validly taken.[2]

1 [2013] EWHC 3640 (Ch), [2013] Pens LR 73 at [40].
2 The judge also analysed the issue by reference to the presumption of regularity, as to which see **2.18**.

Can compliance with the formalities be inferred or presumed?

2.16

If no evidence of compliance with the formalities can be adduced, can the court presume or infer such compliance to validate the exercise of the power?

Inference or presumption?

2.17

The process of inferential reasoning enables the court to make further factual findings from existing evidence, whether by logical deduction or through the judgment and experience of the court. Where a rebuttable presumption of law applies in favour of a party, on the proof or admission of one fact, another fact is to be presumed: once the presumption applies, the burden is on the other party to disprove the presumed fact.

2.18

In this context, of particular relevance is the presumption of regularity,[1] whereby the court will presume that formal requisites have been validly complied with. This presumption gets stronger with the passage of time, where it would be unreasonable to expect primary evidence to be adduced in order to establish such compliance.[2] The presumption is rebuttable, and only comes into operation where there is otherwise no proof one way or the other.[3] The presumption applies to the formalities for the exercise of a power, and does not assist where there is no evidence that the power was in fact exercised.[4]

1 Expressed by the Latin maxim *Omnia praesumuntur rite esse acta*.
2 See *Popely v Heltfield Properties Ltd* [2005] EWHC 368 (Ch) at [81] per Proudman J.
3 *Harris v Knight* (1890) 15 PD 170, 180 per Lindley LJ.
4 Thus, in *Shannan v Viavi Solutions UK Ltd* [2018] EWCA Civ 681, [2018] Pens LR 344, Asplin LJ (obiter at [81]) would not have applied the presumption to overcome the absence of any evidence that a company had consented to its substitution as principal employer of a scheme, as was required by the relevant power.

2.19

In *Entrust Pension Ltd v Prospect Hospice Ltd (No 2)*,[1] Henderson J questioned whether the presumption of regularity added anything to the court's ability to find facts based on inferences drawn from circumstantial evidence, and described the presumption as:

> '... really no more than a rebuttable statement, founded on common sense and experience, of the inference that it will normally be appropriate to draw in a given situation where primary evidence is lacking.'

There is therefore probably no practical distinction in this context between the drawing of inferences and the application of the presumption of regularity.

1 [2013] EWHC 3640 (Ch), [2013] Pens LR 73 at [39], cited with apparent approval by Asplin LJ in *Shannan v Viavi Solutions UK Ltd* [2018] Pens LR 344 at [83].

2.20

For a discussion of the factors which may persuade the court to draw such inferences or apply the presumption in a pensions context, see **2.28–2.29**.

Presumed exercise of a power

2.21

Where a pension scheme power is purportedly exercised by the requisite document, the absence of any reference in the document to the exercise of the power will not be fatal,[1] as the court will presume that the power was exercised, even where an intention to exercise the power cannot be proved.

1 Provided that the power was properly vested in the parties to its exercise: *Shannan v Viavi Solutions UK Ltd* [2016] EWHC 1530 (Ch), [2016] Pens LR 193 at [100] per Deputy Judge Fancourt QC.

2.22

Thus, in *Davis v Richards & Wallington Ltd*,[1] two scheme deeds had been executed by the employer and two of the three trustees, in circumstances where everyone had (wrongly) believed that the third trustee had validly resigned. Scott J held that the deeds were validly executed, on the basis that the employer had the power to remove the third trustee from office, and could properly have exercised that power to bring about the result contemplated by the two deeds.[2] The judge imputed the requisite intention to the employer to exercise the power even though it was not possible to make such an inference on the facts.

1 [1990] 1 WLR 1511. See also *LRT Pension Fund Trustee Co Ltd v Hatt* [1993] Pens LR 227 at [139] per Knox J and *Stannard v Fisons Pension Trust Ltd* [1991] Pens LR 225 at [9] per Dillon LJ.

2 [1990] WLR 1511, 1530–1531.

2.23

That case also demonstrates that if, for whatever reason, it lies within the capability of those who have purported to exercise one power to confer that power by first exercising another power, the principle will be applied to presume the exercise of both powers.[1]

1 *Shannan v Viavi Solutions UK Ltd* [2016] EWHC 1530 (Ch), [2016] Pens LR 193 at [101].

2.24

Such a presumption will be displaced if the evidence shows that the person had an intention not to exercise the power. It appears that an intention not to exercise the power will not be established where the document records the wrong power rather than simply no power at all.[1]

1 *Capital Cranfield Trustees Ltd v Beck* [2008] EWHC 3181 (Ch), [2009] Pens LR 71 at [52] per Morgan J; *Kain v Hutton* [2008] 3 NZLR 589 at [35] per Blanchard J.

2.25

This principle has been applied to validate a deed purporting to make a change which was not permitted under the amendment power, by the application of a statutory power to modify the scheme which did permit the intended change, even though the deed itself referred only to the exercise of the scheme amendment power.[1]

1 *Coats UK Pension Scheme Trustees Ltd v Styles* [2019] EWHC 35 (Ch) at [111] per Morgan J.

2.26

However, the principle will not apply where there is a doubt as to whether the parties would have chosen to exercise the power in question had they taken into account matters relevant to its exercise which were not also relevant to the power they believed themselves to be exercising.[1] Further, the principle cannot normally be applied unless it allows the whole of what the relevant decision-maker was trying to do to be achieved: where the decision involved a set of changes, the principle should not be invoked to salvage some changes but not others, as it is possible that the changes were intended to be made only as a complete package.[2]

1 *Briggs v Gleeds (Head Office)* [2014] EWHC 1178 (Ch), [2015] Ch 212 at [95] per Newey J.
2 *Briggs v Gleeds (Head Office)* [2014] EWHC 1178 (Ch), [2015] Ch 212 at [95] per Newey J.

2.27

Several attempts to apply this principle to overcome ineffective exercises of powers have been unsuccessful:

(a) in *Capita ATL Pension Trustees Ltd v Gellately*,[1] Henderson J said (obiter) that the wording of a document announcing a change to members' normal retirement ages, which stated that the change would be implemented by the exercise of the scheme amendment power, negatived a presumed intention that a different power would be used to effect the change;

(b) in *Capital Cranfield Trustees Ltd v Beck*,[2] Morgan J doubted whether the principle could apply so that a person purporting to exercise a power in the wrong capacity could be presumed to have acted in a capacity which would validate the exercise of the power;

(c) in *Burgess v BIC UK Ltd*,[3] the Court of Appeal declined to apply the principle to presume an intention to make an amendment at a time when the necessary power to do so had only been introduced into the scheme after the amendment in question had been made.

1 [2011] EWHC 485 (Ch), [2011] Pens LR 153 at [67].
2 [2008] EWHC 3181 (Ch), [2009] Pens LR 71 at [52].
3 [2019] EWCA Civ 806, [2019] ICR 1386 at [63].

Practice point 1: establishing an inference or presumption that formalities have been satisfied

2.28

Although each case will turn on its own facts, the following matters may be relevant to the court when considering whether to infer or presume compliance with the requisite formalities.

(a) Where significant steps have been taken to comply with the formalities, the court may be prepared to infer or presume that the parties had completed those steps. For example, where an amendment power required a deed to be executed, the fact that the parties had instructed lawyers to draft the deed and had exchanged drafts may lead the court to assume that the deed had then been formally made, on the basis that the parties would not have gone to that trouble without proceeding to execute the deed. By contrast, if there is no evidence of any attempt to comply with that requirement, the court might infer that the parties did not comply because they were unaware of the need to do so.

(b) The court may well not infer that the required compliance with the formalities for the exercise of an amendment power had been complied with, merely from the future administration of the scheme by the trustees on the footing that the change had been validly made, as that is equally compatible with the possibility that the trustees mistakenly assumed that the change had been validly made.[1]

(c) Where there is a requirement for members to consent to a change, and a recital in a deed which refers to the notification of the change to the members but fails to refer to them consenting to the change, the court may assume that such consent was not obtained.[2]

(d) Where an interim deed refers to an annexed announcement which could no longer be located, a court may assume that a contemporaneous announcement was in the same terms as the announcement referred to in the deed.[3]

(e) Where an amendment power required the trustees to notify members of the change, but the notification in question was issued by the employer, the fact that the trustees had the power to delegate matters meant that the '*natural inference*' was that the notice was issued with the authorisation of the trustees.[4]

1 *Capita ATL Pension Trustees Ltd v Gellately* [2011] EWHC 485 (Ch), [2011] Pens LR 153 at [67] per Henderson J (obiter).
2 *Harwood-Smart v Caws* [2000] Pens LR 101 at [34] per Rimer J.
3 *Hodgson v Toray Textiles Europe Ltd* [2006] EWHC 2612 (Ch), [2006] Pens LR 253 at [51]–[56] per Lewison J.
4 *Vaitkus v Dresser-Rand UK Ltd* [2014] EWHC 170 (Ch), [2014] Pens LR 153 at [74] per HHJ Jarman QC (sitting as a deputy High Court judge).

2.29

Finally, consideration should be given to whether the failure to comply with a formality can be overcome as a matter of construction or implication of terms. For example, where a pension scheme power requires a deed to be executed by all the associated employers, those employers who fell within that definition but who no longer participated in the scheme because they had been sold out of the group were held to be excluded from that requirement.[1]

1 *Davis v Richards & Wallington Ltd* [1990] 1 WLR 1511, 1532 per Scott J; *Capital Cranfield Trust Corp Ltd v Sagar* [2002] OPLR 151 at [62]–[63] per Neuberger J.

Practice point 2: drafting meeting minutes

2.30

The drafting of minutes of employer board meetings or trustee meetings tends not to receive the same careful attention as the drafting of pension scheme amendments. However, where a formal record of a decision to amend is required, such as a resolution or memorandum, the minutes containing that decision may be as important as the amendment itself. It would therefore be prudent to ensure that the minutes and any decision recorded therein are consistent with the language of the amendment power.

2.31

Further, to avoid the issue of whether the correct power was consciously engaged or not, it is recommended that employer and trustee minutes, as well as all resolutions and deeds of amendment, expressly refer to the parties '*exercising all powers enabling*' the change to be made, in addition to the power thought to be the correct one upon which to rely.

3 Amendment

3.1

The cheapest and most convenient way to correct a document error is to make a formal amendment to the scheme's governing provisions. Whilst this method is usually available to deal with mistakes that are cost-neutral or have operated to the detriment of the members, it cannot generally be used to correct mistakes that have benefitted the members. This is because a combination of restrictions in amendment powers and in pensions legislation operate to prevent changes being made which would adversely affect members' benefits. This is the principal reason why other remedial measures are usually needed to correct such mistakes.

Restrictions in amendment powers

3.2

Most, but not all, amendment powers in pension schemes contain restrictions which prevent the power being used to the detriment of members' benefits. Examples of such restrictions are those that prohibit amendments which:

(a) *in any way prejudice the rights of any Member accrued in respect of Pensionable Service up to the date of any such alteration*;

(b) *reduce the benefit secured in respect of any Member up to the date of the amendment*; or

(c) *diminish or prejudicially affect the rights already earned by any member of the Scheme*.

3.3

The following types of amendment potentially attract the application of such restrictions:

(a) changes which only operate to reduce benefits earned by reference to members' service after the change – 'future service benefits';

(b) changes which also operate to reduce benefits earned by reference to members' service prior to the change – 'past service benefits'; and

(c) changes, usually made when the accrual of future service benefits is terminated, to the calculation of the salary-related element of the benefit, from the members' salary at retirement to their salary at the date of the change – 'breaking the final salary link'.

Application to future service benefits

3.4

Where the amendment power prohibits changes which adversely affect members' future benefits, that provision cannot be used to cure document mistakes which have provided members with greater than intended benefits. Such a provision also prevents the scheme closing to future accruals of benefits, so that other methods of closure, such as individual agreements with members or any specific closure powers already in the rules, must be used instead.

3.5

The leading English case is *Lloyds Bank Pension Trust Corp Ltd v Lloyds Bank plc*,[1] in which the court had to construe a restriction which prohibited amendments '*which in the opinion of the Scheme Actuary may have the effect of … decreasing the pecuniary benefits secured to or in respect of such Members under this Scheme …*'. Rimer J held that the words '*pecuniary benefits secured*' covered future service benefits as well as past service benefits, so that any amendment which prejudiced benefits earned after the date of the amendment was prohibited. In so doing, the judge distinguished a previous case,[2] where the relevant restriction applied to benefits '*already secured by past contributions*' on the basis that, in that case, the drafter clearly intended the limitation to apply only to pre-amendment benefits. In the absence of any express or implicit temporal limitation, Rimer J held that future service benefits were protected by the restriction in that case.

1 [1996] Pens LR 263.
2 *Re Courage Group's Pension Schemes* [1987] 1 WLR 495, [1987] 1 All ER 528: see **3.18**.

3.6

Lloyds Bank is the only English case in which a restriction in an amendment power has been held to cover future service benefits, and it has been heavily criticised by pensions practitioners.[1] However, it has not been successfully challenged in this context in any subsequent case and has since been cited with apparent approval.[2] Such restrictions are therefore colloquially known as '*Lloyds Bank* restrictions'.

1 The late Edward Nugee QC, who represented the employer in *Lloyds Bank*, said that his greatest professional regret was that the decision was not appealed.
2 For example, by Arnold J in *HR Trustees Ltd v German* [2010] EWHC 321 (Ch), [2010] Pens LR 23 at [133].

3.7

Lloyds Bank suggests that it is necessary to find some express or implied temporal limitation on the rights protected by the restriction, to prevent it from applying to future service benefits. However, despite a substantial body of Australian authority which supports the principle that restrictions should be construed in a way most favourable to the members and should extend if possible to protect future service benefits,[1] more recent English caselaw suggests that the court will strive to exclude future service benefits from the scope of the restriction.

1 Australian cases where members' future pension benefits have been held to be within the scope of the protection include: *Wilson v Metro Goldwyn Mayer* (1980) 18 NSWLR 730 ('*benefits secured by contributions made*'); *Gas & Fuel Corporation of Victoria v Fitzmaurice* (1991) 22 ATR 10 ('*any benefits then provided*'); *UEB Industries Ltd v Brabant* [1991] Pens LR 109 ('*that Member's interest in the Fund at the date of alteration*'); *Asea Brown Boveri Superannuation Fund Ltd v Asea Brown Boveri* [1999] 1 VR 144 ('*benefit of members already secured*'); *BHLSPF Pty Ltd v Brashs Pty Ltd* [2001] VSC 512 ('*the benefits secured to a member by the contributions paid by him*'). The one contrary case, *Lock v Westpac Banking Corporation* (1991) 25 NSWLR 593, contained a clear temporal limitation on the protection: alterations could only be made '*if the Actuary certifies that the value of the rights of Members and their Dependents and Pensions accrued at the time of making such alteration or replacement are not reduced thereby*'.

3.8

In *Wedgwood Pension Plan Trustee Ltd v Salt*,[1] the restriction in question prohibited amendments which '*prejudice or adversely affect any pension or annuity then payable or the rights of any Member*'. One of the issues was whether that restriction protected future service benefits, which would have prevented the termination of future benefit accrual by the employer. Deputy Judge Reed QC held that the restriction did not protect future service benefits, on the ground that, on their natural meaning, the words '*the rights of any member*' meant, at the time the amendment was introduced, the rights which had accrued to a member as a result of past service, and did not naturally cover benefits which might in the future be obtained as a result of future service with the employer. The deputy judge considered this to be consistent with the established requirement to give a reasonable and practical effect to the scheme bearing in mind that the scheme had to be operated against a constantly changing commercial background, and not to unduly fetter a power to amend the provisions of the scheme as it is important for the parties to be able to make changes which might be required by the exigencies of commercial life.[2] The deputy judge concluded that an amendment power which prevented the employer from curtailing the right of existing members to continue to accrue benefits in circumstances where the employer was in financial difficulties and was finding it difficult to fund the scheme, made far less sense than a construction which protected past service rights but enabled the employer to stop those benefits accruing in the future.

1 [2018] EWHC 79 (Ch), [2018] Pens LR 283.
2 See **5.7**.

3.9

Although the deputy judge distinguished *Lloyds Bank* on the basis of the different wording used in the restriction, and in particular the use of the words '*benefits*' rather than '*rights*', it is difficult to see a material distinction between the two, as '*rights*' in this context might be regarded as shorthand for '*rights to benefits*'. It is suggested that the deputy judge was more influenced by commercial practicalities than the literal meaning of the words used. If this case represents the prevailing approach of the courts, there seems to be little scope for the continued application of *Lloyds Bank,* at least beyond the particular words of the restriction in that case.

3.10

Future benefits may also be protected from amendment by reason of statutory provisions incorporated in the scheme's rules, most notably in relation to schemes operated in privatised industries such as electricity and the railways.[1]

1 For example, the Electricity (Protected Persons) (England and Wales) Pension Regulations 1990 (SI 1990/346) and the Railway Pensions (Protection and Designation of Schemes) Order 1994 (SI 1994/1432).

Application to past service benefits

3.11

An amendment power which only protects past service benefits will also restrict the ability of that power to be used to correct past overprovision of benefit, although its non-applicability to future service benefits will at least enable the document error to be corrected going forward, thereby capping the additional liabilities caused by the error.

3.12

Restrictions which apply to '*accrued*' or '*secured*' benefits will protect past service benefits, but will not extend to protect future service benefits.[1] Thus, unless the wording in the amendment power creates a *Lloyds Bank* restriction, the error can be cured for future accrual.[2]

1 Throughout his judgment in *Lloyds Bank,* Rimer J referred to the concept of '*accrued benefits*' in contradistinction to future service benefits: [1996] Pens LR 263 at [13], [25], [31], [36] and [46].
2 The power will of course still need to be exercised by the employer and/or the trustees in accordance with any legal constraints imposed upon their exercise of the power.

3.13

Although the scope of each restriction will turn on its precise wording, it is likely that any restriction which is intended to protect the benefits of all members – if it is not held to cover future service benefits – will be held to cover those members' past service benefits. This approach is illustrated by *Sterling Insurance Trustees Ltd v Sterling Insurance Group Ltd,*[1] in which Nugee J concluded that the drafter of a restriction which applied to benefits which '*accrued due*' in respect of members included the word '*due*' in error, and he construed the phrase so that it applied to all past service benefits, rather than just those that had fallen due for payment.[2]

1 [2015] EWHC 2665 (Ch) at [24].
2 This process of corrective construction is discussed at **5.15–5.56**.

3.14

Where it is possible to tell from the outset that the amendment adversely affects past service benefits, the restriction will operate to invalidate the amendment. However, it may not be possible to say whether the amendment will operate in that way, because that will turn on post-amendment events, such as future salary increases or investment returns. This gives rise to two possible interpretations of the restriction:

(a) the effect of the amendment must be assessed at the time of the amendment: the restriction would be engaged only if it could definitely be said that the amendment would diminish members' past service benefits; or

(b) the restriction is concerned with the subsequent effect and operation of the amendment in relation to past service benefits, so that an amendment will be given effect to in relation to past service benefits, but not where that would operate to diminish those benefits. In this way, the restriction operates as an overriding limitation on the intended amendment, but subject to that overriding limitation the amendment takes effect. This gives the affected members the 'best of both worlds' as between their amended and unamended past service benefits.

3.15

The conventional view favours the second interpretation. In *HR Trustees Ltd v German*,[1] members' past service defined benefits (DB) rights were converted into defined contribution (DC) benefits in contravention of an amendment power which provided that '*no amendment shall have the effect of reducing the value of benefits secured by contributions already made*'. In theory, it was possible that the value of the DC benefits may have exceeded the value of the former benefits, depending on the future investment performance of the fund. In such circumstances, Arnold J held that the infringement should be corrected by applying an underpin whereby the members would be entitled to the better of the benefits to which they would have been entitled had the amendment been valid, and the benefits to which they would have been entitled had the amendment not been made at all.[2]

1 [2010] EWHC 321 (Ch), [2010] Pens LR 23 at [141].
2 The underpin will be calculated so as to represent the minimum interference with the existing provisions of the scheme: *Dutton v FDR Ltd* [2017] EWCA Civ 200, [2017] Pens LR 221 at [16] per Lewison LJ.

3.16

However, the first interpretation remains arguable, at least in some circumstances. Thus, in *Punter Southall Governance Services Ltd v Hazlett*,[1] a restriction which prohibited amendments '*which would diminish*' members' past service benefits was held not to prevent the introduction of a forfeiture provision, on the basis that that provision would only result in a forfeiture of arrears where the member failed to claim the arrears for six years: whilst that might happen, it could not be said that it '*would*' happen. Similarly, in *Mettoy Pension Trustees Ltd v Evans*,[2] Warner J held that an amendment which transferred the power to apply surplus from the trustees to the employer did not infringe a restriction prohibiting amendments which '*shall ... lead to*' the payment of scheme assets to the employer, as the amendment did not necessarily mean that the employer would apply the surplus for its own benefit.

1 [2021] EWHC 1652 (Ch), [2022] Pens LR 1 at [221] per Morgan J.
2 [1990] 1 WLR 1587, 1630–1631.

Application to the final salary link

3.17

In the decade before the acceleration of the closure of DB schemes to future accruals in the early 2000s, employers began to reduce the costs of such schemes by making some, and later all, of the members' remuneration non-pensionable. Thereafter, when the closure of schemes became more widespread, that was often accompanied by amending the salary-related element of the benefit, so that the benefit was calculated by reference to the members' salary as at the date of closure, rather than their salary as at the date of their retirement or leaving service. These actions raised the question of whether restrictions in amendment powers which apply to past service benefits protect not only benefits referable to the service accrued to the date of the amendment, but also the right to have the benefits based on that service calculated by reference to members' final salaries, including any post-amendment increases to those salaries: if that were the case, any amendments which sought to break this 'final salary link' would contravene the restriction.

3.18

The leading English case in this respect is *Re Courage Group's Pension Schemes*,[1] in which Millett J held, in respect of a restriction which applied to benefits '*already secured by past contributions*', that, as a matter of principle, past service benefits included allowances for prospective future salary in the absence of an express definition to the contrary, and that there was nothing implicit in the use of the word '*secured*' which justified the contrary conclusion:

> 'I see no reason to exclude any benefit to which a member is prospectively entitled if he continues in the same employment and which has been acquired by past contributions, and no reason to assume that he has retired from such employment on the date of the employer's secession when he has not. The contrary argument places a meaning on "secured" which is not justified.'[2]

1 [1987] 1 WLR 495, [1987] 1 All ER 528.
2 [1987] 1 All ER 528, 543. The corresponding passage of the judgment as reported in the Weekly Law Reports is incorrect: *Briggs v Gleeds (Head Office)* [2014] EWHC 1178 (Ch), [2015] Ch 212 at [117] per Newey J.

3.19

Attempts in English cases to argue that *Courage* is wrong have failed,[1] and the principle is now well-established, at least at first instance.[2] The same analysis has been applied to restrictions which include the phrase '*accrued benefits*'.[3] Provisions which protect past service benefits and future salary increases in this way are colloquially known as '*Courage* restrictions.'

1 *Walker Morris Trustees Ltd v Masterson* [2009] EWHC 1955 (Ch), [2009] Pens LR 307; *HR Trustees Ltd v German* [2010] EWHC 321 (Ch), [2010] Pens LR 23.
2 *G4S plc v G4S Trustees Ltd* [2018] EWHC 1749 (Ch), [2019] ICR 141 at [8] per Nugee J.
3 *Briggs v Gleeds (Head Office)* [2014] EWHC 1178 (Ch), [2015] Ch 212 at [111]–[128] per Newey J.

3.20

Despite the controversy, the decision in *Courage* may be justified as a matter of principle: when a member of a DB scheme accrues one year's pensionable service, the benefit based on that year's service is calculated by reference to their final salary, and any attempt to remove or dilute that right reduces the amount of benefit referable to that year's already-accrued service.

3.21

However, where an attempt has been made to break the final salary link on the termination of accrual, *Courage* does not necessarily mean that members' benefits are in all circumstances to be calculated as if they remained in pensionable service for so long as their employment continued. This will depend on how pensionable salary is defined in the scheme's rules.[1] Millett J's analysis is based on the continued accrual of pensionable service, not merely the continued employment of the member where no further benefits are being accrued merely by reason of that employment. The judge held that it was not to be assumed, counterfactually, that members had left pensionable service when in fact they remained in pensionable service. Thus, where pensionable service *has* been terminated by the amendment – so that, under the scheme's rules, the member's final pensionable salary is to be calculated as their salary at the date of such termination – it would be just as counterfactual to assume that the member continued to accrue pensionable service for the purpose of calculating their final pensionable salary, simply because they continued to be employed. If the termination of accrual automatically crystallises a members' final pensionable salary under the existing definition by reference to the termination date, that will not constitute an amendment which purports to break the final salary link and will not fall foul of a *Courage* restriction: it is simply applying the existing definition of when the final salary link ends.

1 See the Pensions Ombudsman's determination in *Mr L Barton* (74532/2, 21 December 2009) at [24].

3.22

Where an attempt has been made to break the final salary link in breach of a *Courage* restriction, the affected members' benefits for the period of infringement will be calculated as the greater of their ordinary leaving service benefits, based on salary at the date of exercise of the power and carrying revaluation, and an underpin based on salary at the date when the member concerned actually leaves service or reaches normal retirement age but not carrying revaluation.[1] This means that, if the member in question has been granted below-inflation salary increases during the material period, the final salary link may have little or no value.

1 *IBM UK Holdings Ltd v Dalgleish* [2014] EWHC 980 (Ch), [2014] Pens LR 335 at [289(iii)], cited with apparent approval by the Court of Appeal in the same case: [2017] EWCA Civ 1212, [2018] ICR 1681 at [173]–[174].

3.23

If a *Courage* restriction exists in the amendment power, any attempt to break the final salary link will be invalid, and will not be curable by another amendment. In such a situation, the only way to achieve that objective will be by way of contractual agreement between the employer and members.

1 As to which see **9.5**.

Amendment by member consent

Existing provision for member consent

3.24

Restrictions on amendments which prejudice members' past or future benefits often contain an exception which disapplies the restriction where the member (or a specified majority of members) consents to those amendments. Such restrictions usually provide that the consent need only be obtained from the members affected by the amendments, and that the consent be provided in writing (or by vote by hand at a meeting) before the amendment is made.

3.25

In the case of an amendment infringing the restriction without obtaining express consent to disapply the restriction, it is highly unlikely that a court would be prepared to infer that the requisite consent had been validly obtained, as the members would not have known that the result of the change was to prejudice benefits which were protected by the restriction. Although there is no authority on the issue, such knowledge on the part of the members is likely to be a precondition for the disapplication of the restriction, by analogy with the trust law principle that beneficiaries are only precluded from asserting a breach of trust by reason of their concurrence where they fully understand the facts to which they were consenting.[1] Such a requirement for informed consent is not satisfied where the members were unaware that, by not consenting to the proposed amendment, their accrued rights could not thereby be taken away.

1 *Re Pauling's Settlement Trusts* [1962] 1 WLR 86, 107 per Wilberforce J.

3.26

Another restriction on the use of consent powers arises where the change to which the member consented also adversely affected the rights of persons who were entitled to benefits on the death of the member. Whilst such persons are contingent beneficiaries under the scheme during the lifetime of the member, they are treated as having their own present interest in the funds of the scheme.[1] Thus, a restriction which permits the member to consent to a prejudicial amendment does not necessarily apply to the member's death beneficiaries, unless the restriction did not protect their interests or the consent requirement expressly provided for the member's consent to apply to them.

1 So that their consent would be required if, for example, the trusts of the scheme were to be terminated or varied under the rule in *Saunders v Vautier* (referred to in **3.27** below): *Thorpe v HMRC* [2010] EWCA Civ 339, [2010] STC 964 at [25] per Lloyd LJ.

Can provision for consent be implied?

3.27

Where the restriction in the amendment power does not include an express provision for member consent, it is unlikely that an English court would imply such a provision into the power. Whilst two New Zealand cases have permitted pension scheme members to combine to consent to an amendment which would otherwise have been prohibited by a restriction in the amendment power even in the absence of an express consent provision,[1] the argument has foundered elsewhere,[2] and the Law Commission has doubted whether it could apply to amendments.[3] In any event, the practical utility of such an implied provision will be limited by the need to obtain the consent of all the affected members, including death beneficiaries.

1 *Re Phillips New Zealand Ltd* [1997] 1 NZLR 93; *Capral Fiduciary Ltd v Ladd* (1999) 1 NZSC 40,455. This was based on an extension of the rule in *Saunders v Vautier* (1841) Cr & Ph 240, which enables the beneficiaries of a trust, being of full capacity, to combine to terminate the trust and divide the assets between them, irrespective of the wishes of the settlor.
2 The Supreme Court of Canada has held that the rule does not apply to private pension schemes which are governed by the terms of the schemes and by legislation: *Buschau v Rogers Communications Inc* [2006] 1 SCR 973.
3 *Fiduciary Duties of Investment Holders* (Law Com No 350, 2014), para 6.37.

Introducing a member consent provision by amendment

3.28

The scope for amending powers of amendment to include a member consent provision is considered at **3.53–3.57**.

Application of restrictions to other scheme powers

3.29

Occasionally, pension schemes will provide for powers to change members' benefits in specific respects, which do not contain the restrictions contained in the general amendment power. An example of such a power is where the definition of normal retirement age refers to a particular age, or such other age as is notified to the members by the employer. As such notification would not involve the exercise of the general amendment power, could it be used to circumvent the restrictions contained in the general power?

3.30

The first issue is whether the specific power is wide enough to encompass the changes which are sought to be justified.

3.31

In two cases, the power to select a different normal retirement age was used to justify changes made to the retirement ages of female members to satisfy EU law equalisation requirements, which did not comply with the restrictions in the schemes' general amendment power:

(a) In *Capital Cranfield Trustees Ltd v Beck*,[1] a scheme defined the normal retirement age of female members as their 60th birthday '*or such day as the Employers shall determine in any particular case and notify in writing to the Member concerned*'. The employer sought to rely on that determination power to validate a change to the retirement age of female members which was merely recorded in an announcement to members, rather than being set out in a deed as was required by the general amendment power. Morgan J rejected that argument on the basis that the words '*in any particular case*' did not authorise the normal retirement age to be changed for a class of members, or all members, and so did not authorise a change in normal retirement age for all female members. Although he did not need to rely on the point, the judge also considered it strongly arguable that the determination power could only be exercised at the time when the member first joined the scheme.

(b) In *Capita ATL Pension Trustees Ltd v Gellately*,[2] a scheme defined the normal retirement age by reference to particular ages, '*except where otherwise stated or otherwise agreed by the Employers and the Trustees*'. In response to an argument advanced by the employer in similar terms to the *Beck* case, Henderson J held that the power to agree a different normal retirement age did not prevail over the formal requirements of the general amendment power where the proposed change was of general application, as the parties to the deed would have contemplated a scheme-wide amendment to something as fundamental as normal retirement ages to be subject to those requirements. The judge therefore held that the power in the definition should be construed as being confined in its scope to special arrangements made in relation to individual members, and was not wide enough to authorise a general equalisation of normal retirement ages. Although he too did not have to decide the point, the judge also said that he saw much force in the argument that the power ceased to be exercisable once a member had joined the scheme and acquired a normal retirement age.

1 [2008] EWHC 3181 (Ch), [2009] Pens LR 71 at [37]–[38].
2 [2011] EWHC 485 (Ch), [2011] Pens LR 153 at [59]–[60].

3.32

By contrast, in *IBM UK Holdings Ltd v Dalgleish*,[1] Warren J accepted the employer's argument that a power to direct that '*any specified person or class of persons shall ... cease to be a Member or Members*' of a pension scheme, enabled the employer to exclude all members of the scheme from membership.

1 [2014] EWHC 980 (Ch), [2014] Pens LR 335 at [292].

3.33

However, even if, as a matter of construction, the specific power was wide enough to enable the change to be made, the case law strongly suggests that any restrictions in the general amendment power which protected members' benefits should also be read into the specific power.[1]

1 See *National Grid Co plc v Mayes* [2001] UKHL 20, [2001] 1 WLR 864 at [57] per Lord Hofmann and at [76] per Lord Scott of Foscote; *Stevens v Bell* [2002] EWCA Civ 672, [2002] Pens LR 247 at [134] per Arden LJ. Warren J's finding in the *IBM* case that the exclusion power extended to all members was influenced by the employer's acceptance that the exercise of that power was subject to the member protections contained in the general amendment power.

Statutory restrictions

Section 67 of PA 1995

3.34

When it originally came into effect on 6 April 1997, s 67 of PA 1995 prohibited the exercise of any power to modify an occupational pension scheme which would or might affect any '*entitlement*' or '*accrued right*' of any member acquired before the power was exercised, unless either the members had consented in the prescribed terms, or an actuary had certified that the amendment in question did not adversely affect such an entitlement or right.

3.35

As to the benefits which were protected by this section:

(a) '*entitlement*' was not defined in the legislation, but was held to mean a benefit to which the right to payment has arisen, including a pension in payment;[1]

(b) '*accrued right*' was specifically defined as a right which had accrued to future benefits under the scheme; but where the member's pensionable service was continuing, those rights were to be determined as if they had opted, immediately before that time, to terminate that service:[2] thus, the section did not prevent the breaking of the final salary link.

1 *Barclay's Bank plc v Holmes* [2000] Pens LR 339 at [134] per Neuberger J.
2 Section 124(2)(b) of PA 1995.

3.36

With effect from 6 April 2006, s 67 was amended in the following material respects:[1]

(a) the modifications to which s 67 relates are now defined as:

  (i) '*protected modifications*', which involve reductions of pensions in payment or the conversion of DB rights into DC rights;[2] and

  (ii) '*detrimental modifications*', which would or might adversely affect members' '*subsisting rights*', which replicate the entitlements and accrued rights which were protected by the original s 67;[3]

(b) instead of a blanket prohibition, an exercise of an amendment power to which s 67 relates and which does not satisfy prescribed conditions, is voidable,[4] in which case the Pensions Regulator may declare the amendment to be void to the extent specified in the order;[5]

(c) the prescribed conditions are as follows:

  (i) for protected modifications, the affected members must consent in the prescribed terms;[6]

  (ii) for detrimental modifications, either the affected members must consent in the prescribed terms, or a certificate must be obtained from an actuary, in prescribed circumstances, to the effect that the value of members' subsisting rights have not been diminished;[7]

  (iii) in addition, both protected and detrimental modifications must satisfy the following requirements:

    (A) the trustees must either exercise the modification power or consent to it, which they cannot do unless the requisite conditions for the modifications have been satisfied;[8] and

    (B) the trustees must notify the members of any modification to which the members have consented within a reasonable period of it being made and before it takes effect; and the trustees must take reasonable steps similarly to notify members where the modification was accompanied by an actuarial certificate.[9]

1 By s 262 of PA 2004. For further guidance on the application of these provisions, see the Pensions Regulator's 'Code of Practice No.10 (Modification of Subsisting Rights)'.
2 Section 67A(2)(3).
3 Sections 67A(4) and (6). The protection of accrued rights under the amended s 67 accordingly still does not cover the final salary link: ss 67A(7) and 124(2)(b).
4 Section 67(2).
5 Section 67G.
6 Section 67B.
7 Section 67C and D. Provided that the actuary was asked the correct question, the certificate will be valid irrespective of whether the actuary's answer was correct: *Cornwell v Newhaven Ports & Properties Ltd* [2005] EWHC 1469 (Ch), [2005] Pens LR 329 at [17] per Lewison J, applied by Trower J in *Mitchells & Butlers Pensions Ltd v Mitchells & Butlers plc* [2021] EWHC 3017 (Ch) at [374].
8 Section 67E.
9 Section 67F. The Pensions Regulator has suggested that trustees should usually aim to notify members within one month of making the decision: 'Code of Practice No.10 (Modification of Subsisting Rights)', para 77.

3.37

Although amendments which fail to comply with these conditions are merely voidable, the Pensions Regulator[1] will usually declare defaulting protected amendments to be wholly void,[2] and defaulting detrimental amendments to be void at least to the extent that they purport to affect subsisting rights.[3] In the latter context, it will be necessary to consider whether the defaulting amendment also contravenes an express restriction in the governing provisions of the scheme, as it is unlikely that the Pensions Regulator would validate any part of an amendment which also contravened such a restriction. Even if the express restriction is limited to amendments which contravene s 67, it is possible that that restriction will extend beyond the scope of the current version of s 67 by prohibiting such amendments, which will render the amendment void rather than voidable.

1 Query whether the court would make a declaration as to the voidability of an amendment in such a situation, as to which see *Mitchells & Butlers Pensions Ltd v Mitchells & Butlers plc* [2021] EWHC 3017 (Ch) at [378]–[383] per Trower J.

2 For example, Determination Notice relating to the DCT Civil Engineering Staff Pension Fund (C26276259) (5 April 2016).

3 For example, Determination Notice relating to the ELCB Staff Pension Scheme (TM7208) (20 July 2010).

Employer-employee consultation requirements

3.38

In addition to the member notification requirement referred to at **3.36**(c)(iii)(B), s 259 of PA 2004 obliges employers with 50 or more employees to consult all affected active and prospective members for a minimum of 60 days before making any of the changes set out in the regulations made under that provision.[1] Those changes include increasing the normal retirement age, closing the scheme to future new entrants or accruals, introducing or increasing member contributions, reducing rates of pensions increases and revaluation, changing the basis of benefit accrual, and changing the definition of pensionable earnings on or after 6 April 2010.

1 Regulation 8 of the Occupational and Personal Pension Schemes (Consultation by Employers and Miscellaneous Amendment) Regulations 2006 (SI 2006/349) (the Consultation Regulations). These are additional to the wider employee consultation requirements imposed on the employer under the Information and Consultation of Employees Regulations 2004 (SI 2004/3426), although reg 20(5)(c) of those Regulations provides that the employer need not consult separately under both sets of Regulations in respect of the same changes, provided that it complies with the prescribed notification requirements.

3.39

Although failure to comply with this consultation requirement exposes the employer to civil penalties, the amendment itself is not thereby invalidated.[1] However, where the failure is particularly egregious, the affected employees may have a claim against the defaulting employer for breach of its contractual duty of trust and confidence to its employees.[2]

1 Section 259(3) of PA 2004; reg 18 of the Consultation Regulations.

2 *IBM UK Holdings Ltd v Dalgleish* [2014] EWHC 980 (Ch), [2014] Pens LR 335 at [1556] per Warren J. This aspect of the Judge's decision was not challenged on appeal.

Section 37 of PSA 1993

3.40

The s 37 regime prohibited alterations to the rules of contracted-out salary-related (COSR) schemes unless prescribed requirements were satisfied, and it continues to apply, with modifications, to those schemes which were formerly COSR schemes prior to the abolition of the contracting-out regime on 6 April 2016.

3.41

This provision is referred to here, not because it will affect the future ability of an amendment to correct past mistakes, but because a prior failure to comply with it may invalidate an otherwise-valid amendment to a scheme which provided COSR benefits between 6 April 1997 and 6 April 2013.

3.42

During that period, the rules of a COSR scheme could not be altered in relation to '*section 9(2B) rights*' unless (amongst other things): the trustees had informed the actuary in writing of the proposed amendment; and the actuary had considered the proposed amendment and confirmed to the trustees in writing that the actuary was satisfied that the scheme would continue to satisfy the 'reference scheme test' in s 12A of PSA 1993 if the alteration were made.[1] A failure to obtain this actuarial confirmation may therefore invalidate such an alteration.

1 Regulation 42(2) of the Contracting-out Regulations.

3.43

For amendments made during this period, there remains doubt as to the scope of s 37. This is because the '*section 9(2B) rights*' affected by s 37 were at that time defined to include '*... rights to the payment of pensions and accrued rights to pensions (other than rights attributable to voluntary contributions) under a scheme contracted-out by virtue of section 9(2B) of the 1993 Act ...*'[1]

1 Regulation 1(2) of the Contracting-out Regulations.

3.44

On a literal construction, future service benefits do not come within that definition. However, there is an argument that the concept of '*section 9(2B) rights*' should be extended to cover such benefits:

(a) the purpose of the contracting-out regime was to ensure that benefits accruing under a COSR scheme met and continued to meet the reference scheme test, which required the ongoing supervision of those benefits: to construe s 37 so as only to apply to past benefits would be to remove the statutory control of alterations in relation to prospective benefits in a manner which was inconsistent with the rest of the contracting-out regime;

(b) accordingly, when the Contracting-out Regulations were originally made in April 1996, the definition of '*section 9(2B) rights*' simply referred to rights, and was not limited to accrued rights;

(c) although that definition was changed to refer to accrued rights with effect from 6 April 1997,[1] that was not intended to impose a temporal limitation on the rights, but was only intended to identify the nature of the rights concerned, ie pension rights as opposed to any other rights which arose from service, such as death benefits.

1 Regulation 3 and para 4(2) of Sch 1 to the Personal and Occupational Pension Schemes (Miscellaneous Amendments) Regulations 1997 (SI 1997/786).

3.45

Because of this argument, amendments which related to future service benefits may nevertheless have been subject to the s 37 regime, insofar as those changes potentially affected the satisfaction of the reference scheme test going forward. This in turn may mean that such changes may be invalidated in their entirety and would not be held to apply prospectively.

3.46

There is as yet no case law on this point;[1] accordingly, the scope of the benefits protected by the s 37 restriction on amendments is still unclear. Until the scope of that restriction is determined by a court, it would be prudent for trustees and their advisers to assume that, for the relevant period, the restriction can apply to changes to both past and future service benefits.[2]

1 The issue was raised in *Punter Southall Governance Services Ltd v Hazlett* [2021] EWHC 1652 (Ch), [2022] Pens LR 1 but did not need to be determined because of the compromise of certain issues before trial: see [12] and [49]–[52] per Morgan J.

2 Alterations to past service benefits made after 6 April 2013 will not be affected, as reg 42(2) of the Contracting-out Regulations was amended so that the requirement for actuarial confirmation only applied to future service benefits: reg 3(b) of the Occupational and Stakeholder Pension Schemes (Miscellaneous Amendments) Regulations 2013 (SI 2013/459).

Other amendment powers

3.47

Not all amendment powers contain restrictions protecting members' benefits,[1] and s 67 of PA 1995 does not apply to any amendments made prior to 6 April 1997.[2] It is therefore possible that an amendment, to which s 67 did not apply, was made pursuant to such an amendment power, and which operated retrospectively to remove the mistaken grant of benefits to members: will such an amendment have been validly made?

1 It is not, however, generally possible to amend an amendment power to as to remove such a protection in order to remove hitherto protected benefits: see **3.55**.

2 *South West Trains Ltd v Wightman* [1998] Pens LR 113 at [75]–[80] per Neuberger J.

3.48

It used to be thought that amendments to pension schemes which adversely affected past service benefits were prohibited at common law.[1] However, it is now accepted that such amendments are permitted, if they fall within the terms of the power. In *Safeway Ltd v Newton*,[2] a scheme amendment made prior to the introduction of s 67 sought retrospectively to increase female members' retirement ages from 60 to 65, pursuant to a power which expressly permitted retrospective amendments. The Court of Appeal referred to the Court of Justice of the European Union the issue of whether such an increase was permissible as a matter of EU law, because the female members' benefits were, as a matter of domestic law, defeasible, being subject to retrospective removal under the amendment power.[3] This approach is consistent with the earlier case of *Doyle v Manchester Evening News*,[4] in which HHJ Blackett-Ord V-C held that a change to the definition of pensionable salary to exclude certain remuneration, which operated to reduce members' past service benefits, was authorised by an amendment power which expressly permitted retrospective changes.

1 When introducing what became s 67 of PA 1995, the Minister for Social Security described the provision as '*putting on a statutory basis what has been understood to be the present position under trust law*': House of Commons Standing Committee D, 8 June 1995, col 469. See also *Municipal Mutual Insurance Ltd v Harrop* [1998] Pens LR 149 at [48]–[51] per Rimer J.
2 [2017] EWCA Civ 1482, [2018] Pens LR 2 at [46] per Lord Briggs of Westbourne JSC.
3 The amendment was subsequently held by the European Court to be contrary to EU law (insofar as it applied to post-17 May 1990 service) unless it was done to alleviate the risk of seriously undermining the financial balance of the scheme: *Safeway Ltd v Newton (C-171/18)* [2020] ICR 673.
4 [1989] Pens LR 47 at [85]. See also *Vaitkus v Dresser-Rand UK Ltd* [2014] EWHC 170 (Ch), [2014] Pens LR 153 at [48] per HHJ Jarman QC (sitting as a deputy High Court judge).

3.49

Where the amendment power is silent on the issue, there is no automatic presumption against retrospective changes: whether they are permitted depends upon questions of fairness in the circumstances of the particular case, although such a power cannot be used to rewrite history.[1] In *Shannan v Viavi Solutions UK Ltd*,[2] Deputy Judge Fancourt QC cited an amendment which adversely affected accrued rights as an example of rewriting history.[3]

1 *Bank of New Zealand v Board of Management of the Bank of New Zealand Officers' Provident Association* [2003] UKPC 58, [2003] OPLR 281 at [26] per Lord Walker of Gestingthorpe.
2 [2016] EWHC 1530 (Ch), [2016] Pens LR 193 at [67] per Deputy Judge Fancourt QC.
3 See also *HR Trustees Ltd v German* [2010] EWHC 321 (Ch), [2010] Pens LR 23 at [148] per Arnold J.

3.50

The concept of rewriting history in this context has since been further considered by the Court of Appeal in *Burgess v BIC UK Ltd*.[1] In that case, Henderson LJ said that the parties to a pension scheme document can agree that their past relationship is to be treated as having departed from historical reality in specified respects. It was therefore possible for a subsequent amendment power to be exercised (prior to s 67 coming into effect) to validate a prior exercise of an amendment power which had been invalid for failure to comply with requisite formalities, and for that validation to operate retrospectively.

However, it was necessary to establish that the parties to the subsequent exercise of the amendment power intended it to operate in that way, and there was no evidence of such an intention, no doubt because the parties were not aware at the time of that exercise that the original amendment was invalid and therefore needed to be validated.

1 [2019] EWCA Civ 806, [2019] ICR 1386 at [55]–[72].

3.51

It is therefore possible that the mistaken granting of pension benefits to members may have been validly corrected by a retrospective amendment at a time when s 67 would not have invalidated such an amendment, even where the amendment power in question did not expressly permit retrospective changes: however, this will only be achieved where a contemporaneous intention to make such a correction can be established.[1]

1 In *Mr K* (PO-22802, 15 October 2020) at [56], the Pensions Ombudsman accordingly went too far in stating that '*there is sufficient case law to show that where the necessary formalities are met, the courts will not find a retrospective amendment invalid*': although the Ombudsman cited *Burgess v BIC UK Ltd* in support, he only referred to the first instance decision, which was reversed on appeal.

Saving part of the amendment

3.52

Where the amendment purports to affect both benefits which are protected by the restriction and benefits which are not so protected – such as an amendment applying to both past and future service benefits where the restriction protects only past service benefits – it may be possible to invalidate only the objectionable part of the amendment and to allow the unobjectionable part of the amendment to operate. This is discussed in **Chapter 4**.

Amending powers of amendment

3.53

It is sometimes said that it is not possible to amend a power of amendment in the absence of a specific power to do so, but that is not so. Whilst the scope for such an amendment will turn on the wording of the amendment power, the case law does not support a blanket prohibition on all such amendments.

3.54

Whilst the courts have emphasised the need for amendment powers in long-term arrangements such as pension schemes not to be unduly fettered, to enable the parties to make such changes as are required by the exigencies of commercial life,[1] the proper approach to the scope of the amendment power has been authoritatively described as follows:[2]

> 'In this context, the process on which the court is engaged is one of interpretation according to the normal principles and not, for instance, the process on which the court is engaged when it is interpreting a statute to be compatible so far as possible with the rights conferred by the European Convention on Human Rights. When the court is engaged on interpretation according to normal principles, it has to be even-handed between the parties, and in general it has to give each word its full weight. If by 'broad interpretation' the judge meant that the power of amendment should be interpreted with greater liberality than other documents purposively construed with a view to holding that an amendment is binding on Participating Employers who have not consented to it,[3] I would disagree. In my judgment, a power of amendment should be interpreted precisely in accordance with its terms, neither more nor less. To construe otherwise is to favour the majority at the expense of the non-assenting minority. The parties have only agreed to amendments approved in accordance with the power of amendment on its true construction.'

1 *Re Courage Group Pension Schemes* [1987] 1 WLR 495, 505 per Millett J.
2 *Stena Line Ltd v Merchant Navy Ratings Pension Fund Trustees Ltd* [2011] EWCA Civ 543, [2011] Pens LR 223 at [48] per Arden LJ.
3 The amendment power in question was vested solely in the trustees.

3.55

There is accordingly no blanket principle that, once an amendment power has been created, it is completely entrenched and wholly incapable of amendment. Thus, an amendment which is purely administrative in nature, such as a change to the form in which the amendment is to be recorded from a trustee resolution to a deed, is unobjectionable. However, where a restriction protecting members' benefits has been included in an amendment power from the outset, it appears that this cannot be removed by amendment, irrespective of the scope of the amendment power. The leading case is *HR Trustees Ltd v German*,[1] which involved the purported replacement of an amendment power which contained a fetter which prevented amendments which had the effect of '*reducing the value of benefits secured by contributions already made*', with an amendment power which contained no such fetter. Arnold J held that that replacement was beyond the scope of the amendment power, as it allowed the original fetter to be circumvented by first removing the fetter and then amending the scheme in a manner precluded by the fetter. In doing so, the judge followed a series of cases,[2] which rejected such amendments on the basis that the parties could not achieve by two steps what they could not achieve by one.

1 [2010] EWHC 321 (Ch), [2010] Pens LR 23 at [123]–[125]. See to the same effect, in a private trust context, *Re Brunners' Declaration of Trust* [1941] 2 All ER 745; and in a public law context, *R (oao Jackson) v A-G* [2005] UKHL 56, [2006] 1 AC 262.
2 *UEB Industries Ltd v WS Brabant* [1992] 1 NZLR 294; *Air Jamaica Ltd v Charlton* [1999] 1 WLR 1399; *BHLSPF Pty Ltd v Brashs Pty Ltd* [2001] VSC 512.

3.56

However, this principle is itself subject to several potential qualifications:

(a) The argument that a restriction in an amendment power was intended to be entrenched and incapable of removal is weakened where the restriction in question did not appear in the original amendment power and was itself added by amendment. Assuming that the addition of the restriction was valid in the first place,[1] there seems to be little objection in principle to permitting it to be removed by the same process.

(b) The principle that the parties cannot do in two steps what they could not do in one step has its limits: a series of perfectly valid amendments over a period of time may, at least where they were not all planned as a single scheme of amendments, result in an end-point which it would not have been possible to reach by a single amendment at the beginning.[2]

(c) The *HR Trustees* principle should not prevent the introduction of a power for affected members to consent to an amendment which would otherwise fall foul of the restriction. Such an amendment does not allow the original restriction to be circumvented, because any person who would be affected by the amendment and who is protected by the restriction retains the ability to prevent the amendment from affecting their benefits and can therefore rely upon the protection of the restriction. Such an amendment does not lessen the effect of the restriction, in the sense that the affected member – who is the person for whose benefit the restriction is in place – is not precluded from relying upon it.[3]

1 It is sometimes suggested that new restrictions cannot be added by amendment, on the basis that they would be beyond the purpose of the amendment power or would fetter the powers of the trustees or would constitute an invalid release of a power. None of these suggestions has been the subject of judicial scrutiny, although the last of them was rejected, in a different pensions context, by Briggs J (obiter) in *Stena Line Ltd v Merchant Navy Ratings Pension Fund Trustees Ltd* [2010] EWHC 1085 (Ch), [2010] Pens LR 411 at [131]–[133].

2 *Re Courage Group Pension Schemes* [1987] 1 WLR 495, 506 per Millett J; *IBM United Kingdom Holdings Ltd v Dalgleish* [2014] EWHC 980 (Ch), [2014] Pens LR 335 at [207] per Warren J.

3 By contrast, the removal of a power for members to consent to detrimental changes may well fall outside the scope of the amendment power: cf. *Lloyds Banking Group Pensions Trustees Ltd v Lloyds Bank* [2020] EWHC 3135 (Ch), [2021] Pens LR 295 at [249] per Morgan J.

3.57

Finally, just because the scope of the amendment power is wide enough to enable it to be amended does not mean that such an amendment can always be made. Where the amendment power involves the trustees and the employer, they must take care not to act in breach of their duties to the members by making or agreeing to such an amendment.

Practice point: ascertaining the proper scope of the amendment power

3.58

When considering the validity of a past amendment, care must be taken not to confine the investigation of the trust documents to the amendment power which applied at the time of the amendment. Because of the principle, identified at **3.55**, that a restriction included in an amendment power from the outset cannot be removed by subsequent amendment, it will be necessary to trace the history of the amendment power from the original provision, through all subsequent iterations, to see whether any restrictions have been removed along the way.[1] Moreover, despite the argument, identified at **3.56**(a), that that principle may not apply with equal force where the removed restriction was not in the original amendment power, there remains a risk that the court would apply the principle to that situation too, particularly if the restriction was inserted for the protection of members.

1 This is an exception to the principle that it is not permitted to delve into the archaeology of a scheme's governing provisions in order to assist in the construction of its current terms: *Barnardo's v Buckinghamshire* [2018] UKSC 55, [2019] ICR 495 at [26] per Lord Hodge JSC.

3.59

Where, as is often the case, the scheme was originally established by an interim trust deed which was subsequently replaced by a definitive trust deed and rules, the need for such an investigation gives rise to the question: where is the original amendment power to be found?

3.60

The answer may turn on the scope of the application of the definitive deed:

(a) where the definitive deed is expressed to supersede the interim deed from the date of the establishment of the scheme, an exoneration clause contained in the former has been held to apply to breaches of trust which occurred prior to its execution;[1]

(b) however, where an establishing deed provided for the scheme to be administered in accordance with rules to be subsequently adopted, it has been held that the amendment power in the rules did not replace the inconsistent amendment power in the deed, on the basis that the rules supplemented, rather than replaced, the deed;[2] this led the court to apply the principle that the amendment power in the rules did not validly remove the restriction contained in the amendment power in the deed.

1 *Imperial Foods Ltd v Jeeves,* (27 January 1986, unreported), Walton J. That decision was described as controversial by Lawrence Collins J in *The Trustee Corp Ltd v Nadir* [2001] BPIR 541 at [24].
2 *HR Trustees Ltd v German* [2010] EWHC 321 (Ch), [2010] Pens LR 23 at [114] per Arnold J.

3.61

It is suggested that the most prudent course of action would be to assume that any restriction in an amendment power contained in the interim deed cannot be validly removed, unless the application of that power is, under the terms of the interim deed itself, unequivocally limited to the lifetime of that deed.

4 Saving Part of the Amendment

4.1

Where a pension scheme amendment would otherwise be invalidated by reason of a mistake as to its scope or terms, a court may limit the invalidity to that part of the amendment which goes beyond what is permitted. For example, an amendment which reduces members' benefits might be expressed to operate both retrospectively and prospectively, in circumstances where the amendment power prohibits detrimental changes to past service benefits only. This might occur where the decision to reduce the benefit is intended to apply from the date of the decision, and the formal amendment is made some time later, but backdated to the date of the decision. In these circumstances, whilst that part of the amendment which purports to operate retrospectively will be void, the court may nevertheless permit the change to apply prospectively.

4.2

This is an important principle which is often applied to ameliorate the otherwise severe consequences of an amendment which infringes a restriction in the amendment power.

4.3

Two methods of saving part of the amendment in this situation have been deployed by the courts: construction and severance. Although the legal principles involved are separate and the conditions for their application have differed, more recent case law has indicated a move towards the adoption of a single method.

The early cases

4.4

The cases which initially dealt with how to treat a change which contravened a restriction in the amendment power approached the issue as a matter of construction. This meant that the restriction was effectively to be read into the change, which was accordingly held to be valid only to the extent that it did not infringe that restriction.

4.5

The first case was *Doyle v Manchester Evening News*,[1] which involved an amendment to a scheme which excluded an element of members' earnings from the definition of pensionable salary. This change was expressed to apply to all members' benefits, whether referable to past or future service. This was held to have infringed a restriction in the amendment power prohibiting changes which prejudiced pensions in payment, as the retrospective element of the change operated to reduce the pensions in payment of two members. HHJ Blackett-Ord V-C rejected the argument that the amendment was wholly invalid, holding that:

> '... the effect of the provisions is simply to exclude from their effect pensions already being paid. The proposed amendment is valid in general, but does not affect the two pensioners whose interests are already vested.'[2]

1 [1989] Pens LR 47: the case was decided in 1985.
2 [1989] Pens LR 47 at [84].

4.6

A similar analysis was applied by the House of Lords in *National Grid Co plc v Mayes*,[1] in which the employer changed a specific provision by exercising a particular power which existed alongside a general amendment power, but which did not contain the restrictions contained in that general power. Lord Hoffmann said that, if the general amendment power provided important safeguards for the members, that might be a good reason to construe the scheme as requiring the employer to adopt the safeguards when exercising the specific power.[2] Lord Scott said that the provisions of the scheme must be construed as a whole, so that the specific power cannot be regarded as conferring on the employer a power of amendment free from the safeguards to which the general amendment power was subject.[3]

1 [2001] UKHL 20, [2001] 1 WLR 864.
2 [2001] UKHL 20, [2001] 1 WLR 864 at [57]. Lord Clyde agreed with this conclusion at [72].
3 [2001] UKHL 20, [2001] 1 WLR 864 at [76].

4.7

In the subsequent case of *Stevens v Bell*,[1] Arden LJ said that *National Grid* established the general principle that a power to make particular changes to a scheme should be interpreted as subject to other implied limitations which appear from the scheme on its true interpretation.

1 [2002] EWCA Civ 672, [2002] Pens LR 247 at [134].

Bestrustees plc v Stuart

4.8

Six days after the *National Grid* case, Neuberger J delivered his judgment in *Bestrustees plc v Stuart*.[1] This case involved an increase in female members' normal retirement ages which purported to apply to benefits referable to past as well as to future service, in breach of a restriction in the amendment power protecting past service benefits. The judge treated the prospective application of the amendment as valid by applying the severance principle, derived from equity's treatment of the execution of a power which exceeds the scope of the power or is in breach of a rule of law: such an 'excessive execution' of the power is void, as the donee has attempted to do something which cannot lawfully be done.[2] However, where the exercise of the power is only excessive in part, the severance principle allows the non-excessive exercise of the power to be severed from the excessive exercise and for the former to be validated.[3]

1 [2001] Pens LR 283.
2 *Lewin on Trusts* (20th edn, Sweet & Maxwell, 2020) (*Lewin*), para 30-017.
3 *Bestrustees plc v Stuart* [2001] Pens LR 283 at [44] to [48] and [51]. The severance principle has also been applied in contract law, especially in the context of illegal restraints on trade (*Marshall v NM Financial Management Ltd* [1997] 1 WLR 1527), and in public law, such as where byelaws are held to be only partly ultra vires (*DPP v Hutchinson* [1990] 2 AC 783).

4.9

The judge identified two requirements for the operation of the severance principle in a pensions context.[1]

(a) The first is that there must be an easily-understood conceptual distinction between the valid and invalid exercise of the power. In the case of amendments which have retrospective and prospective effect, the judge held that the temporal distinction was easy to understand as a matter of concept, which permitted the prospective to be severed from the retrospective.

(b) The second arose from the fact that the severance principle was initially developed in the context of powers, which were often exercised by donees who owed no fiduciary duties to the objects of the power. By contrast, pension scheme powers were usually exercised by trustees, who did stand in a fiduciary position vis-a-vis the members. The judge said that, in such a case, the so-called 'rule in *Hastings-Bass*'[2] came into play, in which the exercise of a fiduciary power by trustees would only be overturned if it is clear that they would not have acted as they did had they acted correctly. Accordingly, the judge said that the severance principle would not apply where there was anything in the exercise of the power which led one to believe that, had the trustees been aware that they were not entitled to exercise the power retrospectively, they would not have exercised the power as they purported to do, either at all or in the way that they did.

The judge did not consider the application of the construction principle, and neither the *Doyle* nor the *National Grid* cases were referred to by him.

1 [2001] Pens LR 283 at [48].
2 *Re Hastings-Bass* [1975] Ch 25, as applied by Warner J in *Mettoy Pensions Trustees Ltd v Evans* [1990] 1 WLR 1587 at 1624: see further **7.4–7.5**.

Subsequent cases

4.10

The cases which followed *Bestrustees* adopted both the construction and severance principles and, when the latter principle was adopted, the judges did not consistently apply the *Hastings-Bass* requirement as identified by Neuberger J.

4.11

In *Betafence Ltd v Veys*,[1] the amendment in issue purported to introduce an employer consent requirement to the provision of unreduced early retirement benefits for all members, where the amendment power prohibited amendments which prejudicially affected secured benefits. In holding that the amendment infringed that prohibition, but only to the extent that it applied to benefits accrued prior to the amendment date, Lightman J did not feel the need to apply the severance principle to uphold the prospective application of the amendment, because he could get to the same result by use of the construction principle. However, the judge went on to say that, if the severance principle was to be applied, all that was necessary was to establish that the distinction between what was and what was not objectionable was clear and that the meaning and application of what was unobjectionable was clear. The judge did not refer to the need to satisfy the *Hastings-Bass* requirement as identified in *Bestrustees* – indeed, the judge made no reference to *Bestrustees* in his judgment.[2]

1 [2006] EWHC 999 (Ch), [2006] Pens LR 137 at [69].

2 In *Wedgwood Pension Plan Trustee Ltd v Salt* [2018] EWHC 79 (Ch), [2018] Pens LR 283 at [61], Deputy Judge Reed QC said that *Bestrustees* did not appear to have been cited to the judge in *Betafence*. However, Michael Furness QC, who appeared for the representative defendant in *Betafence*, has confirmed that *Bestrustees* was cited to the judge in the course of submissions.

4.12

After *Betafence*, two cases applied the principle in *National Grid* to construe specific powers to change pension scheme provisions as being impliedly subject to the limitations in the general amendment power.[1] Sandwiched between those two cases was another apparent example of the court treating the application of a restriction in an amendment power as a matter of construction rather than severance, without reference to the *Hastings-Bass* requirement. In *HR Trustees Ltd v German*,[2] an amendment purported to convert members' past service defined benefits (DB) rights to defined contribution benefits, which was held to infringe a proviso to the amendment power which provided that no amendment could reduce the value of benefits secured by contributions already made. Arnold J held that that provision rendered ineffective amendments which reduced the value of benefits which accrued to members by virtue of their pensionable service down to the date of the amendment; but the judge went on to preserve the amendment insofar as it did not reduce the value of the benefits in what appeared to be an application of the construction principle, by subjecting the amendment to an underpin which preserved the future monetary value of benefits accrued in respect of pre-amendment service.[3]

1 *Capital Cranfield Trustees Ltd v Beck* [2008] EWHC 3181 (Ch), [2009] Pens LR 71; *Capita ATL Pension Trustees Ltd v Gellately* [2011] EWHC 485 (Ch), [2011] Pens LR 153. See **3.31**.
2 [2010] EWHC 321 (Ch), [2010] Pens LR 23.
3 [2010] EWHC 321 (Ch), [2010] Pens LR 23 at [141].

4.13

The next case illustrates the confusion in the authorities at this time. In *IBM UK Holdings Ltd v Dalgleish*,[1] the employer exercised a power, introduced by amendment, to exclude members from the membership of the scheme, which (amongst other things) operated to break the final salary link in respect of those members. Thereafter, the members were treated as deferred members, whose benefits were subject to statutory revaluation. It was accepted by the employer that that exercise of the exclusion power was contrary to a proviso to the amendment power which protected the final salary link.[2]

1 [2014] EWHC 980 (Ch), [2014] Pens LR 335 (Warren J); [2017] EWCA Civ 1212, [2018] ICR 1681 (CA).
2 As to which, see **3.17–3.23**

4.14

Warren J, after citing the *Bestrustees, Betafence* and *HR Trustees* cases, rejected the argument that the amendment was wholly invalid, and described the scope of the amendment in terms of the construction principle, concluding that proviso was to be implied into the rules so that the benefits applicable on the exercise of the exclusion power were the greater of the ordinary leaving service benefits (based on salary at the date of that exercise plus revaluation) and an underpin based on salary at the date when the member actually left service or reached normal retirement date but without revaluation.[1]

1 [2014] EWHC 980 (Ch), [2014] Pens LR 335 at [289(iii)].

4.15

The Court of Appeal, whilst upholding this aspect of Warren J's judgment, appeared to treat the matter as one of excessive execution requiring the *Hastings-Bass* requirement to be satisfied. The issue arose during a submission that the exercise of the exclusion power by the employer was invalid because it was exercised for an improper purpose, as it purported to break the final salary link, whereas Warren J had held that it was implicitly subject to a proviso such that it could not do so. The Court of Appeal said that that argument was at best based on excessive execution, referring to Warren J's conclusion that the exclusion power was subject to an implied limitation such that it could not be used to break the final salary link.[1] The Court of Appeal rejected the argument in the following terms:

> 'By the same reasoning, it seems to us that there is no reason why the exercise of the Exclusion Power by the notices actually given in this case should not be held valid to the extent permitted by the implicit

limitation on the power. If one were to ask whether Holdings would have given the same Notices if it had been aware that it would not be able thereby to break the final salary link, the answer would have to be that it would.'

1 [2017] EWCA Civ 1212, [2018] ICR 1681 at [173]–[174].

4.16

Thus, although the Court of Appeal referred to Warren J's application of the construction analysis, apparently without criticism, the reference to whether the employer would have exercised the power in the same way had it known of the limitations to the amendment power suggests that it was applying the *Hastings-Bass* requirement of the severance principle.

4.17

Decided between the first instance and Court of Appeal decisions in *IBM*, a further first instance case appeared to endorse the severance principle. In *Shannan v Viavi Solutions UK Ltd*,[1] a power in the scheme's rules to appoint a new principal employer was purportedly exercised with retrospective effect. The amendment power in the rules prohibited amendments which operated to prejudice accrued benefits. Although not necessary for his decision, Deputy Judge Fancourt QC said that the exercise of the power could not have had the effect of interfering with accrued rights under the scheme, and that he was very doubtful whether the purported exercise of the power could have been saved by severance in such circumstances, as it was unclear in what respects retrospective effect could be given to the appointment and unclear from precisely what date.

1 [2016] EWHC 1530 (Ch), [2016] Pens LR 193 at [125].

Wedgwood Pension Plan Trustee Ltd v Salt

4.18

The interaction between the construction and severance principles, and the role of the *Hastings-Bass* requirement, were reviewed by Deputy Judge Reed QC in *Wedgwood Pension Plan Trustee Ltd v Salt*.[1]

1 [2018] EWHC 79 (Ch), [2018] Pens LR 283 at [61]–[70].

4.19

The case was unusual, in that the amendment in question was not prejudicial to accrued rights because of an amendment to the rights themselves, but because of the impact on the value of those rights of an extension to the ability of the employer to cease participation in the scheme. The employer in 2006 had purported to serve a notice terminating its contributions to the scheme pursuant to a rule introduced in 2001. It was common ground that, had the notice been valid, it would have been effective to break the final salary link. The relevant issue was whether the introduction of the rule in 2001 was itself valid, when the predecessor provision only permitted contributions to be terminated where it was '*impracticable or inexpedient*' for the employer to continue to participate in the scheme. The question was whether the rule was valid given that the removal of that precondition adversely affected the rights of the members, which was contrary to the restriction in the amendment power.

4.20

Having referred to both the *Bestrustees* and *Betafence* cases, the deputy judge held that they were operating in the same jurisdiction, and that the answer was the same whether approached as a matter of construction or severance, with the former being more applicable in *Betafence* because the amendment could not be saved merely by deleting the objectionable part. For this reason, the deputy judge held that the rule introduced by amendment in 2001 was subject to the implied limitation that the employers could only terminate contributions where it was shown that they had found it inexpedient or impracticable to participate in the scheme.

4.21

The deputy judge also held that the *Hastings-Bass* requirement had to be complied with in any event, citing the Court of Appeal's decision in the *IBM* case. When faced with the post-*Bestrustees* cases in which the construction principle had been applied without having to satisfy the *Hastings-Bass* requirement, the deputy judge said that there may have been no argument in those cases that the power would not have been exercised in any event, implying that the *Hastings-Bass* requirement must still have been relevant in those cases.

4.22

The need to satisfy the *Hastings-Bass* requirement raised the issue of the effect of the restatement of the rule in *Hastings-Bass* by the Supreme Court in *Pitt v Holt*,[1] which held that the exercise of the trustees' discretion could only be set aside under that principle if it was established that the trustees had exercised their power in breach of their fiduciary duty, which would be unlikely to occur if the trustees had acted on the basis of appropriate professional advice. The treatment of this point by the deputy judge is not easy to follow, but she appeared to reject the argument that *Pitt v Holt* affected the *Hastings-Bass* requirement, citing with approval a passage from *Lewin*[2] which set out the severance principle as applied in *Bestrustees* without reference to *Pitt v Holt*.[3]

1 [2013] UKSC 26, [2013] 2 AC 108. See **7.10**.
2 (19th edn, Sweet & Maxwell, 2015), para 29-241. The same passage appears in the current edition (20th edn) at para 30-107.
3 [2018] EWHC 79 (Ch), [2018] Pens LR 283 at [67]–[70].

The role of the *Hastings-Bass* requirement

4.23

Following the *Wedgwood* case, the law appears to be that, whether or not the saving of part of a scheme amendment is treated as a matter of construction of the amendment power, or as a matter of severance, it must be established that the trustees would have introduced the amendment had they known of its true scope, irrespective of whether its introduction amounted to a breach of their fiduciary duty.

4.24

In many cases, this requirement will be easy to satisfy, when it can be readily inferred that the trustees would have wished to go as far as they could in exercising the power in question. However, this will be more difficult where the result of the partial invalidity of the change would result in certain members being better off than if the change was wholly invalid,[1] when the purpose of the change was to reduce members' benefits. Similarly, if the invalid reduction of benefits was part of a package of changes which included increases to benefits, there may be an issue as to whether those increases would have been provided had it been known that the reduction was invalid.

1 Such as where an underpin is applied to give those members the better of the amended benefits and the benefits to which they would have been entitled had the change not been made: see **3.14–3.15.**

4.25

There are several objections to the application of the *Hastings-Bass* requirement in this context:

(a) As stated at **4.9**(b), the *Hastings-Bass* requirement derives from the court's jurisdiction to interfere with the exercise of fiduciary powers. Whilst this is appropriate where the power in question was exercised by trustees, what if the power was also or instead exercised by the employer, or otherwise subject to the consent of the employer? Employers are not usually subject to fiduciary duties when exercising amendment powers,[1] so the *Hastings-Bass* requirement should not apply to them. If that is the case,[2] this requirement places undue emphasis on what the trustees would have done, and ignores the fact that the employer will usually play a key role in the amendment process, and will often be responsible for the amendment being advanced in the first place: why, in this case, should only the trustees' attitudes be relevant, when the employer will have had at least as much say in whether the change is or is not made?[3]

(b) The requirement involves a view to be taken of the trustees' state of mind at the time of the introduction of the amendment, which may give rise to practical difficulties if the amendment was made many years ago, and the trustees who were involved are no longer able to give evidence or do not recollect the matter given the passage of time.

(c) The evidential exercise is further complicated by the need to consider the hypothetical counterfactual situation of what the trustees would have done had they known something which they would not have known or suspected at the time.

(d) The requirement is difficult to apply in the case of changes which introduced a package of measures, only one of which is affected by the mistake: is the matter of what the trustees would have done to be resolved by reference to the effect of the mistake on the whole package, or only on the changes affected by the mistake?

(e) It might be said that the answer to this issue should flow from the effect the changes would have if the amendment was validated in part: the amendment should survive if it would still achieve the original object of the trustees; but if it does not, it should be struck down. However, it will often not be possible to ascertain the effect of the changes until many years into the future, and it may affect different members in different ways. For example, where DB rights were replaced with career average revalued earnings (CARE) benefits, a member who received no future salary increases, or increases at a rate below the revaluation element of the CARE benefits, may be better off under the new regime; yet other members, with different remuneration patterns, may be worse off because of the change.

1 See **13.25–13.26**.

2 In some of the cases, the *Hastings-Bass* requirement has been applied generally to the holders of the amendment power, irrespective of whether they were acting in a fiduciary capacity: see, for example, the *IBM* case [2017] EWCA Civ 1212, [2018] ICR 1681 at [174]; and the *Wedgwood* case [2018] EWHC 79 (Ch), [2018] Pens LR 283 at [74].

3 The contrary argument is that trustees' conduct should be scrutinised more closely than that of the employer, by reason of the more onerous duties owed by them to the members.

New joiners

4.26

Separately from the application of the amendment to the future service of existing members, there is the question of whether an invalid amendment should nevertheless apply to persons who joined the scheme after its purported introduction.

4.27

Support for this proposition can be found in *Air Jamaica v Charlton*,[1] in which Lord Millett said as follows:

> 'Their Lordships are satisfied that the 1994 amendments are incurably bad … This does not mean that an amendment is wholly without effect. An employee who joins the plan after an amendment makes his settlement upon the trusts of the plan as amended …'

1 [1999] 1 WLR 1399, 1411.

4.28

This aspect of *Air Jamaica* was not applied in two cases involving invalid amendments affecting the distribution of surplus on the winding-up of schemes, on the basis that those provisions were intended to apply generally to all scheme members whenever they joined.[1] In one of those cases,[2] the judge said that Lord Millett's statement was obiter, and that if an amendment to introduce a new provision was invalid, under general principles of trust law the trustee had no authority to act upon the new provision since it would be an act in breach of trust.

1 *Harwood-Smart v Caws* [2000] Pens LR 101; *BHLSPF Pty Ltd v Brashs Pty Ltd* [2001] VSC 512.
2 The *BHLSPF Pty Ltd* case at [44] per Warren J.

4.29

The proposition that an invalid amendment can nevertheless apply to new entrants is doubtful as a matter of principle. The governing documentation on which the new member joins ought to be effective against them only to the extent that its terms are legally valid; and there seems to be no good reason why a new entrant should not be entitled to rely on the invalidity of an amendment in the same way as the existing members.

Section 67 of PA 1995

4.30

As discussed at **3.34–3.37**, s 67 of PA 1995 applies to modifications of occupational pension schemes which adversely affected entitlements or accrued rights of members. Prior to 6 April 2006, such modifications were prohibited; thereafter, such modifications were voidable at the instance of the Pensions Regulator.

4.31

Whilst there is no authority on the issue, it is thought that:

(a) the court would permit the prospective application of any such amendment which fell foul of the pre-April 2006 version of s 67;[1] and

(b) the Pensions Regulator would be likely to avoid such an amendment which contravened the post-April 2006 version of s 67, only to the extent that it purported to affect the rights protected by that section.[2]

1 In *Mr K* (PO-22802, 15 October 2020) at [50], the Pensions Ombudsman determined that such an amendment was validly made for new joiners and for existing members in respect of their future service. The Ombudsman did not refer to the *Hastings-Bass* requirement.
2 See, for example, the Determination Notice relating to the ELCB Staff Pension Scheme (TM7208) (20 July 2010).

Practice point: partial invalidity clauses

4.32

It has become increasingly common practice for pension documents to contain terms which expressly provide that, if any term of the document is found to be invalid or unenforceable, the invalid term will be severed from the remaining terms, which will be valid.

4.33

Such provisions – known as 'partial invalidity' or 'severance' clauses – are common in commercial and employment agreements where there is a danger that the invalidity or unenforceability of a particular term may cause the entire agreement to fail.

4.34

In a pensions context, such a provision may have the benefit of alleviating the practical difficulty of having to establish the intention of the trustees for the purposes of the *Hastings-Bass* requirement.

4.35

However, employers should be aware that such a clause may operate to increase the liabilities of the scheme above those that were originally intended, if the term is included in an amendment which provides for both increases and reductions to benefits: even if the intention was for those changes to operate as a package, the provision may operate to confirm the application of the increases even if the reductions are declared invalid. It may be possible to avoid this by including a provision which requires the employer and the trustees to re-negotiate the package, although the enforceability of such a provision is open to question.[1]

1 Whilst 'agreements to agree' are generally unenforceable under English law (*Walford v Miles* [1992] 2 AC 128), in *Butters v BBC Worldwide Ltd* [2009] EWHC 1954 (Ch), [2009] BPIR 1315 at [144]–[151], Peter Smith J said (obiter) that an obligation to negotiate a substitute clause which achieved the objectives of the original clause was enforceable where the required substitute provision was comparatively easy to ascertain.

5 Construction

5.1

When faced with a pension scheme document which may mistakenly fail to accord with the intention of the parties, the first step is to see if it can be construed in such a way that resolves the matter in favour of the meaning that the document was intended to have.

5.2

From a practitioner's perspective, issues of pensions construction are rarely determined in court. Typically, mistakes are identified by those responsible for the administration of the scheme, who will be looking for an inexpensive and discreet solution to the problem which maintains the status quo, an attitude often shared by the employer and the trustees who are of the same view as to what the document was intended to achieve. Thus, unlike in the case of bilateral contractual agreements, resolution of a construction issue in one particular way will not necessarily give rise to complaint and challenge by the party who would benefit from the contrary construction. In such a situation, the parties will not always require the kind of certainty which can only be obtained by seeking the determination of the court: instead, the parties may be looking to move forward pragmatically, with a defensible position that carries an acceptable level of risk.

5.3

The first part of this chapter focuses on how to construe pension documents where the language is ambiguous, in the sense that it can be read in two ways, one of which does and one of which does not accord with the intention of the parties.[1] This part is intended to assist the adviser in fortifying their analysis to support the outcome which the employer and trustees would wish to achieve, without having to undertake the kinds of lengthy, costly and public remedial procedures discussed elsewhere in this book, by considering the tools which are available to construe the document in favour of the intended meaning.[2]

1 Traditionally, a distinction was drawn between patent ambiguities (which appear from the language of the document) and latent ambiguities (which only become apparent when the language is applied to the factual situation): however, this distinction no longer has any practical relevance in the construction of documents: *Lewison The Interpretation of Contracts* (7th edn, Sweet & Maxwell, 2020) (*Lewison*), para 8.12.

2 In addition to the process of construction, the scope and meaning of a document may be determined by recourse to the implication of terms: this is not likely, however, to be of much assistance in reconciling ambiguities caused by mistakes in the drafting of pension documents, as terms are only to be implied where the document does not expressly provide for what is to happen when some event subsequently occurs.

5.4

In the case of documents where the language (as a result, for example, of clerical error) is clearly and unambiguously mistaken, the only way in which that mistake can possibly be cured by way of construction is to apply the principle of 'corrective construction': that principle is considered in the second part of this chapter.

Using general principles of construction to resolve ambiguities

5.5

Construction involves ascertaining the meaning which a document would convey to a reasonable person having all the background knowledge which would reasonably have been available to the parties in the situation in which they were at the time of the contract.[1] Recent Supreme Court decisions have seen a move away from contextualism and purposive interpretation, towards a greater emphasis on the language of the document.[2]

1 *Investors Compensation Scheme Ltd v West Bromwich Building Society* [1998] 1 WLR 896, 912–913 per Lord Hoffmann.
2 *Arnold v Britton* [2015] UKSC 36, [2015] AC 1619; *Wood v Capita Insurance Services Ltd* [2017] UKSC 24, [2017] AC 1173.

5.6

Although it has been said that there are no special rules governing the construction of pension scheme documents,[1] the general rules have been adapted to the particular characteristics of pension schemes in ways which effectively amount to separate principles.[2] The principles of construction applicable to pension documents can accordingly be taken from the following leading cases.

1 For example, *Mettoy Pension Trustees Ltd v Evans* [1990] 1 WLR 1587, 1610 per Warner J.
2 Briggs J described them as 'sub-principles' in *Stena Line Ltd v Merchant Navy Ratings Pension Fund Trustees Ltd* [2010] EWHC 1805 (Ch), [2010] Pens LR 411 at [82].

5.7

The first case is *Re Courage Group's Pension Schemes*,[1] in which Millett J said that the provisions of a pension scheme should wherever possible be construed to give '*reasonable and practical effect to the scheme, bearing in mind that it has to be operated against a constantly changing commercial background*'. Although this statement was made in the course of considering the scope of a scheme's amendment power, the reference to the '*reasonable and practical effect*' has proved to be a powerful and enduring approach to the construction of pension scheme documents in general.[2]

1 [1987] 1 WLR 495, 505.
2 Thus, in *National Grid Co plc v Mayes* [2001] UKHL 20, [2001] 1 WLR 864 at [53], where there was a choice of possible constructions, Lord Hoffmann said that the correct choice depended '*upon the language of the scheme and the practical consequences of choosing one construction rather than the other*'.

5.8

The second case is *Mettoy Pension Trustees Ltd v Evans*,[1] in which Warner J approved Millett J's analysis, describing the proper approach to the construction of pension scheme documents as '*practical and purposive, rather than detached and literal*'. The judge went on to state that the background circumstances in the light of which pension scheme documents have to be construed included the following particular features:

(a) the fact that the rights of scheme members have contractual and commercial origins, earned by service with their employer;

(b) where the scheme is approved and contracted-out, the requirements of HMRC and statutory requirements applicable to such schemes; and

(c) the common practice from time to time in the field of pension schemes generally, as evinced in particular by the evidence of actuaries and by textbooks written by practitioners in that field.

1 [1990] 1 WLR 1587, 1610–1611.

5.9

The third case is *Stevens v Bell*,[1] in which Arden LJ identified characteristics which tended to differentiate pension scheme documents from other analogous instruments in the following terms, building upon the earlier cases:

(a) The benefits members receive under the scheme are part of the remuneration for their services, and their relationship with the employer must be seen as running in parallel with their employment relationship.

(b) As Millett J said in *Re Courage*, the document should be construed so as to give a reasonable and practical effect to the scheme. This requires competing permissible constructions to be tested against the consequences they produce in practice. Technicality is to be avoided, and if the consequences are impractical or over-restrictive or technical in practice, that is an indication that some other interpretation was appropriate.

(c) Difficulties can arise where different provisions have been amended at different points in time. The general principle is that each new provision should be considered against the circumstances prevailing at the date when it was adopted rather than the date of the original trust deed; likewise, the meaning of a clause in the scheme must be ascertained by examining the deed as it stood at the time the clause was first introduced.[2]

(d) The factual situation in the light of which the provision must be construed includes HMRC practice and common practice among practitioners in the field as evidenced by the works of practitioners at that time.

(e) Ultimately, the function of the court is to construe the document without any predisposition as to the correct philosophical approach.

(f) The scheme should be interpreted as a whole, and the meaning of a particular provision should be considered in conjunction with other relevant provisions.

1 [2002] EWCA Civ 672, [2002] Pens LR 247 at [26]–[32]
2 Arden LJ revisited this particular issue in *Stena Line Ltd v Merchant Navy Ratings Pension Fund Trustees Ltd* [2011] EWCA Civ 543, [2011] Pens LR 223 at [31]–[35].

5.10

The final case is *Barnardo's v Buckinghamshire*,[1] in which the Supreme Court has given general guidance on the construction of pension scheme documents following the recent restatement of general construction principles referred to at **5.5**. Lord Hodge JSC began by identifying the following distinctive characteristics of a pension scheme which were relevant to determining how the court would approach the construction of its provisions:

(a) it is a formal legal document which has been prepared by skilled and specialist legal drafters;

(b) unlike many commercial contracts, it is not the product of commercial negotiation between parties who may have conflicting interests and who may conclude their agreement under considerable pressure of time, leaving loose ends to be sorted out in future;

(c) it is an instrument which is designed to operate in the long term, defining people's rights long after the economic and other circumstances, which existed at the time when it was signed, may have ceased to exist;

(d) it confers important rights on the members of the scheme, who were not parties to the instrument and who may have joined the scheme many years after it was initiated; and

(e) members may not have easy access to expert legal advice or be able readily to ascertain the circumstances which existed when the scheme was established.

1 [2018] UKSC 55, [2019] ICR 495 at [13]–[18].

5.11

The judge went on to say that, in such circumstances, it is appropriate for the court to give weight to textual analysis, by concentrating on the words which the drafter has chosen to use and by attaching less weight to the background facts than might be appropriate in commercial contracts. The judge approved a statement in an earlier case[1] that the central importance to the scheme of the members and their families was inherently antipathetic to a departure from the plain language of the document by reason of a common understanding between the trustees and employer or even some widespread practice within the pensions industry. However, the judge said that the emphasis on textual analysis did not derogate from the need both to avoid undue technicality and to have regard to the practical consequences of any construction: Millett J's analysis in *Re Courage* was cited with approval. Instead, the focus on textual analysis operated as a constraint on the contribution that background factual circumstances, which would not readily be accessible to its members as time passed, can make to the construction of the scheme.

1 *Safeway Ltd v Newton* [2017] EWCA Civ 1482, [2018] Pens LR 2 at [22] per Lord Briggs of Westbourne JSC.

5.12

To summarise the position:

(a) the main obstacle to construing a pension scheme provision in the way in which the parties intended is that construction is an objective exercise, by reference to how a reasonable person would read the document rather than the parties themselves; the subjective intentions of the parties are therefore generally inadmissible for this purpose, as is subsequent conduct;[1]

(b) this principle is particularly material to pension schemes, as the persons primarily affected – the members – would not have been involved in the production of the relevant document: accordingly, the Supreme Court in *Barnardo's v Buckinghamshire*[2] has affirmed the limited utility of background factual material in the construction of pension scheme documents, although the central role of the members may enable documents which would have been sent to them at the time, such as announcements or even (in some circumstances) explanatory booklets, to be admitted as relevant background evidence;[3]

(c) in any event, the following principles which have been identified as relevant to ascertaining the meaning of a pension scheme document afford considerable scope for argument that cases of ambiguity should be resolved in a way which accords with the parties' intentions:

    (i) giving reasonable and practical effect to the scheme;

    (ii) taking a practical and purposive, rather than a detached and literal, approach;

    (iii) taking account of common practice amongst pensions practitioners;

    (iv) avoiding constructions which have impractical, over-restrictive or technical consequences;

    (v) construing provisions in conjunction with other relevant provisions; and

    (vi) recognising that the document is intended to define members' rights in the long term;

(d) moreover, there is ample capacity for judges to impose their own notions of what must have been intended when construing pension scheme provisions.[4]

1 It is not clear whether the old principle, which permitted subjective declarations of intent to be admitted in cases of latent ambiguity where all the background circumstances had been admitted and

there remained two or more meanings each of which was entirely consistent with the language of the document, has survived the criticisms of Lord Hoffmann in *Mannai Investment Co Ltd v Eagle Star Life Assurance Co Ltd* [1997] AC 749, 776–780: see *Lewison*, paras 8.22–8.30.

2 [2018] UKSC 55, [2019] ICR 495.

3 Despite the *Barnardo's* case, reference may also be made to previous iterations of the scheme's governing provisions: see *Wedgwood Pension Plan Trustee Ltd v Salt* [2018] EWHC 79 (Ch), [2018] Pens LR 283 at [38] per Deputy Judge Reed QC.

4 A notable example of this is *Sterling Insurance Trustees Ltd v Sterling Insurance Group Ltd* [2015] EWHC 2665 (Ch), discussed at **5.44–5.46**. In *AGCO Ltd v Massey Ferguson Works Pension Trust Ltd* [2003] EWCA Civ 1044, [2004] ICR 15, Sedley and Aldous LJJ (at [82] and [87] respectively) differed in their views as to whether it was 'ridiculous' for a member of a scheme who had been dismissed for cause to be entitled to an early retirement benefit.

5.13

Reliance can also be placed on the general principle that, in the case of ambiguity, the court will strive to uphold the validity of the document, and to avoid it being void for uncertainty:[1] the court will do all it can to 'tie up any loose ends' left open by the drafter of the document.[2]

1 Applied in a pensions context in *Premier Foods Group Services Ltd v RHM Pension Trust Ltd* [2012] EWHC 447 (Ch), [2012] Pens LR 151 at [30] per Warren J.

2 *Dresdner Kleinwort Ltd v Attrill* [2013] EWCA Civ 394, [2013] 3 All ER 607 at [60] per Elias LJ: see generally *Lewison*, paras 8.83–8.92.

Practice point: helpful judicial statements

5.14

When advising clients on the meaning of ambiguous pension scheme provisions, legal advisers may find the following statements taken from pensions cases to be helpful in justifying a construction which resolves the ambiguity in favour of what the parties intended:

(a) 'It would be inappropriate and indeed perverse to construe [pension] documents so strictly as to undermine their effectiveness or their effectiveness for their purpose. I do not think that, in saying that, I am saying anything different from, what was said by Lord Upjohn when in *In re Gulbenkian's Settlements* [1970] AC 508, 522, he referred, in the context and experience in the relevant matter, innate common sense and desire to make sense of the settlor's or parties' expressed intentions, however obscure and ambiguous the language that may have been used, to give a reasonable meaning to that language it if can do so without doing complete violence to it.'[1]

(b) 'The rules cannot always be expected to have the consistency and coherence which in an ideal world they would possess and arguments based on a too detailed analysis of the terms used may frustrate themselves.'[2]

(c) 'Any scheme such as the present will have anomalies, but obviously a construction which reduces, rather than increases, their number is (all other things being equal) to be preferred.'[3]

(d) 'If more than one interpretation is possible, the correct choice may depend on the practical consequences of choosing one interpretation rather than another.'[4]

(e) 'The court will be legitimately averse to the frustration of bona fide transactions by technical points which passed unperceived by all concerned at the time of the transaction in question. However there are limits to the extent to which rules of law, whether or not properly described as technicalities or even merest technicalities, can be circumvented.[5]

(f) 'The settled practice of experienced pension scheme practitioners may well constitute a valuable guide to what the law is and how its provisions should be construed, just as the settled practice of conveyancers has long been recognised and given effect by courts dealing with conveyancing matters but that is not to say that pension scheme practitioners operate in a form of Alsatia or have the power to override the provisions of statute law or equity.'[6]

(g) 'There is no dispute that pension documents should be construed in a "practical and purposive rather than a detached and literal" manner (see per Warner J in *Mettoy Pension Trustees v Evans* [1990] 1 WLR 1578 at 1610). To construe these rules as applying to transferred pensioners would give rise to enormous practical difficulties which the draftsmen cannot have intended.'[7]

(h) '… the scheme should be construed as a whole with a view, if possible, to producing a practical and sensible result.'[8]

(i) 'There may come a point where a particular construction is so disproportionately expensive to an employer that one must reconsider it …'[9]

(j) 'The fact that a particular construction can give rise to an anomaly must cause one to reconsider its correctness.'[10]

(k) 'I do, however, accept that the fact that one interpretation of a provision renders that provision otiose is a strong indication that that interpretation is not the correct one.'[11]

(l) 'I am not attracted, to say the least, by a construction which necessarily involves a Trustee acting other than in accordance with the provisions of the trust even when, in practical terms, any breach can be retrospectively validated … Certainly, when faced with competing constructions one of which does, and one of which does not, involve a breach of trust, I prefer the one which does not in the absence of compelling reasons to the contrary.'[12]

(m) '… the fact that the members are not volunteers, and the fact that pension is a form of deferred remuneration, cannot be conclusive.'[13]

(n) 'I also bear in mind that it is important to avoid unduly fettering a power to amend the provisions of the scheme as it is important for the parties to be able to make changes which might be required by the exigencies of commercial life. A power of amendment which prevented the employer from curtailing the right of existing members to continue to accrue benefits in circumstances where the employer was in financial difficulties and finding it difficult to fund the Plan makes far less sense than a construction which protects rights which members have gained through past employment but enables the employer to stop those benefits accruing in the future.'[14]

1 *Mettoy Pension Trustees Ltd v Evans* [1990] 1 WLR 1587, 1611 per Warner J.
2 *Hoover Ltd v Hetherington* [2002] EWHC 1052 (Ch), [2002] Pens LR 297 at [21] per Pumfrey J.
3 *Hoover Ltd v Hetherington* [2002] EWHC 1052 (Ch), [2002] Pens LR 297 at [38].
4 *Armitage v Staveley Industries plc* [2005] EWCA Civ 792, [2006] Pens LR 191 at [29] per Sir Andrew Morritt V-C. See, generally, *Rainy Sky SA v Kookmin Bank* [2011] UKSC 50, [2011] 1 WLR 2900.
5 *LRT Pension Fund Trustee Co Ltd v Hatt* [1993] Pens LR 227 at [112] per Knox J.
6 *LRT Pension Fund Trustee Co Ltd v Hatt* [1993] Pens LR 227 at [113].
7 *Express Newspapers Pensions Trustees Ltd v Express Newspapers plc* [1999] Pens LR 9 at [31] per Jacob J.
8 *AGCO Ltd v Massey Ferguson Works Pension Trust Ltd* [2002] EWHC 2878 (Ch), [2003] Pens LR 47 at [16] per Neuberger J.
9 *AGCO Ltd v Massey Ferguson Works Pension Trust Ltd* [2002] EWHC 2878 (Ch), [2003] Pens LR 47 at [42].
10 *AGCO Ltd v Massey Ferguson Works Pension Trust Ltd* [2002] EWHC 2878 (Ch), [2003] Pens LR 47 at [46].
11 *Singapore Airlines Ltd v Buck Consultants Ltd* [2011] EWCA Civ 1542, [2012] Pens LR 1 at [43] per Arden LJ.
12 *Premier Foods Group Services Ltd v RHM Pension Trust Ltd* [2012] EWHC 447 (Ch), [2012] Pens LR 151 at [54] per Warren J.
13 *Entrust Pension Ltd v Prospect Hospice Ltd* [2012] EWHC 1666 (Ch), [2012] Pens LR 341 at [65] per Henderson J.
14 *Wedgwood Pension Plan Trustee Ltd v Salt* [2018] EWHC 79 (Ch), [2018] Pens LR 283 at [44] per Deputy Judge Reed QC.

Using corrective construction to deal with unambiguous mistakes

5.15

Where the language of the document is clear and unambiguous, the construction principles discussed above will not allow the document to be read in a different way, even if that would result in the correction of a mistake.[1]

1 The leading case on the general requirement to apply the clear and unambiguous language of a document, irrespective of whether that reading lacks commercial sense, is *Arnold v Britton* [2015] UKSC 36, [2015] AC 1619. For similar statements in a pensions context, see *Harwood-Smart v Caws* [2000] Pens LR 101 at [22] per Rimer J and *Britvic plc v Britvic Pensions Ltd* [2021] EWCA Civ 867, [2021] ICR 1648 at [29]–[32] per Sir Geoffrey Vos MR, [56]–[57] per Coulson LJ and [67]–[70] per Nugee LJ.

5.16

In such a situation, the principle of corrective construction may nevertheless come into play. Whilst courts have long been prepared to correct obvious and easily-curable mistakes made in documents as a matter of construction, the principle of corrective construction has gained a new lease of life in the 21st century, and has become a more popular method of correcting mistakes, both in pensions and general commercial cases.

5.17

The application of this principle has the same effect as rectification, in that the provision in question will be treated as having always been in the corrected form, and its great advantage over rectification is that it does not necessarily require court proceedings, if the client's legal advisers are prepared to advise accordingly; and even if proceedings are required, they will generally be cheaper and quicker than a claim for rectification.

The scope of the principle

5.18

This principle originally existed to deal with blatantly obvious typographical errors and omissions.[1] For many years, the jurisdiction was exercised very sparingly, in circumstances where the mistake was purely clerical in nature.[2] Beyond such cases, the courts generally refused to supply missing words as a matter of construction, even where the intentions of the parties were plain, on the basis that this was trespassing improperly into the realm of rectification.[3] Moreover, the mistake had to be apparent from the document itself: extrinsic evidence was inadmissible for this purpose.[4]

1 For example, *Coles v Hulme* (1828) 8 B & C 568 (a reference in a contract between two English parties to a price of '*one thousand*' was construed to mean '*one thousand pounds*').
2 For example, *Bache v Proctor* (1780) 1 Doug KB 382; *Flight v Lord Lake* (1835) 2 Bing NC 72; *Mourmand v Le Clair* [1903] 2 KB 216; *Re Alexander's Settlement* [1910] 2 Ch 225; *Slough Estates Ltd v Slough Borough Council (No. 2)* [1969] 2 Ch 305.
3 *Young v Smith* (1865-66) LR 1 Eq 180; *Re Ethel and Mitchells and Butler's Contract* [1901] 1 Ch 945; *IRC v Raphael* [1935] AC 96, 142–148 per Lord Wright.
4 *East v Pantiles (Plant Hire) Ltd* [1986] 2 EGLR 111; *Schnieder v Mills* [1993] 3 All ER 377, 381–382 per Robert Walker J.

5.19

The genesis of the extension of the corrective construction jurisdiction was the fifth principle of the restatement of the general principles of construction by Lord Hoffmann in *Investors Compensation Scheme Ltd v West Bromwich Building Society Ltd.*[1]

> 'The "rule" that words should be given their 'natural and ordinary meaning' reflects the common sense proposition that we do not easily accept that people have made linguistic mistakes, particularly in formal documents. On the other hand, if one would nevertheless conclude from the background that something must have gone wrong with the language, the law does not require judges to attribute to the parties an intention which they plainly could not have had.'

1 [1998] 1 WLR 896, 913.

5.20

Although Lord Hoffmann did not specifically refer here to corrective construction, his view that it was possible to discern from the admissible background facts that something must have gone wrong with the language, paved the way for looking beyond the four corners of the document in order to determine whether such a mistake had been made and how to correct it.[1] This enabled the corrective construction principle to be applied beyond obvious clerical or grammatical errors.

1 As was noted by Carnwath LJ in *KPMG v Network Rail Infrastructure Ltd* [2007] EWCA Civ 363, [2008] 1 P & CR 11 at [48]–[49]. See also *Generali Italia SpA v Pelagic Fisheries Corporation* [2020] EWHC 1228 (Comm), [2020] 1 WLR 4211 at [109] per Foxton J.

5.21

Thus, in a rent review case,[1] Clarke LJ described the principle in the following terms:

> 'where it is obvious to a reasonable man with the relevant knowledge that there has been a mistake, it is appropriate to correct that mistake by a process of construction.'

1 *Holding & Barnes plc v Hill House Hammond Ltd* [2001] EWCA Civ 1334, [2002] 2 P&CR 145 at [21]; see also at [47] per Sir Martin Nourse.

5.22

An early example of the application of this wider principle in a pensions context is *Snowville UK Ltd v Holidaybreak plc.*[1] In that case, a service agreement between a company (B) and one of its employees provided that B would fund his benefits in a defined contribution scheme operated by B to a prescribed level. B was then sold to S, at which time the employee identified a substantial shortfall in the funding of his benefits under the scheme. B was thereafter sold by S to H, pursuant to an agreement which provided that H would indemnify S in respect of any liability which S incurred as a result of the underfunding. It was accepted that H could have no liability on a literal construction of the indemnity, as only B was obliged to fund the benefits. However, Deputy Judge Garnett QC was prepared to read the reference to S in the indemnity as a reference to B, on the basis that an objective observer would have concluded that something must have gone wrong with the drafting and that a reasonable person, knowing all the facts, would have concluded that the parties intended the indemnity to cover B's liability to fund the benefits.

1 [2004] EWHC 1336 (Ch).

5.23

An authoritative restatement of this extended corrective construction principle was provided by Lord Hoffmann in the leading case of *Chartbrook Ltd v Persimmon Homes Ltd*,[1] in which he stated that:

(a) the conditions for the application of the principle are that it is clear that something has gone wrong with the language[2] and it is clear what a reasonable person would have understood the parties to have meant;

(b) in order to establish the mistake, the court was not confined to reading the document without regard to its background or context;[3] and

(c) there was no limit to the amount of rearrangement or correction which the court is allowed when applying this principle.

1 [2009] UKHL 38, [2009] 1 AC 1101 at [22]–[25]. For a summary of the relevant conditions in a pensions context, see *Independent Trustee Services Ltd v Knell* [2010] EWHC 650 (Ch), [2010] Pens LR 195 at [10(f)] per Norris J.

2 It is not necessary that the court should be certain precisely what words have been omitted; it is sufficient that it knows their gist: *Homburg Houtimport BV v Agrosin Ltd* [2003] UKHL 12, [2004] 1 AC 715 at [192] per Lord Millett.

3 The suggestion by Hildyard J in *Re Sea Containers Services Ltd* [2012] EWHC 2547 (Ch), [2012] Pens LR 569 at [61], that the principle only comes into play where the mistake is clear and obvious on the face of the instrument, is accordingly incorrect.

5.24

Lord Hoffmann's restatement is not without its critics[1] and in *Marley v Rawlings*,[2] Lord Neuberger JSC described it as controversial. There is certainly a tension between the principle that background material cannot be used to establish an ambiguity where the words used in the document are unambiguous,[3] and the use of such material to establish a mistake in the language of the document where no such mistake is apparent from the document itself.[4]

1 See Buxton, '"Construction" and rectification after Chartbrook' [2010] Cambridge LJ 253. Professor Richard Calnan describes the principle as looking '*very like a form of summary rectification ("rectification lite")*': Calnan, *Principles of Contractual Interpretation* (2nd edn, OUP, 2017), para 7.159.

2 [2015] UKSC 2, [2015] AC 129 at [37].

3 *Rainy Sky SA v Kookmin Bank* [2011] UKSC 50, [2011] 1 WLR 2900 at [23] per Lord Clarke of Stone-cum-Ebony JSC.

4 See the Court of Appeal's discussion in *Britvic plc v Britvic Pensions Ltd* referred to at **5.53**.

Construction versus rectification

5.25

The principle of corrective construction is not a complete substitute for rectification, as there are a number of limits to its application.

The presumption

5.26

In both corrective construction and rectification cases, the court begins with the presumption that the words used in the document constitute a true and accurate record of what the parties intended to say. In rectification cases, the presumption is that the best evidence of the parties' intentions is what they have written;[1] and in construction cases, the court will not easily accept that people have made linguistic mistakes, especially in formal documents.[2] Accordingly, as with rectification, it requires a strong case to persuade the court that the corrective construction principle should be applied.[3] In one case,[4] the court went so far as to state that a higher standard of proof than the usual balance of probabilities was necessary, and that the court had to be sure that there must have been a mistake.

1 See **6.11**.
2 *Chartbrook Ltd v Persimmon Homes Ltd* [2009] UKHL 38, [2009] 1 AC 1101 at [14] per Lord Hoffmann.
3 *Chartbrook Ltd v Persimmon Homes Ltd* [2009] UKHL 38, [2009] 1 AC 1101 at [15] per Lord Hoffmann; see also *Schmidt v Rosewood Trust Ltd* [2003] UKPC 26, [2003] 2 AC 709 at [14] per Lord Walker of Gestingthorpe; *Altera Voyageur Production Ltd v Premier Oil E&P UK Ltd* [2020] EWHC 1891 (Comm), [2021] 1 Lloyd's Rep 451 at [67] per Deputy Judge Salter QC. This applies equally to the correction which ought to be made: *Arnold v Britton* [2015] UKSC 36, [2015] AC 1619 at [78] per Lord Hodge JSC.
4 *Network Rail Infrastructure Ltd v Fremont Ltd* (20 June 2013, unreported) at [51] per Deputy Judge Strauss QC, cited by HHJ Parkes QC in *Dodd v Raebarn Estates Ltd* [2016] EWHC 262 (QB), [2016] HLR 223 at [30].

5.27

As with rectification,[1] whilst it is not necessary that the court should be satisfied how the mistake happened, the fact that there is a plausible explanation as to how the error occurred can support the conclusion that there has indeed been such an error.[2]

1 See **6.25**.
2 *Monsolar IQ Ltd v Woden Park Ltd* [2021] EWCA Civ 961, [2021] L & TR 29 at [40] per Nugee LJ.

The threshold test

5.28

The threshold test for corrective construction is stricter than the test for rectification. For the latter, it is enough that the wording of the document is contrary to the common intention of the parties. However, for the corrective construction principle to be engaged, the court must be satisfied that something has gone wrong with the language the parties have used, as opposed to the implementation of the bargain or the decision to exercise the power, which in turn requires the result to be irrational, absurd or nonsensical.[1]

1 *Honda Motor Europe Ltd v Powell* [2014] EWCA Civ 437, [2014] Pens LR 255 at [37]–[38] per Lewison LJ. See also *G&S Brough Ltd v Salvage Wharf Ltd* [2009] EWCA Civ 21, [2010] Ch 11 at [80] per Jackson LJ; *LSREF III Wight Ltd v Millvalley Ltd* [2016] EWHC 466 (Comm) at [62] per Cooke J; *Monsolar IQ Ltd v Woden Park Ltd* [2021] EWCA Civ 961, [2021] L & TR 29 at [30]–[32] per Nugee LJ.

5.29

A failure to think through the consequences of the provision, as opposed to any deficiency in its drafting, will not bring the corrective construction principle into play.[1] It is not therefore enough that the document is unfavourable to one side or another,[2] or that the wording makes the arrangement difficult to operate.[3]

1 *ING Bank NV v Ros Roca SA* [2011] EWCA Civ 353, [2012] 1 WLR 472 at [24] per Carnwath LJ and at [80] per Rix LJ.
2 *Pink Floyd Music Ltd v EMI Records Ltd* [2010] EWCA Civ 1429 at [20] per Lord Neuberger MR (this part of the judgment is not reported at [2011] 1 WLR 770); *Trillium (Prime) Property GP Ltd v Elmfield Road Ltd* [2018] EWCA Civ 1556 at [15] and [17] per Lewison LJ.
3 *JIS (1974) Ltd v MCP Investment Nominees 1 Ltd* [2003] EWCA Civ 721 at [19] per Carnwath LJ.

The scope of the admissible evidence

5.30

The process of construction is an objective exercise, ie what a reasonable person would have understood the document to mean; by contrast, what the parties themselves thought the document meant to achieve is relevant for the purposes of rectification.[1]

1 See *North Circular Properties Ltd v Internal Systems Organisation Ltd* (26 October 1984, unreported), per Deputy Judge Rattee QC, quoted in *Lewison*, para 9.12.

5.31

It follows that the evidence the court will admit to establish the mistake and the correction in a construction case is narrower than is permitted to establish the mistaken intention in a rectification case. Thus, rectification is the only available remedy if there is only evidence of subjective intention.[1] Moreover, a court of construction cannot take account of any pre-document negotiations, or of any matters subsequent to the execution of document, such as how it has been operated by the parties. By contrast, evidence of both of these matters is admissible and relevant in rectification cases.[2]

1 See **6.13**.
2 See **6.19**.

5.32

In practice, a successful construction claim will be based on extrinsic objective evidence, such as previous versions of deeds, draft deeds, and commentary on those drafts, together with a sufficiently strong case, based on the implications of the literal document, in order to overcome the threshold test described at **5.28**.

The scope of the correction

5.33

Although, as Lord Hoffmann stated in *Chartbrook*, there are no limits to the amount of correction which can be made, the court will not as a matter of construction read into the document a whole term omitted in error, where the document makes sense without it.

5.34

A good illustration of this is *Cherry Tree Investments Ltd v Landmain Ltd*,[1] in which the Court of Appeal was asked to construe a legal charge to include an enlarged power of sale for the mortgagee, which had not been expressly set out in the legal charge itself, but which had been set out in the terms of a related facility agreement. A majority of the court refused to read that power into the charge, because it involved reading an entire provision which had been omitted by the parties into a document which made perfect sense without it.

This was considered to be beyond the correction of what the parties had put into the document, and amounted to a rewriting of the contract to include something which had never been there, which was regarded as the exclusive province of rectification.

1 [2012] EWCA Civ 736, [2013] Ch 305.

Application of the principle in pensions cases

5.35

Since *Chartbrook,* the corrective construction principle has been considered in several pensions cases.

ICM Computer Group Ltd v Stribley[1]

5.36

In compliance with EU law, the trustees and the employer of a pension scheme agreed to equalise the normal retirement ages of male and female employees at age 65 with effect from 1 March 1997. The scheme's amendment power required the issue of a 'scheme amendment authority' document, by which the employer authorised the trustees to alter or add to the terms of the scheme. The authority in question, whilst providing for changes referable to past service benefits and to eligibility for membership in line with the equalisation of retirement ages, failed to make any reference to equalising those retirement ages for future service. The employer claimed that there was sufficient evidence to establish that the parties were in error in failing to provide for a common retirement age of 65 for future service, and that the authority should be read as making such provision.

1 [2013] EWHC 2995 (Ch), [2013] Pens LR 409 at [18]–[25].

5.37

Having secured the support of the defendant joined to represent the members of the scheme, the employer sought and obtained summary judgment in respect of its claim. Asplin J was able to discern from the four corners of the authority itself that there had been an attempt by the parties to deal with the issue of retirement ages compendiously, as (for example) the specified amendments only made sense if what was being done by the parties was to change the position in respect of future service; the judge said that the case was therefore very different from the situation in the *Cherry Tree Investments* case. The judge went on to say that, had it been necessary, she would have taken account of extrinsic evidence, namely an earlier resolution of the trustees agreeing to equalise retirement ages: she held that this was not inadmissible evidence of antecedent negotiations, but was an actual decision which the authority was intending to put into effect. The judge rejected the concern that reading a term which had not been properly written into the document in the first place infringed the formalities of the amendment power, which required a document signed by all the trustees: she held that the words were first to be read into the document, and then the document was to be analysed to ensure that it complied with the amendment formalities, which it did.

Royal Mail Group v Evans[1]

5.38

Following privatisation, certain employees of Royal Mail became entitled under its main pension scheme to the same benefits as those available to civil servants. Civil servants' pensions were increased annually in line with the general level of prices set by the Secretary of State: the retail price index (RPI) was initially used to set those increases, but from 2010 the index was changed to the consumer price index (CPI).

1 [2013] EWHC 1572 (Ch), [2013] Pens LR 239 at [83].

5.39

The issue was whether the benefit increases under the Royal Mail scheme were to continue to be set by reference to RPI, on the basis of a rule which provided that the members in question '*who had been entitled to have their pension in payment or in deferment increase without limitation in line with* [RPI] *shall continue to be so entitled under this Scheme*'. However, there were, strictly speaking, no members who had been entitled to have their pensions increased in line with RPI, as the civil service scheme on which their benefits were based did not require RPI to be used. Asplin J accepted Royal Mail's argument that the rule must have been mistakenly drafted as it cannot have been intended to apply to no members, and that the reference to RPI should be construed as a reference to the indexation applied to civil service pensions.

5.40

This case has been regarded as a controversial decision,[1] and in *Carr v Thales Pension Trustees Ltd*,[2] Nugee J – who had been the successful counsel in the case – preferred to base the decision on the fact that the rule was intended to continue an existing entitlement, not to confer a new one, and that the misdescription of that entitlement as RPI increases would not invalidate that intention.[3]

1 The commentary to the report of the case in the Pensions Law Reports described it as '*deeply flawed*'.
2 [2020] EWHC 949 (Ch), [2020] Pens LR 19 at [76].
3 Nugee J relied on the principle of construction traditionally expressed in the maxim *falsa demonstratio non nocet cum de corpore constat*: 'a misdescription does no harm'.

Honda Motor Europe v Powell[1]

5.41

The main issue in this case concerned whether a deed of adherence by which an employer participated in a pension scheme could be read as incorporating a particular benefit structure into the scheme in respect of the members employed by that employer, set out in an announcement to those members.

1 [2013] EWHC 3149 (Ch), [2013] Pens LR 417 (Asplin J); [2014] EWCA Civ 437, [2014] Pens LR 255 (CA).

5.42

At first instance, the argument on that issue before Asplin J turned on the construction of the existing wording of the deed, and did not involve the corrective construction principle. However, an ancillary issue was raised regarding a typographical error in the announcement, which defined future pensionable pay as '*your average basic pay in the best eight consecutive years in the ten years before retirement*': it was common ground that '*eight*' should be replaced by '*three*'. The judge agreed that the error and the means of correcting the error would have been obvious to a reasonable reader with all the relevant knowledge, as the definition was intended to track the relevant Inland Revenue requirements.[1]

1 [2013] Pens LR 417 at [58]. See also *R & S Pilling (t/a Phoenix Engineering) v UK Insurance Ltd* [2019] UKSC 16, [2020] AC 1025, in which the Supreme Court applied a corrective construction to a motor insurance policy which certified that it met prescribed statutory requirements, so that it conformed with those requirements.

5.43

In the Court of Appeal, the employer sought to rely on the corrective construction principle on the main issue, arguing that the judge's conclusion that the reference in the deed of adherence to '*the benefits of the scheme*' meant the benefits in general, and not any particular scale of benefits, was '*untenable and silly*'. This was rejected on the basis that there was nothing which had obviously gone wrong with the language of the deed, and that what may have gone wrong was that those charged with implementation overlooked the need for a separate exercise of the amendment power: the remedy for that lay in rectification, not construction.[1]

1 [2014] Pens LR 255 at [38] per Lewison LJ and at [46] per Sir Stanley Burnton.

Sterling Insurance Trustees Ltd v Sterling Insurance Group Ltd[1]

5.44

The issue in this case concerned the meaning of the words '*accrued due*' in a restriction in an amendment power which prohibited alterations which '*operate so as to substantially reduce in aggregate the value (as to which the decision of the Trustees acting on the advice of the Actuary shall be final) of the benefits accrued due in respect of any Member up to the date of such alteration, modification or addition.*' Did that restriction protect all past service benefits, such as to prevent an amendment which sought to break the final salary link?

1 [2015] EWHC 2665 (Ch).

5.45

Nugee J accepted the employer's argument that, on its true construction, the natural and ordinary meaning of the phrase '*accrued due*' was limited to benefits which had fallen due for payment.[1] However, the judge was prepared to adopt a corrective construction to the phrase in the context of its use in the amendment power, and to disregard the word '*due*', so that the restriction applied to all accrued benefits.[2] He did so principally on the following grounds:[3]

(a) the practical effect of the employer's construction would be to give the protection very limited effect, and it was unlikely that the drafter would have gone to the trouble of protecting a payment which the trustees should have already paid;

(b) s 67 of PA 1995, which was in force at the time of the introduction of the amendment power, already protected changes to benefits which had become payable;

(c) the references in the provision to acting on actuarial advice, the aggregate value of the benefits and substantial reduction to the benefits, pointed away from the drafter having envisaged a payment which had already fallen due.

1 [2015] EWHC 2665 (Ch) at [24].
2 [2015] EWHC 2665 (Ch) at [44]–[45].
3 [2015] EWHC 2665 (Ch) at [29]–[37].

5.46

This decision represents a significant extension of the corrective construction principle. The judge did not rely on the absurdity or illogicality of the provision: on the contrary, he accepted that, on its literal construction, it was capable of operating according to its terms. The judge instead corrected the provision as a matter of construction, on the basis of the impractical consequences of its limited application. This is arguably a relaxation of the threshold test discussed at **5.28**, and an application of the principle to a case where the wording merely made the arrangement more difficult to operate.

Re BCA Pension Plan[1]

5.47

This case concerned the construction of a pensions increase rule which provided for different rates of increase in sub-rule (2) and sub-rule (3) of the rule. The second paragraph of the original sub-rule (1) set out the criteria to determine which of sub-rules (2) or (3) was to apply to the pensionable service in question. An amendment to the rules repeated sub-rules (2) and (3) but did not repeat the second paragraph of sub-rule (1), so that the rules no longer provided for when the different rates would apply.

1 [2015] EWHC 3492 (Ch), [2016] 4 WLR 5 at [28]–[34].

5.48

The trustee applied under s 48 of the Administration of Justice Act 1985 (AJA 1985)[1] for authority to administer the scheme by construing the new rules as if the words from the second paragraph of sub-rule (1) in the original rules had not been omitted, on the basis that the omission had clearly been an error and that the pension increase rule made no sense without the omitted words. Snowden J acceded to the application, holding that, in the light of the context – including the original rules which were admissible for this purpose[2] – it was self-evident that there had been a mistake in the drafting of the new rules, and it was obvious what was necessary to cure the mistake.

1 As to which, see **14.75–14.89**.
2 See *KPMG v Network Rail Infrastructure Ltd* [2007] EWCA Civ 363, [2008] 1 P & CR 11 at [35]–[43] per Carnwath LJ.

Barnardo's v Buckinghamshire[1]

5.49

This case was not concerned with corrective construction. It is relevant because the restatement by Lord Hodge JSC of the material criteria for the construction of pension scheme documents, which placed greater emphasis than previous decisions on a textual analysis than on the background factual matrix,[2] did not, in his view, preclude the application of the corrective construction principle:

> '… a focus on textual analysis in the context of the deed containing the scheme must not prevent the court from being alive to the possibility that the draftsman has made a mistake in the use of language or grammar which can be corrected by construction, as occurred in *Chartbrook Ltd v Persimmon Homes Ltd* [2009] AC 1101, where the court can clearly identify both the mistake and the nature of the correction.'

1 [2018] UKSC 55, [2019] ICR 495 at [17].
2 See **5.5**.

5.50

However, as the next case shows, it may well be that the primacy now given by the courts to the language of the pension scheme provision will operate to limit the scope for its correction by construction.

Britvic plc v Britvic Pensions Ltd[1]

5.51

A scheme provided for a pensions increase cap of a prescribed rate '*or any other rate decided by the principal employer*'. The issue was whether the prescribed rate could be replaced by any other rate, or only by a higher rate.

1 [2020] EWHC 118 (Ch), [2020] Pens LR 154 (HHJ Hodge QC, sitting as a deputy High Court judge); [2021] EWCA Civ 867, [2021] ICR 1648 (CA).

5.52

The deputy judge, having considered the underlying legislative provisions and the documents produced as part of the creation of, and the transfer into, the scheme, construed the phrase '*any other rate*' to mean only some other higher rate, and not a lower one. Alternatively, if that phrase could not be so construed, the deputy judge said that he would have adopted a corrective construction, on the basis that an objective observer, with full knowledge of the admissible background, would have been clear as to what the nature of that error was and how it should be corrected.[1]

1 [2020] Pens LR 154 at [135]–[137].

5.53

The Court of Appeal allowed the appeal, focusing on the unambiguous language of the phrase, which did not naturally mean '*or any higher rate*'. Sir Geoffrey Vos MR held that the process of corrective construction was only normally adopted in the case of an obvious mistake on the face of the document; and whilst an objective observer might well think that the provision could have been better drafted, that was not enough to allow the court to depart from the clear language of the phrase.[1] Nugee LJ agreed that there was no basis for concluding that a drafting mistake had been made, relying on the fact that the drafter evidently took the language directly from the predecessor provision.[2]

1 [2021] ICR 1648 at [33]. See also at [59]–[61] per Coulson LJ. The Master of the Rolls also held (at [32]) that, even if a mistake had been made, it was impossible to discern what the cure for the mistake was: rather than simply providing for a higher rate, the rule could equally have provided for a range of rates.

2 [2021] ICR 1648 at [78].

Procedure

5.54

As stated above, if the legal advisers to the trustees are sufficiently confident on the point, the corrective construction principle can be applied on the basis of their advice alone, and does not require an order of the court, although of course it would remain open for that advice subsequently to be challenged. Accordingly, the trustees may require the employer to indemnify them for any liability for breach of trust which may arise if they continue to administer the scheme on the corrected basis, but such an indemnity may need to continue for many years, and will only be of value to the trustees for so long as the employer is able to pay under it.

5.55

If the trustees or the employer wish for certainty on the issue, proceedings can be brought in one of three ways:

(a) by Part 8 claim brought by the employer;

(b) by Part 7 claim bought by the employer, generally in conjunction with a rectification claim, with the intention that the construction claim will be dealt with first, by way of a preliminary issue; or

(c) by Part 8 claim brought by the trustees, seeking directions from the court as to the proper meaning of the document, pursuant to CPR Part 64.

The procedures applicable to these claims are dealt with in **Chapter 14**.

5.56

A cheaper and quicker option than full-blown proceedings is available where the employer is prepared to take the risk that no future challenge will be made to its preferred construction but the trustees wish to be protected from criticism when administering the scheme on the basis of that construction. In such circumstances, the trustees may apply for authorisation from the court to operate the scheme on that basis, pursuant to s 48 of AJA 1985. This application is dealt with at **14.75–14.89**.

Practice point: including express provisions on construction in a deed of amendment

5.57

The ability of the parties to influence the determination of construction questions by express provisions in the scheme is subject to the principle that such matters are issues of law for a court to determine, and that any provision in a trust which attempts to oust the jurisdiction of the court is invalid.[1]

1 *Re Wynn* [1952] Ch 271.

5.58

However, the inclusion in the trust deed and rules of the scheme of a term which provides for how the document is to be construed may still have merit.

(a) Whilst blatant attempts to oust the court's jurisdiction – such by giving the trustees the exclusive power to determine questions of construction or by giving effect to the subjective intentions of the parties – will not succeed, there may be scope for more subtle attempts to influence the way in which the court would approach the issue, by providing for the court to take particular account of matters which might otherwise be outweighed by other factors.

(b) There is no case law which expressly prohibits terms which operate to influence the court rather than to override its authority, and it is certainly arguable that such provisions ought to be given effect to as objective evidence of the parties' intentions, provided that they do not seek to subvert established principles of construction. One example which may be justified on such an argument is a term which provides that, where the interpretation of a provision may otherwise generate more than one meaning, it shall be construed so as to result in what the scheme actuary advises to be the lowest cost to the employer in terms of additional liabilities or other expenses.

(c) Relatively few questions of construction will end up in court: if a provision such as that under discussion assists in allowing an adviser to the employer or trustees in persuading another party, such an insurer in a buy-out situation, of a particular construction, the provision will have been worthwhile.

5.59

The parties to the document may also seek to influence a matter of construction by:

(a) identifying and stating the purpose of the amendment, and providing that the parties do not intend the document to make any amendment beyond that purpose (deeming void any drafting that would have excessive or collateral effect); and insofar as they do not deliver the stated purpose, the rules shall nevertheless be treated as amended so as to fulfil that stated purpose;[1] or

(b) incorporating other documents by express reference, so that the document in question is construed together with and by reference to those documents.[2]

1 Cf. the deed of intention in issue in *Premier Foods Group Services Ltd v RHM Pension Trust Ltd* [2012] EWHC 447 (Ch), [2012] Pens LR 151 at [17].

2 This is a familiar procedure in the case of wills: see, for example, *Re Wippell* [2018] EWHC 730 (Ch).

5.60

Care must be taken to identify with precision the purpose or documents which the parties wish to be used in assisting the construction of the document, bearing in mind that the mistake in question will of course not be known at the time of the document's preparation, and it is possible that references to purposes and other documents may even create ambiguities which would not otherwise exist. That said, it is sensible to consider such an approach particularly on a large consolidation exercise (to provide, for example, that the effect of the consolidation does not increase members' entitlements), on the replication of benefits in another arrangement following a merger of schemes, or on a complex amendment exercise.

6 Rectification

6.1

Where the parties mistakenly execute pension scheme documents which do not accord with their intentions, the court has the power to rewrite, or rectify, the document so that it accords with those intentions. The document is then treated as if it had always been written as rectified.[1]

1 *Craddock Bros Ltd v Hunt* [1923] 2 Ch 136, 151 per Lord Sterndale MR and 160 per Warrington LJ. Accordingly, there is no need to comply with any of the statutory conditions for the modification of pension schemes.

6.2

Rectification is not used to correct a mistake in the transaction, but a mistake in the way in which the transaction has been expressed in writing:[1] it is therefore about setting the record straight. This may involve putting words into the document which the parties have mistakenly left out, or deleting words which were not intended to be in the document, or putting right a misunderstanding as to the meaning of the words or expressions used in the document.

1 *Allnutt v Wilding* [2007] EWCA Civ 412, [2007] BTC 8003 at [11]–[12] and [19]–[20] per Mummery LJ.

6.3

Rectification has traditionally been regarded as the principal method for correcting pension scheme mistakes which have unintentionally benefitted members, and which cannot be unwound because of restrictions in the amendment power and/or s 67 of PA 1995 protecting past service benefits. The primacy of rectification in this context has led to courts being reluctant to permit other forms of relief to achieve the same effect.[1] However, the process of rectifying pension scheme documents is expensive and time-consuming, and has led to other methods of correction being explored.

1 In *Smithson v Hamilton* [2007] EWHC 2900 (Ch), [2008] 1 WLR 1453 at [61]–[80], Sir Andrew Park (sitting as a deputy High Court judge) refused to set aside a pension scheme amendment under the rule in *Hastings-Bass*, which he described as permitting rectification by the back door: see **7.9**(a).

6.4

Rectification nevertheless remains the most popular remedy for dealing with pensions mistakes, and the courts have regularly been prepared to grant the relief: although the remedy has been described as '*cautiously watched and jealously exercised*',[1] there are only two reported cases in which pensions rectification claims have failed.[2]

1 *Whiteside v Whiteside* [1950] Ch 65, 71 per Sir Raymond Evershed MR.
2 *Lansing Linde Ltd v Alber* [2000] Pens LR 15; *Collins v Jones* [2001] WTLR 1229.

6.5

A rectification claim is often brought together with an alternative construction claim. In such circumstances, it is legitimate for the court to grant rectification while leaving aside a more doubtful case on construction, even though the court would thereby be rectifying a document which might have accorded with the true intention of the parties.[1]

1 *Re Hampel Discretionary Trust 1999* [2012] EWHC 2395 (Ch), [2013] WTLR 1405 at [16] per Henderson J, applied in a pensions context by Deputy Judge Martin QC in *MNOPF Trustees Ltd v Watkins* [2013] EWHC 4741 (Ch) at [11] and by Chief Master Marsh in *Blatchford Ltd v Blatchford* [2019] EWHC 2743 (Ch), [2020] Pens LR 5 at [18].

Legal principles

Scope of the remedy

6.6

The remedy is available not only in cases where particular words have been misused, but also in cases where those words were used intentionally but it was mistakenly believed that they had a different meaning to that which they in fact have on their true construction.[1] It is also available where there was a mistake as to the legal effect of the words used in the document having regard to their true construction, even if the document contains the very wording it was intended to contain: this is to be contrasted with mistakes as to the commercial consequences of the document, or as to the advantages to be gained by entering into it, where rectification is not available.[2]

1 *Re Butlin's Settlement Trusts* [1976] Ch 251, 260 per Brightman J.
2 *AMP (UK) plc v Barker* [2001] Pens LR 77 at [71] per Lawrence Collins J.

The relevant test

6.7

The conditions for the rectification of pension scheme documents are as follows:[1]

(a) that the parties had a common continuing intention, whether or not amounting to an agreement, in respect of a particular matter in the document to be rectified;

(b) that that common intention continued at the time of the execution of the document sought to be rectified; and

(c) that, by mistake, the document did not reflect that common intention.

1 These are adapted from the judgment of Peter Gibson LJ in *Swainland Builders Ltd v Freehold Properties Ltd* [2002] EWCA Civ 560, [2002] 2 EGLR 71 at [33]–[34]. A further requirement – an outward expression of accord – only applies in cases of rectification of contracts: where the remedy is sought in respect of an amendment to the rules of a pension scheme, which involves the approval by one party

(trustees or employer) of what the other has done rather than a mutual agreement, there is no need to establish that requirement: *FSHC Group Holdings Ltd v GLAS Trust Corp Ltd* [2019] EWCA Civ 1361, [2020] Ch 365 at [78] per Leggatt LJ; *Univar UK Ltd v Smith* [2020] EWHC 1596 (Ch), [2020] Pens LR 23 at [207] per Trower J.

Whose intention is relevant?

6.8

Where the document which is sought to be rectified constituted an amendment of the governing provisions of the scheme, the persons whose intentions are primarily relevant for rectification purposes are those in whom the amendment power is vested.

6.9

Where the amendment power is vested in one person, only their intention is relevant for the purposes of rectification.[1] Where the amendment power is exercisable jointly by the employer and trustees, or is exercisable by the trustees subject to the consent of the employer (or vice versa), it is the intentions of the employer and trustees which are relevant.[2] However, there is no need for the parties to have agreed between them on the manner of the exercise of the power, or even to have communicated that intention to each other: it is sufficient that their independent intentions converge.[3]

1 *MNOPF Trustees Ltd v Watkins* [2013] EWHC 4741 (Ch) at [12] per Deputy Judge Martin QC.
2 *Drake Insurance plc v MacDonald* [2005] EWHC 3287 (Ch), [2005] Pens LR 401 at [33]–[34] per Warren J.
3 *AMP (UK) plc v Barker* [2001] Pens LR 77 at [67] per Lawrence Collins J; *IBM UK Pensions Trust Ltd v IBM UK Holdings Ltd* [2012] EWHC 2766 (Ch), [2012] Pens LR 469 at [19(i)] per Warren J.

6.10

The difference of approach between unilateral and bilateral powers of amendment is only likely to have significance in practice where the evidence shows a difference of intention between the employer and the trustees or the weight of the evidence lies in one direction or the other.[1]

1 *SPS Technologies Ltd v Moitt* [2020] EWHC 2421 (Ch), [2021] Pens LR 185 at [28] per Chief Master Marsh.

Proving common intention

The need for convincing proof

6.11

Because the natural presumption is that the written document is an accurate record of what the parties agreed, a high level of proof that the document did not reflect the parties' common intention is needed. Whilst the standard of proof is the ordinary civil standard of the balance of probabilities, in order to tip the balance in a rectification claim the court will require the proof to be convincing.[1] It is not enough to show that the parties did not intend what was recorded: they also have to show what they did intend, with some degree of precision.[2] However, it is not necessary to prove the exact form of words in which the common intention was to be expressed, provided that the substance and detail of the common intention can be ascertained.[3]

1 *Thomas Bates & Sons Ltd v Wyndham's (Lingerie) Ltd* [1981] 1 WLR 505, 521 per Brightman LJ; *FSHC Group Holdings Ltd v GLAS Trust Corp Ltd* [2019] EWCA Civ 1361, [2020] Ch 365 at [46]. The old cases spoke of needing 'strong irrefragable' (ie unbreakable) evidence: see, for example, *Countess of Shelburne v Earl of Inchiquin* (1784) 1 Bro CC 338, 341 per Lord Thurlow LC.
2 *Racal Group Services Ltd v Ashmore* [1995] STC 1151, 1158 per Peter Gibson LJ.
3 *Swainland Builders Ltd v Freehold Properties Ltd* [2002] EWCA Civ 560, [2002] 2 EGLR 71 at [34] per Peter Gibson LJ.

6.12

The nature and quality of the document which is sought to be rectified may affect the cogency of it as evidence of the parties' intention and therefore the degree of convincing counter-proof required. Whilst a short and clearly-drafted instrument offers the strongest proof of the parties' true intentions, that is not necessarily so in the case of a lengthy and highly complex instrument where the error is deeply hidden in the small print.[1] Many pension scheme documents will fall into this latter category.

1 *Konica Minolta Business Solutions (UK) Ltd v Applegate (No 2)* [2013] EWHC 2536 (Ch) at [37] per Deputy Judge Bartley Jones QC.

The test is subjective

6.13

The test for establishing that the parties had a continuing common intention is subjective, turning on what the parties thought and did, as opposed to what a reasonable observer would have thought the common intention to have been.[1]

1 *FSHC Group Holdings Ltd v GLAS Trust Corp Ltd* [2019] EWCA Civ 1361, [2020] Ch 365 at [176], disapproving contrary dicta by Lord Hoffmann in *Chartbrook Ltd v Persimmon Homes Ltd* [2009] UKHL 38, [2009] 1 AC 1101 at [57]–[66] and not following the Court of Appeal in *Daventry District Council v Daventry and District Housing Ltd* [2011] EWCA Civ 1153, [2012] 1 WLR 1333. The test is subjective, irrespective of whether the case involved a bilateral or unilateral amendment power: *SPS Technologies Ltd v Moitt* [2020] EWHC 2421 (Ch), [2021] Pens LR 185 at [34(1)] per Chief Master Marsh.

6.14

Despite this, the intention of a collective body, such as a group of trustees or a board of directors, would usually be objectively manifested.[1] More generally, the manifestation of the parties' subjective intentions will most clearly be established by the documentation with which they were provided and which they discussed, together with the documentary record of those discussions.[2] The claimant can accordingly rely upon extrinsic documentary evidence of the intention as well as upon evidence from the decision-maker as to what they intended in their own mind.

1 *AMP (UK) plc v Barker* [2001] Pens LR 77 at [67] per Lawrence Collins J.
2 *Univar UK Ltd v Smith* [2020] EWHC 1596 (Ch), [2020] Pens LR 23 at [209]–[210] per Trower J.

Retention of the status quo

6.15

Where the parties intended the document to change the status quo, but the document mistakenly omitted the change, it is necessary to adduce evidence that the parties intended that change to be made.[1] It is not enough to prove the intention which the parties would have had if they had considered the issue: in order to prove the specific intention to change, evidence of a positive decision by the parties to the document is required.[2]

1 In *Lansing Linde Ltd v Alber* [2000] Pens LR 15 at [166], the claim to rectify a pension scheme amendment so as to change the documented benefits was rejected by Rimer J because the evidence disclosed that trustees intended to sign, wholly blindly, the document which was put before them on the basis that, as it was prepared by the scheme administrator's solicitors, it must be one they could safely sign.
2 *Tucker v Bennett* (1887) 38 ChD 1, 13 per Cotton LJ.

6.16

However, where the parties intended to retain the status quo, either generally or as to a particular provision, and the document mistakenly changed the status quo, it may be impossible in the context of a long and complex document such as the rules of a pension scheme to prove that the parties intended the particular provision in question to remain unchanged. In such a case, the court is prepared to infer the requisite intention from the absence of any evidence of an intention to make the offending change.[1]

1 *Industrial Acoustics Company Ltd v Crowhurst* [2012] EWHC 1614 (Ch), [2012] Pens LR 371 at [45] per Vos J.

6.17

In such cases, the court has discerned a generalised 'intention by reference' sufficient to make out a claim for rectification, ie an intention to reflect the status quo, warts and all (the exact details of which may not have been in the parties' minds), save for a number of demonstrably-intended changes. For example, in *ZF Lemforder UK Ltd v Lemforder UK Pension Trustees Ltd*,[1] the trustee and employer intended the provisions of a new scheme to '*mirror*' or '*broadly reflect*' the provisions of a related scheme (subject to minor differences). However, by mistake, the new scheme failed to replicate a provision of the related scheme. Warren J ordered rectification of the new scheme provisions by inserting the omitted provision: the fact that the parties had given little attention to the drafting of the rules of the new scheme and had relied on their lawyers to transpose the provisions was not an obstacle to rectification, but a ground for it.[2]

1 [2005] EWHC 2882 (Ch), [2006] Pens LR 85 at [79] and [85]–[86].
2 See also *Scania Ltd v Wager* [2007] EWHC 711 (Ch) at [12] and [18] per Sir Andrew Morritt C; *Konica Minolta Business Solutions (UK) Ltd v Applegate (No.2)* [2013] EWHC 2536 (Ch) at [31] and [45] per Deputy Judge Bartley Jones QC; *Univar UK Ltd v Smith* [2020] EWHC 1596 (Ch), [2020] Pens LR 23 at [214] per Trower J.

6.18

For example, where the parties and their advisers discuss the intended changes or prepare documents listing those changes, the omission of any reference to the change which is sought to be rectified during those discussions or in those documents can be relied upon in support of the removal of that change by rectification.[1] The absence of any change to the administration of the scheme after execution of the revised scheme documentation will also be powerful evidence that a mistake that ought to be rectified was made.[2]

1 *MNOPF Trustees Ltd v Watkins* [2013] EWHC 4741 (Ch) at [17] and [18] per Deputy Judge Martin QC; *Saga Group Ltd v Paul* [2016] EWHC 2344 (Ch), [2017] 4 WLR 12 at [54] per HHJ Hodge QC (sitting as a deputy High Court judge); *Univar UK Ltd v Smith* [2020] EWHC 1596 (Ch), [2020] Pens LR 23 at [240] per Trower J.
2 *Blatchford Ltd v Blatchford* [2019] EWHC 2743 (Ch), [2020] Pens LR 5 at [28] per Chief Master Marsh.

Prior and subsequent conduct

6.19

The admissible evidence for rectification claims is much wider than would be permitted in construction cases. For example, evidence of the parties' pre-contractual negotiations is admissible; and conduct after the date of the relevant document can constitute evidence of the intention of the person effecting it.[1] Accordingly, evidence that the employer and the trustees have applied a particular interpretation to an amendment is some evidence of what the parties intended, although standing by itself it might not ordinarily amount to the strong and clear evidence which is required in cases of rectification.[2]

1 *Gallaher Ltd v Gallaher Pensions Ltd* [2005] EWHC 42 (Ch), [2005] Pens LR 103 at [141] per Etherton J.
2 *Drake Insurance plc v MacDonald* [2005] EWHC 3287 (Ch), [2005] Pens LR 401 at [35] per Warren J.

Attribution of intention

6.20

In ascertaining the intention of a corporate entity, the intention of the person or persons who were the decision-makers, and who had authority to bind the entity in relation to the relevant transaction, will be attributed to that entity.[1] In ascertaining the decision-maker, regard will be had to the decision-making process adopted by the entity and the extent to which individuals involved in the decision-making process relied on others.[2] In this respect, it is necessary to identify the persons who actually approved the nature and terms of the transaction, not the persons upon whose authority the transaction was entered into.[3]

1 *Hawksford Trustees Jersey Ltd v Stella Global UK Ltd* [2012] EWCA Civ 55, [2012] 2 All ER (Comm) 748 at [41] per Patten LJ.
2 *Univar UK Ltd v Smith* [2020] EWHC 1596 (Ch), [2020] Pens LR 23 at [211] per Trower J.
3 *Girls Day School Trust v GDST Pension Trustees Ltd* [2016] EWHC 1254 (Ch), [2016] Pens LR 181 at [10] per Norris J.

6.21

If the relevant entity comprises a number of decision-makers, it is possible that they will not have been unanimous as to the relevant decision, or that they will have acted with different intentions so that some were mistaken and some were not. In that situation, it is likely that the intention of the number of decision-makers which is necessary to bind the remainder – such as a majority of board directors, if the company's articles so provide – will constitute the requisite intention of the entity as a whole. Moreover, if the actual intent of those who were not mistaken was simply to be guided by others on a particular issue without having any independent intent of their own, they are not to be treated as decision-makers in relation to the relevant issue.[1]

1 *Univar UK Ltd v Smith* [2020] EWHC 1596 (Ch), [2020] Pens LR 23 at [212] per Trower J (obiter).

Successive documents

6.22

Where a consolidating deed repeats a rectifiable error made in an earlier deed or deeds, rectification may be available for the later deed if the evidence of intention at the time of its execution was that the consolidating deed should reflect the members' substantive legal entitlements under the earlier deed including the right to rectify, even though the parties to the later deed did not have the mistaken provision in mind at the time it was executed. If, however, the only intention at the time of the consolidating deed was to replicate the language of the earlier deed as it then stood, a claim to rectify would fail.[1]

1 *IBM UK Pensions Trust Ltd v IBM UK Holdings Ltd* [2012] EWHC 2766 (Ch), [2012] Pens LR 469 at [448]–[451] per Warren J. Although that decision was made on the (now disavowed) basis that objective evidence of common intention was required, the same analysis should apply where common intention is to be proved subjectively. See also *Mitchells & Butlers Pensions Ltd v Mitchells & Butlers plc* [2021] EWHC 3017 (Ch) at [274]–[346].

6.23

Where serial rectification of successive deeds is sought, a powerful evidential factor is that the error has not disturbed the status quo from the first occasion when an error is said to have occurred and through the successive deeds: the continuity of established practice over an extended period will support the case for there having been an intention for the successive deeds to reflect the rights the members had as a matter of law, ie with the first deed in the chain duly rectified.[1]

1 *SPS Technologies Ltd v Moitt* [2020] EWHC 2421 (Ch), [2021] Pens LR 185 at [33] per Chief Master Marsh.

Relevance of professional advisers

6.24

It is no bar to rectification that the mistake in respect of which rectification is sought occurred as a result of negligence on the part of the claimant or its advisors. Indeed, the negligence does not prevent rectification: it is a ground for it.[1]

1 *AMP (UK) plc v Barker* [2001] Pens LR 77 at [72] per Lawrence Collins J.

6.25

Although the intention of the parties to the document is most relevant, evidence of the thinking of the adviser responsible for the drafting of the document can also be useful in establishing what must have been in the mind of the parties.[1] If the mistake in question arose from an error in the drafting of the document, evidence from the drafter is also helpful to explain how the mistake arose.[2] However, such evidence may need to be treated with some caution, as the adviser may have an interest in admitting a mistake where a successful rectification claim would reduce the quantum of any claim that may be brought against them.[3]

1 See *Misys Ltd v Misys Retirement Benefit Trustees Ltd* [2012] EWHC 4250 (Ch) at [29] per Briggs J. Cf. *Mitchells & Butlers Pensions Ltd v Mitchells & Butlers plc* [2021] EWHC 3017 (Ch) at [86] per Trower J.
2 See, for example, *MNOFP Trustees Ltd v Watkins* [2013] EWHC 4741 (Ch) at [19] per Deputy Judge Martin QC.
3 *Konica Minolta Business Solutions (UK) Ltd v Applegate (No 2)* [2013] EWHC 2536 (Ch) at [38] per Deputy Judge Bartley Jones QC; *Univar UK Ltd v Smith* [2020] EWHC 1596 (Ch), [2020] Pens LR 23 at [215] per Trower J.

Discretionary nature of the remedy

6.26

As an equitable remedy, even where the conditions for its application are satisfied, the court has a discretion whether to grant rectification, and may refuse to do so where an equitable defence is successfully invoked. Two such defences are of particular relevance to pensions rectification claims.

Laches

6.27

A substantial period of delay in bringing a rectification claim may bar the remedy on the grounds of laches.

6.28

Mere delay, even if substantial,[1] is not sufficient to establish the defence: it is also necessary for the circumstances of the delay to render it inequitable to grant rectification, which usually requires detriment to have been suffered by the members.[2] Such detriment will not usually take the form of a reduction to their benefits if rectification is granted, as the members will normally have been receiving benefits on the assumption that the document reflected the parties' common intention.[3] It is possible that the members will have suffered detriment, if the delay has resulted in the loss or destruction of relevant evidence or the dimming of relevant witnesses' memories,[4] but it is more likely that that would operate to the detriment of the claimant, given the exacting burden of proof required to grant rectification.

1 In *Weld v Petrie* [1929] 1 Ch 33, a delay of 18 years did not deter the court from granting equitable relief; and in *Gallaher Ltd v Gallaher Pensions Ltd* [2005] EWHC 42 (Ch), [2005] Pens LR 103, the documents in issue had been executed 17 years earlier.

2 *Fisher v Brooker* [2009] UKHL 41, [2009] 1 WLR 1764 at [64] per Lord Neuberger of Abbotsbury.

3 *ZF Lemforder UK Ltd v Lemforder UK Pension Trustees Ltd* [2005] EWHC 2882 (Ch), [2006] Pens LR 85 at [94] per Warren J; *Gallaher Ltd v Gallaher Pensions Ltd* [2005] EWHC 42 (Ch), [2005] Pens LR 103 at [146] per Etherton J.

4 *Lynch v James Lynch & Sons (Transport) Ltd* (8 March 2000, unreported), at [47] per Peter Gibson LJ; *Price v Saundry* [2019] EWHC 1039 (Ch), [2019] WTLR 683 at [37] per HHJ Matthews (sitting as a Deputy High Court Judge).

6.29

Moreover, time does not begin to run for the purposes of laches until the mistake in question has been discovered:[1] the period between the mistake and its discovery is not taken into account when assessing whether a detrimental delay has occurred.

1 *Beale v Kyte* [1907] 1 Ch 564.

Bona fide purchaser

6.30

Rectification will not be granted where it would operate to the detriment of a bona fide purchaser for value. In *AMP (UK) plc v Barker*,[1] scheme members who had, without their knowledge, received greater benefits than had been intended, sought to resist a claim for rectification on the basis that they had earned their benefits and should therefore be treated as bona fide purchasers in respect of the unintended benefits. This argument was rejected by Lawrence Collins J, who held that the members were only purchasers of the benefits which had been intended to be granted to them, and had given no consideration for the benefits which had been mistakenly conferred on them.[2] In any event, a court is even less likely to apply this argument as a blanket defence to a pensions rectification claim, given that the remedy can be granted on terms that the parties grant some form of concession to any members affected by the amendment.[3]

1 [2001] Pens LR 77 at [79].

2 This case was followed by Etherton J in *Gallaher Ltd v Gallaher Pensions Ltd* [2005] EWHC 42 (Ch), [2005] Pens LR 103 at [147]–[148]; and by Trower J in *Univar UK Ltd v Smith* [2020] EWHC 1596 (Ch), [2020] Pens LR 23 at [376]. Note the doubt expressed on this point by Deputy Judge Halpern QC in *Citifinancial Europe plc v Davidson* [2014] Pens LR 625 at [11].

3 See *Central & Metropolitan Estates Ltd v Compusave* [1983] 1 EGLR 60, where a lease was rectified to include a five-yearly rent review, on terms that the tenant would be given an opportunity to surrender the lease at the end of the first five-year period. In *Konica Minolta Business Solutions (UK) Ltd v Applegate* [2012] EWHC 3741 (Ch), [2013] Pens LR 105 at [122], Asplin J recorded the agreement of the parties that rectification could be granted on terms that ensured compliance with preservation requirements. See also *Konica Minolta Business Solutions (UK) Ltd v Applegate (No 2)* [2013] EWHC 2536 (Ch) at [47]–[53] per Deputy Judge Bartley Jones QC.

6.31

In *Mitchells & Butlers Pensions Ltd v Mitchells & Butlers plc*,[1] a principal employer of a scheme, who assumed that position following a corporate restructuring which occurred after the errors in question had been made, sought to defend a rectification claim on the basis that it was a bona fide purchaser. That argument was dismissed by Trower J on the ground (amongst others) that the employer was not a 'purchaser' in any relevant sense, as the power to appoint a principal employer was concerned with substitution and succession to a position, and did not concern the sale of property or the transfer of property rights.

1 [2021] EWHC 3017 (Ch) at [231]–[247].

Partially invalid if rectified?

6.32

Where rectification is granted, the re-wording of the document will take effect from its inception. However, it is possible that the rectified document would to some extent be invalid, such as where the parties' intention was for the document to apply a retrospective reduction to members' benefits, in contravention of a restriction in the amendment power. In such circumstances, the court will not rectify to comply with that restriction, as that would not accord with the intention of the parties: instead, the court will rectify the document as intended, but also declare that that document cannot apply to the extent that it infringes the restriction.[1]

1 *Hogg Robinson plc v Harvey* [2016] EWHC 129 (Ch), [2016] Pens LR 61 at [29] per Deputy Judge Fancourt QC.

Procedure

6.33

This section describes the procedure for rectification of a document which has mistakenly granted members more generous benefits than had been intended.

Pre-action process

Effect of the mistake

6.34

Once the mistake has been identified, the employer and trustees will want an early estimate of likely cost to the scheme of the mistake, to determine the most proportionate way of proceeding.

6.35

Where the mistake has an ongoing adverse effect on the liabilities of the scheme, the employer and the trustees should consider entering into a 'capping deed', which – without prejudice to the rectification claim – terminates the adverse effect of the mistake going forward and caps the additional liabilities. If the rectification claim is unsuccessful, and the employer and trustees subsequently seek to recover the cost of the additional liabilities from a professional adviser, a failure to execute a capping deed within a reasonable time of discovering the mistake may reduce the damages award on the ground of failure reasonably to mitigate the loss.[1]

1 See **15.56–15.58**.

6.36

Where the trustees, employer or professional advisers are of the view that the mistake has caused a failure to comply with a legal duty relevant to the administration of the scheme, they must consider whether to make a 'breach of law' report to the Pensions Regulator pursuant to s 70 of PA 2004.

6.37

A decision will need to be taken on whether the rectification claim is advanced by the employer or the trustees. Usually it will be the employer that brings the claim, as it will bear the burden of funding the additional liabilities if the mistake is not corrected. However, it is possible that the trustees will take the lead where, for example, the employer is insolvent. The remainder of this section assumes that the claim is brought by the employer.

Gathering evidence

6.38

If the consequences of the error make a rectification claim worthwhile, the next task is to search for and gather the evidence that will be necessary to establish the grounds for rectification. Because of the requirement to provide convincing proof, no stone should be left unturned in the search for evidence, which will typically include the following:

(a) documents showing the reasons for the production of the document to be rectified, including any minutes evidencing discussion by and decisions of the employer or the trustees,[1] and any instructions to and advice from their advisers,[2] as to the matters to be dealt with in the document: one example would be where the changes were intended to reduce benefits as part of a cost-cutting exercise by the employer, which would be inconsistent with the document operating to increase benefits;

(b) discussions and negotiations relating to the drafting of the document, including travelling drafts and any advice obtained in respect of those drafts;

(c) any contemporaneous advice provided to the employer or trustees by the drafter as to what they believed the document was intended to achieve;

(d) documents sent to members which sought to explain the changes which were intended to be made by the document, such as announcements and explanatory booklets, particularly if they were formally signed off by the employer or the trustees;[3]

(e) oral evidence from the key decision-makers amongst the parties to the document as to what they intended;

(f) oral evidence from the drafter explaining why the document was drafted in a way which did not accord with the instructions of the parties; and

(g) evidence of the way in which the scheme had been subsequently administered in accordance with the true intention of the parties, such as the valuation, funding, provision and communication to members of benefits.

1 In *Lansing Linde Ltd v Alber* [2000] Pens LR 15 at [155], Rimer J held that a minute of a trustee meeting was the best evidence as to what the meeting resolved to do, although it was not conclusive and could be rebutted by convincing oral evidence to the contrary. In *Dukeries Healthcare Ltd v Bay Trust International Ltd* [2021] EWHC 2086 (Ch), [2021] WTLR 809 at [97], a case on equitable mistake, Deputy Master Marsh said that where pro-forma minutes of meetings have been produced, it is likely to be necessary for the claimant to provide evidence that those minutes actually reflected the intention and understanding of the board at the time.

2 Consideration may need to be given to waiving privilege over any legal advice provided in respect of the document.

3 *Pioneer GB Ltd v Webb* [2011] EWHC 2683 (Ch), [2011] Pens LR 425 at [21] and [23] per Sales J. In *Lansing Linde Ltd v Alber* [2000] Pens LR 15 at [161], Rimer J rejected the relevance of the explanatory booklet as evidence of the employer's and trustees' intentions, on the ground (amongst others) that there was no evidence that the booklet derived from those persons. However, in *Mitchells & Butlers Pensions Ltd v Mitchells & Butlers plc* [2021] EWHC 3017 (Ch) at [47], Trower J held that the booklet was an important document as it reflected a common understanding of what the rules provided and identified the benefits which were of sufficient significance to merit specific mention.

6.39

Other matters which may be relevant to establishing the requisite mistake are:

(a) the absence of any advice taken by the employer or the trustees as to the consequences for the funding or administration of the scheme of the document as drafted;

(b) any illogicality or illegality involved in the changes made by the document as drafted: for example, a document providing more generous benefits for deferred members than for active members may raise questions, as it is unlikely that an employer would wish to prefer members who were no longer in its employment;[1]

(c) a shift in the balance of power between the employer and the trustees occasioned by the changes made by the document as drafted, without any accompanying explanation to them from the drafter as to the consequences of such a shift;[2] and

(d) any difficulties in communicating to members the effect of the changes made by the document as drafted.

1 See *Wright v MGN Pension Trustees Ltd* [2007] EWCA Civ 1247, [2008] Pens LR 77 at [9]–[14] per Lloyd LJ; *SPS Technologies Ltd v Moitt* [2020] EWHC 2421 (Ch), [2021] Pens LR 6 at [18] per Chief Master Marsh.

2 See *Mitchells & Butlers Pensions Ltd v Mitchells & Butlers plc* [2021] EWHC 3017 (Ch) at [93] per Trower J.

Witnesses

6.40

Substantial statements should be taken from the key decision-makers, which will include those who were parties to any decision to approve the terms of the document, and may include those who executed the document.

6.41

Although it is not necessary to take substantial statements from those persons who executed the document in a purely formal capacity, such as the company secretary of the employer or any trustees who were not substantively involved in the decision, it is still necessary for them to give a statement explaining their lack of substantive involvement, to ensure that there are no avoidable gaps in the witness evidence and to avoid adverse inferences being drawn from such gaps.

6.42

No time should be wasted in undertaking the process of gathering evidence, and the temptation to delay interviewing witnesses until all the documents are gathered should usually be resisted. Although the witnesses will eventually need to be proofed by reference to all the documents, it is important to ensure that statements are taken at an early stage, as that may assist in identifying and focusing on the relevant evidence, and will avoid difficulties if elderly witnesses later prove unable to give evidence. This is particularly important where the mistake was made many years previously, and the investigations involve liaising with third parties. Proofing witnesses in this way will be an iterative process, with statements developing by reference to documents and other oral evidence which emerges during the investigation.

6.43

The principles applicable to the preparation and contents of witness statements for cases listed in the Business and Property Courts has recently been restated,[1] in terms applicable to all statements signed on or after 6 April 2021, irrespective of when the claim was issued.[2] The key points are as follows:

(a) As to the preparation of the statement:[3]

  (i) the witnesses should have explained to them by their legal adviser, the purpose and proper content of the statement and the proper practice in relation to its preparation, before they are asked to prepare or consider any draft statement and, wherever practicable, before any evidence is obtained from them (by interview or otherwise);

(ii) the statement should be based on a record or notes made by the legal adviser of evidence they obtained from the witness from (and if possible during) an interview;

(iii) when interviewing the witness, the legal adviser should avoid leading questions where practicable, and particularly in relation to important contentious matters, and should use open questions as much as possible, generally limiting closed questions to requests for clarification of, or additional detail about, prior answers;

(iv) the legal adviser should assist the witness as to the structure, layout and scope of the statement and may take primary responsibility for drafting it, but in that case the content should be taken from, and should not go beyond, the content of any record or notes made by the legal adviser;[4]

(v) if the legal adviser wishes to indicate in a draft statement that further evidence is sought from the witness to clarify or complete the statement, that should be done by non-leading questions for the witness to answer in their own words and not by proposing content for approval, amendment or rejection by the witness;

(vi) if the witness provides information otherwise than by interview, that should be stated at the beginning of the statement and the process should be described.

(b) As to the content of the statement:[5]

(i) it must contain only evidence of such factual issues as the witness would be permitted to give if they were called to give oral evidence at trial;

(ii) it must set out only matters of fact of which the witness has personal knowledge that are relevant to the case: to comply with this requirement, the statement must set out by list what documents, if any, the witness has been referred to;

(iii) it should not quote at length from any document to which reference is made, seek to argue the case, take the court through the documents in the case or set out a narrative derived from the documents, or include commentary on other evidence in the case;

(iv) on important disputed matters of fact, it should state how well the witness recalls the matters addressed, and whether, and if so how and when, the witness has refreshed their memory by reference to documents;

(v) in addition to the usual statement of truth, it must contain a signed confirmation from the witness in the following form:

I understand that the purpose of this witness statement is to set out matters of fact of which I have personal knowledge.

I understand that it is not my function to argue the case, either generally or on particular points, or to take the court through the documents in the case. This witness statement sets out only my personal knowledge and recollection, in my own words.

On points that I understand to be important in the case, I have stated honestly (a) how well I recall matters and (b) whether my memory has been refreshed by considering documents, if so how and when.

I have not been asked or encouraged by anyone to include in this statement anything that is not my own account, to the best of my ability and recollection, of events I witnessed or matters of which I have personal knowledge.

(vi) it must also contain a certificate of compliance, signed by the legal adviser, in the following form:

I hereby certify that:

1. I am the relevant legal representative within the meaning of Practice Direction 57AC.

2. I am satisfied that the purpose and proper content of trial witness statements, and proper practice in relation to their preparation, including the witness confirmation required by paragraph 4.1 of Practice Direction 57AC, have been discussed with and explained to ***[name of witness]***.

3. I believe this trial witness statement complies with Practice Direction 57AC and paragraphs 18.1 and 18.2 of Practice Direction 32, and that it has been prepared in accordance with the Statement of Best Practice contained in the Appendix to Practice Direction 57AC.

(c) Where the statement fails to comply with these requirements, in addition to its usual powers of case management and sanctions, the court may refuse permission to rely upon some or all of the evidence, order the statement to be re-drafted, make an adverse costs order or require a witness to give some or all of their evidence orally.[6]

1 CPR PD 57AC.
2 CPR PD 57AC, para 1.1. The Practice Direction does not apply to trustees' claims for directions under CPR Part 64 (discussed in **14.67–14.72**) unless the court directs otherwise: CPR PD 57AC, para 1.3(8).
3 CPR PD 57AC, Appendix, paras 3.9–3.13.
4 If there are a number of witness statements, it is important to ensure that they are not too similar to each other, as that tends to lessen their credibility.
5 CPR PD 57AC, Appendix, paras 3.1–3.7 and 4.1–4.3.
6 CPR PD 57AC, Appendix, para 5.2.

6.44

The purpose of these principles is not to change the law on the admissibility of evidence at trial, but to eradicate the improper use of witness statements as vehicles for narrative, commentary and argument.[1] The principal effect that these principles are likely to have on witness statements in rectification claims is to curtail the common practice of the lead witness referring to, and commenting upon, the primary documentary evidence relating to the parties' intention with regard to the instrument to be rectified. This has hitherto been considered to provide a helpful overview of the case for rectification, particularly where the intention is to apply for summary judgment, but it will fall foul of the prohibition on the witness taking the court through the documents in the case and setting out a narrative derived from the documents. Such an overview will therefore have to appear, either in a draft Particulars of Claim or in the claimant's written submissions to the court.

1 *Mansion Place Ltd v Fox Industrial Services Ltd* [2021] EWHC 2747 (TCC) at [37] per O'Farrell J.

6.45

If a key person is proving to be an unwilling witness, consideration should be given to issuing a witness summons to compel their attendance at court.[1] This course of action is risky, as a witness who refuses to attend trial voluntarily may prove to be uncooperative and even hostile. The best approach, where possible, is to communicate with the witness and find out the reasons for their reluctance to attend, to see if their concerns can be alleviated.

1 The procedure is set out in CPR 34.2–34.7A.

Taking stock

6.46

At an advanced stage of the evidence-gathering process, the legal advisers should rigorously analyse the case by applying the relevant legal principles to the evidence, perhaps with the assistance of counsel. One way of ensuring a thorough examination of the facts and law is to draft a formal pleading, which, if done properly, will highlight any weaknesses in the case which may require further investigation.

6.47

At this stage, a decision can be taken as to whether the case is sufficiently strong for an application to court for rectification to be made, and whether it is possible to obtain summary judgment; and if a decision to proceed is taken by the employer, it will be necessary to inform the trustees, so that discussions can take place about how best to inform the members of the issue. These matters are considered further at **6.62–6.65** and **6.74–6.82**.

Appointing a representative defendant

6.48

As pensions rectification claims relate to trust property, the court may make an order appointing a person to represent any other person or persons in the claim, where the represented persons are in a class of persons with the same interest in the claim, where those persons cannot easily be ascertained, and where the appointment would further the CPR's overriding objective.[1] Unless the court orders otherwise, any order made in a claim including a representative will bind all the persons so represented.[2]

1 CPR 19.7(2).
2 CPR 19.7(7)(a).

6.49

Representation orders can be granted at an interim stage of the proceedings or else at the disposal of the claim (either by summary judgment or at trial).[1]

1 See *IBM UK Pensions Trust Ltd v Metcalfe* [2012] EWHC 125 (Ch) at [12] and [24] per Warren J.

6.50

Any claim for rectification of a pensions mistake will involve joining as a defendant to the claim a person or persons who will represent the members of the scheme in whose interests it is for the claim to fail, ie those members who have benefitted from the mistake.

6.51

The representative defendant serves two primary purposes. First, they, through their legal advisers, act on behalf of the members in considering, and if necessary arguing, the case against granting rectification. They are accordingly required to satisfy themselves as to whether the legal and factual bases for the rectification claim are met.[1] Secondly, the binding effect of the representation order means that, if rectification is granted, the members will not be able to argue in the future for benefits based on the document as originally drafted. The appointment of a representative defendant accordingly benefits the employer as well as the members.

1 *Nomura International plc v Nomura London Retirement Benefits Plan Trustees Ltd* (18 March 2019, unreported), at [8] per Master Teverson.

6.52

As the answer to most rectification claims is binary – either the document will be rectified, or it will not – it is not usually necessary to have more than one representative defendant. If, exceptionally, there are classes of members with different interests from each other, care should be taken to ensure that the number of representative defendants are kept to the minimum necessary to enable the court to be satisfied that it has heard full argument on behalf of all those interested.[1] If the claimant is unsure as to which members need to be joined as defendants, they may apply to issue the claim form without naming any defendants under CPR 8.2A, together with an application to the court for directions as to which persons to join.

1 Chancery Guide, para 29.93. In a suitable case, it may be possible for the trustees to argue on behalf of a particular class of members, and for an order that the trustees represent that class: this occurred (albeit in a different context) in *Bridge Trustees Ltd v Yates* [2008] EWHC 964 (Ch), [2008] Pens LR 261 at [3].

6.53

Once a decision has been taken in principle to proceed with a rectification claim, the employer (with the assistance of the trustees) should identify and appoint a representative defendant, who can act as the focal point for communications with members, and can be consulted in advance of the commencement of the claim about any summary judgment application the employer may wish to make. These matters are considered further at **6.74–6.82**.

6.54

Representative defendants are usually individual members of the scheme, who themselves would be adversely affected if rectification were granted. A reasonable and proportionate search should be undertaken by the employer and trustees for a member to act as a representative defendant. When canvassing for volunteers, it is important that the members are reassured that they will not have to appear as witnesses or be exposed to any personal liability for costs, while at the same time ensuring that they have the sufficient time and capacity to take on the task.

6.55

Members who are closely connected with the parties to the documents which are being rectified, such as officers of the employer and past or present trustees, are not suitable to act as representative defendants, because of the potential conflict of interest. Care should also be taken to ensure, as far as is possible, that a member has not volunteered to be a representative defendant because of some personal motive, such as harbouring a grudge against the employer.

6.56

If, after reasonable steps have been taken, it is not possible to identify an affected member who is willing to act as a representative, the employer may join as a defendant a member who is either not affected by the issue or whose interests are adverse to the position they are advancing.[1] If no member at all can be found to assist, the court will be willing to appoint a non-member, such as a solicitor, as representative defendant.[2] In this respect, the court's overriding concern is to see that the interests of all those represented are protected.[3]

1 *Thompson v Fresenius Kabi Ltd* [2013] Pens LR 157 at [12]–[16] per Briggs J.
2 For a recent example, see *Punter Southall Governance Services Ltd v Hazlett* [2021] EWHC 1652 (Ch), [2021] Pens LR 1 at [9].
3 Chancery Guide, para 29.95.

6.57

Once appointed, the representative defendant should be treated as any other defendant to proceedings: they must be given access to the relevant documents and be advised by their legal advisers as to the merits of the case, and they must give instructions to their advisers as to whether, and if so how, the case should be defended. To this end, it is often helpful for the claimant's legal advisers to explain the factual background and the basis of the claim to the representative's legal advisers at an early stage of the process.

6.58

Representative defendants are representative in the sense that they are typical of their class: they do not represent members in the sense of acting as their delegate:[1] the defendant is not required to canvass the members and should not put forward on the members' behalf any grievances they may have which are not relevant to the rectification claim. Representative defendants will be expected to follow legal advice, and not strike out on their own. If the representative defendant does not comply, and acts to the detriment of the membership as a whole, another defendant can be added to represent the members, and the recalcitrant member will continue as a defendant in an individual capacity, with no protection in costs if they persist in acting in their own interests, rather than the interests of the members.[2]

1 *The Girls' Day School Trust v GDST Pension Trustees Ltd* [2016] EWHC 1254 (Ch), [2016] Pens LR 181 at [15] per Norris J.

2 The court may decide that the representation order should not cover the recalcitrant member, who will therefore not be bound by any decision; however, if that member should subsequently seek to challenge the decision, having had the chance to do so in the initial claim, their claim is likely to be struck out: see *Wytcherley v Andrews* (1871) LR 2 P&D 327.

6.59

There is usually little that the representative defendant need do as regards gathering evidence, other than to put in a short witness statement to explain who they are and to summarise their representative role. The representative defendant's principal role in this regard is to ensure that the employer and trustees have taken all reasonable and proportionate steps to investigate and to obtain the evidence relevant to the claim. As to this:

(a) regarding documentary evidence, it is not uncommon for the employer to adduce a statement from an officer or its legal adviser to explain what investigations have been undertaken; alternatively, the defendant may request that the claimant serve at an early stage a disclosure statement required under the CPR standard disclosure procedure;[1]

(b) with regard to oral evidence, although it is open to the representative defendant to approach any existing witness with further questions or any potential witness who has not given a statement, that is uncommon; and it may be preferable in those cases for the representative defendant to request the employer or the trustees to fill in any evidential gaps which have been identified, and to take more direct action only if that request is not dealt with properly.

1 CPR 31.10.

6.60

Provided that they act reasonably, the representative defendant's costs will be paid out of the scheme assets, assessed on the indemnity basis. The defendant may wish to proceed with the protection of a prospective costs order, which will usually be agreed between the legal advisers and approved by the Master at an interim hearing.[1]

1 Chancery Guide, para 29.94. See further **14.99–14.104**. It is possible for the trustees to provide an indemnity for the representative defendant's costs from the assets of the scheme without the need for a court order, but only where the scheme rules expressly give the trustees power to do so.

6.61

Sometimes the employer will seek in advance to limit the costs that the representative defendant will incur, such as by imposing a cap on the costs, requiring prior approval of costs, or limiting the seniority of the defendant's legal advisers. Although the reasonableness of such an action will depend on the circumstances of the particular case, the employer must take care not to be seen to be hindering the representative defendant's ability properly to defend the claim.

Informing the members

6.62

Although there is no requirement to consult with or notify members, it is good practice for the trustees (whether or not in conjunction with the employer and the representative defendant) to write to the affected members, in order to inform them of the mistake, its effects, the steps which are being taken to correct it and the role of the representative defendant.[1] Such an announcement may also give the members the contact details of the representative defendant's legal advisers, so that the members may ask questions or provide any information that they may think is relevant to the claim. Where the announcement is to be issued by the employer or the trustees, it is good practice to share a draft with the representative defendant's legal advisers for comment and approval.

1 *Industrial Acoustics Company Ltd v Crowhurst* [2012] EWHC 1614 (Ch), [2012] Pens LR 371 at [60] per Vos J; *Citifinancial Europe plc v Davidson* [2014] Pens LR 625 at [7] per Deputy Judge Halpern QC; *The Girls' Day School Trust v GDST Pension Trustees Ltd* [2016] EWHC 1254 (Ch), [2016] Pens LR 181 at [15] per Norris J; and see Chancery Guide, para 29.99. In *Archer v Travis Perkins plc* [2014] EWHC 1362 (Ch), [2014] Pens LR 311 at [27], Rose J said that keeping members informed was as much the representative defendant's responsibility as it was the responsibility of the employer and trustees.

6.63

Further communications should be sent to members if and when a substantive court hearing is due to take place, either for a summary judgment application or for the trial of the claim. Notice of the former will give any members who feel particularly aggrieved or badly affected by the proposal to appear at the hearing of the application to make a separate case (albeit at their own risk as to costs).

6.64

The notice must balance the need to give the members sufficient information and the need to avoid unnecessary alarm; insofar as it explains why the representative defendant has decided not to contest a summary judgment application, the notice must not create the suspicion of a deal done 'behind closed doors'.

6.65

If a member who is not a representative defendant objects to the rectification application, the court has the following options:[1]

(a) adjourn the disposal hearing with a view to giving the representative defendant a further opportunity to make representations or to obtain further instructions;

(b) make a qualified rectification order so as to exempt the dissentients;

(c) give a class of persons or named persons permission to apply to the court; or

(d) consider the merits of the objections and, if they are without merit, make the rectification order without adopting any of the other courses of action.

1 *Iggesund Paperboard (Workington) Ltd v Messenger* [2021] EWHC 627 (Ch), [2021] Pens LR 449 at [27]–[28] per Chief Master Marsh.

Preparatory steps for summary judgment

6.66

If the employer is advised that there are good grounds for obtaining summary judgment,[1] it will be necessary to obtain the consent of the representative defendant, as it is very unlikely that the court would make such an order if the representative defendant considers there to be reasonable grounds for defending the claim.

1 See **6.74–6.82**.

6.67

It is therefore advisable for the employer to take the following steps to prepare for the summary judgment application, prior to issuing proceedings:

(a) send to the representative defendant's legal advisers a request for their agreement not to oppose a summary judgment application, together with:

  (i) the documentary evidence which, in the normal course of events, would be disclosed to the representative defendant in the proceedings;

  (ii) signed witness statements from all the relevant personnel, including statements from those who are unable to give evidence in support of the claim;

(iii) a draft of the Particulars of Claim which the claimant would file and serve if the matter were contested: it is usually a good idea to prepare and provide this even if the proposal is to proceed by way of Part 8 claim, which would not usually require such a document to be produced;[1]

(iv) an explanation of the steps taken to gather documentary and oral evidence and the reasons for any gaps in that evidence; and

(v) if relevant, an explanation of the reasons for any substantial period of time which has elapsed between the discovery of the mistake and the proposed claim;

(b) respond to any queries the representative defendant has regarding those documents or any other aspect of the case; and

(c) secure the representative defendant's agreement not to contest the summary judgment application.

1 See **14.54–14.58**.

6.68

The representative defendant's legal advisers must scrutinise the summary judgment proposal with great care, even scepticism: they are in the difficult position of having had no prior involvement in the production or negotiation of the document in respect of which rectification is sought, and are entitled to rely on any technical legal arguments against rectification and to draw adverse inferences from any unexplained absence of evidence. However, it will not be in the interests of the members to force a long and expensive trial without sufficient grounds to defeat the claim, and no responsible representative defendant should oppose summary judgment for the sake of it, hoping that something might turn up in subsequent disclosure or in the cross-examination of the witnesses.[1]

1 See the remarks of Master Teverson on this issue in *Nomura International plc v Nomura London Retirement Benefits Plan Trustees Ltd*, (18 March 2019, unreported) at [18], cited by Chief Master Marsh in *Blatchford Ltd v Blatchford* [2019] EWHC 2743 (Ch), [2020] Pens LR 5 at [33].

Commencing the claim

Where to bring the claim

6.69

Claims for the rectification of pension scheme documents will invariably be brought in the High Court,[1] and will be assigned to the Chancery Division Business List of the Business and Property Courts.[2]

1 The rectification jurisdiction of the County Court is limited to small value real property transactions: s 23(d) of the County Courts Act 1984.
2 Sch 1(g) to the Senior Courts Act 1981.

6.70

Rectification claims will in the first instance be heard by a Master, and will only be transferred to a judge if the case raises issues of particular difficulty.[1] In practice, this means that all summary judgment applications will be dealt with by Masters, whereas trials involving complex issues of fact and/or law will be heard by judges.

1 Chancery Guide, para 29.71.

Part 7 or Part 8?

6.71

Rectification claims can be brought as either Part 7 or Part 8 claims.[1] However, the latter type of claim is unsuitable where there is any likely to be any dispute of fact,[2] and is therefore only appropriate if the claim is uncontested.[3]

1 See **14.37–14.63**.
2 CPR 8.1(2)(b).
3 Chancery Guide, para 29.91.

Parties to the claim

6.72

If the scheme contains an amendment power which involves both the employer and the trustees, so that they are the parties to the document to be rectified, they should be made parties to the rectification claim, along with the representative defendant.

6.73

If the employer has taken the lead in advancing the claim, it will be claimant. The trustees will usually be joined as defendants, and will adopt a neutral role in the proceedings: their interests will be limited to providing any relevant evidence from the trustees and other scheme personnel, ensuring the proceedings are properly conducted, assisting the court where necessary and making sure that the eventual order is administratively workable.

Summary judgment

6.74

Summary judgment may be granted where there is no real prospect of successfully defending the claim and there is no other reason why the case should be disposed of at trial.[1] In this context, real prospects of success means realistic and carrying some degree of conviction, as opposed to fanciful or merely arguable.[2]

1 CPR 24.2.
2 *Swain v Hillman* [2001] 1 All ER 91 at 92–94 per Lord Woolf MR; *ED&F Man Liquid Products Ltd v Patel* [2003] EWCA Civ 472, [2003] CP Rep 51 at [8] per Potter LJ.

6.75

Where, prior to the issue of the claim, the representative defendant's legal advisers have indicated that they will not contest a summary judgment application, the claimant can then issue the claim form and apply for summary judgment.[1]

1 Such an application can be made after the defendant has filed an acknowledgment of service: CPR 24.4(1)(a).

6.76

The summary judgment process is available where the claim is commenced under either CPR Part 7 or Part 8.[1] However, in *Sovereign Trustees Ltd v Lewis*,[2] Chief Master Marsh said that a summary judgment application was unnecessary in a Part 8 claim, as the claimant could simply apply for a 'disposal hearing',[3] at which the court may determine whether or not the relief sought by the claimant should be granted, where the relief sought is unopposed or could not realistically be opposed.

1 CPR 24.3.
2 [2016] EWHC 2593 (Ch), [2016] Pens LR 345 at [3].
3 CPR PD 8A, para 8.1.

6.77

The claimant should file with the court the documentary evidence and witness statements on which it wishes to rely, together with a short witness statement explaining that summary judgment or disposal is being sought and (if one has been prepared) exhibiting a draft of the Particulars of Claim, so that the court has a convenient narrative of the case. The representative defendant should also file a short statement explaining that they have received legal advice on the merits of the claim and that they are willing not to contest the application on the basis of that advice.

6.78

It is now established practice for the representative defendant's counsel to write an opinion setting out the reasons why they have advised their client not to contest the application, and for that opinion to be sent in advance to the court. Because the opinion will contain a frank appraisal of the strengths of the claim and the weaknesses of the defence, it is not appropriate for it to be disclosed to the claimant, in case the summary judgment application is not successful and the claim proceeds to trial. The practice is therefore to keep the opinion confidential as between the representative defendant and the court, and for it not to be seen by any other party.[1]

1 See *Colorcon Ltd v Huckell* [2009] EWHC 979 (Ch), [2009] Pens LR 201 at [6] per HHJ Toulmin QC (sitting as a deputy High Court judge); *Misys Ltd v Misys Retirement Benefit Trustee Ltd* [2012] EWHC 4250 (Ch) at [20] per Briggs J; *The Girls' Day School Trust v GDST Pension Trustees Ltd* [2016] EWHC 1254 (Ch), [2016] Pens LR 181 at [17] per Norris J. In *Saga Group Ltd v Paul* [2016] EWHC 2344 (Ch), [2017] 4 WLR 12 at [22], HHJ Hodge QC, having reviewed the authorities, concluded that all the evidence, including the representative defendant's legal advice, should be made public at the hearing. However, in a series of subsequent cases Chief Master Marsh strongly endorsed the practice of keeping

the evidence confidential: *Sovereign Trustees Ltd v Lewis*, [2016] EWHC 2593 (Ch), [2016] Pens LR 345 at [37]); *Unipart Group Ltd v UGC Pension Trustees Ltd* [2018] EWHC 2124 (Ch), [2018] Pens LR 18 at [9]; *Blatchford Ltd v Blatchford* [2019] EWHC 2743 (Ch), [2020] Pens LR 5 at [34]; *Lloyds Bank plc v Comben* [2019] EWHC 3775 (Ch), [2020] Pens LR 215 at [15]; *SPS Technologies Ltd v Moitt* [2020] EWHC 2421 (Ch), [2021] Pens LR 185 at [6]. In *The Girl's Day School Trust* case, Norris J said (at [17]) that the agreement of the other parties to confidentiality does not preclude the court from taking the view that, after judgment, the evidence ought to be made public and available for inspection by scheme members.

6.79

It is usual for the summary judgment application to be determined at a hearing, as it is often not an efficient use of the court's time for it to have to consider a mass of material raising potentially complex issues unassisted by oral submissions, and a public hearing will serve to dispel any concern on the part of members there has been some 'deal done in a dark corner'.[1] However, where the underlying issues are not complex and the evidence is wholly compelling, the application can be disposed of without a hearing, as the publicity of a written judgment may achieve far more than the delivery of an oral judgment to an almost empty courtroom.[2]

1 *The Girls' Day School Trust v GDST Pension Trustees Ltd* [2016] EWHC 1254 (Ch), [2016] Pens LR 181 at [13] per Norris J.
2 *The Girls' Day School Trust v GDST Pension Trustees Ltd* [2016] EWHC 1254 (Ch), [2016] Pens LR 181 at [14]. The same purpose may be achieved by a period of delay before implementation of the judgment, or by notice to all scheme members of an intended hearing, with permission for the claimant to vacate the hearing in the event that no scheme member gives notice of an intention to attend.

6.80

On the hearing of the application, the claimant employer and the representative defendant will appear by counsel. The trustees may also choose to do so, but may decide not to appear in order to save costs. After the claimant's counsel has made their submissions in support of the claim in open court, it is usual for the representative defendant's counsel to be heard in private in the absence of the other parties, so that they can make submissions on the confidential opinion and the merits of the case generally, and answer any questions the court may have on those matters.[1]

1 *Konica Minolta Business Solutions (UK) Ltd v Applegate* [2013] EWHC 2536 (Ch) at [7] per Deputy Judge Bartley Jones QC.

6.81

Even where no objection is taken by the representative defendant to the grant of the relief, it remains necessary for the court to satisfy itself that rectification is justified on the evidence. The court will therefore wish to scrutinise carefully the changes that are proposed, the reasons for them and the evidence in support.[1] The court will also wish to see that the representative defendant has pursued with the employer and trustees all reasonable lines of investigation.[2]

1 Chancery Guide, para 29.69: see *Saga Group Ltd v Paul* [2016] EWHC 2344 (Ch), [2017] 4 WLR 12 at [11] per HHJ Hodge QC (sitting as a deputy High Court judge).
2 *Hogg Robinson v Harvey* [2016] EWHC 129 (Ch), [2016] Pens LR 61 at [27] per Deputy Judge Fancourt QC.

6.82

It sometimes happens that an individual member disagrees with the decision of the representative defendant not to contest the summary judgment application. Where this occurs, the court may well not want to shut the member out from making submissions, and may order that the remedy not become effective for a certain period, thereby giving the member an opportunity to advance their arguments.[1] The court may make such an order even in the absence of a known challenge, to enable members to be informed of the judgment and be given the chance to object.[2]

1 See *Colorcon Ltd v Huckell* [2009] EWHC 979 (Ch), [2009] Pens LR 201 at [9] per HHJ Toulmin QC (sitting as a deputy High Court judge).
2 This was done in *The Girls' Day School Trust v GDST Pension Trustees Ltd* [2016] EWHC 1254 (Ch), [2016] Pens LR 181: see at [52] per Norris J.

Compromising the claim

6.83

If the case is not suitable for summary judgment, the parties should consider whether it would be preferable to compromise the claim. Compromises are dealt with in **Chapter 15**.

The trial

6.84

Any disputes which cause the rectification claim to go to trial are likely to relate to factual issues, in which case the witnesses who have given statements will be called to give oral evidence, so that the parties who are contesting the evidence – which will usually be confined to the representative defendant – will be able to cross-examine the witnesses.

6.85

In keeping with their neutral role, the trustees will rarely ask the witnesses a substantial number of questions, unless it is to assist the court or to challenge any matters raised which are adverse to the trustees' witnesses.

6.86

Contested rectification claims usually arise because the case is not sufficiently clear on the documents, so that the oral evidence is likely to be key. In theory, the requirement for the intention of the parties to be established subjectively should heighten the relevance of oral evidence as to what the parties thought, as opposed to what they communicated in documents.[1] However, in particular where the alleged mistake occurred many years ago, the court may view with some scepticism the recollection of witnesses, to the extent that they are inconsistent with the contemporaneous documents.[2]

1 See *Murray Holdings Ltd v Oscatello Investments Ltd* [2018] EWHC 162 (Ch) at [192], where Mann J said that the (then applicable) objective test for common intention probably made it easier to maintain a rectification case without calling any witnesses.
2 See the well-known comments of Leggatt J in *Gestmin SGPS SA v Credit Suisse (UK) Ltd* [2013] EWHC 3560 (Comm) at [15]–[22]. See also *Blatchford Ltd v Blatchford* [2019] EWHC 2743 (Ch), [2020] Pens LR 5 at [37] per Chief Master Marsh.

6.87

As regards costs, the usual order is for all of them, including those of the employer, to be paid out of the assets of the scheme on the indemnity basis, although it may be more convenient for them to be paid by the employer where, for example, those costs are to be included as damages in a claim against an adviser whose duty of care is more clearly owed to the employer than to the trustees.[1]

1 *St Modwen Properties Ltd v Herbert* [2016] EWHC 428 (Ch), [2016] Pens LR 113 at [21]–[23] per Rose J.

Post-claim

6.88

If rectification is granted, although the rectified document takes effect from its original effective date without the need to execute a new document, for the sake of administrative good order it may be preferable to execute a new document, or amend the existing rules, to reflect the rectified document.

6.89

If the losing party wishes to appeal the decision of the trial judge to the Court of Appeal, they will need permission to do so.[1] The costs incurred by the representative defendant on an appeal will not usually be covered by the original prospective costs order so that, if the appeal was being brought by the claimant, it is likely that they would be required to cover the representative defendant's costs of defending the appeal.[2] If the appeal was being bought by the representative defendant, the claimant is unlikely to consent to those costs, and the defendant would have to apply to court for a fresh prospective costs order.

1 CPR 52.3.
2 This could be made a condition of the grant of permission to appeal, or else the court would be likely to grant a prospective costs order in favour of the defendant, as it did in *Re National Grid Co plc Group of the Electricity Supply Pension Scheme* [1997] OPLR 161.

Practice point: can rectification be avoided?

Rectification is an expensive remedy

6.90

Where the rectification claim is disputed on behalf of the scheme members, obtaining this relief is usually an expensive and slow-moving process. There are several reasons for this:

(a) The need for convincing evidence of the parties' intentions means that the cardinal rule for rectification claims is that you cannot have too much evidence.

(b) Because of the factual issues that arise, rectification claims are normally begun by Part 7 proceedings, which are generally more elaborate and expensive than the Part 8 procedure used to determine construction issues.

(c) Because pension schemes are by their nature long-term arrangements, mistakes in scheme documents are often made many years before the discovery of the mistake. The passage of time may well lead to difficulties in tracking down relevant documents and witnesses.

(d) For these reasons, disputed rectification claims can often involve long and costly trials.[1]

(e) It is not always possible for the cost of the rectification claim to be recovered from a negligent adviser who was responsible for the error.

As a result of this, three potential methods of addressing the document error have been adopted as alternatives to court proceedings for rectification.

1 For example, a rectification claim relating to the IBM pension schemes took up 13 days of court time, involved 20 witnesses and resulted in a 139-page judgment: *IBM United Kingdom Pensions Trust Ltd v IBM UK Holdings Ltd* [2012] EWHC 3540 (Ch), [2013] Pens LR 33. *Univar UK Ltd v Smith* [2020] EWHC 1596 (Ch), [2020] Pens LR 23 involved a 14-day trial with 16 witnesses and a 101-page judgment.

'Deeds of correction'

6.91

At one time it was fashionable for employers and trustees to seek to correct mistakes in pension scheme documents without going to court, by entering into so-called 'deeds of correction'. These were intended to alter the provisions of the scheme retrospectively to deal with the error; however, they were not expressed to be amendments, but changes to the wording which were designed to accord with what the parties had intended all along.

6.92

Only rectification orders made by the court can have retrospective effect: that is a consequence which cannot be brought about by agreement between the parties.[1] Thus, whilst a deed of rectification is unobjectionable where it does not do anything which could not have been done by amendment, a deed which purports retrospectively to reverse the effect of an unintended conferral of benefits on members may fall foul of a restriction in the amendment power or s 67 of PA 1995, and will therefore be ineffective to achieve that aim.

1 *Persimmon Homes Ltd v Woodford Land Ltd* [2011] EWHC 3109 (Ch), [2012] BLR 73 at [21] per Henderson J; *Shannan v Viavi Solutions UK Ltd* [2016] EWHC 1530 (Ch), [2016] Pens LR 193 at [119] per Deputy Judge Fancourt QC.

6.93

The contrary argument is that, where the more generous benefits are conferred by mistake and are thereby liable to be removed by rectification, they do not constitute *benefits* or *rights* which have been earned by or otherwise accrued to the members, and so do not engage the restriction in the amendment power or s 67.

6.94

Support for that argument can be found in *South West Trains Ltd v Wightman*,[1] in which a collective agreement between the employer and the members' representatives operated to reduce the benefits set out in the rules of the scheme. It was argued on behalf of the members that s 67, which had come into force by the time of the claim, precluded the agreement from reducing their accrued benefits as set out in the rules. Neuberger J held that, by reason of the agreement, the members had no '*entitlement*' or '*accrued right*' to such benefits, saying as follows:

> 'If, as a matter of law and fact, a person can be prevented from doing something by a third party who has a direct and substantial interest in such prevention, and there is no policy reason as to why that third party should be restrained from exercising his right and every practical reason for thinking that he will exercise it, then it would seem to me to follow that one should assess the person's position on the assumption that the third party will indeed exercise his right.'

1 [1998] Pens LR 113 at [77].

6.95

In addition, there is authority to similar effect, albeit in different contexts, where the document in question is rectifiable.

(a) In *Lobler v HMRC*,[1] Proudman J held that, where the taxpayer was entitled to rectification of his tax returns because of a mistake, his tax position would be treated as if that remedy had been granted, because of the maxim 'equity treats as done that which ought to be done'.

(b) In *Hamed El Chiaty & Co v The Thomas Cook Group*,[2] the Court of Appeal stayed English proceedings between parties to a charter agreement which contained no exclusive jurisdiction clause, because of an oral agreement conferring jurisdiction on the Egyptian courts: the court rejected the argument that the written agreement needed to be rectified before the oral term could be enforced, and Neill LJ said that the same maxim applied to permit the document to be treated as having been rectified.

1 [2015] UKUT 152 (TCC), [2015] STC 1893 at [45]–[50] and [74]. Although HMRC chose not to appeal *Lobler*, it regularly asserts in correspondence with taxpayers that it considers the case to be wrongly decided: see *Hymanson v HMRC* [2018] UKFTT 667 (TC) at [80]; and see *Fashion on the Block Ltd v HMRC* [2021] UKFTT 306 (TC), [2021] STI 2103 at [46].
2 [1994] 1 Lloyd's Rep 382, 390.

6.96

Despite these, there are several legal and practical objections to the effectiveness of deeds to correct mistakes by reducing past service benefits:

(a) The administration of the scheme on the basis of a deed of correction is inconsistent with the principle – described as '*trite law*'[1] – that, for so long as the document in issue remains unrectified by the court, the parties ought not to proceed on the basis that that document does not accord with their intentions.[2]

(b) The cases which support the effectiveness of a retrospective deed of rectification can all be distinguished:

   (i) the *South West Trains* case did not involve rectification, and turned on the fact that the members were contractually bound by the collective agreement to accept the reduced benefits;

   (ii) the *Lobler* case probably turned on the fact that the First Instance Tribunal does not have the power to order rectification, and on the wish not to clog up the courts with claims for rectification of tax returns, as well as the punitive rate of taxation which was sought to be imposed on the taxpayer – some 779%;

   (iii) the principal basis for the decision in the *Hamed El Chiaty* case was that the existence of the oral term was sufficient to permit the court to exercise its statutory discretion to order a stay despite the provisions of the charter agreement.[3]

(c) In addition, those cases all involved the court establishing that the written rights were overridden, either by agreement or a rectifiable mistake: by contrast, at the time a deed of rectification is entered into, the parties cannot be sure that a court would subsequently grant rectification.

(d) Indeed, it may be difficult for employers to demonstrate to the trustees' satisfaction that the case for rectification is sufficiently clear-cut without the kind of extensive investigations and analysis which would justify seeking rectification in any event.

(e) Even a good rectification claim may be lost by reason of delay because of the deterioration in the quality of the evidence which would be necessary to establish the conditions for rectification (by reason of dimming of memories or loss of documents).[4]

1 *Singla v Brown* [2007] EWHC 405 (Ch), [2008] Ch 357 at [23] per Deputy Judge Ivory QC.
2 *Law v Warren* (1843) Dr t Sugd 31, 41 per Sugden LC; *R v Croydon and District Rent Tribunal, ex p Langford Property Company Ltd* [1948] 1 KB 60, 65 per Lynskey J; *Goodman v Gallant* [1986] Fam 106, 111 per Slade LJ.
3 [1994] 1 Lloyd's Rep 382, 389–390 per Neill LJ and 393 per Staughton LJ.
4 See **6.27–6.28**.

6.97

The trustees should accordingly not contemplate entering into a deed of correction unless they are satisfied that the case for rectification is sufficiently certain to succeed; given that it is relatively easy for a member to challenge the administration of the scheme in accordance with such a deed, by making a complaint to the Pensions Ombudsman, the trustees might conclude that an application to court for rectification is the more prudent option.

'Rectification at a later date'

6.98

Another course of action sometimes suggested by the employer is for the trustees to continue to administer the scheme despite the documentation, on the basis that the trustees could seek rectification in due course if a challenge was subsequently made to the way in which they were operating the scheme.

6.99

This is a tempting solution for an employer where, as is often the case, the mistake in the scheme documentation is buried away and is not likely to be spotted by members; the trustees may be lulled by the strength of the rectification claim into acting as though rectification had already been granted, safe in the knowledge that that claim could always be brought in the unlikely event of a challenge.

6.100

However, the practical disadvantage of not seeking rectification as soon as possible, referred to at **6.95**(e), applies equally here; and in any event, it is doubtful whether the trustees can properly proceed on this basis, as that would be inconsistent with the general principle that trustees are obliged to administer the trust on the basis of the trust documents.[1] At the very least, the trustees should require the employer to provide an indemnity for any costs and liabilities which the trustees may incur by use of this process.

1 *Target Holdings Ltd v Redferns* [1996] AC 421 at 434 per Lord Browne-Wilkinson. See also the Pension Regulator's 'Trustee Guidance' (December 2007).

Contractual compromise

6.101

The final option is for the employer to enter into a contractually-binding compromise with the affected members without bringing proceedings, whereby members are given an incentive payment in return for agreeing not to commence a claim, with provision for that payment to be refunded if the member resiles from the agreement. This process would not require an application to court, although the employer will need to ensure that all the affected members are parties to the agreement, and that the members have been independently advised as a class on the nature of the compromise and the benefits that they are potentially giving up as a result.

7 Setting Aside for Mistake

7.1

Equity will intervene in a number of situations to set aside trust documents created in the purported exercise of powers by trustees and other donees.[1] One of those situations, where the exercise goes beyond the scope of the power (known as 'excessive execution') is considered in the pensions context at **4.8**; and mistakes made by scheme trustees and employers in their decision-making processes are dealt with in **Chapter 13**. This chapter will consider three other situations of particular relevance to pension schemes, where documents made in the mistaken exercise of powers may be subject to the equitable jurisdiction to set the documents aside: the so-called 'rule in *Hastings-Bass*'; the equitable remedy of recission for mistake; and mistakes concerning the purpose of the power.

1 These are summarised in Tucker, le Poidevin QC and Brightwell (eds), *Lewin on Trusts* (20th edn, Sweet & Maxwell, 2020) (*Lewin*), para 30-101.

7.2

It was noted in the leading case of *Pitt v Holt*[1] that the first two of these situations cover different areas. The rule in *Hastings-Bass* is restricted to decisions by trustees and other fiduciaries, and does not necessarily require the decision-maker to be under a positive misapprehension. Equitable rescission, by contrast, is not limited to transactions entered into by fiduciaries, and does generally require there to have been something that can be identified as an operative mistake. Nevertheless, there is a degree of overlap between them in their practical application, and parties seeking to overturn mistakes in pension scheme documents often sought to rely on both principles.[2]

1 [2013] UKSC 26, [2013] 2 AC 108 at [6] per Lord Walker of Gestingthorpe.
2 For example, *AMP (UK) plc v Barker* [2001] Pens LR 77; *Gallaher Ltd v Gallaher Pensions Ltd* [2005] EWHC 42 (Ch), [2005] Pens LR 103; *Smithson v Hamilton* [2007] EWHC 2900 (Ch), [2008] 1 WLR 1453.

7.3

For a time, those two principles provided an easier and cheaper, and therefore more popular, alternative to rectification of pension scheme documents, and at one point it appeared as though they might supplant rectification altogether in this area. However, a later reconsideration of those principles has meant that, unless the Court of Appeal is prepared to hold otherwise, the rule in *Hastings-Bass* is no longer available as a practical means of correcting pensions mistakes, although there remains some scope for the application of equitable mistake in this context.

The rule in *Hastings-Bass*

7.4

Prior to *Pitt v Holt*, the rule in *Hastings-Bass* enabled the court to set aside the exercise of a power given to a trustee or other fiduciary under the terms of a trust where the effect of that exercise was different from that which they intended, if it was clear that they would not have acted as they did, had they not failed to take into account considerations which they ought to have taken into account, or had they not taken into account considerations which they ought not to have taken into account.[1]

1 *Sieff v Fox* [2005] EWHC 1312 (Ch), [2005] 1 WLR 3811 at [49] per Lloyd LJ.

7.5

The identification of this principle with the Court of Appeal's decision in *Re Hastings-Bass*[1] is somewhat of a misnomer, as that case is not authority for the proposition which came to bear its name.[2] That case was an example of excessive execution, and did not involve inadequate deliberation by the trustees. The true source of the rule is *Mettoy Pension Trustees Ltd v Evans*,[3] in which Warner J reformulated a passage from Buckley LJ's judgment in *Re Hastings-Bass* in the following terms:

> 'where a trustee acts under a discretion given to him by the terms of the trust, the court will interfere with his action if it is clear that he would not have acted as he did had he not failed to take into account considerations which he ought to have taken into account.'[4]

Notwithstanding this, the principle identified by Warner J has continued to be called 'the rule in *Hastings-Bass*'.

1 [1975] Ch 25.
2 See *Pitt v Holt* [2013] UKSC 26, [2013] 2 AC 108 at [1], [18]–[25], [32] and [60].
3 [1990] 1 WLR 1587, 1621.
4 To which should be added: '*or failed to take into account considerations which he ought not to have taken into account*': *Buckley v Hudson Forge Ltd* [1999] Pens LR 151 at [111] per Lloyd J. In *Stannard v Fisons Pension Trusts Ltd* [1991] Pens LR 225 at [39], Dillon LJ put the test in terms of what the trustees might, rather than would, have done if they had taken account of only relevant considerations. In *Pitt v Holt* [2013] UKSC 26, [2013] 2 AC 108 at [92], the Supreme Court held that this was an arid distinction, given the high degree of flexibility in the range of the court's possible responses to the application of the rule.

7.6

In the *Mettoy* case,[1] Warner J also held that, where that rule applied, the court could either declare void the whole of the purported exercise of discretion by the trustees or, in an appropriate case – such as where the trustees would have decided, had they thought about it properly, to omit some particular provision from a deed – declare that provision alone to be void.

1 [1990] 1 WLR 1587, 1624-1625.

7.7

In the early 2000s, the rule in *Hastings-Bass* became a popular method of setting aside tax-planning arrangements which had gone wrong,[1] a practice deprecated by Park J when refusing to set aside such a transaction in *Breadner v Granville-Grossman*:[2]

> 'There must surely be some limits. It cannot be right that whenever trustees do something which they later regret and think that they ought not to have done, they can say that they never did it in the first place.'

1 For example, *Green v Cobham* [2002] STC 820; *Abacus Trust Co (Isle of Man) v National Society for the Prevention of Cruelty to Children* [2001] STC 1344; *Burrell v Burrell* [2005] EWHC 245 (Ch), [2005] STC 569; *Jiggens v Low* [2010] EWHC 1566 (Ch), [2010] STC 1899.
2 [2001] Ch 523 at [61].

7.8

At around the same time, the principle was being regularly relied upon by employers of pension schemes to set aside changes made which did not achieve their intended purpose, either because of drafting errors or because of misunderstandings as to the effect of those changes.[1] This practice became so commonplace that representative defendants would often agree not to oppose applications for summary judgment in such cases. Moreover, the exercise of this jurisdiction produced results which were indistinguishable from rectification, as the court would agree to set aside the unintended changes in return for an undertaking by the employer that it would agree to an amendment which retrospectively reintroduced the intended changes.[2]

1 For example, *Hillsdown Holdings plc v The Pensions Ombudsman* [1997] 1 All ER 862; *AMP UK plc v Barker* [2001] Pens LR 77; *Bestrustees plc v Stuart* [2001] Pens LR 283; *Hearn v Younger* [2002] EWHC 963 (Ch), [2005] Pens LR 49; *Gallaher Ltd v Gallaher Pensions Ltd* [2005] EWHC 42 (Ch), [2005] Pens LR 103; *Betafence Ltd v Veys* [2006] EWHC 999 (Ch), [2006] Pens LR 137.
2 See, for example, *Gallaher Ltd v Gallaher Pensions Ltd* [2005] EWHC 42 (Ch), [2005] Pens LR 103 at [159].

7.9

Again, it was Sir Andrew Park, now sitting as a deputy High Court judge, who pushed back against the application of the rule in *Hastings-Bass* in this context. In *Smithson v Hamilton*,[1] he rejected an attempt by the trustees and employer to apply the rule in *Hastings-Bass* to correct the terms of a definitive deed and rules which mistakenly allowed deferred members to take their benefits early without actuarial reduction. In fact, the representative defendant also sought to rely on the rule in *Hastings-Bass* for a different purpose, causing the deputy judge to remark that he felt as if he was '*ploughing a lone furrow*' in querying the application of the rule.[2] Whilst accepting that there had been a drafting error in the deed and rules, the deputy judge nevertheless refused to set it aside, on the following grounds:

(a) The claim to change the deed and rules was an attempt to rectify those documents by the back door, and the only way to change them retrospectively was by rectification.[3] The rule in *Hastings-Bass* operated, not to change things which the trustees have done, but to set them aside altogether, leaving the trustees as either having done nothing, or having done a part of what they set out to do but not the whole of it. It was not legitimate to outflank this result by an undertaking to introduce a new deed and rules containing the intended provision, an approach which the deputy judge described as having '*at least a hint of tacit bargaining with the court*'.[4] Given that the rule in *Hastings-Bass* was a relatively new and still-expanding jurisdiction, its use to circumvent the strict conditions required for rectification went beyond wherever the limits would eventually be set.

(b) The rule in *Hastings-Bass* only applied to things done by trustees, and the adoption of the definitive deed and rules was essentially the act of the employer. The trustees' main role in connection with the scheme was to administer it in accordance with the deed and rules, and their role regarding the adoption of the deed and rules was lesser than the role of the employer, who was primarily responsible for the decision to have a pension scheme and consequential decisions about its structure and design. Whilst in a formal sense the scheme might be regarded as a joint scheme of the employer and the trustees, in substance the reality was that the employer was the party responsible for its contents: the deed and rules were therefore overwhelmingly employer documents, not trustee documents.[5]

(c) Whilst the trustees had fiduciary responsibilities in connection with the making of the definitive deed and rules, they were not such as to cause the rule in *Hastings-Bass* to apply to set aside the relevant rule. The fiduciary duties were owed by the trustees to the members, and did not include identifying a mistake which operated to the members' advantage: that was not a consideration, the failure to take into account of which would give rise to the application of the rule in *Hastings-Bass*. The deputy judge acknowledged that there could be cases where the rule in *Hastings-Bass* caused an act taken by trustees on mistaken professional advice to be set aside, but on the facts of his case, the advisers in question were acting for the employer, not the trustees.[6]

1 [2007] EWHC 2900 (Ch), [2008] 1 WLR 1453. An appeal was subsequently compromised: [2008] EWCA Civ 996, [2009] ICR 1.

2 [2008] 1 WLR 1453 at [11].

3 [2008] 1 WLR 1453 at [61]–[80].

4 [2008] 1 WLR 1453 at [77]. No such concerns were raised by Etherton J about the same type of undertaking given in *Gallaher Ltd v Gallaher Pensions Ltd* [2005] EWHC 42 (Ch), [2005] Pens LR 103. It is well-established that a court may set aside the exercise of a power in a private trust context, on terms that the trustees would exercise the power in a particular way in the future: *Pitt v Holt* [2013] UKSC 26, [2013] 2 AC 108 at [92].

5 [2008] 1 WLR 1453 at [81]–[96]. In *Arcadia Group Ltd v Arcadia Group Pension Trust Ltd* [2014] EWHC 2683 (Ch), [2014] BTC 40 at [34]–[37], Newey J distinguished *Smithson v Hamilton*, holding that, whilst in the ordinary course the employer may be principally responsible for the initial design of a scheme, thereafter the functioning of the scheme and the respective powers of the employer and the trustees will depend upon the terms of the scheme's governing documentation.

6 [2008] 1 WLR 1453 at [97]–[104].

7.10

The rule in *Hastings-Bass* has since been comprehensively restated by the Supreme Court in *Pitt v Holt,*[1] which has made the application of the rule subject to establishing a breach of fiduciary duty on the part of the trustees: it is not enough to show that the trustees' deliberations fell short of the highest possible standards, or that the court would, on a surrender of discretion by the trustees, have acted in a different way.[2] The Supreme Court also confirmed that the rule renders the exercise of the discretion voidable rather than void.[3]

1 [2013] UKSC 26, [2013] 2 AC 108.
2 [2013] 2 AC 108 at [73].
3 [2013] 2 AC 108 at [93].

7.11

The Supreme Court did nothing to disturb the reasoning in *Smithson v Hamilton*, and provides no indication that the rule in *Hastings-Bass* has any further role to play in the correction of mistakes in pension scheme documentation. Despite being criticised from both a scholarly and practical perspective,[1] *Smithson v Hamilton* remains the latest word on the application of the rule in *Hastings-Bass* to pension schemes: no subsequent court has applied the rule to set aside a pension provision.[2] Unless the Court of Appeal is prepared to reconsider the decision, *Smithson v Hamilton* has effectively sounded the death knell for the application of the rule in *Hastings-Bass* to correct mistakes in pension scheme documents.[3]

1 For the former, see Hacker, 'Mistakes in the Execution of Documents: Recent Cases on Rectification and Related Doctrines' (2008) 19 Kings LJ 293, 325–333; as to the latter, the editor of the Pensions Law Reports trenchantly commented at the end of the report of the case in the following terms: '*There is little merit in this judgment; it reeks of specious pedantic legal argument, pomposity and a complete misunderstanding of the ways in which pension schemes work and errors which can arise in the drafting. Most other judges with commercial experience take a more pragmatic view to mistakes, rather than force the parties to sue for negligence, a remedy which in any event may not be available.*'
2 It was unsuccessfully invoked in *Walker Morris Trustees Ltd v Masterson* [2009] EWHC 1955 (Ch), [2009] Pens LR 307 and in *Prudential Staff Pensions Ltd v The Prudential Assurance Company Ltd* [2011] EWHC 960 (Ch), [2011] Pens LR 239.
3 Although see **7.37–7.40** for a suggested potential drafting solution.

Equitable rescission

7.12

Equity has long allowed non-contractual voluntary dispositions, such as the exercise of powers, to be rescinded for mistake. This jurisdiction can therefore be used to set aside pension scheme documents made pursuant to an amendment power where the operative mistake was that of one or more of the holders of the power – typically the employer and/or the trustees.

7.13

This jurisdiction is separate from the rescission of contracts for common mistake. At one time, it was thought that equity would rescind contracts for mistake in circumstances that fell short of those in which the common law held a contract void: in *Solle v Butcher*,[1] Denning LJ identified an equitable jurisdiction which permitted the court to intervene where the parties had concluded an agreement that was binding in law under a common misapprehension of a fundamental nature as to the material facts or their respective rights. However, that case was not followed by the Court of Appeal in *Great Peace Shipping Ltd v Tsavliris Salvage (International) Ltd*,[2] which confirmed that there is no separate jurisdiction to set aside a contract in equity other than under the more exacting circumstances in which a contract will be void for mistake at common law.

1 [1950] 1 KB 671.
2 [2002] EWCA Civ 1407, [2003] QB 679.

The applicable test pre-Pitt v Holt

7.14

The original test for setting aside voluntary dispositions was that, in the absence of any suspicious activity such a fraud or undue influence, the mistake by the holder of the power was of so serious a character as to render it unjust on the part of the donee to retain the property.[1]

1 *Ogilvie v Littleboy* (1897) 13 TLR 399, 400 per Lindley LJ, affirmed by the House of Lords, *sub nom Ogilvie v Allen* (1899) 15 TLR 294.

7.15

A further gloss was put on the doctrine by Millett J in *Gibbon v Mitchell*,[1] in which he summarised the law in the following terms:

> '... wherever there is a voluntary transaction by which one party intends to confer a bounty on another, the deed will be set aside if the court is satisfied that the disponor did not intend the transaction to have the effect which it did. It will be set aside for mistake whether the mistake is a mistake of law or of fact, so long as the mistake is as to the effect of the transaction itself and not merely as to its consequences or the advantages to be gained by entering into it.'

1 [1990] 1 WLR 1304, 1309.

Application to pension schemes

7.16

The principle was considered in several cases involving amendments to pension scheme provisions which did not accord with the intention of the parties, although in all those cases the principle was invoked in conjunction with either rectification or the rule in *Hastings-Bass*.[1]

1 In *Spooner v British Telecommunications plc* [2000] Pens LR 65 at [133], an election by members of a pension scheme to opt out of a section of that scheme in the mistaken belief that their existing benefits would be retained, was set aside in equity. Although the voluntary disposition cases were cited to the court, Rimer J held that the elections were contractual in nature, and based his decision on *Solle v Butcher*.

7.17

In *AMP (UK) plc v Barker*,[1] a trustee resolution amended the rules of a scheme to provide incapacity benefits, but unintentionally provided enhanced benefits to all members who left service early. Lawrence Collins J rectified the resolution to accord with the intention of the trustees and employer, but said that he would also have set aside the resolution for mistake as there was no reason why the jurisdiction should be limited to voluntary settlements in the strict sense.

1 [2001] Pens LR 77 at [84] and [118].

7.18

In *Gallaher Ltd v Gallaher Pensions Ltd*,[1] Etherton J similarly would have set aside deeds of amendment which mistakenly applied pensions increases to the GMP element of members' benefits, if he had not already ordered rectification. The judge also held that, in the light of the employer undertaking to restore the increases to the non-GMP element of the benefits, the court would not refuse to exercise the jurisdiction merely because 17 years had elapsed since the amendments had been made.

1 [2005] EWHC 42 (Ch), [2005] Pens LR 103 at [150]–[161].

7.19

This jurisdiction was also relied upon by the employer in *Smithson v Hamilton*.[1] Equitable rescission did not suffer from the problem, fatal to the claim based on the rule in *Hastings-Bass*, that the mistake was essentially that of the employer rather than the trustees, as a mistake by the employer would have been sufficient. The relevant facts of this case were materially indistinguishable from those in the *AMP* and *Gallaher* cases which were sufficient to permit the application of the equitable doctrine, yet Sir Andrew Park refused to apply it to set aside the deed and rules. The deputy judge held that the equitable jurisdiction applied to private trusts and did not extend to pension schemes, as they were not established by way of unilateral voluntary disposition, but pursuant to the members' bilateral contracts of employment with the employer.

1 [2007] EWHC 2900 (Ch), [2008] 1 WLR 1453 at [107]–[121].

7.20

The deputy judge disagreed with the contrary view of Lawrence Collins J in the *AMP* case, expressing his unhappiness about the jurisdiction being extended to commercial and contractual matters in which the mechanism of a trust has been used as part of the commercial structure: indeed, the deputy judge went so far as to suggest that the judge in that case must have based his decision on the equitable jurisdiction to set aside contracts pursuant to *Solle v Butcher*, despite the absence of any reference to that decision in the relevant part of the judgment. The deputy judge also disagreed with the application of equitable rescission in the *Gallaher* case for the same reason.

7.21

The deputy judge's rejection of the application of the jurisdiction is highly questionable, for the following reasons:

(a) The relevant claim was not to set aside the pension scheme, but to set aside the exercise of the amendment power vested in the employer and trustees. The requirement for a voluntary disposition is directed at the amendment power, not the scheme; it is therefore irrelevant whether the scheme was established pursuant to a contractual obligation.[1] What is relevant is that the amendment power was voluntary, in the sense that there was no obligation on the part of its holders to exercise it. There is therefore no valid distinction between private trust powers and pension scheme amendment powers for the purpose of the application of the equitable jurisdiction.

(b) The court will apply the equitable doctrine where no consideration has been given for the benefit conferred by the transaction.[2] Where the exercise of the power gave members greater benefits than were intended, those members received an unearned and undeserved windfall, for which no consideration had been provided.[3]

Since *Smithson v Hamilton*, the Court of Appeal has referred to cases involving the exercise of pension scheme powers as examples of voluntary dispositions.[4]

1 Although this is itself a doubtful proposition: the employment contracts are more likely to give members the right to join a scheme which had already been established: as the deputy judge said in a different context earlier in his judgment ([2008] 1 WLR 1453 at [87]), the decision to have a pension scheme is a matter for the employer.

2 *Van der Merwe v Goldman* [2016] EWHC 926 (Ch), [2016] 4 WLR 71 at [31] per Morgan J.

3 It is for this reason that such members cannot raise a bona fide purchaser defence to a rectification claim: *AMP (UK) plc v Barker* [2001] Pens LR 77 at [79] per Lawrence Collins J, discussed at **6.30**.

4 *Day v Day* [2013] EWCA Civ 280, [2014] Ch 114 at [22] per Sir Terence Etherton C and [46]–[50] per Lewison LJ.

7.22

Thus, notwithstanding *Smithson v Hamilton*, there remains scope for a mistaken exercise of a pension scheme amendment power to attract the application of the equitable rescission jurisdiction. It is notable in this respect that, in giving the lead judgment of the Court of Appeal in *Pitt v Holt*, Lloyd LJ included the *AMP* case in his discussion on that jurisdiction, without any negative comment on its application to pension schemes.[1]

1 [2011] EWCA Civ 197, [2012] Ch 132 at [193]. The *AMP* case was also briefly referred to, without critical comment, in the Supreme Court: [2013] UKSC 26, [2013] 2 AC 108 at [119].

The applicable test following Pitt v Holt[1]

7.23

The test for setting aside for mistake in equity was restated by the Supreme Court in *Pitt v Holt*, following the problems created by Millett J's distinction in *Gibbon v Mitchell* between the effect of a transaction and its consequences or the advantages gained by entering into it.[2] The relevance of that distinction was swept away by the Supreme Court, which held that:

> '... the true requirement is simply for there to be a causative mistake of sufficient gravity; and, as additional guidance to judges in finding and evaluating the facts of any particular case, that the test will normally be satisfied only when there is a mistake either as to the legal character or nature of a transaction, or as to some matter of fact or law which is basic to the transaction.'[3]

1 A ten-point summary of the relevant test was set out by Deputy Master Marsh in *Dukeries Healthcare Ltd v Bay Trust International Ltd* [2021] EWHC 2086 (Ch), [2021] WTLR 809 at [83]. However, as the Deputy Master remarked (at [84]) those points must be applied with caution, as each point was not self-contained and, in most instances, they overlapped to a greater or lesser degree. See also *Kennedy v Kennedy* [2014] EWHC 4129 (Ch), [2015] WTLR 837 at [36] per Sir Terence Etherton C.

2 See **7.15**.

3 [2013] 2 AC 108 at [122].

7.24

This test requires the court to evaluate the gravity of the mistake objectively in terms of its injustice or unconscionability, by a close examination of the facts, including the circumstances of the mistake and its consequences for the person who made the disposition.[1]

1 [2013] 2 AC 108 at [124]–[126]. Whilst the possibility of a claim being bought against an adviser for breach of duty is a factor in determining whether it is unconscionable to leave the mistake uncorrected, the uncertainties of such a claim means that only limited weight should be attached to that factor: *JTC Employer Ser Trustees Ltd v Khadem* [2021] EWHC 2929 (Ch) at [55] per HHJ Jarman QC (sitting as a deputy High Court judge).

7.25

As the mistake must have been operative at the time of the relevant disposition, the court is required to inquire into the mindset of the claimant at the moment they entered into the transaction which is sought to be avoided, although evidence of the claimant's mindset at some subsequent time may allow the court to form a view as to whether the claimant was operating under a mistake at the relevant time.[1]

1 *Bhaur v Equity First Trustees (Nevis) Ltd* [2021] EWHC 2581 (Ch), [2021] BTC 31 at [108] per Marcus Smith J.

7.26

The requirement for the mistake to be causative is satisfied where it is established that the claimant would not have entered into the transaction in the form they did, had they been aware of the mistake: it is not necessary to show that the transaction would not have been entered into at all.[1]

1 *Lewin*, para 5-074, approved by Marcus Smith J in *Bhaur v Equity First Trustees (Nevis) Ltd* [2021] EWHC 2581 (Ch), [2021] BTC 31 at [109].

7.27

The Supreme Court in *Pitt v Holt* also held as follows:[1]

(a) whilst ignorance, inadvertence or misprediction are insufficient to establish a mistake for the purposes of the equitable jurisdiction, the court should not shrink from drawing the inference of conscious belief or mistaken tacit assumption (which are sufficient) when there is evidence to support such an inference;

(b) the mistake may be as to a matter of fact or law;

(c) it does not matter if the mistake is due to carelessness on the part of the person making the voluntary disposition, unless the circumstances are such as to show that they deliberately ran the risk, or must be taken to have run the risk, of being wrong;

(d) it is not necessary that the mistake be known to, still less induced by, the person or persons taking a benefit under the disposition.

1 [2013] UKSC 26, [2013] 2 AC 108 at [108]–[114]. See *Van der Merwe v Goldman* [2016] EWHC 926 (Ch), [2016] 4 WLR 71; *Payne v Tyler* [2019] EWHC 2347 (Ch), [2019] WTLR 1221 and *Mackay v Wesley* [2020] EWHC 1215 (Ch).

7.28

As an equitable remedy, setting aside will be subject to the usual equitable defences such as laches, acquiescence and confirmation. Of particular relevance in this context is the effect of rescission on third parties, such as those who have received benefits under the provisions which are sought to be rescinded: the court may in that situation require an undertaking that no claims will be brought against those persons.[1]

1 *Pitt v Holt* [2013] UKSC 26, [2013] 2 AC 108 at [141].

The practical application of equitable rescission

7.29

The ability to rescind the exercise of a scheme amendment power because of a mistake is likely to be of benefit to employers and trustees where rectification is not possible because, for example, it is not clear what the parties would have done had the mistake not been made.

7.30

This jurisdiction is not to be regarded, however, as a less onerous means of correcting mistakes than rectification, in terms of the evidential burden on the claimant. As with rectification, convincing proof will be needed to establish that a mistake has been made for the operation of this jurisdiction, as in both cases the court assumes that what the parties intended was what they recorded in the document.[1] Moreover, the court is required to focus intensively on the facts of the case,[2] which will require the court to be provided with adequate evidence about the mistake: mere assertion by the person said to have been mistaken may, on its own, not suffice.[3] A claimant bringing a claim seeking relief based upon mistake must be scrupulous to ensure that the court is given a complete and accurate picture.[4]

1 *Anker-Petersen v Christensen* [2002] WTLR 313 at [35]–[36] per Davis J; *Gallaher Ltd v Gallaher Pensions Ltd* [2005] EWHC 42 (Ch), [2005] Pens LR 103 at [154] per Etherton J; *Bhaur v Equity First Trustees (Nevis) Ltd* [2021] EWHC 2581 (Ch), [2021] BTC 31 at [107] per Marcus Smith J.
2 *Pitt v Holt* [2013] UKSC 26, [2013] 2 AC 108 at [126]. This applies even where the application to set aside the transaction is effectively unopposed: *Wright v National Westminster Bank plc* [2014] EWHC 3158 (Ch), [2015] WTLR 547 at [10] per Norris J.
3 *Dukeries Healthcare Ltd v Bay Trust International Ltd* [2021] EWHC 2086 (Ch), [2021] WTLR 809 at [95] per Deputy Master Marsh; *Bhaur v Equity First Trustees (Nevis) Ltd* [2021] EWHC 2581 (Ch) at [83] per Marcus Smith J. See also *Pitt v Holt* [2013] UKSC 26, [2013] 2 AC 108 at [127].
4 *Dukeries Healthcare Ltd v Bay Trust International Ltd* [2021] EWHC 2086 (Ch), [2021] WTLR 809 at [131].

7.31

Another potential limit on the jurisdiction was Sir Andrew Park's comment in *Smithson v Hamilton*[1] that it has only been applied in cases where an entire transaction has been set aside, which suggests that it is not possible to set aside individual provisions. The deputy judge did not explain why the equitable mistake doctrine should be restricted in this way, when the application of the rule in *Hastings-Bass* enabled specific terms within a document to be set aside.[2] Since then, it has been held that a self-contained and severable part of a voluntary transaction can be rescinded for mistake without affecting the rest of the transaction.[3]

1 [2007] EWHC 2900 (Ch), [2008] 1 WLR 1453 at [109].
2 See **7.6**.
3 *Kennedy v Kennedy* [2014] EWHC 4129 (Ch), [2015] WTLR 837 at [46] per Sir Terence Etherton C. See also *Bainbridge v Bainbridge* [2016] EWHC 898 (Ch), [2016] WTLR 943.

Mistake as to purpose

7.32

A donee of a power created for the benefit of others is required to exercise it for the purpose for which it was created:[1] a failure to do so will render the exercise of the power void.[2] This doctrine is known as 'fraud on a power', although this does not denote any bad faith on the part of the donee: 'fraud' in this context simply means that the power has been exercised for a purpose, or with an intention, beyond the scope of or not justified by the instrument creating the power.[3] Accordingly, it is now more commonly called the 'proper purposes' principle.

1 The classic statement of the principle was made by Lord Westbury LC in *Duke of Portland v Lady Topham* (1864) 11 HLC 32, 54.
2 *Cloutte v Storey* [1911] 1 Ch 18. Query whether this is the correct form of relief for cases which more closely resemble the trustees failing to take only proper considerations into account: *Pitt v Holt* [2013] UKSC 26, [2013] 2 AC 108 at [62].
3 *Vatcher v Paull* [1915] AC 372, 378 per Lord Parker of Waddington.

7.33

If the exercise of the power was for an improper purpose, it is irrelevant that the donee was acting in what they believed to be the best interests of those affected by the exercise of the power, or even that the proposed exercise would demonstrably be for their benefit.[1]

1 *Howard Smith Ltd v Ampol Petroleum Ltd* [1974] AC 821, 834 per Lord Wilberforce.

7.34

Determining whether a power has been exercised for a proper purpose requires proof of both the purpose of the power and the purpose for which the donee has exercised the power. As to these:

(a) the purpose of the power is not determined solely by a process of construction: the purpose is rarely expressed in the instrument creating it, and a power which on its face is unlimited in its scope may still be subject to limitations as to how it can be exercised, to be inferred from the mischief of the provision conferring it, which is itself deduced from its express terms, an analysis of its effect, and the court's understanding of the business context;[1]

(b) ascertaining the purpose for which the donee exercised the power will often involve a subjective element:[2] extrinsic evidence beyond that admissible on a question of construction may accordingly be adduced, including contemporaneous documents directly revealing the state of the donee's mind.[3]

1 *Eclairs Group Ltd v JKX Oil & Gas plc* [2015] UKSC 71, [2016] 3 All ER 641 at [30]–[31] per Lord Sumption JSC. The proper purposes of the power are to be ascertained as at the date when the power was conferred: *Independent Trustee Services Ltd v Hope* [2009] EWHC 2810 (Ch), [2010] ICR 553 at [78] per Henderson J.
2 *Eclairs Group Ltd v JKX Oil & Gas plc* [2016] 3 All ER 641 at [15] per Lord Sumption JSC.
3 *Re Burton's Settlements* [1955] Ch 82, 100 per Upjohn J.

7.35

The scope of the enquiry into the purposes of a pension scheme power was considered by the Court of Appeal in *British Airways plc v Airways Pension Scheme Trustee Ltd*,[1] in which the exercise by the trustee of an apparently unlimited unilateral amendment power to enable it to grant increases to pensions was successfully challenged by the employer. Whilst it was agreed that the starting point was the objects clause of the scheme, it was accepted that that was not decisive.[2] Lewison LJ considered that the constitutional functions of the trustee were to manage and administer the scheme, which did not include a power to redesign the benefit structure.[3] Peter Jackson LJ said that the purpose of the scheme was not restricted to the result that the scheme existed to produce, but encompassed both the result and the essential means by which it was to be produced, which required the balance of powers between the trustee and the employer to be ascertained and maintained.[4] Thus, it is necessary not only to look at any constraints affecting the power, either directly in the power itself or indirectly in the objects clause, but also to any constraints affecting the donee of the power.

1 [2018] EWCA Civ 1533, [2018] Pens LR 506.
2 [2018] Pens LR 506 at [52] per Patten LJ, at [100] per Lewison LJ and at [116] per Peter Jackson LJ.
3 [2018] Pens LR 506 at [101]–[102]; also at [121] per Peter Jackson LJ.
4 [2018] Pens LR 506 at [116].

7.36

The improper purposes principle has been considered in a pensions context on several occasions:

(a) In *Re Courage Group's Pension Schemes,*[1] Millett J held that the use of a power to substitute a new company for an existing employer, for the purpose of enabling the scheme's surplus assets to be removed for the new company's sole benefit, was beyond the purpose of that power.

(b) In *Hillsdown Holdings plc v Pensions Ombudsman,*[2] the trustees of one scheme exercised the power to transfer the assets and liabilities to another scheme, to facilitate an agreement between the employers of those schemes that the surplus assets so transferred would be paid to them, in circumstances where such a payment was prohibited by the terms of the transferor scheme. Knox J upheld the Pension Ombudsman's finding that the transfer was an improper exercise of the transfer power for a collateral purpose.

(c) In *Bank of New Zealand v Bank of New Zealand Officers Provident Association Management Board,*[3] an amendment to a scheme, which enabled surplus to be distributed not only to current members but also to former employees who had received lump sums on retirement instead of pensions, was held to be consistent with the purpose of the power, notwithstanding that the reference in the objects clause to the scheme being for the benefit of 'members and pensioners' did not include former employees in receipt of lump sum payments.

(d) In *Law Debenture Trust Corp plc v Lonrho Africa Trade & Finance Ltd,*[4] a scheme rule gave the trustees the sole power to augment benefits. The evidence disclosed that the provision was introduced solely for the purpose of 'predator protection', by allowing the trustee to augment members' benefits unilaterally in the event of aggression by the principal employer towards the fund. It was argued by the employer that the exercise of the power outside of that situation would be beyond the purpose for which it was conferred. That argument was rejected by Patten J, who drew a distinction between the purpose for which a power was granted and the circumstances in which it was granted. The motivation for the introduction of the power was not the same as the purposes for which the power was granted, and to require the trustees to decide whether the scheme was under attack before exercising the power would be to place them in an impossible position, which could not have been intended.

(e) In *Allan v Rea Brothers Trustees Ltd*,[5] the Court of Appeal held that the transfer of funds into a scheme, on the strength of a false declaration that the relevant member was an employee of the transferee scheme's employer, may constitute an improper purpose, although there was insufficient evidence of the terms of the transfer power in the transferor scheme to determine that issue.

(f) In *Phoenix Venture Holdings Ltd v Independent Trustee Services Ltd*,[6] it was contended by an employer of a multi-employer scheme in winding-up, that the exercise of the amendment power by the trustee to introduce a power to apportion the liabilities between the employers, and the exercise of that power to apportion the entire liability to the claimant employer, were improper exercises of those powers for the purpose of driving the claimant into insolvency, so that the scheme might qualify for entry into the Pension Protection Fund (PPF). Sir Andrew Morritt V-C said (obiter) that that contention was arguable, and that it supported the claimant's application to restrain the presentation of a winding-up petition by the trustee.

(g) In *Independent Trustee Services Ltd v Hope*,[7] the trustee of an underfunded scheme with an insolvent employer proposed to exercise its power to buy-out the benefits of certain high-earning employees before the scheme entered the PPF. This would have the effect of providing those benefits in full, but would not adversely affect the other members, as their benefits would be provided under the PPF at the same level as if the buy-out had not taken place. Henderson J rejected the proposal, holding that the purpose of the buyout power was to apply an amount that fairly represented the benefits to which a member was entitled under the scheme in the purchase of an insurance policy which provided benefits in substitution, and it was implicit, as being otherwise contrary to the fundamental purposes of the scheme as a whole, that the amount that might be so applied was limited to a fair share of the scheme assets. The proposal would employ a disproportionately high and unfair share of scheme assets in exercising the buy-out power, and would be an improper exercise of the power as going far beyond the purpose for which it existed in the context of the scheme.

(h) In *Dalriada Trustees Ltd v Faulds*,[8] the trustees of each of two unconnected pension schemes exercised their investment powers to make a reciprocal loan to a member of the other scheme, to facilitate the access by the member of their funds prior to retirement. Bean J held that the loans were made for an ulterior purpose, and the fact that everyone involved with the transactions wished to validate the loans did not affect that conclusion.

(i) In *Barnardo's v Buckinghamshire*,[9] Warren J was considering whether the trustees had the power to replace the retail price index (RPI) with the consumer price index (CPI) as the index used to determine the rate of increases to pensions in payment and in deferment. The judge said that the purpose of the increase provisions was to protect the members to some extent from the effects of price inflation; the index was there to provide a measure by which those increases were to be awarded; and a power to switch the index ought properly to be exercised only to ensure that the index in use best reflected the policy of providing protection from inflation.

(j) In *British Airways plc v Airways Pension Scheme Trustee Ltd,*[10] the trustees exercised a unilateral power of amendment to allow discretionary increases to be paid to members, and subsequently exercised that power to award such an increase. Those powers were exercised in the light of the reduction in automatic pension increases by reason of the switch from RPI to CPI, and the discretionary increases were set at 50 per cent of the difference between the two indices. The Court of Appeal held (by a majority) that those exercises were beyond the purpose of the amendment power, which did not enable the trustees to design benefits in circumstances in which the fund was in deficit and the employer would be required to make additional contributions for the purpose of funding benefits which had not already been promised but which were additional benefits decided upon by the trustees.

1 [1987] 1 WLR 495.
2 [1997] 1 All ER 862.
3 [2003] UKPC 58, [2003] OPLR 281.
4 [2002] EWHC 2732 (Ch), [2003] Pens LR 13 at [45].
5 [2002] EWCA Civ 85, [2002] Pens LR 169 at [49].
6 [2005] EWHC 1379 (Ch), [2005] Pens LR 379 at [65]–[66].
7 [2009] EWHC 2810 (Ch), [2010] ICR 553.
8 [2011] EWHC 3391 (Ch), [2012] ICR 1106 at [72].
9 [2015] EWHC 2200 (Ch), [2015] Pens LR 501 at [78]. In the Court of Appeal, it was common ground that the judge's analysis was correct ([2016] EWCA Civ 1064, [2017] Pens LR 26 at [83]); there was no reference to this point in the Supreme Court.
10 [2018] EWCA Civ 1533, [2018] Pens LR 506.

Practice point: can an express provision overcome *Smithson v Hamilton?*

7.37

As stated at **7.11**, *Smithson v Hamilton* has, for the time being at least, put paid to the setting aside of pension scheme documents under the rule in *Hastings Bass* on the basis that the trustees failed to take only proper considerations into account. Moreover, the rule has been made more difficult to apply generally after *Pitt v Holt*, because of the need to establish a breach of fiduciary duty and because the result was that the exercise of the power was voidable rather than void.

7.38

However, those requirements do not apply to the doctrine of excessive execution, referred to at **4.8**:

(a) there is no need to establish a breach of fiduciary duty for the excessive execution principle to apply: it is sufficient that the exercise of the power is beyond what the trustees are permitted by the scope of the power to do;

(b) excessive execution of a power renders the exercise void rather than voidable.[1]

Although a failure by the trustees to take account of only relevant considerations in exercising a power does not of itself constitute excessive execution, it is theoretically possible to introduce into the governing provisions of the scheme an express term requiring the trustees to act in that way, so that a failure to comply with that requirement operates as a precondition of the valid exercise of the power. For example, a term may be inserted which provides that no exercise of the power shall be valid unless the trustees have only taken into account considerations which they ought to have taken into account.

1 *Lewin*, para 30-017.

7.39

The argument in favour of such a term would be that:

(a) a breach of that term would operate in the same way as a breach of any other express restriction in the exercise of a power phrased in terms of a precondition to the validity of the amendment, in that it would be void for excessive execution;[1]

(b) the document created in the exercise of that power could more easily be treated as having no effect without the need for an application to court, whereas a document which is merely voidable under the rule in *Hastings-Bass* could not be set aside unless done by the court;

(c) the doctrine of severance can apply as it does in all cases of excessive execution, so that any exercise of the power which was not vitiated by the breach of the term could be treated as operative, provided that the requirements for severance were satisfied.[2]

1 See **1.19**.
2 See **Chapter 4**.

7.40

There is no guarantee that a court would accept that a breach of such a term would have such an effect, and there are several arguments which could be ranged against it, such as:

(a) the restriction is too vague to have such an effect: what is a relevant consideration? How material must it be? Who is to determine those questions?

(b) enshrining the rule in *Hastings-Bass* into the express terms of the scheme should mean that the breach of that term has the same effect as under that rule, ie that the term is voidable rather than void; and

(c) it is another attempt to introduce rectification of pension scheme documents by the back door.[1]

However, unless and until such a provision is held to be ineffective, it may provide another defensible route for employers and trustees to correct document errors in circumstances where they wish to avoid litigation.

1 Although the avoidance of the document, subject to the principle of severance, is not so flexible a remedy as to replicate rectification in all circumstances.

8 Other Equitable Principles

8.1

This chapter considers three further equitable principles which might conceivably be of help in correcting mistakes in pension scheme documents without the need to apply to court to do so. However, whilst the first of these principles has been successfully invoked in a pensions context and may continue to be of use going forward, the other two principles are likely to be of little assistance in this field.

'Equity treats as done that which ought to be done'

8.2

The equitable maxim 'equity treats as done that which ought to be done' is of long standing[1] and has its most frequent application in the case of contracts, where equity will treat a contract to do a thing as if the thing were already done, although only in favour of persons entitled to enforce the contract and not in favour of volunteers. In this context, its best-known application was in *Walsh v Lonsdale*,[2] where it was held that a specifically enforceable agreement for a lease could take effect in equity as a completed lease before the requisite formalities for executing it had been satisfied.

1 Dating back to *Banks v Sutton* (1732) 2 P Wms 700.
2 (1882) 21 ChD 9.

8.3

The maxim had been applied in pensions cases to validate defective documents where there was a duty, as opposed to a mere power, to execute them.[1] However, in *HR Trustees Ltd v Wembley plc*,[2] Vos J went further in applying the maxim to validate an amendment which otherwise fell foul of the formality requirements of amendment power. At the time, this decision was thought to have made a significant inroad into the principle that amendments had strictly to comply with those requirements, but subsequent cases have sought to row back from it.

1 *Davis v Richards and Wallington Industries Ltd* [1990] 1 WLR 1511, 1535 per Scott J; *Harwood-Smart v Caws* [2000] Pens LR 101 at [43] per Rimer J.
2 [2011] EWHC 2974 (Ch). For so important a case, it is strange that it has never been reported.

The Wembley case

8.4

A scheme contained an amendment power[1] which permitted the employer to issue a written authority to the trustees to amend, following which the trustees were required to make a declaration of the amendment signed by all of them. The trustee body, which comprised of five individuals, had formally resolved to amend the scheme to change the rate of pension increases for benefits accruing after 6 April 2000: that decision was made at two trustee meetings, held in November 1999 (attended by four trustees) and in January 2000 (attended by all five trustees). Thereafter, the scheme's insurer produced a 'scheme amendment authority' document which was intended to put the trustees' decision into formal effect. The authority was signed at the July 2000 trustee meeting by the four trustees present at that meeting, and the company secretary signed on behalf of the employer. The absent trustee, however, did not sign the authority because of an administrative oversight. It was accepted that she would have signed the authority had she been asked, and that she remained willing to sign it if required by the court.

1 This was a standard form amendment power used in scheme documents prepared by Legal & General: the power has also been considered, in this and other contexts, in *Bestrustees Ltd v Stuart* [2001] Pens LR 283; *ICM Computer Group v Stribley* [2013] EWHC 2995 (Ch), [2013] Pens LR 409; *Honda Motor Europe Ltd v Powell* [2014] EWCA Civ 437, [2014] Pens LR 255; and *Briggs v Gleeds (Head Office)* [2014] EWHC 1178 (Ch), [2015] 1 Ch 212.

8.5

Having rejected the employer's arguments as to why the amendment power should be construed so as to validate the amendment, Vos J held that the amendment was nevertheless effective by the application of the maxim, because the trustees had already validly exercised their discretion to make the amendment authorised by the employer at the November 1999 and January 2000 trustee meetings; having done so, the trustees were obliged to make the appropriate declaration in a particular form, and could have been compelled on behalf of the members, who were not volunteers, to specifically perform their exercise of the power.[1] The judge went on to say that:

> 'It may be that there has never been before a case on all fours with the present, but law and equity would be made to look ridiculous if it were powerless to correct what has been an obvious administrative error like the one made in this case.'

1 [2011] EWHC 2974 (Ch) at [66].

8.6

The judge said that none of the scheme members whose benefits may have been adversely affected by the amendment had reason to feel aggrieved, as they were notified of the change at the time and never expected to accrue rights on any other basis. The judge therefore held that the amendment was valid to amend benefits with effect from July 2000.[1]

1 Although the application of the maxim means that the thing should take effect from when it ought to have been done, the problem of the amendment operating retrospectively was sidestepped by the employer's concession that the amendment only took effect from the date of the July 2000 trustee meeting, rather than the April 2000 date originally resolved by the trustees: [2011] EWHC 2974 (Ch) at [22].

8.7

The decision has been regarded as controversial, and the scope of its application is unclear. Could it, for example, be applied in cases of non-execution rather than defective execution? Was an attempt to make the amendment a pre-requisite of the application of the maxim and, if so, how close to success must the attempt get? Was it a requirement for the trustees to have already resolved to make the amendment? If the employer had authorised an amendment which was unequivocally for the benefit of the members, such that the only decision the trustees could have properly made in the circumstances was to approve the amendment, could the maxim apply at the earlier stage to treat that decision as having been made, as well as at the later stage to treat the amendment as having been made?

Subsequent treatment

8.8

Since the *Wembley* case, attempts to apply the maxim to defective pension scheme amendments have failed, although the bases on which the case has been distinguished are not wholly satisfactory.

8.9

In *Briggs v Gleeds (Head Office)*,[1] Newey J refused to apply the maxim to validate a defective amendment which operated to reduce members' benefits. The judge noted the potentially far-reaching implications of the *Wembley* case, given that the application of the maxim did not depend on the defective execution of the amendment. The judge was concerned that this meant that a scheme's formally-executed documents may not provide a reliable guide to its terms, and that there could be confusion as to the applicable time of the amendment where, for example, there was a delay between the trustees making the decision to amend and executing the amendment or where a decision was made to change the amendment between those times. The judge refused to apply the maxim because of the detrimental nature of the intended change to members' benefits. He considered that trustees should be treated as having done what they ought to have done only in favour of someone who would have been able to enforce the obligation; and trustees should not be taken to have made amendments against the interests of the scheme's members, where it was unrealistic to assume that the members would have compelled them to do so.

1 [2014] EWHC 1178 (Ch), [2015] 1 Ch 212 at [76]–[82].

8.10

In *Burgess v BIC UK Ltd*,[1] the maxim was invoked to cure a defective amendment which granted increases to members' benefits. In that case, the scheme rules gave the trustees the power (with the consent of the employer) to amend the rules by a document signed by them and by the employer. The trustees resolved to make the amendment at a trustee meeting, but that document was not signed and no other signed document was produced. Arnold J declined to apply the maxim, distinguishing the *Wembley* case on the basis that the amendment power in his case did not oblige the trustees to execute the amending document, but merely conferred a discretionary power: the maxim had no application as the court could not have compelled the trustees to make the amendment merely because they had in fact decided how it should be exercised.

1 [2018] EWHC 785 (Ch), [2018] Pens LR 13 at [114]. This issue did not arise on appeal.

8.11

It appears from these cases that the maxim will only be applied where the amendment was for the benefit of the members, and where amendment power itself created an obligation on the part of the trustees to make an amendment. But these restrictions on the application of the maxim are problematical:

(a) The attempt in the *Briggs* case to rely on the fact that the amendment in question was against the interests of members ignores the fact that the amendment in issue in the *Wembley* case also reduced members' benefits. Moreover, Newey J's analysis ignores the interests of the employer in there being a valid amendment which would reduce its liabilities to the scheme; the ability of the employer to compel the trustees to perfect the amendment should be sufficient to regard the amendment as having been made pursuant to the maxim.

(b) The fact that the amendment power in the *Burgess* case conferred only a discretionary power on the trustees is not a relevant distinguishing feature, as it had previously been established that the amendment power in the *Wembley* case also gave the trustees a discretion to refuse to make the amendment.[1] The reason why the maxim was applied in that case was that the trustees had already exercised that discretion, and so had become obliged to comply with the formalities for making the amendment.

1 *Bestrustees plc v Stuart* [2001] Pens LR 283 at [39] per Neuberger J, followed by Vos J in the *Wembley* case [2011] EWHC 2974 (Ch) at [45].

Practice point: strengthening the case for the application of the maxim

8.12

The key question for the application of the maxim, which was not explored in either of the above cases, is whether the circumstances surrounding the agreement between the trustees and the employer gave rise to a right on the part of the employer to compel the trustees to make the formal amendment, thereby allowing the maxim to apply to treat the requisite formalities as having already been satisfied. This requires the agreement to be supported by valuable consideration, as a contract contained in a deed which is without consideration will not be ordered to be specifically performed.[1]

1 *Kekewich v Manning* (1851) 1 De GM & G 176, 188 per Knight-Bruce LJ.

8.13

There is certainly an argument that, where the amendment in question will affect the benefits of the members and has been the product of negotiation between the trustees and the employer, a concluded agreement on the changes will be supported by valuable consideration. This may take the form of (for example) the professional costs incurred during the negotiations by the employer and by the trustees.

8.14

The trustees and employer can accordingly strengthen the prospects for the application of the maxim, should the amendment document fail to comply with the required formalities in some way,[1] by including in the amendment document a recital that they have agreed the changes contained in the document for valuable consideration, and explaining the nature of that consideration.

1 Even careful compliance with the existing amendment powers may not be sufficient where provisions in earlier amendment powers had been wrongly removed and are to be read back into the existing power: see **3.55**.

Equitable relief against defective execution

The principle

8.15

Where, by reason of accident or mistake, there is a formal defect in the execution of a power, equity will grant relief in favour of certain individuals who are regarded as having provided good consideration.

8.16

The principle was established in the old case of *Tollet v Tollet*.[1] In that case, a husband was granted a power to settle property on his wife by deed, but instead he purported to do so by will. The wife had no other financial provision on her husband's death. Jekyll MR held that equity would intervene to remedy the defect, holding as follows:

> '… the difference is betwixt a non-execution and a defective execution of a power; the latter will always be aided in equity under the circumstances mentioned, it being the duty of every man to pay his debts, and a husband or father to provide for his wife or child. But this Court will not help the non-execution of a power, since it is against the nature of a power, which is left to the free will and election of the party whether to execute or not, for which reason equity will not say he shall execute it, or do that for him which he does not think fit to do himself.'

1 (1728) 2 P Wms 489, 490.

8.17

The following conditions must be satisfied for equity to intervene:[1]

(a) an intention by the person with the power to exercise it;

(b) an attempted execution of the power: there is no jurisdiction to remedy a failure either to exercise the power at all or to exercise it in time;

(c) the defect is formal rather than going to the substance of the power;

(d) there was a proper exercise of the power: the court will not assist where there would be a fraud on the power[2] or a breach of trust;

(e) the doctrine will only operate in favour of certain categories of persons, namely:

 (i) purchasers for value;

 (ii) creditors;

 (iii) charities; and

 (iv) persons for whom the appointor is under a natural or moral obligation to provide.

1 *English v Keats* [2018] EWHC 673 (Ch), [2018] WTLR 91 at [58] per HHJ Hacon (sitting as a deputy High Court judge), citing the Royal Court of Jersey in *Bas Trust Corp Ltd v MF* [2012] JRC 081.
2 See **7.32**.

8.18

Tollet v Tollet was revisited by Park J in *Breadner v Granville-Grossman.*[1] In that case, the trustees of a discretionary trust had power before a 'closing date' to create fresh trusts. The trustees purported to execute fresh trusts in favour of a person, but did so too late. The judge refused to apply the equitable principle for several reasons, the following of which are relevant for pension schemes:

(a) the principle applies because equity acts upon the consciences of the beneficiaries entitled in default and prevents them from taking what their entitlement would otherwise have been; there was nothing unconscionable on the part of those entitled under the existing trusts wishing to retain their interests which were not removed by a valid exercise of the power;

(b) the requirement for the power to be exercised in discharge of a natural or moral obligation requires there to be a close relationship between the holder of the power and the person in whose favour they intended to exercise it: there has been no case where the power was exercisable by the trustees themselves;

(c) equity will only relieve against defects which are not of the essence of the power, and will not be applied to defeat a material part of the drafter's intention:[2] the exercise of the power before the closing date was of the essence of the power, and the court cannot override the drafter's intentions in this respect; the drafter deliberately chose to apply a time-limit to the exercise of the power because they thought that it was at least possible that there was a good reason for it.

1 [2001] Ch 523, 546-551.
2 *Cooper v Martin* (1867-68) 3 Ch App 47, 56 per Lord Cairns and Sir John Rolt LJJ.

8.19

This principle was applied by HHJ Hacon in *English v Keats.*[1] In that case, the claimants, who were three siblings, claimed the benefit of deeds of appointment purportedly made by trustees who included the parents of the siblings. However, the deeds only identified three of the four trustees, and only three of the trustees executed the deeds. The deputy judge held that all the trustees intended to exercise a valid power to amend the settlements, and that they purported to do so by three signatures. In those circumstances, it was held that there was an attempted exercise of the power and that the deeds of appointment were effective to confer on the claimants an interest under the deeds.

1 [2018] EWHC 673 (Ch), [2018] WTLR 91.

8.20

English v Keats was distinguished in *Smith v Stanley*,[1] in which Deputy Judge Rees QC refused to apply the principle to validate informal distributions of trust property made by trustees of a will trust to the testator's sister and children prior to the execution of a deed of appointment. The deputy judge held that equity could not intervene where there was a failure to execute a deed, and there had been no moral obligation on the trustees to provide for any of the persons to whom the payments were made.
1 [2019] EWHC 2168 (Ch) at [52].

Application to pension schemes

8.21

Formidable obstacles face the application of this principle to validate a purported amendment to the provisions of a pension scheme which fails to comply with the formal requirements of the amendment power.

8.22

First, as equity intervenes in favour of the objects for whom the power is exercised, where the amendment in question purports to reduce the benefits of members, or otherwise operates to their detriment, it is unlikely that the principle will apply to prejudice those members to the advantage of the employer.

8.23

Further, the requirement for there to be a close relationship between the holder of the power and the person in whose favour the power is intended to be exercised means that it is unlikely that the principle can be invoked where the power was exercised by the trustees of the scheme. Thus, in *Burgess v BIC UK Ltd*,[1] Arnold J refused to apply this principle to validate the defective exercise of an amendment power vested in the trustees and employer of a pension scheme which would have provided pension increases to certain members, on the basis that the trustees did not owe any legal or moral obligation to grant increases to those members.

1 [2018] EWHC 785 (Ch), [2018] Pens LR 380 at [116]. This issue did not arise on appeal.

8.24

In the *Burgess* case, the judge did not expressly consider whether the relationship between the members and the employer, as joint holder of the amendment power, could have been sufficient: it is possible that the facts of a particular case may give rise to a legal or moral obligation on the part of the employer to provide the benefits to the members which are the subject of the defectively-executed instrument. But even here, it is very arguable that the formal requirements of the amendment power may be regarded as the essence of the power which cannot be defeated by the intervention of equity: whilst those requirements may be formal in nature, the courts have emphasised the importance to members of ensuring fully-compliant amendments as a reason for the need strictly to comply with those requirements.[1]

1 *Bestrustees Ltd v Stuart* [2001] Pens LR 283 at [33] and [40] per Neuberger J; *Capital Cranfield Trust Corp Ltd v Sagar* [2002] OPLR 151 at [40] per Neuberger J. In *Thackwell v Gardiner* (1851) 5 De G & Sm 58, Sir James Parker V-C refused to apply the equitable principle where the instrument did not comply with the requirement for two witnesses, as that was intended to protect a married woman against her husband's influence.

Equitable *non est factum*

8.25

In *Turner v Turner*,[1] a farmer made a discretionary settlement which he did not understand, and appointed as trustees family friends who never realised that they had any responsibility at all except to do as the settlor asked, thinking that it would be intruding into the settlor's affairs if they were to read the documents that they were asked to sign. In those circumstances, the court set aside the appointments 'made' by the trustees.

1 [1984] Ch 100.

8.26

This case has been regarded as extreme and highly unusual, and has been described as 'equitable *non est factum*.'[1] Attempts in several pensions cases to rely on this principle have failed, reflecting the truly exceptional circumstances which must exist before it can be applied. The grounds on which the principle was rejected in those cases are as follows:

(a) whilst the trustees who had exercised the power in question had been subject to very strong persuasion, it was sufficient that they knew that they had had a discretion to exercise;[2]

(b) where trustees intended to exercise the amendment power but made a mistake in thinking that they were merely formalising an earlier amendment, that brought into play the rule in *Hastings-Bass*[3] but not the principle in *Turner v Turner*;[4]

(c) the principle did not arise where the trustees instructed specialist consultants to prepare the documentation, delegated the responsibility for liaising with the consultants to one of their own number, and asked the consultants to confirm that the documents were suitable when they were presented for execution;[5]

(d) the principle did not arise where new trustees on their appointment had given effect to an amendment of a pension trust which had been fully considered by their predecessor, although not by them.[6]

It is accordingly virtually impossible to see how this principle could be applied in the modern pension scheme context.

1 *Sieff v Fox* [2005] EWHC 1312 (Ch), [2005] 1 WLR 3811 at [38] per Lloyd LJ.
2 *Stannard v Fisons Pension Trust Ltd* [1990] Pens LR 201 at [168] per Warner J. This point was not pursued on appeal.
3 See **7.4–7.5**.
4 *Betafence Ltd v Veys* [2006] EWHC 999 (Ch), [2006] Pens LR 137 at [74] per Lightman J.
5 *Smithson v Hamilton* [2007] EWHC 2900 (Ch), [2008] 1 WLR 1453 at [130] per Sir Andrew Park
6 *HR Trustees Ltd v German* [2010] EWHC 321 (Ch), [2010] Pens LR 23 at [216] per Arnold J.

9 Contract and Estoppel

9.1

Where a document error cannot be corrected by any of the methods already discussed, it may be possible to argue that the members are nevertheless bound to accept the intended changes, either as a matter of contract with the employer that binds the trustees, or by virtue of an estoppel preventing the members relying on the original document.

9.2

Such arguments will usually be run by the employer who stands to lose out by reason of the increase in liabilities caused by the invalidity of the change. It will only be in very rare cases that the trustees seek to run contract or estoppel arguments in this context. It is more likely that, in seeking directions from the court on the issue of the validity of an amendment, the trustees will seek to exclude from the order any contract or estoppel claim or defence which may arise from the factual circumstances specific to the members or the employer.

9.3

Despite early cases which seemed to support them, later cases have shown a reluctance to accept contract or estoppel arguments, particularly where they operate against the members' interests. For historical mistakes, they are accordingly unlikely to be of much assistance.

Contract

The principle

9.4

The leading case is *South West Trains Ltd v Wightman*.[1] By a binding contract with their employer, the scheme members agreed to incorporate a number of allowances into their annual salary, with only part of that new salary being treated as pensionable. A proposal by the trustee to amend the rules of the scheme to give effect to this agreement was challenged by the members, who contended that, under the rules as they stood, they were entitled to have all their salary treated as pensionable. Neuberger J dismissed the challenge on the basis that there was an implied term in the contract that the members would not claim pensions at a higher level than had been agreed. The judge went on to say that it may well be that the trustees could refuse to pay the members the claimed benefits under the scheme even without the intervention of the employer. An agreement between the employer and the members which affected the benefits could accordingly override the members' scheme rights.[2]

1 [1998] Pens LR 113 at [94]–[109].
2 See also the judgments of Lightman J in *The Trustees of the NUS Officials and Employees Superannuation Fund v Pensions Ombudsman* [2002] Pens LR 93 at [13], and *AF Blakemore & Son Ltd v Machin* [2007] EWHC 963 (Ch), [2007] Pens LR 189 at [6].

9.5

Following that case, employers who wish to change the terms of a pension scheme in a way which could not be done by amendment because of a restriction in the amendment power, have done so by agreeing individual contracts with members, which have become known as '*South West Trains* agreements'. Of more relevance for present purposes are the attempts by employers to argue that members were contractually bound to accept amendments which turned out to be invalid, by reason of matters which occurred at the time of those amendments.

Application of the principle to historic mistakes

9.6

In *HR Trustees v German*,[1] a conversion of defined benefits (DB) rights into defined contribution (DC) benefits was held to be invalid under the terms of the scheme amendment power. The employer argued that the affected members had become contractually bound to accept the converted benefits, by signing and returning application forms on which they had indicated that they had read the explanatory booklet which set out the terms of the new DC scheme and that they wished to join that scheme, and by attending presentations explaining the new pension arrangements. Arnold J rejected that argument on two grounds:

(a) the employer needed to show that the parties intended their rights to be governed by a contract which was separate from the terms of the scheme, and no such intention was proved on the evidence, as:

   (i) the members were simply told by the employer what it had decided to do, and were thereby presented with a fait accompli: there was no suggestion in the documents that the change in benefits was dependent upon the members' agreement;

   (ii) the explanatory booklet clearly stated that it was not comprehensive and that the scheme was governed by the trust deed and rules; and

   (iii) the members cannot have intended to give up existing DB rights, and in particular the rights protected by the restriction in the amendment power, when the booklet contained no reference to those rights: neither, for the same reason, were the members being asked to consent to the conversion of their benefits;

(b) where the claimed benefits were contrary to the terms of the scheme, there was a need to show the type of informed consent on the part of the members which would preclude them from asserting a breach of trust: there was no such informed consent, as the members were not informed of the restriction in the amendment power and were given no choice whether or not to consent to the changes.

1 [2010] EWHC 321 (Ch), [2010] Pens LR 24 at [163]–[169] and [173]–[174].

9.7

In *Capita ATL Pension Trustees Ltd v Gellately*,[1] the employer, following an invalid amendment, sought to rely on an announcement to members and on an application form as having contractual effect. Henderson J rejected the argument because the amendment did not disclose an intention to create any legal relations as it was stated to be a brief summary of the changes, it referred to the formal scheme documents prevailing in the event of a conflict, the form was to be signed and returned before proposed presentations had taken place, there was no clarity as to who the contracting parties were, there was no need to bind the members by contract when the proposed amendment would have been sufficient, and the only consent sought on the application form was to deduct the increased contributions from members' earnings.

1 [2011] EWHC 485 (Ch), [2011] Pens LR 153 at [77]–[84].

9.8

In *Briggs v Gleeds (Home Office)*,[1] the employer argued that members were contractually bound to a number of changes made in various deeds which had been held to be invalid.

(a) The first invalid amendment involved the establishment of a new DC section, and the employer relied on the application form signed by members by which they applied for membership of the section and agreed to abide by the rules, authorised the deduction of contributions from their salaries, and agreed to transfer the value of their DB rights to the new section. Newey J held that the employer needed to establish an intention to create contractual relations, and that the forms were explicable by reference to the rights the members believed themselves to have already under the scheme.[2]

(b) The same analysis was applied by the judge in respect of subsequent invalid amendments to pension accrual, employer contribution rates and pension increases, where the members had signed and returned forms in which they opted either to accept the changes or to be treated as having left the scheme, and (in the former case) authorised the deduction of contributions.[3]

(c) The final invalid amendment in issue involved the closure of the DB section, with the associated breaking of the final salary link, and the transfer of the remaining members of that section to a new DC section. The members in question were offered membership of that section and a transfer of their benefits, in return for which they would receive a one-off salary increase. Contrary to the other changes, the judge held that the members who accepted this offer were contractually bound to this change. Three relevant principles underlie this aspect of the judge's decision:[4]

(i) an intention to create contractual relations was established, as the parties' behaviour could not be wholly explained by reference to members' pre-existing rights: no-one could have thought that the affected members were already entitled to the salary increases;

(ii) the judge rejected the requirement for informed consent identified by Arnold J in *HR Trustees Ltd v German*, on the basis that such a requirement had nothing to do with contract law, which had developed its own principles for vitiating agreements such as the doctrines of mistake, misrepresentation and *non est factum*;

(iii) the judge also rejected an argument based on s 91 of PA 1995, which renders unenforceable agreements to surrender members' pension benefits. The judge applied the principle that that provision does not apply where there is a doubt or dispute about the existence of the rights in issue,[5] holding that the agreement operated as a compromise of a doubt about whether the transfer could break the final salary link.

1 [2014] EWHC 1178 (Ch), [2015] Ch 212 at [147]–[149].
2 The judge held that this conclusion applied to both existing members and to members who had never joined the DB section.
3 [2015] Ch 212 at [159].
4 [2015] Ch 212 at [160]–[177].
5 *HR Trustees Ltd v German* [2010] EWCA Civ 1349, [2011] ICR 329. The judge followed the decision of Warren J in *Bradbury v BBC* [2012] EWHC 1369 (Ch), [2012] Pens LR 283 that there did not need to be an identified dispute in existence at the time for that principle to apply.

Reliance on employment contracts

9.9

One situation in which the employer will not need to establish a new contract is where the change is expressed to be a variation of the members' existing terms and conditions of employment.

9.10

If the employer has no express power to alter the employment contract unilaterally,[1] the variation will not bind the members unless they have agreed to it. The principal issue in such a situation is likely to be whether the members have agreed to the variation.

1 Whilst such a power is lawful, it is an unusual provision which can only be conferred by clear words: *Amberley (UK) Ltd v West Sussex County Council* [2011] EWCA Civ 11 at [22] per Aikens LJ. This principle operates with particular force in the employment context where there is an obvious inequality of bargaining power, and the court will generally be reluctant to interpret such a provision as allowing an employer to make changes detrimental to an employee's rights: *Daniels v Lloyds Bank plc* [2018] EWHC 660 (Comm), [2018] IRLR 813 at [106] per Cockerill J.

9.11

An employee's agreement to a variation of the employment contract is usually obtained by the employer requiring the employee to sign and return to the employer a slip or separate form, by which the employee acknowledges and consents to the variation. Where, however, the employee's agreement has not been obtained by that means, the employer must rely on consent to the variation being implied by reason of the employee's conduct which, in the current context, is likely to be limited to their continuation to work after notification of the variation.

9.12

The leading case on this issue is *Abrahall v Nottingham City Council*,[1] which considered whether employees had impliedly consented to the imposition of a two-year pay freeze by the employer, by continuing to work without protest during that period. After considering the previous relevant authorities,[2] Underhill LJ laid down the following principles:

(a) as a matter of principle, a contractual variation can be accepted by conduct, and in an employment context, it is possible that an employee's conduct in continuing to perform the contract, in circumstances where the employer has made clear that they wish to modify it, may be reasonably understood as indicating acceptance of the change;

(b) what inferences can be drawn must depend on the particular circumstances of the case;

(c) as to the proper approach to the question of when continuing to work may constitute acceptance:

   (i) the inference must arise unequivocally: if the conduct of the employee in continuing to work is reasonably capable of a different explanation, it cannot be treated as constituting acceptance of the new terms: the employees are to have the benefit of any (reasonable) doubt;

   (ii) protest or objection at the collective level may be sufficient to negative any inference that by continuing to work individual employees are accepting a reduction in their contractual entitlement to pay, even if they themselves say nothing;

   (iii) the issue need not be answered once and for all at the point of implementation: it is possible that, after a period of time, the employee's conduct does imply acceptance of a contractual variation.

1 [2018] EWCA Civ 796, [2018] ICR 1425 at [85]–[89].
2 Including *Rigby v Ferodo Ltd* [1988] ICR 29, *Jones v Associated Tunnelling Co Ltd* [1981] IRLR 477, *Solectron Scotland Ltd v Roper* [2004] IRLR 4 and *Khatri v Cooperative Centrale Raiffeisen-Boerenleenbank BA* [2010] EWCA Civ 397, [2010] IRLR 715.

9.13

In that case, it was held that the employees had not accepted the pay freeze, on the grounds that:

(a) the proposed variation was wholly disadvantageous to the employees;

(b) the matter was not put to the employees as something on which their agreement was required; and

(c) there was strenuous protest on the part of the unions not only up to but beyond the date of the implementation of the pay freeze, even though that stopped short of industrial action.[1]

1 [2018] ICR 1425 at [101]–[104].

9.14

Although each case will turn on its facts, the prospects of successfully arguing that a mere continuation to work will constitute implied acceptance of pension changes are extremely remote. In practice, an employee's pension is something which is likely to have little practical impact on them during their working life, more so if the scheme is non-contributory. Typically, the benefits payable to an employee will only be of concern to them when they approach retirement age or otherwise qualify for benefits, or when they seek to have their benefits transferred to another arrangement. Changes made to pension benefits during an employee's working lifetime do not have the kind of immediate practical application which would necessarily lead the court to treat continuing to work as acceptance of that change.

1 [2011] EWHC 485 (Ch), [2011] Pens LR 153 at [69].

9.15

In the pensions context, the issue of implied acceptance was briefly mentioned by Henderson J in *Capita ATL Pension Trustees Ltd v Gellately*.[1] That case did not involve a change to the employment contract, but featured an announcement to members that changes to the pension scheme would be made: in the course of explaining why a contract claim was not run at trial, the judge said that it was hopeless to argue that merely continuing to work for the same employer after the implementation of the changes could constitute sufficient consideration to support a contract, given the general difficulty of ever persuading a court that continuing to work can constitute consideration for a variation of a contract of employment, let alone for a free-standing extrinsic contract.

1 [2011] EWHC 485 (Ch), [2011] Pens LR 153 at [69].

Conclusion

9.16

In the absence of an offer to the members of a financial incentive in return for the changes to their benefits, it is unlikely that a contract extrinsic to the scheme will be established from any documents passing between the employer, the trustees and the members at around the time of the invalid amendment. Those parties will be unlikely to have had any freestanding contractual relationship in mind, and will have intended the members' entitlements to be governed by the provisions of the scheme, as varied by the amendment.

Estoppel

9.17

Arguments that members are estopped from denying the validity of invalid amendments, or from enforcing amendments mistakenly conferring windfall benefits, are based on either estoppel by representation or estoppel by convention. In such cases, the employer will wish to contend that the members, or relevant group of members, as a whole are bound by the estoppel, which creates its own practical problems.

Estoppel by representation

9.18

The employer might contend that, even though the amendment in question is invalid, the members should nevertheless be estopped from relying on that invalidity, by reason of representations contained in documents created at the time of the amendment which describe the changes which were intended to be made, such as announcements, application forms and explanatory booklets.

9.19

The leading case on estoppel by representation in a pensions context is *Steria Ltd v Hutchison*.[1] That case did not involve an invalid change to the scheme rules: the member in question claimed a right to retire from the scheme on a full pension at age 62, in reliance on statements made in a letter from the employer and in explanatory booklets, when the scheme rules had always provided that any pension payable on retirement before age 65 would be reduced. Despite accepting that a layperson reading the documents relied upon might gain the impression contended for by the member,[2] the Court of Appeal rejected his claim.

1 [2006] EWCA Civ 1551, [2007] ICR 445.
2 [2007] ICR 445 at [52] per Mummery LJ and at [115] per Neuberger LJ.

9.20

As a matter of general principle, Neuberger LJ noted that unconscionability was the key factor underlying estoppel claims, and said that it was very unlikely that this would be satisfied unless three requirements could be satisfied:[1]

(a) a clear representation made by the defendant upon which it is reasonably foreseeable that the claimant will act;

(b) an act on the part of the claimant which was reasonably taken in reliance upon the representation; and

(c) after the act, the claimant being able to show that they will suffer detriment if the defendant is not held to the representation.[2]

1 [2007] ICR 445 at [91]–[93].

2 Neuberger LJ (at [93]) described these requirements as '*relatively broad brush*': a more comprehensive description of the conditions for an estoppel by representation includes the requirements that there must be a representation of fact as opposed to a mere statement of intention or future promise, and that the representation must have been the proximate cause of the action which caused the detriment: *Phipson on Evidence* (19th edn, Sweet & Maxwell, 2018) (*Phipson*), para 5-29.

9.21

The court emphasised that, when ascertaining the nature of the representations, it was necessary to read the documents as a whole, and not to take particular parts in isolation.[1] This was particularly relevant when considering the effect of the statements in the explanatory booklet which supported the member's case, as account also had to be taken of the 'health warning' contained in the booklet, which stated that the scheme rules would prevail over the booklet on any question of interpretation: this made it impossible for the member to establish reliance solely on the booklet without reference to the rules.[2] This case therefore sounded the death knell for the so-called 'estoppel by booklet' argument, which involved members relying on statements made in booklets which were inconsistent with the scheme rules:[3] a member cannot rely on a booklet to override the rules, where the booklet itself provides that, in the event of a conflict, the rules override the booklet.[4]

1 [2007] ICR 445 at [60] per Mummery LJ.

2 [2007] ICR 445 at [69]–[71] per Mummery LJ and at [101]–[107] per Neuberger LJ. Although the letter from the employer did not include a health warning, the court held that that document did not found an estoppel, as the member had failed to establish any detriment in reliance on the representation relating to his retirement age, and an attempt by the member to argue that detriment was to be presumed in this situation was rejected: [2007] ICR 445 at [73]–[75] per Mummery LJ and at [118]–[133] per Neuberger LJ

3 The possibility of such an argument succeeding had been left open by Pumfrey J in *Hoover Ltd v Hetherington* [2002] EWHC 1052 (Ch), [2002] Pens LR 297 at [51]. However, other cases had doubted whether an estoppel could apply in the face of a health warning: *Lansing Linde Ltd v Alber* [2000] Pens LR 15 at [222] per Rimer J; *Hearn v Younger* [2002] EWHC 963 (Ch), [2005] Pens LR 49 at [111] per Etherton J.

4 *Trustee Solutions Ltd v Dubery* [2006] EWHC 1426 (Ch), [2007] ICR 412 at [52] per Lewison J.

9.22

In cases involving invalid pension scheme changes, attempts to rely on estoppel by representation based on documents prepared at around the time of the change are highly unlikely to succeed, because the relevant representations in those documents will not be sufficiently clear and unequivocal. Where an employer is seeking to rely on statements relating to the changed benefit structure intended to be introduced into the scheme, unless the document also informs the members that those rights are protected by the terms of the amendment power and that they will be giving up that protection, the members will not know the true position regarding the benefits contained in the documents. In such circumstances, it would not be unconscionable for the members to rely on those protected rights.

9.23

Thus, in *HR Trustees Ltd v German*,[1] an estoppel by representation was held not to arise by reason of the completion by members of application forms on which they had indicated that they had read the explanatory booklet which set out the terms of the new DC scheme and that they wished to join that scheme. This was on the basis (amongst others) that the forms made no reference to giving up DB rights that were protected under the terms of amendment power, and so were not sufficiently clear and unambiguous.

1 [2009] EWHC 2785 (Ch), [2010] Pens LR 23 at [177]–[178] per Arnold J.

Estoppel by convention

9.24

As a further or alternative argument, the employer may seek to rely on estoppel by convention, which arises where parties to a transaction have proceeded on the basis of an underlying assumption on which they have conducted the dealings between them: neither of them will be allowed to go back on that assumption where it would be unfair or unjust to allow them to do so.[1]

1 *Amalgamated Investment & Property Co Ltd v Texas-Commerce International Bank Ltd* [1982] QB 84.

9.25

The principles for establishing such an estoppel are as follows:[1]

(a) It is not enough that the common assumption upon which the estoppel is based is merely understood by the parties in the same way: it must be expressly shared between them. Something must be shown to have 'crossed the line' sufficient to manifest an assent to the assumption, which may consist of either words or conduct from which the necessary sharing can properly be inferred.

(b) The expression of the common assumption by the party alleged to be estopped must be such that they may properly be said to have assumed some element of responsibility for it, in the sense of conveying to the other party an understanding that they expected the other party to rely upon it.

(c) The person alleging the estoppel must in fact have relied upon the common assumption, to a sufficient extent, rather than merely upon their own independent view of the matter.

(d) Reliance must have occurred in connection with some subsequent mutual dealing between the parties.

(e) Some detriment must thereby have been suffered by the person alleging the estoppel, or benefit thereby have been conferred upon the person alleged to be estopped, sufficient to make it unjust or unconscionable for the latter to assert the true legal (or factual) position.

1 These were set out by Briggs J in *HMRC v Benchdollar Ltd* [2009] EWHC 1310 (Ch), [2010] 1 All ER 174 at [52], as subsequently modified by him in *Stena Line Ltd v Merchant Navy Ratings Pension Fund Trustees Ltd* [2010] EWHC 1805 (Ch), [2010] Pens LR 411 at [137] and by Hildyard J in *Blindley Heath Investments Ltd v Bass* [2015] EWCA Civ 1023, [2017] Ch 389 at [92]. These principles have recently been approved by the Supreme Court in *Tinkler v HMRC* [2021] UKSC 39, [2021] 3 WLR 697 at [53].

9.26

An early application of this principle in a pensions context was in *Icarus (Hertford) Ltd v Driscoll*.[1] In that case, a category of members accrued benefits under the scheme's rules at the rate of 1/80ths of pensionable salary, and contributed a prescribed percentage of their pensionable pay. In 1978, an announcement and a revised explanatory booklet notified those members that the accrual rate was to be reduced to 1/270ths and the scheme was to be made non-contributory for those members, to bring them into line with other categories of members. Those changes were not formally incorporated into the scheme's governing provisions. Aldous J held that the affected members were nevertheless bound to the alterations by an estoppel by convention, stating that:

> 'All the parties to the scheme … have since 1978 proceeded on the basis that the rate of accrual was 1/270th and they cannot now go back on it. Further I believe it would not be unjust or unfair to hold them to that. In fact it would be odd for me to decide that the rate was 1/60th or 1/80th when all the parties had accepted and worked on the basis that it was 1/270th.'

1 [1990] Pens LR 1 at [15].

9.27

This case has not been kindly treated by subsequent authorities. In *Foster Wheeler v Hanley*,[1] Patten J said that the outline of the facts in the judgment was '*sparse in the extreme*' and did not really indicate the judge's reasons for his conclusion. In *Trustee Solutions Ltd v Dubery*,[2] Lewison J said that the reasoning was '*extremely compressed*' and could not be said to have laid down any general principle. In *Steria Ltd v Hutchison*,[3] Neuberger LJ said that the decision was '*short and unreasoned*' and came '*in the relatively early days of pension scheme litigation*'.

1 [2008] EWHC 2926 (Ch), [2009] Pens LR 39 at [84].
2 [2006] EWHC 1426 (Ch), [2007] ICR 412 at [52].
3 [2006] EWCA Civ 1551, [2007] ICR 445 at [105].

9.28

Since the *Icarus* case, whilst the courts have been careful to state that, in principle, estoppel by convention can be established in pensions cases, in practice such claims have not succeeded.

9.29

The usual stumbling block is the need to establish detrimental reliance, which was summed up by the following oft-quoted statement by Sir Andrew Morritt V-C in *Redrow plc v Pedley*:[1]

> '… as the formulation of the principle shows, what must be proved is that each and every member has by his "course of dealing put a particular interpretation on the terms of" the Rules or "acted upon the agreed assumption that a given state of facts is to be accepted between them as true". This involves more than merely passive acceptance. The administration of a pension scheme on a particular assumption as to the yardstick by which contributions or benefits are to be calculated may well give rise to a relevant assumption on the part of the trustees. I suggest that it requires clear evidence of intention or positive conduct to bind the general body of members to such an assumption. I doubt whether receipt of the benefit or payment of the contribution, without more, can be enough. It must not be overlooked that if the principle is applicable it may be used to increase the liability or reduce the benefit of a member as well as, in this case, the opposite.'

1 [2002] EWHC 983 (Ch), [2002] Pens LR 339 at [64]. This obiter comment was endorsed by Neuberger LJ in *Steria Ltd v Hutchison* [2007] ICR 445 at [109].

9.30

Subsequent attempts to rely on estoppel by convention in cases of invalid amendments have failed because of the lack of any positive change in the way in which the members' benefits were to their knowledge administered.

9.31

In *HR Trustees Ltd v German*,[1] the employer sought to raise this estoppel to justify the invalid conversion of DB rights into DC benefits, on the basis that the members were informed of the change in writing and at presentations, they had signalled their acceptance of the change by signing application forms, all parties behaved on the basis of the change for 15 years, and some of the members paid additional voluntary contributions which were matched by the employer, a process which was only available under the converted arrangement. Arnold J rejected this argument, holding that the members had not '*put a particular interpretation on*' the scheme rules or '*acted upon the agreed assumption*' that they had given up rights to which they were entitled under those documents: on the contrary, the members did no more than passively accept the fait accompli presented by the employer on the basis that the scheme rules had been amended.

1 [2009] EWHC 2785 (Ch), [2010] Pens LR 23 at [189].

9.32

Similarly, Henderson J in *Capita ATL Pension Trustees Ltd v Gellately*,[1] held that there was no detrimental reliance by the members in signing and returning the application form and agreeing to the deduction of contributions.

1 [2011] EWHC 485 (Ch), [2011] Pens LR 153 at [85].

9.33

Again, in *Briggs v Gleeds (Head Office)*,[1] Newey J held that the employer could not establish an estoppel by convention to overcome an invalid amendment, as there had been no more than passive acceptance from both existing and new members of the scheme: existing members were told that changes were taking place and were not asked to agree to them; new entrants were simply enrolled in the scheme in the form it was understood to be in at the material time.[2] Further, it had not been established that the employer had relied on any assumption shared between itself and the members, as the employer would have acted on the basis of views it arrived at independently of members, on the strength of professional advice.

1 [2014] EWHC 1178 (Ch), [2015] Ch 212 at [184]–[185].
2 The inability of an estoppel to bind future members was also noted by Sir Andrew Morritt V-C (obiter) in *Redrow plc v Pedley* [2002] EWHC 983 (Ch), [2002] Pens LR 339 at [62].

9.34

The requirement to establish more than mere passive acceptance to found an estoppel by convention means in practice that it will be necessary to show that members have acted in a way which they would not have done had they not been aware of the relevant changes.[1] Whilst it is not enough merely to continue to be a member of the scheme, paying contributions and receiving benefits as before, it is certainly arguable that the changes themselves may involve the members acting in such a way as to render it unconscionable for them to rely on the unamended scheme rules.

1 Cf *Steria Ltd v Hutchison* [2006] EWCA Civ 1551, [2007] ICR 445 at [117] where Neuberger LJ said that, for an estoppel by representation, it was probably not necessary to satisfy a 'but for' test: it was sufficient to show that the representation was a significant factor in the member acting in the manner relied upon.

9.35

Take, for example, the *Icarus* case,[1] where the members not only received the announcement and booklet informing them of the reduction in their accrual rate, but also ceased to make contributions to the scheme, to reflect the fact that they were accruing benefits at a lower rate than before. That cessation of contributions constituted the positive conduct which made it unconscionable for the members later to seek to rely on the higher accrual rate in the scheme rules: otherwise, they would be receiving a higher rate of benefits without paying the appropriate rate of contributions for such benefits.[2]

1 [1990] Pens LR 1.
2 Although Sir Andrew Morritt V-C in *Redrow v Pedley* [2002] EWHC 983 (Ch), [2002] Pens LR 339 at [64] doubted whether '*payment of the contribution, without more*' was sufficient to constitute active acceptance, this ought to be read as payment of the same contribution rate as before: he is not to be taken to be referring here to the payment of a different contribution rate.

9.36

Another example is an invalid attempt to comply with equalisation requirements by raising female members' normal retirement age from 60 to

65, in contravention of a restriction in the amendment power: those female members who continue to accrue benefits in the scheme after age 60 have arguably only done so because their retirement ages had validly changed, thereby constituting the requisite positive conduct.

9.37

In this respect, the rejection of the estoppel by convention argument in *HR Trustees Ltd v German*[1] is questionable, in the light of the matched additional voluntary contributions which were only available under the converted arrangement. Arnold J did not deal with this point in his judgment, but perhaps the fact that only some of the relevant members benefitted from matched contributions meant that that evidence was too exiguous to establish an estoppel affecting all the relevant members.

1 [2009] EWHC 2785 (Ch), [2010] Pens LR 23: the judge (at [189]) did describe this as possibly the employer's strongest argument to validate the impugned amendment on the grounds of contract or estoppel.

9.38

A further potentially positive act of members in the *HR Trustees, Gellately* and *Briggs* cases[1] was their express authorisation in the application forms that contributions to the new arrangements were to be deducted from their salaries. In neither the *HR Trustees* case nor the *Briggs* case was this matter considered in the context of the estoppel arguments;[2] and in the *Gellately* case,[3] Henderson J held that the authorisation was expressed to be conditional on the amendments to the rules having been validly made. In the absence of such wording, it remains arguable that the members' authorisation of the deduction of contributions constitutes more than passive acceptance of the benefits to be provided to the members in return for those contributions: such authorisation is of great importance to the employer, as it is prohibited from deducting contributions from employees' salaries without their written consent.[4]

1 See *HR Trustees v German* [2010] EWHC 321 (Ch), [2010] Pens LR 23 at [66]; *Capita ATL Pension Trustees Ltd v Gellately* [2011] EWHC 485 (Ch), [2011] Pens LR 153 at [40]; and *Briggs v Gleeds (Home Office)* [2014] EWHC 1178 (Ch), [2015] 1 Ch 212 at [137] and [153].

2 In *Briggs v Gleeds (Home Office)* [2015] 1 Ch 212 at [149] Newey J referred to the issue briefly when considering the contract argument: he simply said that this was a purely administrative act on the part of the employer.

3 [2011] Pens LR 153 at [85].

4 Section 13(1)(b) of the Employment Rights Act 1996.

Estoppels in favour of members

9.39

A rare example of an estoppel in favour of a potential scheme beneficiary is *Catchpole v Alitalia Pension Trustees*.[1] In that case, a member was incorrectly told by the scheme secretary that she did not need to marry her partner for him to be entitled to benefits after her death. They did not marry and, after the member died, her partner was refused benefits by the trustees because the scheme rules only provided death benefits for spouses. Warren J held that the secretary's statement was a representation made on behalf of the trustees and that the estoppel was capable of binding, and did bind, the scheme as whole.

1 [2010] EWHC 1809 (Ch), [2010] Pens LR 387.

9.40

In upholding the estoppel, the judge emphasised that no action would have been required on the part of the trustees to give effect to the estoppel: all that needed to happen was that the member marry her partner. The judge said that the outcome may have been different had the trustees been required to exercise a discretion to bring about the effect of the estoppel, as it might be more difficult to say that it would be unconscionable for the trustees to deny the claim where that would impute to them a decision (which they had not in fact made) to exercise their discretion or to amend the scheme in favour of the claimant. The finding of an estoppel may therefore depend upon the nature of the entitlement being claimed.

Practice point: establishing a group estoppel

9.41

The requirement referred to at **9.29** for more than passive acceptance is one of a number of practical difficulties associated with proving estoppels which seek to bind a general body of members, rather than a single member, ie 'group estoppels'.

9.42

Proving a group estoppel requires a practical and commonsense approach. Whilst it is not necessary to call evidence relating to each member's intention, the claimant must prove that the estoppel must be applicable to the general body of members as such.[1] For example, if the employer is relying on application forms sent to the members, the estoppel can only apply to those members who can be shown to have signed and returned the forms.[2]

1 *ITN v Ward* [1997] Pens LR 131 at [22] per Laddie J; *Redrow plc v Pedley* [2002] EWHC 983 (Ch), [2002] Pens LR 339 at [63] per Sir Andrew Morritt V-C.
2 *Capita ATL Pension Trustees Ltd v Gellately* [2011] Pens LR 153 at [69]–[70] per Henderson J. In that case, it was argued that, where there was no positive evidence one way or the other, the trustees should for the time being treat the members concerned as not bound, but that, if evidence came to light in future that a member did sign and return the form, they should then be treated accordingly: this argument was rendered academic by the judge's finding that no estoppel arose even in respect of members who did sign and return the forms.

9.43

Other practical problems include the following:[1]

(a) the trusts of the scheme cannot be altered by estoppel because there can be no such estoppel binding future members;

(b) the estoppel cannot apply to former employees who had left the scheme before any of the events which are said to have created the erroneous assumption, as they cannot be said to have shared the assumption;

(c) estoppels which apply to some, but not all, members may result in unequal treatment of some members as compared with others, which may potentially put the trustees in conflict with the sex equality rule enshrined in s 67 of the Equality Act 2010: in general the court will not uphold an estoppel in conflict with statute or public policy;

(d) the court will also be unlikely to enforce an estoppel where to do so would place the trustees in breach of their fiduciary duties to members by preferring the interests of certain members over the interests of other members;

(e) any assumption relied upon as constituting a convention which does not, for example, comply with equalisation requirements, cannot establish an estoppel where the assumption would have to be modified to take account of those requirements;

(f) if the shared assumption is anything other than that which was expressly stated to members of the scheme (because, for example, of the need to strip out any retrospective element of that assumption), it is unrealistic to suggest that the members shared the altered assumption, unless they are to be endowed with unusual knowledge of pensions law and/or the detailed contents of the rules: *ex hypothesi* they do not have the latter, since if they did there would be no estoppel at all.

1 See *Redrow v Pedley* [2002] Pens LR 339 at [62]–[64] per Sir Andrew Morritt V-C; *Trustee Solutions Ltd v Dubery*, [2006] EWHC 1426 (Ch), [2007] ICR 412 at [50]–[51] per Lewison J; *Burgess v BIC UK Ltd* [2018] EWHC 785 (Ch), [2018] Pens LR 380 at [154] per Arnold J.

10 Mistaken Overpayments

10.1

Mistakes in the payment of benefits arise in a number of different situations, ranging from simple calculation errors to the consequences of resolving technical questions of scheme interpretation. The need to deal with the overpayment of benefits can also arise because of mistakes made in the drafting of pension scheme documents which have been the subject of earlier chapters. This chapter considers the legal and practical issues which arise when trustees are faced with having to correct mistaken overpayments to members.

10.2

On discovering an overpayment, if relevant the trustees must first consider reducing the benefits to the correct amount going forward. Members will find it extremely difficult to prevent this, unless they can prove that they have changed their lifestyle in anticipation of future receipts of the increased benefit. See **10.35** (n1). The remainder of this chapter considers the steps open to trustees to recover past overpayments.

Must the trustees recover overpayments?

10.3

The starting point is that trustees are under a duty to recover sums which are owed to the trust fund, including taking proceedings if necessary. Accordingly, pension scheme trustees are prima facie obliged to seek recovery of overpayments of benefits.[1] However, the trustees will not be required to take recovery proceedings if they reasonably believe that that would produce no useful result.[2] In making that assessment, the trustees should take account of the position of the member, the amount of the sum owed and the probability of the proceedings being successful.[3]

1 *Burgess v BIC UK Ltd* [2018] EWHC 785 (Ch), [2018] Pens LR 13 at [176] per Arnold J.

2 *Hobday v Peters (No 3)* (1860) 28 Beav 603, 604 per Sir John Romilly MR. The onus is on the trustees to show that no good would have resulted from any proceedings: *Re Brogden* (1888) 38 ChD 546, 568 per Cotton LJ.

3 *Re Owens; Jones v Owens* (1882) 47 LT 61, 63 per Jessel MR.

10.4

The threshold test for trustees to forego recovery of overpayments is high: they must be reasonably sure that the necessary steps would be fruitless or ineffectual.[1] The trustees will be exposed to criticism if they take no steps to recover overpayments in circumstances where there are no reasonable grounds for believing that such steps will be pointless; and trustees should think very carefully about undertaking such a course of action.

1 See *Spencer v Spencer* [2014] 2 NZLR 190 at [64] per Randerson J.

10.5

In *Capita ATL Pension Trustees Ltd v Gellately*,[1] the trustee was directed not to seek recoupment of overpayments out of future pension payments to widows of deceased members, on the grounds that:

(a) the sums involved were relatively small;

(b) recoupment would be likely to cause distress to the widows; and

(c) it would almost certainly not be cost-effective in view of the time and money that would have to be spent in explaining the position, communicating with the widows and trying to agree with them a suitable timetable for the recoupment.

1 [2011] EWHC 485 (Ch), [2011] Pens LR 153 at [91] per Henderson J.

10.6

Ultimately, this is a matter for the exercise of the trustees' discretion. A similar issue arose in *Lloyds Banking Group Pensions Trustees Ltd v Lloyds Bank*,[1] in the context of underpayments to members, where the trustee had a discretion under the scheme rules to apply a forfeiture provision to impose limits on the compensation of members for past underpayments. Morgan J said that the general rules as to the exercise of a trustee discretion apply, in that the trustee must have regard to only relevant considerations and must make a decision which is rational and not perverse.[2]

1 [2018] EWHC 2839 (Ch), [2019] Pens LR 95 at [420].
2 In *Foster Wheeler Ltd v Hanley* [2008] EWHC 2926 (Ch), [2009] Pens LR 39 at [145], Lewison J refused an application by an employer for what was effectively a direction requiring the trustee to recover overpayments from members.

10.7

Each case will turn on its own facts, but it is likely to be difficult for trustees to justify taking no steps at all, at least where a substantial number of members have been overpaid, resulting in a significant depletion of the assets of the scheme. The trustees' task in this respect will, of course, be made easier if there is a solvent employer which is willing to absorb the cost of the overpayments by, for example, the exercise of the scheme's augmentation power.

10.8

Another matter for the trustees to consider in this context is that many cases of overpayments will arise because of an error on the part of the scheme's professional advisers, which may lead to a claim by the trustees against the advisers for breach of duty. Where the trustees choose not to recover overpayments where they have a legal right to do so, the advisers can argue that the trustees have not reasonably mitigated their loss, and that any damages claim should be reduced accordingly.[1] If the trustees choose not to recover sums purely out of sympathy for the members, they may well have difficulties in claiming the unrecovered sums from the advisers.

1 For mitigation of loss arguments by negligent advisers, see **16.56–16.58**.

10.9

Another issue arises where the overpayment arose because of a mistake in the equalisation of male and female members' benefits as required by EU law. If, for example, male members had been overpaid benefits, would a failure to recover those overpayments require the trustees to provide female members with corresponding increases in order that both sexes are treated equally?

10.10

If there is a good reason not to recover the overpayments, the trustees are probably not obliged to provide corresponding benefits to female members: the equalisation requirement applies to the provision of benefits properly payable under the scheme, not to mistaken benefits. Of some relevance in this regard are the obiter comments of Jacob J in *National Westminster Bank plc v HMRC*,[1] made when refusing to overturn HMRC's decision not to repay in full an overpayment of VAT: the judge rejected the argument that HMRC had infringed the equal treatment principle because other taxpayers seeking a refund in similar circumstances had mistakenly had their claims met without question. The judge said that that principle did not oblige HMRC to perpetuate a mistake in favour of others.[2]

1 [2003] EWHC 1822 (Ch), [2003] STC 1072 at [63]–[66].
2 The Supreme Court has subsequently held that the equal treatment principle is not a distinct principle of administrative law: *R (oao Gallaher Group Ltd) v Competition and Markets Authority* [2018] UKSC 25, [2019] AC 96.

10.11

If, however, the trustees decide to continue the mistaken payment to male members going forward, and the mistake is enshrined as a scheme benefit by the application of the scheme's augmentation power, that probably would give rise to an obligation to provide equal benefits to female members.

Methods of recovering overpayments

Request for repayment

10.12

Trustees should first seek to recover an overpayment by writing to the member concerned to explain the circumstances in which the overpayment arose and to ask them to repay the overpaid sum, either directly or by a reduction in their future pension payments.

10.13

It should be borne in mind that the request is likely to come as a shock to the member, who may well feel vulnerable and be upset by having to repay benefits in circumstances where they are blameless. It is therefore very important that the trustees treat the matter with appropriate sensitivity in correspondence with the member,[1] and the request for repayment should be accompanied by an apology for the mistake. The trustees should also consider offering a modest ex gratia payment for the distress and inconvenience suffered by the member, to be offset against the overpayment.

1 In *Ms L Fenucci-Corsini* (N00031, 11 November 2003) at [33], the Ombudsman determined that the insensitive tone of correspondence demanding overpayment merited an award of compensation.

10.14

Many overpayment cases result in a complaint by the member to the Pensions Ombudsman. Whilst the Ombudsman will not interfere with the legal rights of the trustees to recover overpayments,[1] it is possible that the overpayment itself will be found to constitute maladministration. The trustees should therefore assume that their correspondence with the member will be scrutinised by the Ombudsman, who is likely to look severely on any overly-aggressive conduct. In particular, trustees should think carefully about how to inform the member about the more formal methods of recovery that they may adopt if the member does not comply with the request for repayment.

1 See **10.56**.

10.15

When writing to the member, the trustees should explain the possibility of the member raising a change of position defence,[1] and invite the member to put forward any arguments and evidence in support of such a defence.[2] The trustees should then consider any arguments put forward by the member as to why they should not or cannot repay the overpayments. If the trustees are of the view that the evidential basis for any such defence is lacking, they should not dismiss the member's argument out of hand without giving them a further opportunity to furnish the requisite evidence; and any decision to reject such a defence, either in whole or in part, together with the reasons for that decision, should be carefully minuted. In general, the trustees should approach this matter as if they would be required to defend their conduct before the Pensions Ombudsman or a court.

1 See **10.31–10.42**.
2 Demands for repayment without any attempt to make enquiries of the member about a change of position defence have been held by the Pensions Ombudsman to amount to maladministration: see, for example, *C11258* (22 August 1995), *D11399* (10 September 1996); *Mr S Simpson* (E00018, 19 June 1997); *Mr H V Pountney* (K00816, 9 April 2002). See also *Mr J G Turnball* (PO-5358, 20 November 2015) at [31].

Restitution

10.16

Since it became established that claims for money had and received by reason of mistake applied to mistakes of law as well as fact,[1] it has been possible for trustees generally to recover benefits overpaid as a result of a legal or factual mistake.[2]

1 *Kleinwort Benson Ltd v Lincoln City Council* [1999] 2 AC 349.
2 See, for example, *Derby v Scottish Equitable plc* [2001] Pens LR 163.

10.17

Once it is established that the error by or on behalf of the trustees caused them to make the overpayment, a claim for restitution will lie, subject to any defences which the member can raise. There is no need for the trustees to establish fault on the part of the member;[1] and the court does not have a general discretion to reject the claim simply because it may consider it to be unfair or unjust to grant recovery, however careless or negligent the trustees had been.[2]

1 *Goff & Jones: The Law of Unjust Enrichment* (9th edn, Sweet & Maxwell, 2016) (*Goff & Jones*), para 9-152. Such fault may affect the availability of defences to a restitution claim: see **10.41**.
2 *Derby v Scottish Equitable plc* [2001] Pens LR 163 at [25] per Robert Walker LJ, following *Lipkin Gorman v Karpnale Ltd* [1991] 2 AC 548, 578 per Lord Goff of Chieveley.

10.18

However, where the trustees were in doubt as to the correctness of the payment, but deliberately decided to pay without making any further enquiry, they will lose the right to recover.[1] If, on the other hand, the trustees did investigate, but failed to spot the error because of the inadequacy of the investigation, they can still recover.[2]

1 *Kelly v Solari* (1841) 9 M&W 54, 58 per Lord Abinger CB and 59 per Parke B.
2 *Derby v Scottish Equitable plc* [2001] Pens LR 163 at [24] per Robert Walker LJ.

10.19

It is usually sufficient for the trustees to seek a personal restitutionary remedy against the overpaid member, which will take the form of an order that the member pay the trustees a sum of money representing the value of the overpaid benefit. However, there may be occasions where the overpayment has been used to purchase an asset and it may suit the trustees to claim a proprietary remedy, seeking a declaration that the trustees have ownership of or a security interest in the asset, usually accompanied by consequential orders such as an order that the asset be conveyed to the trustees or that it be sold and a share of the proceeds remitted to the trustees.[1] Such a remedy may be advantageous where, for example, the member has become insolvent, as the trustees can gain priority over unsecured creditors; the remedy will also permit the trustees to obtain an interim freezing order preserving the asset until the outcome of the trial.

1 For a full discussion of the circumstances in which proprietary remedies will lie for restitution claims, see *Goff & Jones*, chs 37–38.

10.20

Although, for reasons discussed below, recoupment is often a more attractive remedy than restitution, there may be cases in which restitution is the only practical remedy, such as where the overpayment relates to a transfer. In that situation, recoupment is not available, and the absence of any ongoing relationship between the member and the scheme means that the member may be less inclined to cooperate with the trustees in repaying the overpaid sum.

Recoupment

10.21

The alternative method of obtaining repayment is for the trustees to use the equitable remedy of recoupment, which allows them to recover overpayments from members by making deductions from future payments of benefit. This is part of the equitable accounting process in the administration of the trust and does not require authorisation by the court.[1]

1 But see **10.65–10.72**.

10.22

This remedy is only available where the overpayment was made from trust assets: it does not lie where the original obligation to pay arose under a contract;[1] or where the payments were made from a statutory scheme which is not established under trust.[2] However, in the latter case, the Pensions Ombudsman has applied the principle of equitable set-off to achieve substantially the same result.[3]

1 *Re Hatch* [1919] 1 Ch 351.
2 In addition, social security legislation often includes provisions permitting the recoupment of overpaid benefits: see, for example, s 71 of the Social Security Administration Act 1992, the application of which has been held not to infringe the recipient's rights to peaceful enjoyment of possessions under art 1 of Protocol No 1 of the European Convention on Human Rights: *McGrath v Secretary of State for Work and Pensions* [2012] EWHC 1042 (Admin).
3 *Mr E* (PO-29198, 30 November 2020) at [81]–[85]; *Dr N* (PO-23533, 17 March 2021) at [36]–[38]; *Mr S* (PO-22206, 11 October 2021) at [36].

10.23

Recoupment has several practical advantages over restitution:

(a) it does not involve a hostile claim against the member, and is therefore potentially less traumatic and raises fewer reputational issues for the trustees;

(b) the trustees can set the level of recoupment so as not to cause unnecessary difficulties for the member: because recoupment is an equitable remedy, it should not be applied in an inequitable manner,[1] so that the reduction made to a member's benefits must not cause undue hardship;[2]

(c) the member probably cannot rely on a change a change of position defence;[3]

(d) the right of recoupment is not barred by any statutory limitation period, and can only be barred by laches.[4]

1 *Re Musgrave* [1916] 2 Ch 417, 425 per Neville J.
2 See, for example, *Ms Myra Phillips* (PO-2876, 1 August 2014).
3 See **10.49–10.50**.
4 See **10.47–10.48**.

10.24

The principal disadvantage of this remedy is that its efficacy depends upon the continued receipt of benefit by the member: hence its non-applicability to a member who has transferred their benefits to a different scheme. Further, the death of the member before the full amount is recouped is likely to mark the end of the remedy, as it is most probably not possible to continue its application to payments made to death beneficiaries, although of course the member's death may itself have a positive effect on the funding of the scheme. By contrast, a claim for restitution of overpaid benefit can be pursued against the estate of the deceased member.[1]

1 *NHS Business Services Authority v Wheeler* [2014] EWHC 2155 (Ch), [2014] Pens LR 639 at [14] per Deputy Judge Gaunt QC.

Defences to the recovery of overpayments

Restitution

Limitation

10.25

It is now well-established that claims in restitution for mistaken overpayments are by analogy subject to the limitation period applicable to contract claims, pursuant to s 5 of the Limitation Act 1980 (LA 1980), which provides that such claims cannot be brought after the expiration of six years from the date on which the cause of action accrued.[1] For this purpose, the trustees' cause of action against the member accrues on the making of the overpayment, and each overpayment of pension gives rise to an individual cause of action against the member.[2]

1 *Aspect Contracts (Asbestos) Ltd v Higgins Construction plc* [2015] UKSC 38, [2015] 1 WLR 2961 at [25] per Lord Mance. Although this was regarded in 2015 as not entirely free from doubt (see *Diamandis v Wills* [2015] EWHC 312 (Ch) at [101]), the application of the statutory limitation period by analogy to contract claims had been clearly established as long ago as 1911: *Re Robinson* [1911] 1 Ch 502.
2 *Webber v Department for Education* [2016] EWHC 2519 (Ch), [2017] ICR 198 at [49] per Deputy Judge Bartley Jones QC.

10.26

This six-year period is subject to s 32(1)(c) of LA 1980, which provides that the period shall not run in claims for relief from the consequences of a mistake until the claimant has discovered the mistake or could with reasonable diligence have discovered it. As the restitutionary claim is based on a mistaken overpayment, this provision postpones the running of the limitation period, but only until the trustees have either discovered or could with reasonable diligence have discovered the mistake. This accordingly imposes an obligation on the trustees to exercise reasonable diligence in monitoring payments made from the scheme.[1]

1 *Webber v Department for Education* [2014] EWHC 4240 (Ch), [2015] ICR 544 at [65]–[77] per Nugee J.

10.27

Where the member is entitled to take a limitation defence to defeat part of the claim for recovery, what date is to be taken as the date from which the limitation period is to be back-calculated? By s 5 of LA 1980, the cut-off date for the application of the limitation period is when the action is brought, which means the date when the claimant requested the claim form to be issued.[1] Similarly, where the claim for recovery of past overpayments is made by way of court proceedings, the cut-off date is when those proceedings are started.

1 *Barnes v St Helens Metropolitan Borough Council (Practice Note)* [2006] EWCA Civ 1372, [2007] 1 WLR 879.

10.28

However, where the trustees have demanded the repayment of overpayments, the member may make a complaint to the Pensions Ombudsman, who will then adjudicate on whether the member has a valid defence. LA 1980 does not cater for time to stop running in that situation, as the focus there is on court proceedings. In other quasi-judicial proceedings, statutory limitation periods are expressly applied by analogy,[1] but there is no equivalent applying to complaints to the Ombudsman. It is therefore necessary to find a proxy for the issuing of the claim form to determine when time stops running in Ombudsman cases.

1 For example, s 13 of the Arbitration Act 1996 applies LA 1980 to arbitral proceedings.

10.29

In this respect, the authorities have differed in their analysis:

(a) In *Webber v Department for Education*,[1] the member brought a complaint against the administrators of a public sector scheme claiming recovery of overpaid benefits. Nugee J said (obiter) that the closest analogy to the issue of a claim form was the formal bringing of the complaint, because at that point the question of the recovery of the overpayments was in issue between the parties before the Ombudsman.

(b) When the issue subsequently came back before the High Court in the same proceedings,[2] Deputy Judge Bartley Jones QC disagreed with the view of Nugee J, on the basis that treating the issuing of the claim form as the relevant step was problematic because the complaint was brought, not by the administrator seeking recovery, but by the member denying recovery. The deputy judge considered that the relevant act ought to be that of the claimant in the overpayment claim, whereas the complaint was made by the equivalent of the defendant to the claim, ie the member. The deputy judge identified the first unilateral act of the administrator as a letter to the Ombudsman indicating that it opposed the allegations in the member's complaint, which the deputy judge said was the first assertion in the complaints procedure of its entitlement to repayment of the overpaid pension. The deputy judge held that the making of the complaint should not protect the administrator against the running of time, as it would not then have been aware of the claim, and would have taken no steps to protect its position by, for example, issuing a protective claim form. The deputy judge accordingly held that the cut-off date was from the date that the Ombudsman received the administrator's reply to the member's complaint.

(c) The deputy judge's analysis has since been applied by the Ombudsman on several occasions.[3]

1 [2015] ICR 544 at [81].
2 *Webber v Department for Education* [2016] EWHC 2519 (Ch), [2017] ICR 198.
3 For example, *Mrs G* (PO-2215, 21 February 2017); *Mrs K* (PO-9785, 18 June 2019).

10.30

Thus, for overpayment cases where limitation is an issue, the trustees may be prejudiced by any delay in the Ombudsman sending the complaint to them, causing the limitation period to continue to bite into the past overpayments. Accordingly, the Ombudsman's office has set up a protocol to identify and prioritise cases received where limitation may be an issue, by inviting the trustees to respond as soon as possible so that a cut-off date for the purposes of limitation can be established. At that stage the trustees need only indicate an intention to respond, with a full response to be provided in due course – essentially, the equivalent of a protective claim form.

Change of position

10.31

Recipients of overpayments can defeat a claim for recovery if they can demonstrate that they had changed their position in good faith following receipt of the overpaid sums.[1] This is the principal defence to restitution claims, and the one most commonly asserted by members facing claims for the repayment of overpaid benefits.

1 The burden of establishing the defence is on the member, who must adduce evidence of the change of position relied upon: Mr N (PO-28155, 21 June 2021) at [36].

10.32

The court will apply this remedy flexibly by reducing the member's liability *pro tanto* where their position has only partly changed;[1] and the court may also apply it by granting restitution on terms.

1 *Lipkin Gorman v Karpnale Ltd* [1991] 2 AC 548, 580 per Lord Goff of Chieveley.

10.33

Although the leading case on this defence did not lay down a set of detailed rules for its operation, preferring to see them develop on a case-by-case basis,[1] that does not mean that the court has complete discretion to reject a claim simply because it considers it to be unfair or unjust: the court must proceed on the basis of principle, not sympathy.[2]

1 *Lipkin Gorman v Karpnale Ltd* [1991] 2 AC 548, 580 per Lord Goff of Chieveley.
2 *Derby v Scottish Equitable plc* [2001] Pens LR 163 at [34] per Robert Walker LJ.

10.34

Although the principal detriment which qualifies for the defence will be a reduction in the member's assets, detriment is not limited in this way.[1] However, the disappointment the member may feel in having to repay money they would rather keep is not sufficient.[2]

1 Thus, giving up a job to lead a life of leisure in circumstances where it would be difficult to find another job may be a qualifying detriment: *Commerzbank AG v Price-Jones* [2003] EWCA Civ 1663 at [39] per Mummery LJ.
2 *Mahme Trust Reg v Tayeb* [2002] EWHC 1543 (Ch), [2003] WTLR 21 at [143] per Rimer J.

10.35

Usually the most difficult hurdle for members to surmount when arguing this defence is the need to establish a causal link between the receipt of benefit and the change of position, in that the change of position would not have occurred but for the receipt of benefit.[1] For example, a change of position defence will not normally lie where the member has used the overpaid sums to pay off a debt which would have to be paid off sooner or later.[2] In this regard, a comparison should be made between, for example, the value of purchases and the amount of the overpayment, as modest purchases may still have been made even if the member had received the correct level of benefit.[3]

1 *Derby v Scottish Equitable plc* [2001] Pens LR 163 at [31] per Robert Walker LJ. That does not mean that the receipt of benefit must necessarily precede the change of position: the defence may be established where the recipient has already changed their position in good faith in the expectation of receiving a future benefit: *Commerzbank AG v Price-Jones* [2003] EWCA Civ 1663 at [38] per Mummery LJ. In such a case, the Ombudsman has directed that the member be compensated for the expenditure incurred because of the expectation: *Mrs G Holt* (PO-84553/1, 8 October 2012) at [23]; and see also *Mrs R* (CAS-44749-W4N2, 1 September 2021).
2 *Derby v Scottish Equitable plc* [2001] Pens LR 163 at [35] per Robert Walker LJ. The court might, in these circumstances, allow recovery on terms, to enable the recipient to regain the position which they previously occupied before requiring them to make restitution: *Goff & Jones,* paras 27.12–27.15.
3 See, for example, *Mr Michael Carroll* (PO-1106, 4 October 2013) at [68].

10.36

The requirement for a causal link does not mean that a change of position defence cannot be established on the grounds that the overpaid sums were used for ordinary living expenses, where the recipient relied on those sums to raise their everyday outgoings.[1]

1 For example, *Phillip Collins Ltd v Davis* [2000] 3 All ER 808, 827–830 per Jonathan Parker J.

10.37

The expenditure must also be irreversible: for example, if the member spent the money on items which they could resell, the defence would only succeed to the extent that they could not recover the payment.[1]

1 *Lipkin Gorman v Karpnale Ltd* [1991] 2 AC 548, 560 per Lord Templeman.

10.38

Whilst each case will turn on its own facts, the following are examples of expenditure which the Pensions Ombudsman has determined can establish a change of position defence:

(a) giving up work and living off pension income;[1]

(b) agreeing to substantial financial commitments in negotiations during divorce proceedings;[2]

(c) reducing working hours;[3]

(d) making gifts to family members which are used to purchase property;[4]

(e) adopting a higher standard of living;[5]

(f) taking out loans;[6]

(g) making charitable donations;[7] and

(h) upgrading holidays.[8]

1 *Mr T J Hunt* (S00486, 12 August 2008).
2 *Mrs N McNicholas* (PO-408, 11 April 2013).
3 *Mrs Julie Barrow* (PO-2567, 30 April 2014).
4 *Mr Alan John* (PO-351, 28 May 2013) at [34]–[36].
5 *Mrs B Wytch* (PO-528, 22 March 2013) at [25]; *Mrs K Mead* (PO-845, 17 July 2013) at [23].
6 *Mrs Dianne Fewings* (PO-2451, 20 March 2015) at [22].
7 *Mr Y* (PO-10171, 13 February 2018) at [38].
8 *Mrs K* (PO-9785, 18 June 2019) at [85] and [88].

10.39

In *NHS Business Services Authority v Wheeler*,[1] Deputy Judge Gaunt QC overturned a decision of the Deputy Pensions Ombudsman that the executors of the member's estate had a good change of position defence to an overpayment claim in respect of payments made in the general administration of the estate, as that amounted to an illegitimate preference of the estate's creditors over the scheme; the Ombudsman also did not properly identify the injustice to the estate said to have resulted from the mistaken overpayment.

1 [2014] EWHC 2155 (Ch), [2014] Pens LR 639.

10.40

The Ombudsman's office is not always wholly consistent in its treatment of expenditure. Thus, in one case, the Ombudsman said that purchasing a share of an aunt's property did not qualify, as the monies expended could be realised on the sale of the property.[1] Two months later, the Deputy Pensions Ombudsman said in another case that the purchase of a conservatory was to be treated as irreversible, disregarding the possibility of selling the house and realising any enhanced value.[2]

1 *Mr R Corp* (P00299, 18 August 2006) at [57].
2 *Mr B Ford* (P00334, 30 October 2006) at [26]–[30].

10.41

The requirement that the change of position be in good faith means that the defence can be lost where the member spent the overpaid sums when they knew of the facts which entitled the trustees to recover.[1] Even where the member does not know for sure, the defence may be lost where they have grounds for believing that the payment may have been made by mistake but failed to make appropriate enquiries.[2] The defence would also not be available where the overpayment was caused by the recipient's own actions, such as failing to inform the scheme about the death of a member.

1 *Niru Battery Manufacturing Co v Milestone Trading Ltd (No 1)* [2002] EWHC 1425 (Comm), [2002] 2 All ER (Comm) 705 at [135] per Moore-Bick J; approved on appeal: [2003] EWCA Civ 1446, [2004] QB 985 at [164] per Clarke LJ. This was applied in a pensions context by Nugee J in *Webber v Department for Education* [2014] EWHC 4240 (Ch), [2015] ICR 544 at [61].
2 *Niru Battery Manufacturing Co v Milestone Trading Ltd (No. 1)* [2002] 2 All ER (Comm) 705 at [135].

10.42

Although mere negligence on the part of the recipient does not undermine the defence,[1] the Ombudsman will expect an overpaid member to act reasonably, and to question the receipt of a benefit which is considerably greater than they had been expecting.[2] In *Webber v Department for Education,*[3] Nugee J held that the defence was not available to a member who appreciated that the payment he was receiving may be an overpayment, and who could have made a simple inquiry of the payer to check whether that was so, but chose not to do so. However, in a recent determination,[4] the Ombudsman reiterated that it was not sufficient to establish that the member was in possession of sufficient information to spot the error, if it is not also established that the member spotted the error and appreciated, or at least suspected, its implications.

1 This was common ground in *Abou-Rahmah v Abacha* [2006] EWCA Civ 1492, [2007] 1 Lloyd's Rep 115 at [42] per Rix LJ.
2 *Professor B Kenny* (28034/5, 24 February 2010); *Miss J Cunningham* (86236/2, 8 October 2012).
3 [2014] EWHC 4240 (Ch), [2015] ICR 544 at [62].
4 *Mrs E* (CAS-30002-K6Z8, 22 June 2021) at [54].

Estoppel

10.43

A restitution claim may also be defeated if the trustees are estopped from making such a claim. The requirements of estoppel by representation and by convention are set out at **9.20** and **9.25** respectively.

10.44

The grounds of this defence are not dissimilar to the change of position defence, as an estoppel generally requires the member to have changed their position to their detriment in reliance on the representation or convention. However, the member will also have to establish either a representation by the trustees, or an underlying assumption on which the trustees and the member have conducted the dealings between them, that the member is entitled to the benefit they have received; and the payment of money is highly unlikely by itself to constitute such a representation or course of dealing.[1] It is therefore usually simpler for the member to rely on a change of position defence.[2]

1 *Goff & Jones*, para 30-02.
2 An estoppel defence, based on a series of benefit statements provided by the scheme's insurer, was upheld by the Ombudsman in *Mrs N McNicholas* (PO-408, 11 April 2013).

10.45

At one time, it was thought that the estoppel defence had one significant advantage over change of position, in that the former acted as a complete defence to the claim,[1] whereas the latter only operated as a *pro tanto* discharge of the liability to repay by reference to the extent of the change of position. However, more recently the courts have held that the estoppel defence should only operate *pro tanto* and should not bar the claim completely, where the latter would be a disproportionately favourable outcome to the member given the amount of detriment that they have suffered.[2] Despite academic criticism of this approach,[3] it is now well-established, and removes the only practical reason for members to raise this defence instead of, or together with, change of position.

1 *Avon CC v Howlett* [1983] 1 WLR 605.
2 *Derby v Scottish Equitable plc* [2001] Pens LR 163; *National Westminster Bank plc v Somer International (UK) Ltd* [2001] EWCA Civ 970, [2002] QB 1286.
3 *Goff & Jones*, para 30-16.

Reasonable repayment plans

10.46

Even in the absence of any defence on the part of the member to a claim for repayment, the Ombudsman has directed reasonable repayment terms to be agreed with the member, by reference to the member's ability to make such repayments.[1] In one case, the Deputy Pensions Ombudsman applied to repayment terms a general rule that the period of repayment must be at least as long as the period during which the overpayment took place and should not cause undue financial hardship;[2] and in another case, the Ombudsman directed the trustees to spread the recovery of overpayments over ten years, where the overpayments had been made for seven years.[3]

1 *Miss A K Ewing* (H00439, 16 September 1999) at [39]. The Ombudsman and his Deputy have both expressed expectations that there would be sensible discussions about the terms of repayment: *Mr S* (PO-14310, 16 March 2018); *Mrs T* (PO-21858, 26 March 2019); *Mr Y* (PO-21875, 30 June 2020); *Dr N* (PO-23533, 17 March 2021).
2 *Mr Steve Hudson* (PO-4565, 21 March 2015) at [44]; see also *Mr N* (PO-22841, 15 May 2020) at [51].
3 *Mr S* (PO-18392, 27 March 2018) at [21].

Recoupment

Limitation

10.47

In *Burgess v BIC UK Ltd,*[1] Arnold J declined to apply the contractual limitation period to the recoupment remedy on the basis that equitable recoupment was not a restitutionary claim for unjust enrichment, but an equitable self-help remedy which did not involve any claim for payment back of the monies paid in the past, but an adjustment of accounts in the future. The judge also relied on s 36(1)(b) of LA 1980, which excludes the contractual limitation period in respect of claims for '*specific enforcement of a contract or an injunction or for any other equitable relief*'.

1 [2018] EWHC 785 (Ch), [2018] Pens LR 13 at [172].

10.48

Thus, the only way in which the recoupment of benefits may be lost by reason of passage of time is if its use is barred by the doctrine of laches.[1]

1 Discussed in the context of rectification claims at **6.27–6.29**.

Change of position

10.49

Another advantage of the recoupment remedy for trustees is that a change of position defence is probably not available, as the member is not being asked to pay back that which they have already received, and the fact that they may already have spent the money wrongly received is not thought to be a good reason why they should not suffer a deduction from future payments.[1] In such circumstances, such a defence may only be available where the member has not only spent the money wrongly received, but has also committed to spend the amount to which they would have been entitled apart from the recoupment.[2]

1 *Lewin on Trusts* (20th edn, Sweet & Maxwell, 2020) (*Lewin*), para 42-013. The contrary view expressed in the 15th edition of Underhill and Hayton, *Law Relating to Trusts and Trustees* 416, is not repeated in later editions.
2 *Lewin*, para 42-013.

10.50

In any event, the requirement for the remedy to be applied equitably and without undue hardship on the member allows account to be taken of factors which would otherwise be relevant to a change of position defence. In this regard, the Ombudsman has adopted a general principle that overpayments must be recouped from future instalments over at least no shorter timeframe than the period during which the mistake had gone undetected.[1]

1 See, for example, *Fitzgerald* (86179/1, 21 August 2012) at [47].

10.51

Despite this, the Ombudsman has regularly required the member to establish the conditions for the change of position defence to defeat a recoupment remedy.[1] To require those conditions to be satisfied before the member can defeat some or all of the remedy appears unduly restrictive: the need to operate the remedy in an equitable way should give the Ombudsman sufficient scope to achieve a fair outcome.

1 *Mrs N* (PO-10427, 30 March 2017); *Dr E* (PO-16856, 25 October 2018). *Mr R* (PO-21594, 16 May 2019); *Dr S* (PO-22315, 20 November 2019); *Mrs N* (PO-20306, 3 April 2020); *Mrs R* (PO-24254, 19 June 2020); *Mr Y* (CAS-43117-Y3V5, 20 May 2021).

Estoppel

10.52

Although the requirement to apply the remedy equitably should render an estoppel defence unnecessary, it remains in principle available to a member facing recoupment, and the Deputy Pensions Ombudsman has applied it in such a situation.[1]

1 *Mrs N* (PO-10427, 30 March 2017).

Tax consequences of overpayments

10.53

This is dealt with at **17.2–17.10**. In particular, it should be noted that the trustees are obliged to correct any error they discover within a reasonable period, to prevent the continuing overpayments from being subject to unauthorised payment charges.[1]

1 See reg 14 of the Registered Pension Schemes (Authorised Payments) Regulations 2009 (SI 2009/1171).

Procedure for recovering overpayments

Which method to use?

10.54

When considering how to recover overpayments, the trustees must first decide whether to seek restitution, recoupment, or a combination of these methods. In so doing, the trustees should consider factors such as the age and health of the member (which will potentially affect the ability to recover overpayments from future benefit instalments), the amount of the overpayment, the financial circumstances of the member, and any other points made by the member which may affect the decision. It is for the trustees to choose how to recover the overpayment, even if the choice is not the most financially favourable method for the member.[1]

1 *Mr S* (PO-22206, 11 October 2021) at [37]–[38].

Restitution

10.55

No claim for recovery of an overpayment can be made unless the member has been notified of the mistake or payment has been demanded of them.[1]

1 *Freeman v Jeffries* (1869) LR 4 Exch 189.

10.56

It is open to the member to make a complaint to the Ombudsman alleging maladministration on the part of the trustees if a demand for recovery of an overpayment is made. The Ombudsman's position is that, whilst such an overpayment is maladministration, the trustees are entitled to recover it unless the member can sustain a legally-recognised defence.[1]

1 See, for example, *Mr Alan Belk* (PO-372 and PO-4244, 30 November 2015) at [75] and [77].

10.57

The trustees can prevent the Ombudsman from adjudicating on this issue if they commence legal proceedings before the complaint is made.[1] However, given the Ombudsman's willingness to deal with members' defences on their merits,[2] it may be a more cost-effective solution for the trustees to allow the member to go through the Ombudsman process and hope that the member repays the overpayment if their complaint is not upheld, rather than for the trustees to immediately go to court. However, if the member refuses to repay the overpayment, the Ombudsman has no power to require them to do so.[3]

1 Section 146(6)(a) of PSA 1993: if proceedings are commenced after the complaint has been made, the court may stay those proceedings to allow the complaint to proceed: s 148(2) of PSA 1993.
2 In *NHS Business Services Authority v Wheeler* [2014] EWHC 2155 (Ch), [2014] Pens LR 639 at [13], Deputy Judge Gaunt QC held that the appellant had rightly conceded that the Ombudsman was entitled to investigate such matters on a complaint made in respect of the overpayment.
3 Section 151(2) of PSA 1993. The Ombudsman's determination on the member's defences, however, will be binding on the complainant member, subject to any appeal: s 151(3)(a) of PSA 1993.

10.58

A claim for recovery of the overpaid benefit must be brought in the county court if the total value of the overpayment is less than £100,000;[1] otherwise, the claim must be brought in the High Court.

1 CPR PD 7A para 2.1.

10.59

The particulars of claim should include the following information:

(a) the source, amount and date of the payment;

(b) the nature of the mistake;

(c) the correct amount of the payment;

(d) the absence of knowledge of the mistake by the trustees at the time of payment;

(e) the source and date of the discovery of the mistake; and

(f) the nature and date of the demand by the trustees for repayment and of the failure to repay.

10.60

In addition to the overpaid sum, the trustees can claim interest from the date of the issue of proceedings until judgment.[1]

1 Section 69 of the County Courts Act 1984; s 35A of the Senior Courts Act 1981.

10.61

If the member wishes to raise a defence such as change of position, the onus is on the member to plead it fairly and squarely so that its factual merits can be explored at trial.[1]

1 *Adrian Alan Ltd v Fuglers* [2002] EWCA Civ 1655, [2003] PNLR 14 at [16] per Brooke LJ.

10.62

The onus of proving a change of position defence is also on the member, who must adduce evidence and give disclosure in support of it.[1] Whilst the court will make allowances for the fact that a good faith defendant may not have kept an exact record of their spending, as they could not have been expected to account for it to anyone else,[2] a mere assertion that money has been spent, without supporting evidence, will not suffice.[3]

1 *Prudential Assurance Co Ltd v HMRC* [2016] EWCA Civ 376, [2017] 1 WLR 4031 at [150] per Lewison LJ: this point was not disturbed on appeal.
2 *Derby v Scottish Equitable plc* [2001] Pens LR 163 at [33] per Robert Walker LJ; *National Westminster Bank plc v Somer* [2001] EWCA Civ 970, [2002] QB 1286 at [68] per Peter Gibson LJ.
3 *Goff & Jones*, para 27-32.

Recoupment

10.63

The trustees will need carefully to consider the terms of any recoupment, in particular the period over which the overpaid sum will be recovered out of future instalments of pension. The trustees should bear in mind that the remedy must be applied in a fair and equitable manner, and should take account of the Ombudsman's requirement that overpayments be recouped from future instalments over at least the period for which the mistake had gone undetected.[1]

1 See **10.50**.

10.64

It may be possible to soften the blow by deciding to make recoupment from future increases to pensions in payment, so that the member receives their benefits with reduced or no increases until the overpayment is recovered.

10.65

As stated above, the right of recoupment is a 'self-help' remedy, and does not require the trustees to initiate a claim in court against the member. However, that does not necessarily mean that the trustees can completely avoid all formal adjudicatory processes.

10.66

By s 91(1) of PA 1995, occupational pension rights are prohibited from being assigned, commuted, surrendered, charged or being subject to a lien or a set-off. Initially, there was a widespread view that the right of recoupment did not come within this provision, as it did not involve the alienation of any benefits: that was because the overpayments were regarded as premature payments of future benefit,[1] so that the sums withheld by reason of recoupment were not benefits payable to the member at all. The Ombudsman therefore permitted trustees to recoup benefits without applying s 91.[2]

1 *Livesey v Livesey* (1827) 3 Russ 287, 296 per Lord Lyndhurst LC.
2 See, for example, *Noble* (L00663, 7 October 2002) and *Noakes* (M00851, 24 February 2004).

10.67

However, fresh impetus was given to the contrary view by changes to s 91 made by PA 2004. Section 91(5) provided for several exceptions to the general prohibition in s 91(1), and PA 2004 introduced a new exception applying to:

> 'a charge or lien on, or set-off against, the person in question's entitlement, or right, for the purpose of discharging some monetary obligation due from the person in question to the scheme arising out of a payment made in error in respect of the pension.'[1]

1 Section 91(5)(f) of PA 1995, introduced by s 266(2) of PA 2004.

10.68

That exception looks very like a description of recoupment in the context of mistaken overpayments of pension benefits, even though it repeats the reference in s 91(1) to the remedy being in the form of a charge, lien or set-off, none of which strictly encompass the equitable remedy of recoupment. Nevertheless, the introduction of the new exception led to a change of view within the Ombudsman's office, and in *Clift*,[1] the Deputy Pensions Ombudsman held that the recoupment of overpaid pensions from future instalments did fall within s 91.

1 (PO-2066, 3 June 2014).

10.69

The relevance of that change of practice for the practical application of the recoupment remedy is that the new exception to s 91(1) is made expressly subject to s 91(6), which:

(a) restricts the amount which can be recovered to the lesser of the amount of the monetary obligation in question, and the value (determined in a prescribed manner) of the member's benefits;

(b) requires the member to be given a certificate showing the amount of the charge, lien or set-off and its effect on their benefits; and

(c) provides that, where there is a dispute as to its amount, the charge, lien or set-off cannot be exercised unless the obligation has become enforceable '*under an order of a competent court or in consequence of an award of an arbitrator* …'.

Accordingly, if recoupment comes within the scope of the new exception to s 91(1), a court order will be required before the deduction can be made where the amount in question is in dispute.

10.70

If an overpaid member disputes the recoupment sought by the trustees, the usual course of action would be for either the member to make a complaint to the Ombudsman or the trustees to refer the matter to the Ombudsman as a dispute of fact or law between them and the member. If the Ombudsman's determination on the issue constituted '*an order of a competent court*' for the purposes of s 91(6), the requirement of that provision will be easily satisfied in that situation. However, if the Ombudsman does not constitute a competent court, the cost of litigating to enforce recoupment may well operate as a significant disincentive to the use of that remedy, particularly if the trustees are seeking to recover relatively modest amounts of overpaid benefit.

10.71

The status of the Ombudsman in this respect is not entirely clear:

(a) In *Clift*, the Deputy Pensions Ombudsman allowed the trustee to proceed to recoup based on her determination, which must have been because she considered her determination to be an order of a competent court for the purposes of s 91(6) once the member had submitted to the jurisdiction of the Ombudsman by making the complaint.

(b) However, in *Burgess v BIC UK Ltd*,[1] Arnold J said (obiter) that a determination of the Ombudsman was not an order of a competent court under s 91(6) because the Ombudsman was not a court; however, the judge said that an order made by the county court under s 151(5)(a) of PSA 1993 to enforce an Ombudsman's determination would constitute an order of a competent court.

(c) The judge's view on this issue is highly questionable:

(i) he was not taken to several cases in which statutory tribunals similar to the Ombudsman have been treated as courts for like purposes;[2]

(ii) the judge did not refer to s 151(3) of PSA 1993, which makes the Ombudsman's determinations final and binding on the complainant, and points to the determination having the status of a court order;

(iii) by relying on s 151(5)(a) of PSA 1993, the judge confused the recognition of a claim and its enforcement: in the case of recoupment, all that is necessary is to have the right recognised by the court, and there is no scope for judicial enforcement of that right, as recoupment is a remedy exercisable by the trustees;

(iv) requiring a county court enforcement order to be sought before overpayments can be recouped provides a further layer of complication to the use of the recoupment remedy to deal with overpaid pensions: this is inconsistent with the principle that s 91 of PA 1995 is not intended to make the settlement of pensions disputes any more complicated than is necessary.[3]

(d) Despite Arnold J's comments, in April 2019 the Pensions Ombudsman took the unusual step of issuing a factsheet setting out his views as to why he considered that the Ombudsman is a competent court for the purposes of s 91(6). Accordingly, the Ombudsman now regards himself as able to satisfy the s 91(6) requirement and permits recoupment to take place without the trustees needing to take the matter to court.[4]

1 [2018] EWHC 785 (Ch), [2018] Pens LR 1 at [168]. An appeal from that decision was allowed on a basis which meant that the recoupment issue did not arise for consideration by the Court of Appeal: [2019] EWCA Civ 806, [2019] ICR 1386.

2 One such example is *Peach Grey & Co v Sommer* [1995] ICR 549, in which it was held that an industrial tribunal was an '*inferior court*' for the purposes of RSC Ord 52 requiring committal proceedings for contempt of court in such courts to be brought in the Divisional Court.

3 See *HR Trustees Ltd v German* [2010] EWCA Civ 1349, [2011] ICR 329, in which the Court of Appeal held that s 91 did not prevent the compromise of a bona fide pensions dispute.

4 For example, see *Mr N* (PO-16358, 9 November 2018); *Mr D* (PO-1918, 20 October 2020).

10.72

Notwithstanding this lack of clarity, there remains the more fundamental issue of whether s 91 should apply to the recoupment remedy at all. In the *Burgess* case[1] it was common ground between the parties that recoupment was a form of set-off which was subject to s 91. That position is, however, highly doubtful: although they operate in a similar way, recoupment and set-off are different legal principles and none of the authorities on recoupment describe the remedy in terms of a set-off. This issue therefore remains open pending a considered judgment.

1 [2018] Pens LR 1 at [164].

10.73

A similar issue arises in the context of whether overpayments can be recouped out of guaranteed minimum pensions (GMPs). Section 91(7) of PA 1995 makes s 91 subject to s 159 of PSA 1993, which provides that every assignment of, or charge on, a member's GMP entitlement shall be void. The Ombudsman has determined that the right to offset overpayments of benefits from a statutory public sector scheme out of GMPs constitutes a charge and so is void.[1] It remains to be seen whether the same analysis would be applied to recoupments out of GMPs payable under a trust-based occupational pension scheme.

1 *Mrs S* (PO-23848, 19 August 2021) at [98].

Practice point: handling multiple overpayment cases

10.74

It is not uncommon for systemic errors to cause many members of a scheme to be overpaid benefits. In such circumstances, the trustees should consider establishing a protocol for recovery which can apply to all members in an efficient and cost-effective manner. Such a protocol could include provision for the following:

(a) putting in place mechanisms for dealing with any gaps in the data required to identify and calculate the overpayments, including the use of actuarial assumptions;

(b) identifying and documenting in advance the criteria which will be applied when determining whether or not to recover the overpayments in individual cases;

(c) adopting a uniform approach to compensation payments for distress and inconvenience;

(d) informing the members of the issue, how it affects them, what the trustees are intending to do to put matters right, and the timeframe within which the issue will be settled;

(c) inviting the members to put forward reasons as to why the proposed method of recovery should not apply to them, together with supporting evidence; and

(f) arranging for a suitably qualified person or panel to deal with members' claims in the first instance, and for the internal dispute resolution procedure to deal with appeals from that body.

If the overpayments issue is particularly large or contentious, the trustees may wish to consider obtaining directions from the court to approve the proposed protocol, under the CPR Part 64 procedure.[1]

1 As to which, see **14.67–14.72**.

11 Mistaken Underpayments

11.1

The same types of mistake that cause pensions to be overpaid can also cause pensions to be underpaid. This chapter considers the circumstances in which trustees are obliged to make good any such underpayments, and the extent of that obligation.

11.2

Much of the law on this subject derives from three High Court decisions. The first two concerned the incorrect application to guaranteed minimum pensions (GMPs) of EU law requirements to equalise pension benefits. In two judgments in *Lloyds Banking Group Pensions Trustees Ltd v Lloyds Bank*[1] (*Lloyds 1* and *Lloyds 2*), Morgan J considered issues relating to the consequential obligation on the trustees to compensate members for the failure of their benefits to incorporate equalised GMPs. The other case, relating to the Axminster Carpets Group Retirement Benefits Plan[2] (*Axminster*), involved a compromise of various issues relating to the meaning and validity of amendments to benefits, which meant that those benefits had been underpaid, and which gave rise to similar issues to those considered in *Lloyds 1* and *Lloyds 2*.

1 [2018] EWHC 2839 (Ch), [2019] Pens LR 95; [2020] EWHC 3135 (Ch), [2021] Pens LR 295.
2 *Punter Southall Governance Services Ltd v Hazlett* [2021] EWHC 1652 (Ch), [2022] Pens LR 1.

11.3

In *Lloyds 2*, the judge focused on the underpayment issues as they related to former members of the scheme who had transferred their benefits to other arrangements. This chapter deals with general underpayment issues, and **Chapter 12** deals with those issues as they relate specifically to transferred-out members.

The trustees' primary obligation

11.4

Pension scheme trustees are obliged to pay the benefits in accordance with the governing provisions of the scheme, and will be obliged to make back payments to members whose benefits have been underpaid.[1] In *Axminster,*[2] Morgan J identified two possible types of claim where trustees failed to pay the correct level of benefits: a claim for an account of the sums due to the member under the trust together with an order for payment of the sums found due on the taking of the account; and a claim for equitable compensation for breach of trust. Although it will rarely be necessary in the context of a pension scheme, where the members' rights to benefits have crystallised they will also have a proprietary claim against the assets of the scheme which are required to be realised in order to pay the correct benefits.[3]

1 This was common ground in *Lloyds 1* at [396].
2 *Axminster* at [110].
3 *Granada Group Ltd v Law Debenture Trust Corp plc* [2015] EWHC 1499 (Ch), [2015] 2 BCLC 604 at [53] per Andrews J; *Re HIH Superannuation Pty Ltd* [2003] NSWSC 65 at [29] per Barrett J.

11.5

Despite this, the primary method for a member to seek redress for a failure by the trustees to make good an underpayment is by way of a complaint to the Pensions Ombudsman alleging maladministration.[1]

1 The underpayment of pension benefits will constitute maladministration, even if it was accounted for as soon as it was identified and steps were taken to redress it: *Mrs W McKinney* (84793/2, 16 May 2012) at [12].

Interest on arrears

Entitlement to interest

11.6

In *Lloyds 1*[1] it was common ground that the trustees ought to add interest to the back payments in relation to the period during which each instalment was due and unpaid, in order to compensate the member for being kept out of the funds during the period of underpayment.

1 *Lloyds 1* at [453]. See also *Lloyds 2* at [78].

11.7

However, in *Axminster*,[1] Morgan J accepted the employer's argument that a number of authorities, not cited in the *Lloyds* cases, established that pension scheme members do not have a pre-existing entitlement to interest on the back payment of pensions arrears.[2] The judge therefore went on to consider the issue of interest from the standpoint of what the court could order on a claim by the underpaid member.

1 *Axminster* at [322].
2 *Torre v Browne* (1855) HL Cas 555; *Booth v Coulton* (1861) 2 Giff 514; *Edwards v Warden* (1876) 1 App Cas 281; *Re Berkeley* [1968] Ch 744. This was not always the rule (see, for example, *Litton v Litton* (1719) 1 P Wms 541), and it has been described as anomalous: *Re Berkeley* [1968] Ch 154, 165-166 per Cross J.

11.8

The judge held that it was open to the underpaid member to bring a claim against the trustees for equitable compensation for breach of trust, where the court would have its usual jurisdiction in equity to award interest on the compensation ordered to be paid.[1] In addition, the judge referred to the court's power under s 35A of the Senior Courts Act 1981 to award interest in proceedings for the recovery of a debt or damages, and was prepared to assume that pensions arrears fell within that jurisdiction, although he did not receive any submissions on the point.[2] The judge also noted that interest under s 35A could not be awarded if the debt or damages were paid before the action was brought.[3]

1 *Axminster* at [322]–[324].
2 *Axminster* at [325].
3 *Axminster* at [325].

11.9

The judge went on to make some tentative comments on the scope of an interest award, although he had received no submissions on that point. He said that the issue would depend on the cause of action and the identity of the defendant:

(a) a claim for an account and an order for payment of the sum found due on the taking of the account would not carry interest because of the principle that a member does not have a pre-existing entitlement to the addition of interest on the taking of an account: interest could only be awarded where the jurisdiction under s 35A of the Senior Courts Act 1981 was available;

(b) a claim for equitable compensation against the current trustees did not give rise to any limitation issues and would enable the court to award interest pursuant to its equitable jurisdiction; but

(c) a claim for equitable compensation for breach of trust against predecessor trustees which was statute-barred under LA 1980[1] would not result in an award of equitable compensation, with or without interest, in respect of breaches during that period.[2]

1 See **11.17**.
2 *Axminster* at [327]–[330].

11.10

This leaves trustees seeking to deal proactively with underpaid benefits, in circumstances where no court proceedings have been issued, in a potentially difficult position, as they will need to consider the addition of interest on the assumption that the members concerned had brought the relevant claims. The trustees will accordingly have to identify who were the trustees at the time of the underpayment and determine whether a non-statute-barred claim could be brought against them. Moreover, it cannot be assumed that s 35A of the Senior Courts Act 1981 will apply, as the trustees would be compensating members for underpayments before any claims had been brought, which precludes the application of that provision.

11.11

The general principle that members have no pre-existing entitlement to interest is displaced by exceptional circumstances, including where trustees were at fault.[1] Thus, if the underpayment was caused by an administrative error, it is possible that interest may be added to the back payment without the need to consider what would have happened had the member made a claim.

1 *Torre v Browne* (1855) HL Cas 555, 578 per Lord Cranworth LC.

11.12

There may be circumstances which justify the trustees not adding any interest at all to the late payment of benefits. In one recent determination,[1] the Pensions Ombudsman upheld the decision of a trustee not to pay interest when compensating a number of members for many years of underpaid benefits, on the basis that the scheme was in winding-up and in significant deficit, and the trustee had been advised by its lawyers that that was a reasonable decision to take.

1 *Mr E* (PO-26322, 4 June 2020). See also *Mr X* (PO-9889, 27 July 2016).

The rate of interest

11.13

In *Lloyds 1*, Morgan J was also asked to decide on the appropriate rate of interest. As to this, the judge adopted guidance from case law[1] which said that the issue was to be approached broadly, by reference to the general attributes of the persons to be compensated, but without regard to their particular attributes or any special position in which they may have been.[2] Although he had not been provided with evidence of the members' general attributes, the judge noted that the amount of the underpayments was relatively modest and would not have made a major difference to the lives of the members over the years, and so approached the issue on the assumption that the underpayment would not have driven a typical member to borrow money at overdraft rates of interest.[3]

1 *Carrasco v Johnson* [2018] EWCA Civ 87 at [17] per Hamblen LJ. In *Axminster* at [337], Morgan J noted that the Court of Appeal in *Watson v Kea Investments Ltd* [2019] EWCA Civ 1759, [2019] 4 WLR 145, at [68] and [78], had commented that *Carrasco v Johnson* did not concern interest in relation to equitable compensation: however, it was not suggested that the Judge's approach in *Lloyds 1* was invalidated on that account.

2 *Lloyds 1* at [456].

3 *Lloyds 1* at [457].

11.14

The judge concluded that the equitable result was that interest should be paid at one per cent above the base rate, in view of the historically low base rates in recent years: had base rates been significantly higher, he would not have gone above the base rate.[1] The judge also awarded simple, rather than compound, interest in accordance with usual equity practice.[2]

1 *Lloyds 1* at [461]–[462].

2 *Lloyds 1* at [462]. In *Axminster* at [343], the judge similarly awarded interest at one per cent above the base rate; it was common ground in that case (at [331]) that simple interest was to be awarded.

11.15

Of potential relevance to this issue is the statutory jurisdiction of the Pensions Ombudsman to award a prescribed rate of interest in cases of late payment of pension benefits by trustees,[1] that prescribed rate currently being the base rate.[2] Although this jurisdiction was cited to the judge in *Lloyds 1*,[3] he made no reference to it in his analysis of the appropriate rate. Despite this, the adoption by the trustees of a rate which has been endorsed by Parliament in the specific context of compensating pension scheme members for underpaid benefits would seem to be reasonable, particularly as members would be very likely to pursue any such claim as a complaint to the Ombudsman rather than by court proceedings.

1 Section 151A of PSA 1993.
2 Regulation 6 of the Personal and Occupational Pension Schemes (Pensions Ombudsman) Regulations 1996 (SI 1996/2475).
3 *Lloyds 1* at [458].

Limitation

11.16

This issue was considered, relatively briefly, in *Lloyds 1*, and in considerably more detail in *Axminster*.

11.17

As stated above, a failure to provide members with the correct benefit constitutes a breach of trust on the part of the trustees. The limitation periods applicable to claims in respect of trust property are set out in s 21 of LA 1980. The default position is that an action to recover trust property or in respect of any breach of trust must be brought within six years from the accrual of the cause of action.[1] That is subject to several exceptions,[2] including the following in s 21(1)(b):

> 'an action … to recover from the trustee trust property or the proceeds of trust property in the possession of the trustee, or previously received by the trustee and converted to his use.'[3]

In such a case, no limitation period will apply.

1 Section 21(3) of LA 1980.
2 One such exception is in s 21(3), which provides that the limitation period does not begin to run in respect of a beneficiary entitled to a future interest in the trust property until the interest falls into possession. In a pension scheme context, this is generally thought to prevent the limitation period beginning to run against any active or deferred member until their benefits come into payment.
3 This exception is itself qualified by s 21(2) in the case of a trustee who has honestly and reasonably received or retained trust property or its proceeds as a beneficiary. The limitation period is disapplied in that situation only for the excess of trust assets over and above their proper share, so that the share of trust assets properly distributed to the trustee is protected by the six-year limitation period in s 21(3).

11.18

In *Lloyds 1*, Morgan J held that this exception applied in the case of underpaid benefits, as the trustees are to be treated as having retained the assets which are subject to the trust and out of which the trustee is obliged to make the payment to the members.[1]

1 *Lloyds 1* at [434] and [437].

11.19

The judgment in *Lloyds 1* was primarily focused on the issue of the effect of equalisation on GMPs, and limitation was very much a secondary issue, the analysis of which occupied three paragraphs of a 471-paragraph judgment. In *Axminster*, Morgan J took the unusual step of agreeing to consider the issue afresh. After a thorough review of the legislative history and the case law, the judge held that a claim by a member against trustees for an account and for the payment of arrears of pension would be '*an action to recover from the trustee trust property*' for the purposes of s 21(1)(b), which therefore operated to disapply the limitation period where the trustees had underpaid benefits.[1] The judge left open the question of whether the same analysis applied to a claim against the current trustees for equitable compensation for breach of trust, but held that a member who brought such a claim against a former trustee would not be able to rely on s 21(1)(b), as that trustee would no longer be in possession of the trust property.[2]

1 *Axminster* at [156].
2 *Axminster* at [159]–[160]. The same analysis would presumably apply to former trustees of a scheme that had been wound up, and to trustees of a segregated scheme following a bulk transfer of the assets of the segregated section.

11.20

Even where the statutory limitation period does not apply, the equitable doctrine of laches can in theory still operate to bar the claim.[1] This defence arises where there has been a lapse of time and the member's actions have been such as to make it unconscionable for them to be permitted to assert their claim. However, the application of this principle is likely to be of limited relevance to cases of mistaken underpayments because time does not begin to run for this purpose until the trustees became aware of the underpayment,[2] and any attempt by the trustees to rely on their (or their predecessor's) own prolonged failure to deal with the issue once it had come to their knowledge is highly unlikely to find favour with the court. Moreover, the laches defence depends on the personal circumstances of each member, and is not suitable to be determined on a group basis.[3]

1 See **6.27**.
2 *Beale v Kyte* [1907] 1 Ch 564.
3 *Burgess v BIC UK Ltd* [2018] EWHC 785 (Ch), [2018] Pens LR 13 at [176] per Arnold J: this point was not considered on appeal.

Forfeiture of benefits

11.21

As the statutory limitation periods will not typically be relevant to the back payment of pension benefits, the only way in which a time limit can be imposed on such payments is under the scheme rules. Many schemes will contain forfeiture provisions, which seek to absolve the trustees from any obligation to pay benefits which have not been claimed by the members for a period of time. As a result of Morgan J's decisions in *Lloyds 1* and *Axminster*, such provisions may, depending on their wording, apply to preclude the members from claiming the entirety of the underpaid benefits.

Validity of forfeiture provisions

11.22

Pension scheme forfeiture provisions are operative only insofar as they comply with s 92(5) of PA 1995, which provides for exceptions to the general principle in s 92(1) of PA 1995 that occupational pension scheme benefits cannot be forfeited. The relevant exception is in s 92(5)(b), which provides that:

> 'Subsection (1) does not prevent forfeiture by reference to a failure by any person to make a claim for pension[1] … where the claim is not made within six years of the date on which the pension becomes due.'

1 Which includes any part of a pension: s 94(2) of PA 1995.

11.23

In *Lloyds 1*, the employers sought to rely on forfeiture provisions contained in the rules of the schemes in issue that precluded the trustee from paying any arrears that stretched back further than six years into the past.

11.24

Four of those provisions were in the following terms:[1]

> *No beneficiary shall be entitled to claim any instalment of pension or other benefit to which he is entitled under the Scheme more than 6 years after that instalment has fallen due for payment.*
>
> *Any sum which may have become due to a Member or other person entitled to benefit under the Rules shall be forfeited if it has not been claimed during a period of at least six years from the date upon which that sum became due, but, if the sum formed one payment of a pension or annuity the right to such pension or annuity shall not thereby be extinguished.*
>
> *If any pension or benefit or any instalment remains unpaid to and unclaimed by the person to whom it is payable for a period of six years from the date it became payable, then the entitlement to it shall be extinguished*
>
> *… the Trustees will forfeit any benefit if the person entitled to the benefit does not claim it within six-years of the date on which it becomes due.*

1 *Lloyds 1* at [402]–[405]. Immaterial parts of the provisions have been omitted.

11.25

A fifth provision stated that the trustee may reduce a person's benefits, or decide that a person's benefits will be forfeited, in any other circumstances allowed by s 92.

11.26

The members argued that those provisions did not come within the s 92(5)(b) exception, as:

(a) they dealt with circumstances where no pension had been claimed (for example, where the member was no longer in contact with the scheme), and did not apply to cases where a pension had been claimed and paid but the full amount of the pensioner's entitlement was not paid to him: the member cannot be said to have '*made a claim*' for the unpaid element of pension; and

(b) where the provisions gave the trustees a discretion as to what to do in a case which came within those provisions, the trustees should not exercise that discretion in the circumstances of the case.

11.27

Morgan J held as follows:

(a) as to the four provisions set out in **11.24**:

  (i) on their true construction, members could not claim arrears more than six years after the date when they were due, even where the trustees had made payments in relation to pension entitlements but had underpaid the members because they had miscalculated the pension: as the members were not entitled to those arrears, the trustees were not bound to pay them, and any such payment would be voluntary;[1]

  (ii) they complied with s 92(5)(b): whilst s 92(5) referred to a '*claim for pension*', the definition of '*pension*' in s 94(2) included any part of a pension or any payment by way of pension; thus, the failure of the member to make a claim for the underpayment of pension because it was wrongly calculated meant that the member had not made a claim for a payment by way of pension, so that a rule which provided for forfeiture after six years on that ground came within the exception in s 92(5)(b);[2]

(b) as to the fifth provision set out in **11.25**, which gave the trustee a discretion to pay or withhold a back payment in relation to a period which was more than six years before the arrears were claimed, that discretion was to be exercised in accordance with general principles, in that the trustee must have regard to only relevant considerations and must make a decision which is rational and not perverse.[3]

1 *Lloyds 1* at [408]–[411].

2 *Lloyds 1* at [417]. The judge (at [416]) was prepared to assume that s 91 applied to the first provision, even though it did not use the word '*forfeiture*', noting that s 92(7) defined that word for the purposes of s 92 to extend to '*any manner of deprivation*' of a pension.

3 *Lloyds 1* at [418] and [420]. In *Axminister* at [192], Morgan J referred to, but did not have to deal with, the question of whether the exercise of a forfeiture power was constrained by its purpose: see, further, **7.32–7.36**.

Construction of forfeiture provisions

11.28

In *Axminster*, Morgan J applied the usual principles of interpretation applicable to pension scheme provisions,[1] in determining that a provision which gave the trustees a discretion to apply for different purposes '*any monies payable out of the Plan and not claimed within six years from the date on which they were due*' was not a forfeiture clause, but only applied to cases of missing beneficiaries.[2]

1 Set out in *Barnardo's v Buckinghamshire* [2018] UKSC 55, [2019] ICR 495 at [13]–[18] per Lord Hodge: see **5.10**.

2 *Axminster* at [174]–[176].

11.29

In that case, the judge also had to consider a provision which expressly forfeited a benefit where the member '*fails to claim a benefit within six years of it becoming due*' and which gave the trustees a discretion to use all or part of the benefit for certain purposes, including payment to the member. The judge held that that provision applied to cases of underpaid benefits, on the following grounds:

(a) a '*benefit*' meant the sum which is unpaid on the date on which it fell due;

(b) a '*claim*' meant a claim by the member to be paid the sum which has not been paid, after the time when the sum was due;

(c) '*fails*' meant simply that a claim was not made, and did not require the trustees to show that the member was at fault, or that the trustees were free from fault.[1]

1 *Axminster* at [190].

11.30

The judge went on to hold that the forfeiture provision came within s 92(5)(b) of PA 1995, which did not require the failure to claim the benefit to involve fault on the part of the member.[1]

1 *Axminster* at [211] and [214].

11.31

Finally, as to how to exercise the discretion conferred on the trustees to apply the forfeited benefits, the judge said that:

(a) the trustees should consider how the situation had arisen and the consequences of the discretion being exercised or not exercised;

(b) when considering the former factor, it was relevant to refer to the position of the members and to the position of the trustees from time to time; and

(c) the absence of fault on the part of member and/or the presence of fault on the part of the trustees were capable of being relevant factors, which may lead the trustees to exercise their discretion to pay the benefits to the member unless there were other considerations which overrode that approach.[1]

1 *Axminster* at [264]–[266]. The judge went on (at [285]–[298]) to deal with further factors which were specific to the circumstances of the scheme in issue.

11.32

Although the judge referred to those principles in the context of a discretion as to what to do with the forfeited benefits, they are equally relevant to a power to decide whether or not to forfeit the benefits.

Amending the scheme to include a forfeiture provision

11.33

Because the forfeiture provision in *Axminster* had been added to the scheme by way of an amendment, the judge had to consider whether and to what extent the provision – which could operate to forfeit benefits accrued by reference to pre-amendment service – was affected by the restriction in the amendment power, which prevented changes which '*would diminish the benefits … already accrued (as determined by the Actuary) under the* [scheme] *to the Member*'.[1] Having said that the point was not entirely an easy one, the judge held that the restriction did not affect the forfeiture provision, as:

(a) the amount of the benefits to which the member was entitled before and after the amendment were unaffected and so were not '*diminished*' by the amendment; and

(b) the provision only resulted in a forfeiture of arrears where the member failed to claim the arrears for six years, and while that *might* happen, it cannot be said that it *would* happen.[2]

1 The restrictions on the modification of pension schemes imposed by s 67 of PA 1995 do not apply to forfeiture provisions permitted by s 92: reg 3(b) of The Occupational Pension Schemes (Modification of Schemes) Regulations 2006 (SI 2006/759).
2 *Axminster* at [211].

Practical consequences

11.34

Trustees faced with underpaid benefits need to check the scheme rules carefully for any forfeiture provisions which may affect the requirement to make good underpayments. Whilst such provisions may operate harshly on members who had no knowledge of their benefit entitlements, the trustees will only be able to take this into account where the provision gives them a discretion, rather than an obligation, to forfeit.

11.35

If the scheme in question does not contain a forfeiture provision, the employer and trustees may want to consider introducing such a provision by amendment, and they will be encouraged by Morgan J's comments in *Axminister* on the non-application of the restriction in the amendment power to the introduction of such a provision. However, those comments are somewhat controversial, and may well be revisited in the future.

Tax consequences of underpayments

11.36

These are dealt with at **17.11–17.64**.

Practice point: the steps the trustees will be expected to take to make good underpayments

11.37

How proactive do the trustees need to be in compensating underpaid members? Where underpayments relate to active members and pensioners, the trustees' task in identifying the members will be relatively straightforward; but what of deferred members who have lost touch with the scheme?

11.38

In *Lloyds 2,* Morgan J was asked to determine whether trustees were under an obligation to take active steps to compensate members who had transferred out of the scheme, or whether the trustees could wait until a request had been made. The judge gave some limited general guidance, which applies equally to the identification and compensation of deferred members.

11.39

The judge held that the trustees would be expected to be proactive in dealing with the issue. Because the past inadequate transfer payment constituted a breach of fiduciary duty, and a court would, on an application for directions by the trustees, be inclined to direct them that they should deal with the problem rather than do nothing, it was open to the trustees to decide for themselves to take that approach without the need for directions.[1] However, the judge would not go into detail about what steps the trustees would be expected to take, saying only the following:

> '… all that I can usefully say is that the Trustee does need to be proactive in that it must consider the rights and obligations which I have identified, the remedies available to members and the absence of a time bar and then determine what to do.'[2]

In determining what to do, the trustees must act in accordance with their duty to administer the scheme with reasonable care and skill,[3] bearing in mind that the underpayment constitutes a breach of fiduciary duty.

1 *Lloyds 2* at [272]–[274].
2 *Lloyds 2* at [276].
3 See *Lewin on Trusts* (20th edn, Sweet & Maxwell, 2020) (*Lewin*), para 34-001.

11.40

Although each case will turn on its own facts, all trustees faced with this situation should, as a minimum, consider the following:

(a) just as the first duty of a trustee on being appointed is to ascertain the trusts so that they know the scope of their fiduciary obligations,[1] the same duty logically arises when the trustees discover that they have misapprehended the scope of the trust and their fiduciary obligations;

(b) trustees who have been made aware that they have underpaid benefits should therefore take reasonable steps to identify the affected members and the amount of the underpayment to them;

(c) where the calculation of the required compensation is hampered by the lack of reliable data, the trustees should consider putting in place sensible protocols for assessing compensation, such as making reasonable actuarial assumptions where financial information is unavailable, and taking reasonable steps to track down members whose contact information may be out of date;

(d) trustees should then take reasonable steps to make good the underpayments.

1 *Lewin*, para 13-036.

11.41

What are reasonable steps to make good the underpayments will depend on the circumstances of each scheme, and it will generally be open to the trustees to undertake a cost-benefit analysis, by reference to such factors as:

(a) the complexity of the scheme's history – in terms of mergers and restructurings – which may make the potentially affected membership difficult to assess;

(b) the availability of data in order to locate the affected persons and to calculate the compensation;

(c) the relative cost of locating the persons and making good the underpayments;

(d) the effect of that cost on the solvency of the scheme and the employer covenant; and

(e) whether some or all of those costs are or can be covered by existing or future insurance: where the scheme in question is at or near the point of winding-up, the trustees will be particularly interested in obtaining run-off insurance including cover for any residual liabilities caused by the underpayments.

However, absent special circumstances, the trustees should not prioritise completion of the compensation exercise in respect of active and pensioner members of the scheme over the compensation of deferred members.

11.42

The trustees should also take and act on legal advice in cases of doubt, and ensure that there is a good paper trail evidencing the factors which were taken into account when making their decisions.

11.43

Further guidance on correcting past underpayments pursuant to the GMP equalisation requirement can be found in Section A of the PASA GMP Equalisation Working Group's Guidance Note on Methods (September 2019), some of which applies to correcting past underpayments more generally.

12 Mistakes in Scheme Transfers

12.1

Most schemes will give members leaving pensionable service the right to have their benefits transferred to another pension arrangement. In addition, many such members have a statutory right to transfer the 'cash equivalent' of their benefits.[1] A bulk transfer of assets and liabilities between schemes within the same group of employers may occur where, for example, two or more schemes merge into a single scheme; or the assets and liabilities of a defined contribution (DC) scheme may be bulk transferred to a master trust. Such transfers involve the assignment of assets from the transferring scheme to the receiving arrangement, and the consequent extinction of the member's rights to benefits under the transferring scheme, usually effected by way of a discharge of the trustees' liability to pay such benefits granted by the scheme rules, by statute or by an express discharge from the transferring member.

1 Part 4ZA of PSA 1993.

12.2

There are a number of ways in which mistakes can occur in the course of such a transfer, ranging from administrative errors to a misapprehension as to the law. An example of the latter is *Lloyds Banking Group Pensions Trustees Ltd v Lloyds Bank*[1] (*Lloyds 2*) in which Morgan J had to determine a number of issues – following his earlier decision[2] (*Lloyds 1*) that guaranteed minimum pension (GMPs) had been wrongly calculated – concerning former scheme members whose transfer payments had been wrongly calculated as a result.

1 [2020] EWHC 3135 (Ch), [2021] Pens LR 295.
2 [2018] EWHC 2839 (Ch), [2019] Pens LR 95.

Compensation for underpayments

The trustees' primary obligation to the members

Statutory transfers

12.3

Where the underpayment related to a transfer made under the statutory cash equivalent legislation, Morgan J in *Lloyds 2* held that the trustees were in breach of their duty under s 99(2) of PSA 1993 to *'do what is needed to carry out what the member requires'*, and they could not claim the benefit of the discharge set out in s 99(1).[1]

1 *Lloyds 2* at [86], [90], [155].

12.4

The judge held that the underpayment amounted to a breach of fiduciary duty on the part of the trustees and the members could apply to court for an order that the trustees make good the underpayment from the transferring scheme's assets. The order that a court would make on the application of a member requiring the trustees to perform their obligation is the payment to the receiving arrangement of a 'top-up' to the earlier underpayment. In those circumstances, the trustees remain able, belatedly, to perform that duty without an order of the court.[1]

1 *Lloyds 2* at [95], [149], [272]–[274]. Members in this position have accordingly been described as creditors rather than beneficiaries: section A2 of the PASA GMP Equalisation Working Group's Supplemental Guidance on Transfer Payments (August 2021).

12.5

Neither the trustees nor the member can insist upon compensation being provided by way of a residual benefit under the transferring scheme, although they could agree to this as an alternative to the provision of a top-up payment.[1]

1 *Lloyds 2* at [229].

12.6

Once the top-up payment is made to the receiving arrangement, the trustees need not ensure that the transferring member receives the benefit to which they are entitled to under that arrangement.[1]

1 This was common ground in *Lloyds 2* at [279]. A top-up payment to the receiving arrangement should be sufficient even if the member has by then transferred to a third arrangement, as the receiving arrangement would itself be obliged to make the top-up payment as it would also have failed to make a transfer payment in the correct amount.

12.7

Where the member has ceased to be a member of the receiving arrangement or where the trustees are not able to make a top-up payment because the receiving arrangement will not accept it, in the absence of an agreement between the parties the court might consider making an order for the payment of compensation directly to the member.[1] Another option is for the top-up to be retained by the trustees of the transferring scheme until the member provides details of another arrangement which is willing to accept the payment.

1 *Lloyds 2* at [237]. Query whether such payments would need to comply with the conditions for compromising equality claims pursuant to s 147(3) of the Equality Act 2010, which include the receipt of independent advice by the member on the effect of the compromise.

12.8

By contrast, where the mistaken underpayment arose in the context of a mirror-image bulk transfer, the trustees are discharged from any liability to make good those underpayments, as the transfer credits provided as part of the bulk transfer are provided to the members instead of the transferring scheme providing short service benefits to them, pursuant to s 73(2) of PSA 1993.[1]

1 *Lloyds 2* at [181].

Non-statutory transfers

12.9

Where the transfer payment was made pursuant to the scheme rules rather than statute, the trustees' duty to compensate members for underpaid transfers will turn on the wording of those rules.

12.10

In *Lloyds 2,*[1] Morgan J held that, where the rule required the trustees to transfer such assets *'as they consider appropriate'*, the general principles relating to challenges to the exercise of a trustee power discussed in *Pitt v Holt*[2] apply. Thus, if the transfer is undervalued, the trustees' decision is voidable only if the decision involved a breach of duty.[3] An aggrieved member may apply to court to set aside the transfer payment on this basis,[4] although there may be cases where the trustees should make the application.[5]

1 *Lloyds 2* at [192].
2 [2013] UKSC 26, [2013] 2 AC 108. See **13.23**.
3 *Lloyds 2* at [193].
4 *Lloyds 2* at [221].
5 *Lloyds 2* at [277].

Relevance of the nature of the transfer

12.11

Lloyds 2 accordingly set up a potentially significant distinction between statutory and non-statutory individual transfers. A mistaken underpayment of a statutory transfer requires the trustees automatically to compensate the member by way of a top-up, whereas the trustees will only be liable to compensate the member in respect of an underpaid non-statutory transfer made pursuant to the exercise of a discretion, where the member (or the trustees) have obtained a court order setting the transfer aside; and the cost of obtaining such an order will often be prohibitive compared to the amount at stake. An added practical difficulty arises because trustees may not know whether past transfers were made pursuant to statutory or non-statutory powers. It has been suggested that trustees may in such circumstances choose to correct non-statutory transfers in the same way as statutory transfers,[1] although that does not sit easily with the requirement in *Lloyds 2* for non-statutory transfers to be formally set aside by a competent tribunal.

1 Section A2 of the PASA GMP Equalisation Working Group's Supplemental Guidance on Transfer Payments (August 2021).

Interest on arrears

12.12

Mirroring his general analysis in *Lloyds 1*,[1] Morgan J in *Lloyds 2*[2] ordered that simple interest should be added to the top-up payments at the rate of one per cent above the base rate.

1 See **11.14**.
2 *Lloyds 2* at [263].

Limitation

12.13

In *Lloyds 2*, Morgan J held that s 21(1)(b) of LA 1980 operated to disapply the statutory limitation period to the right of the member to claim a top-up benefit from the transferring scheme: the trustees' breach of duty fell within s 21(1)(b), as an action to *'recover … trust property'* extended to a case where the order sought by the member is that the trustees make a top-up payment to the receiving arrangement.[1]

1 *Lloyds 2* at [381].

12.14

The judge also held that the breach of duty was committed on the date of the original transfer and was a one-off breach, there being no fresh breach of duty on each day the earlier breach remained unremedied.[1]

1 *Lloyds 2* at [272], [367]–[368].

12.15

See also the discussion in **11.16–11.20** of the judge's approach to limitation in the context of underpaid benefits, much of which is also relevant to transfers.

Forfeiture of benefits

12.16

In *Lloyds 2*, Morgan J considered whether the forfeiture provisions in the schemes in issue applied to transferring members' top-up rights, where the transfers had taken place under the cash equivalent transfer legislation. The relevant terms of the forfeiture provisions are set out in **11.24**, in respect of which the judge held as follows:[1]

(a) whilst the language of the forfeiture provisions should be given their ordinary meaning, the judge was not inclined to give the wording a wide or expansive meaning unless ordinary principles of construction justified that course;

(b) the top-up right did not come within a forfeiture provision which applied to *'any instalment of pension or other benefit to which the member is entitled under the scheme'*, as the top-up was neither payable by instalments nor a benefit to which the member was entitled under the scheme;

(c) the top-up right did not come within a forfeiture provision which applied to *'any sum which may have become due to a member or other person entitled to benefit under the Rules'*, as the payment was not due to the member because the trustee was not obliged to pay that sum to the member and the member was not entitled to receive it from the trustee, and the receiving arrangement was not a *'person entitled to benefit under the rules'*;

(d) the top-up right did not come within a forfeiture provision which applied to *'any pension or benefit or any instalment remains unpaid to and unclaimed by the person to whom it is payable'* because the receiving arrangement did not have a right to claim the payment, and it cannot have been intended that the right of the transferring member would be lost because it was not claimed by the receiving arrangement which did not have a right to claim it;

(e) the top-up right did not come within a forfeiture provision which applied to *'benefits under the scheme'* as the right to a cash equivalent was to be regarded as a statutory right to leave the scheme and to acquire benefits under a different arrangement.

1 *Lloyds 2* at [346]–[356].

12.17

Having decided that none of the forfeiture provisions in issue applied to the top-up rights, the judge said that he did not need to answer the question of whether the operation of those provisions in respect of statutory cash equivalent transfers would have been prohibited by s 129(1) of PSA 1993, which provides that any provision of a scheme is overridden to the extent that it conflicts with the transfer legislation.[1] The judge nevertheless expressed a provisional view that forfeiture provisions could apply to the top-up rights, notwithstanding that those provisions are an exception to s 92(1) of PSA 1993[2] which prohibited the forfeiture of *'an entitlement to a pension under an occupational pension scheme or a right to a future pension under such a scheme'*, as he doubted that the right of a transferring member to require the trustees to make a top-up payment to the receiving arrangement constituted such an entitlement or right.[3]

1 *Lloyds 2* at [345].
2 See **11.22** above.
3 *Lloyds 2* at [342].

Express discharges

12.18

In *Lloyds 2,* Morgan J considered a number of discharge forms signed by members on the transfer-out of their benefits, to determine whether the trustees were thereby absolved from their liability to top up the transferring members' benefits under the receiving arrangements.[1]

1 *Lloyds 2* at [296]–[327].

12.19

Whilst the effect of an express discharge will depend on its precise wording, the following points of general application arose from the judge's analysis:

(a) a general release of liability is to be construed by applying ordinary principles of contractual interpretation, which require the court to have regard to the background to the contract and the context in which the provision was entered into; although there was no rule of law that a general release could not extend to rights and claims of which the employee was unaware and could not have been aware, that type of situation established a 'cautionary principle' which should inform the approach of the court: there may be circumstances in which a general release should not be given its full literal meaning;[1]

(b) a form which discharges the trustees from liability *'to provide benefits'* does not cover the trustees' top-up liability;[2]

(c) where the release takes effect *'where the transfer is of the whole of my entitlement under the Scheme'* such a transfer has not occurred where the trustees have not included a sum which they were obliged to include.[3]

1 *Lloyds 2* at [302], applying the principles in *BCCI v Ali* [2001] UKHL 8, [2002] 1 AC 251.
2 *Lloyds 2* at [304].
3 *Lloyds 2* at [306].

Recovery of overpaid transfers

12.20

Provided that the transfer of the assets was effected in accordance with the requisite formal requirements,[1] a mistaken exercise of the transfer power will not affect the receiving arrangement's legal title to the assets, although if the mistake constitutes a breach of trust, such a transfer will not vest the beneficial interest in the administrators of the receiving arrangement.[2]

1 For example, a transfer of real property must be recorded in writing: s 2(1) of the Law of Property (Miscellaneous Provisions) Act 1989.
2 *Independent Trustee Services Ltd v GP Noble Trustees Ltd* [2012] EWCA Civ 195, [2013] Ch 91 at [106] per Lloyd LJ, approved by Lord Mance JSC in *Akers v Samba Financial Group* [2017] UKSC 6, [2017] AC 424 at [52]. See also *Allan v Rea Brothers Trustees Ltd* [2002] Pens LR 169.

12.21

A transferee could nevertheless in such circumstances defeat any prior beneficial claim by claiming to be a bona fide purchaser for value without notice of the breach. However, that defence will not be available where the transfer is set aside, which may occur where, for example, the transfer was vitiated because of a failure by the transferring scheme trustees to give proper consideration to the current value of the fund.[1] In such a case, the appropriate remedy would be to require the transfer amount to be recalculated on the correct basis and for the payment of the sum found to be due to whichever arrangement has lost out. If the transfer is unravelled in this way, it is treated as if it had never had any legal effect, so that the transferee cannot rely on the bona fide purchaser defence to resist a claim for the repayment of the assets to the transferring scheme.[2]

1 As occurred in *Stannard v Fisons Pension Trust Ltd* [1991] Pens LR 225.
2 *Independent Trustee Services Ltd v GP Noble Trustees Ltd* [2013] Ch 91 at [113]. Query whether a bona fide purchaser defence would in any event be available for the receiving administrators of a DC scheme, where the adjustment to member benefits would be relatively easy and would not cause any loss to the receiving arrangement.

Delays in making transfer payments

12.22

In *Tenconi v James Hay Partnership*,[1] a member complained to the Pensions Ombudsman that a delay in the transfer of his personal pension assets to another provider until August 2016 had caused him to lose the opportunity to invest in stocks shortly before the Brexit referendum result in June 2016. The Ombudsman found that the respondent administrator had unduly delayed in making the funds available, amounting to maladministration and that, had the administrator acted sooner, the money might have been available by 23 June (the day of the referendum) or by 30 June. However, the Ombudsman found that any lost opportunity to invest before or after the referendum result had not been within the administrator's reasonable contemplation, and any loss was not measurable, because there could be no certainty regarding which shares the member could or would have bought, what their prices would have been, and what effect the referendum result would have had on them.

1 [2019] Pens LR 19.

12.23

The member's appeal was allowed by Deputy Judge Hollander QC, on the grounds that the Ombudsman had erred in law in applying the tests for foreseeability and measurability of loss. The deputy judge applied ordinary negligence principles of quantum, confirming that the question of quantification of damages was separate to that of recoverability. On the issue of foreseeability, it was possible that any transfer request might be for the purposes of investment with a new provider. If there was a delay, it was foreseeable that the delay could cause loss where there might be spikes in the market. The suggestion that loss had not been in the administrator's contemplation could not be sustained. On measurability, the deputy judge held that the Ombudsman had set too high a test in requiring evidence of the shares the member had intended to purchase following the Brexit vote. It was enough to show on the balance of probabilities that the money would have been invested with the new provider, and the Ombudsman would be able to make findings of fact based on the member's past portfolio and investment patterns. The matter was remitted back to the Ombudsman for reconsideration in light of the court's findings.

12.24

The Ombudsman subsequently determined that, had there been no maladministration, the member would have been likely, on the balance of probabilities, to have wholly invested his pension funds in the stock market at the time and, in doing so, would have gained a subsequent financial profit. As a result, the administrator was directed to compensate for the full investment loss.[1]

1 *Mr T* (CAS-38354-V5L8, 12 August 2020).

Tax consequences of incorrect transfers

12.25

These are dealt with at **17.65–17.70**.

Practice point: the steps the trustees will be expected to take compensate underpaid transfers

12.26

In *Lloyds 2,* Morgan J was asked to determine whether trustees were under an obligation to take active steps to compensate members who had transferred out of the scheme, or whether the trustees could wait until a request had been made by the receiving arrangement or by the transferred-out member.

12.27

The judge held that the trustees would be expected to be proactive in dealing with the issue. Because the past inadequate transfer payment constituted a breach of fiduciary duty, and a court would, on an application for directions by the trustees, be inclined to direct them that they should deal with the problem rather than do nothing, it was open to the trustees to decide for themselves to take that approach without the need for directions.[1] However, the judge would not go into detail about what steps the trustees would be expected to take, saying only the following:

> '… all that I can usefully say is that the Trustee does need to be proactive in that it must consider the rights and obligations which I have identified, the remedies available to members and the absence of a time bar and then determine what to do.'[2]

In determining what to do, the trustees must act in accordance with its duty to administer the scheme with reasonable care and skill,[3] bearing in mind that the underpayment constitutes a breach of fiduciary duty.

1 *Lloyds 2* at [272]–[274].
2 *Lloyds 2* at [276].
3 See *Lewin on Trusts* (20th edn, Sweet & Maxwell, 2020) (*Lewin*), para 34-001.

12.28

Although each case will turn on its own facts, all trustees faced with this situation should, as a minimum, consider the following:

(a) just as the first duty of a trustee on being appointed is to ascertain the trusts so that they know the scope of their fiduciary obligations,[1] the same duty logically arises where the trustees discover that they have misapprehended the scope of the trust and their fiduciary obligations;

(b) trustees who have been made aware that they have underpaid benefits should therefore take reasonable steps to identify the arrangements to which the members had transferred their benefits[2] and the amount of the compensation to be paid to the receiving arrangement in respect of each member;

(c) where the calculation of the required compensation is hampered by the lack of reliable data, the trustees should consider putting in place sensible protocols for assessing compensation, such as making reasonable actuarial assumptions where financial information is unavailable;

(d) trustees should then take reasonable steps to make good the underpayments.

1 *Lewin*, para 13-036.
2 This duty was conceded by the employers in *Lloyds 2*: see [269].

12.29

What are such reasonable steps to make good the underpaid transfers will depend on the circumstances of each scheme, and it will generally be open to the trustees to undertake a cost-benefit analysis, by reference to such factors as:

(a) the complexity of the scheme's history – in terms of mergers and restructurings – which may make the potentially affected persons difficult to assess;

(b) the availability of data in order to locate the affected persons and to calculate the compensation;

(c) the relative cost of locating the affected persons and making good the underpayments;

(d) the effect of that cost on the solvency of the scheme and the employer covenant; and

(e) whether some or all of those costs are or can be covered by existing or future insurance: where the scheme in question is at or near the point of winding-up, the trustees will be particularly interested in obtaining run-off insurance including cover for any residual liabilities caused by the underpayments.

However, absent special circumstances, trustees should not prioritise completion of the compensation exercise in respect of existing members of the scheme over the compensation of transferred-out members.

12.30

The trustees should also take and act on legal advice in cases of doubt, and ensure that there is a good paper trail evidencing the factors which were taken into account when making their decisions.

12.31

Further useful guidance can be found in section A3 of the PASA GMP Equalisation Working Group's Supplemental Guidance on Transfer Payments (August 2021).

13 Decision Errors

13.1

The methods of correction discussed in earlier chapters relate specifically to the documentation produced following the exercise of powers by the trustees and/or employers of the pension scheme. This chapter focuses on the ways in which mistakes in the exercise of the powers themselves can be corrected.

13.2

Where those mistakes are formalised in pension scheme documents, the methods discussed in this chapter should be considered alongside those discussed in earlier chapters, in particular the methods of setting aside documents discussed in **Chapter 7**. However, not all decision errors are implemented in that way: for example, the trustees and/or the employer may wrongly decide that a member does not qualify for enhanced benefits payable on early retirement through ill-health or redundancy, or they may refuse to pay death benefits to a person because it was wrongly concluded that they were not a dependant of the member. It is with these types of errors that this chapter is primarily concerned.

13.3

Typically, this type of error will arise in the context of a challenge by the disappointed person who has been denied benefits or who has had their benefits reduced; but before this is considered, there is the question of the extent to which the trustees or employer can themselves correct a decision error.

Correction by the trustees/employer

13.4

Suppose the trustees or the employer refuse to grant an ill-health pension to a member because they do not consider that the qualifying definition of incapacity is satisfied, but subsequent medical evidence causes them to change their mind. In the absence of an express provision enabling the application for the pension to be reconsidered, can the trustees or employer re-exercise the power to grant the pension, or must the original exercise first be set aside by the court or the Pensions Ombudsman?

13.5

Timing is an important consideration here. An 'in principle' decision will not preclude it being reconsidered, if further relevant evidence comes to light before the decision is acted upon.[1] However, once the decision is made and the power has been definitively exercised, the subsequent evidence will at best render the decision voidable,[2] which will require it to be set aside so as to allow the discretion to be exercised afresh.[3]

1 See *Re Y Trust* (2011) 14 ITELR 687.
2 See **13.24** and **13.33**.
3 In *Mr J Hawkins, Mr S Hawkins and Mr M Hawkins* (PO-2753,3081,3082, 31 March 2012), the Pensions Ombudsman refused to allow a life office to recover a distribution of death benefits on the grounds of mistake because the decision to distribute had not been set aside.

13.6

In practical terms, the exercise of the power in question is likely to be regarded as definitive at the time when the decision is formally minuted,[1] although if the provision containing the power included some formal requirement, such as notification to the member, compliance with that formality will probably be held to be the material time.[2]

1 See *Entrust Pension Ltd v Prospect Hospice Ltd (No 2)* [2012] EWHC 3640 (Ch), [2013] Pens LR 73 at [35] per Henderson J.
2 Cf. *Briggs v Gleeds (Head Office)* [2014] EWHC 1178 (Ch), [2015] Ch 212 at [77] per Newey J.

Correction following a challenge by the member

13.7

There are two types of decision error involved in the exercise of a pension scheme power which the member may seek to challenge: an error involving a judgment as to a state of facts; and an error in the exercise of a discretion vested by the power.

Judgment as to a state of facts

13.8

The ability to exercise a pension scheme power is often dependent upon the existence of a given state of facts, such as whether an applicant for an ill-health pension satisfies the test of incapacity, or whether an applicant for a death benefit qualifies as a dependant. Indeed, this fact may be the only relevant question for the exercise of the power if, once it is established in favour of the applicant, the power must be exercised in their favour. Even where the power includes a residual discretion whether to exercise it, the requirement to form a judgment as to whether a person has satisfied the factual requirements for the grant of a pension is not the same as the exercise of that discretion,[1] although (as will be seen) there are similarities to the legal approaches to those issues.

1 See *Trustees of the Saffil Pension Scheme v Curzon* [2005] EWHC 293 (Ch), [2005] Pens LR 267 at [46] per Park J.

The trustees

13.9

The leading case on the trustees' duties when forming a judgment on a state of facts is *Harris v Lord Shuttleworth*,[1] in which the trustees of a scheme were required to determine whether the member had retired '*by reason of incapacity*' in order to qualify for an ill-health pension. Glidewell LJ held that the relevant principles are as follows:

(a) the trustees must ask themselves the correct questions;

(b) they must direct themselves correctly in law, in particular they must adopt a correct construction of the scheme rules;

(c) they must not arrive at a perverse decision, ie a decision at which no reasonable body of trustees could arrive; and

(d) they must take into account only relevant factors.

1 [1994] ICR 991, 999.

13.10

A judgment as to a state of facts which is reached in compliance with these duties cannot be impugned by the court or the Pensions Ombudsman, even if the tribunal would have come to a different decision had the decision rested with it: a wide measure of discretion is given to the trustees, in recognition of the fact that the scheme has vested that decision in them.[1]

1 *Dundee General Hospitals Board of Management v Walker* [1952] 1 All ER 896, 904–905 per Lord Reid.

13.11

If the judgment falls foul of one or more of those principles, the appropriate remedy is usually for the decision to be set aside and the matter remitted to the trustees for reconsideration.[1] However, where the decision on a question of fact is overturned on the basis of perversity and there is only one rational decision to be made on the evidence, the court will substitute that decision and, if nothing else need be done, direct the trustees to pay the benefit on the basis of that decision.[2]

1 As occurred in *Kerr v British Leyland (Staff) Trustees Ltd* (1986) [2001] WTLR 1071.
2 As occurred in *Trustees of the Saffil Pension Scheme v Curzon* [2005] EWHC 293 (Ch), [2005] Pens LR 267.

13.12

In practice, the most common ground on which the trustees' judgment is challenged is the failure to take account of only relevant factors. Such cases will turn on their own facts, but the following general principles can be stated:

(a) the trustees must make proper enquiries and not simply act on the information to hand;[1]

(b) however, the trustees are not required to continue to seek more information indefinitely[2] and may also not need to undertake enquiries unless and until a claimant puts forward sufficient material to show that there is a case to be investigated;[3]

(c) this duty has clear similarities to the so-called 'rule in *Hastings-Bass*', considered in **Chapter 7**, which applies to the actual exercise of the power by the trustees: in accordance with the original version of that rule, it was held be an additional requirement to establish that the trustees would or might have adjudged the factual issue differently had they taken the correct matters into account;[4] but it is not clear whether the more stringent test for the application of that rule laid down in *Pitt v Holt*,[5] referred to at **13.23**, will now be applied.[6]

In a recent case concerning the payment of a death benefit,[7] the Ombudsman said that the decision-maker should seek to identify all potential beneficiaries and then collect sufficient information about their personal and financial circumstances to put itself in a position to make a decision about who to pay the benefit to. The required level of enquiry may vary depending on the facts, and in more complicated cases, a higher level of enquiry may be appropriate. The duty to identify all potential beneficiaries was not absolute, although due care and skill should be taken in attempts to do so.

1 *Wild v Smith* [1996] Pens LR 275 at [26] per Carnwath J.
2 Hence it is unduly stringent to require *all* relevant factors to be taken into account, as the cost and delays involved in investigating every possible consideration would be inordinate: the duty is best regarded as part of the perversity test, so that the trustees would be in breach of duty only if a particular factor is so significant that a failure to take it into account would be irrational: *Lewin on Trusts* (20th edn, Sweet & Maxwell, 2020) (*Lewin*), para 29-042.
3 *ALCOA of Australia Retirement Plan Pty Ltd v Frost* (2012) 36 VR 618 at [60] per Nettle JA.
4 In *Kerr v British Leyland (Staff) Trustees Ltd* [2001] WTLR 1071, it was held that, for the challenge to succeed, it was only necessary to establish that the trustees might have acted differently. In *Sieff v Fox* [2005] EWHC 1312 (Ch), [2005] 1 WLR 3811, Lloyd LJ said (at [77]) that this only applied to cases where the trustees had no residual discretion to exercise. Although that case concerned the rule in *Hastings-Bass*, and there seems no reason in principle why that distinction should be relevant to a judgment on a state of facts: see *Lewin*, para 29-024 n 86.
5 [2013] UKSC 26, [2013] 2 AC 108.
6 In *Pitt v Holt*, Lord Walker of Gestingthorpe said (at [75]) that the court would be much more ready to intervene in the exercise of a judgment on an issue of fact than in the defective exercise of a discretion.
7 *Miss CS* (PO-21507, 27 July 2021) at [32] and [43].

The employer

13.13

As will be seen, the different interests of trustees and employers mean that they are not subject to the same duties in the exercise of dispositive powers under the scheme. However, that is not the case with regard to the establishment of a state of facts, which is an objective exercise of judgment that should not turn on differences in the interests to which the persons responsible for the judgment are entitled to have regard.

13.14

An early leading case involving an employer was *Mihlenstedt v Barclays Bank International Ltd*,[1] which concerned a decision not to grant an ill-health pension pursuant to a scheme rule which provided that such a pension would only be permitted where the employer was of the opinion that the member satisfied the prescribed test for incapacity. This gave rise to three issues: whether an obligation to pay the pension arose if the test was satisfied; whether the employer was under a duty to consider the application for a pension; and whether the employer had correctly determined that the test had not been satisfied. Having held that the provision did require the pension to be paid if the test was satisfied, Nourse LJ went on to distinguish the source of the trustees' and employer's duties in the context of the second issue, holding that the employer's obligation to consider the application for a pension arose, not as a matter of trust, but pursuant to its obligations to the member under the contract of employment.[2] As to the third issue, the judge did not rely on the trust/contract distinction when holding that the employer's decision that the member was ineligible for the pension could not be impugned by the court if the employer had actually or effectively asked itself the correct questions and if there was material before it on which it could properly answer them in the negative.[3]

1 [1989] Pens LR 91.
2 [1989] Pens LR 91 at [14]–[15]. See also per Nicholls LJ at [77]–[78].
3 [1989] Pens LR 91 at [22]: indeed, the judge had earlier (at [18]) supported his reliance on the employment contract by analogy with the case of trustees who are required by the terms of their trust to form an opinion, for example, as to the value of a particular asset for the purpose of a general division of the trust assets between the beneficiaries.

13.15

This decision was subsequently applied by Sir Nicholas Browne-Wilkinson V-C in the seminal case of *Imperial Group Pension Trust Ltd v Imperial Tobacco Ltd*,[1] in holding that the exercise of a pension scheme power vested in the employer was subject to the implied duty of mutual trust and confidence imposed on the employer by the contract of employment. In addition, the obligation of the employer to exercise its judgment as to a state of facts has been said additionally to require it to act in accordance with that duty, which requires the employer's decision not to be perverse or irrational.[2]

1 [1991] 1 WLR 589, discussed at **13.25**.
2 *Wilde v British Broadcasting Corp* [2003] EWHC 1436 (Ch), [2003] OPLR 265 at [40] per Etherton J.

13.16

These cases establish that the first three grounds for challenging a factual judgment identified at **13.9** apply irrespective of whether the employer or the trustees are the judge.[1] Whilst there is no pension scheme authority on whether a challenge can also be based on a failure by the employer to take account of only relevant factors, it is likely that any future consideration of this issue will be influenced by the Supreme Court's decision in *Braganza v BP Shipping Ltd*.[2] That case concerned a term in an employment contract which provided that a death in service benefit would not be payable if, in the opinion of the employer, the death resulted from suicide: the court was required to identify the test to be applied in deciding whether the employer was entitled to come to that conclusion. The Supreme Court held that a term would normally be implied that the power should be exercised not only in good faith but also without being arbitrary, capricious, or irrational in the public law sense. Thus, the decision could be impugned either as a matter of substance, where it was one that no reasonable decision-maker could have reached, or as a matter of process, where the decision-maker had failed to exclude extraneous considerations or to take account of all obviously relevant ones.

1 See *Lewin*, para 29-029.
2 [2015] UKSC 17, [2015] 1 WLR 1661.

Exercise of the power

13.17

Because of the different interests to which they are entitled to have regard when exercising pension scheme powers, different standards apply to trustees and employers.[1]

1 The following analysis assumes that there are no express constraints on the exercise of the powers imposed by the scheme's governing provisions. In this respect, pension scheme powers which provide a role for both the trustees and the employer are generally regarded as to be exercised jointly by them, even where (for example), the power is expressed to be vested in the trustees with the consent of the employer. However, where the exercise of a trustee power in a private trust is subject to the consent of another person, such as a protector, there is an ongoing and yet unresolved debate as to whether that person is exercising an independent discretion or has merely a supervisory role: see *PTNZ v AS* [2020] EWHC 3114 (Ch), [2020] WTLR 1423; *Re X Trusts* [2021] SC (Bda) 72 Civ; *Re Piedmont and Riviera Trusts* [2021] JRC 248.

The trustees[1]

13.18

In exercising pensions powers, the primary duty of the trustees is to promote the purpose for which the scheme was created, which will generally be securing the benefits provided by the scheme.[2] In this respect, the trustees should be aware that their role is primarily to manage and administer the scheme, and not (for example) to take an active role in designing or altering the benefit structure where the scheme was in deficit.[3]

1 For an exhaustive analysis of this issue, from both a pensions and non-pensions perspective, see David Pollard, *Pensions, Contracts and Trusts: Legal Issues on Decision Making* (Bloomsbury Professional, 2020).
2 *Merchant Navy Ratings Pension Fund Trustees Ltd v Stena Line Ltd* [2015] EWHC 448 (Ch), [2015] Pens LR 239 at [228] and [233] per Asplin J.
3 *British Airways plc v Airways Pension Scheme Trustee Ltd* [2018] EWCA Civ 1533, [2018] Pens LR 506. See **7.35**.

13.19

Pension scheme trustees are also subject to a number of specific statutory duties, most notably with regard to their investment powers.[1]

1 See ss 33—36 of PA 1995. See also the general duty to act with reasonable skill and care imposed by s 1(1) of the Trustee Act 2000, which (by s 36(2)) applies to pension scheme trustees to a limited extent.

13.20

Provided that:

(a) due regard is given to those duties and to the purpose of the scheme and of the power which is being exercised;

(b) the trustees act rationally and in good faith; and

(c) the trustees take account of only relevant factors;

the trustees' exercise of the power will not be open to challenge.[1] For example, in deciding whether to exercise dispositive powers, pension scheme trustees do not owe a duty to act impartially between members, as the essence of such powers is that they can be used to favour some members over others.[2]

1 *Edge v The Pensions Ombudsman* [2000] Ch 602 at 627 per Chadwick LJ. See also *Entrust Pension Ltd v Prospect Hospice Ltd* [2012] EWHC 1666 (Ch), [2012] Pens LR 341 at [74] per Henderson J.
2 *Edge v The Pensions Ombudsman* [2000] Ch 602 at 627 per Chadwick LJ.

13.21

The duty to act rationally does not equate to a requirement to act reasonably, and has been described as '*an absence of arbitrariness, of capriciousness or of reasoning so outrageous in its defiance of logic as to be perverse*'.[1] Irrationality will be difficult to prove, particularly where the challenge is to an exercise of discretion as opposed to a factual judgment.[2]

1 *Hayes v Willoughby* [2013] UKSC 17, [2013] 1 WLR 935 at [14] per Lord Sumption (discussing rationality in the context of a defence to the tort of harassment provided by s 1(3)(a) of the Protection from Harassment Act 1997). See also *Stephens v Michelin Pensions Trust Ltd* [2006] EWHC 1640 (Ch) at [31] per Lindsay J: '*To succeed the appellant would have had to have shown that the trustees' decision … was so misguided an exercise of the absolute discretion that no trustees properly advising themselves of all the relevant circumstances could have reasonably so concluded.*'
2 *Pitt v Holt* [2013] UKSC 26, [2013] 2 AC 108 at [75] per Lord Walker of Gestingthorpe. See also *Bramston v Haut* [2012] EWCA Civ 1637, [2013] 1 WLR 1720 at [71] per Kitchen LJ.

13.22

The duty to take account of only relevant factors requires the trustees to inform themselves, before making a decision, of matters which are relevant to the decision, and may require them to take advice from appropriate experts, such as lawyers or actuaries.[1] Subject to this general requirement, the relevance of any particular factor will depend upon the nature of the power being exercised, but provided that it has been taken into account, the weight to be given to that factor is a matter for the trustees.[2]

1 *Scott v National Trust for Places of Historic Interest or Natural Beauty* [1998] 2 All ER 705, 717 per Robert Walker J. The trustees cannot, however, delegate their decision to the expert: as Robert Walker J said in that case: '*it is … for advisers to advise and for trustees to decide.*'
2 *Sampson v Hodgson* [2008] All ER (D) 395 (Apr) at [24] per Deputy Judge Ivory QC.

13.23

The ability to challenge the trustees' exercise of a power on this ground is likely to be further constrained by the Supreme Court's decision in *Pitt v Holt*[1] that the inadequate deliberation by the trustees must be sufficiently serious as to amount to a breach of fiduciary duty, which will not be established where the trustees conscientiously obtain and follow, in making a decision which is within the scope of their powers, apparently competent professional advice which turns out to be wrong.[2] There is surprisingly little authority on the application of *Pitt v Holt* in this particular context;[3] and if it does apply, equitable rescission (discussed at **7.12–7.31**) may be a more attractive remedy, as that does not require a breach of duty to be established.

1 [2013] 2 AC 108.
2 [2013] 2 AC 108 at [73] and [80] per Lord Walker of Gestingthorpe. The old requirement that the failure on the part of the trustees would or might have led to a different result has been replaced by a more flexible approach, designed to achieve the best practical solution in the particular circumstances: [2013] 2 AC 108 at [92].
3 Apart from Morgan J In *British Airways plc v Airways Pension Scheme Trustee Ltd* [2017] EWHC 1191 (Ch), [2017] Pens LR 271 at [482]–[493], whose decision was overturned on appeal without reference to this point.

13.24

Breach of this duty renders the exercise of the power voidable[1] and will generally cause the court to direct the trustees to reconsider the exercise of discretion.

1 See *Pitt v Holt* [2013] UKSC 26, [2013] 2 AC 108 at [93], in the context of the rule in *Hastings-Bass*. The failure to ask the right question would generally render the decision voidable if it involved a breach of duty: *Lloyds Banking Group Pensions Trustees Ltd v Lloyds Bank plc* [2020] EWHC 3135 (Ch), [2021] Pens LR 295 at [196] per Morgan J. Whilst there is no authority that the failure to act rationally and in good faith renders the exercise of the power voidable rather than void, the editors of *Lewin* (para 29-040) consider that it does; for a contrary view, see Underhill and Hayton, *Law of Trusts and Trustees* (19th edn, Butterworths LexisNexis, 2018) paras 57.35–57.40.

The employer

13.25

In very limited circumstances, powers vested in the employer under a pension scheme are treated as fiduciary in nature, so that the employer will be subject to the same duties as trustees.[1] Usually, however, the employer's exercise of the power is constrained by the so-called '*Imperial* duty', named after the landmark decision in *Imperial Group Pension Trust Ltd v Imperial Tobacco Ltd*[2] which established that the exercise of pension scheme powers by employers is subject to the duty of mutual trust and confidence which is implied in all employment contracts.[3] This duty has been authoritatively stated as requiring the employer not, without reasonable and proper cause, to conduct itself in a manner calculated and likely to destroy or seriously damage the relationship of confidence and trust between employer and employee.[4]

1 One such example is the power to distribute surplus on the winding-up of the scheme: *Mettoy Pension Trustees Ltd v Evans* [1990] 1 WLR 1587.
2 [1991] 1 WLR 589.
3 In *Imperial Group Pension Trust Ltd v Imperial Tobacco Ltd* [1991] 1 WLR 589, 597, Sir Nicholas Browne-Wilkinson V-C described it as '*the implied obligation of good faith*'; subsequently, in *Hillsdown Holdings plc v The Pensions Ombudsman* [1997] 1 All ER 862, 889, Knox J said that this was a convenient shorthand only and did not carry the implication that a failure to observe the implied obligation would amount to bad faith in the pejorative sense in which that expression is often used.
4 *Malik v BCCI* [1998] AC 20, 45 per Lord Steyn.

13.26

The *Imperial* duty operates as a limited constraint on the employer's exercise of pension scheme powers. It is not a fiduciary duty, so that the employer is entitled to take its own interests into account when exercising the power;[1] it does not require the employer to take account of the members' financial interests;[2] and it does not import a requirement on the employer to act reasonably.[3] The duty will not be breached unless the employer's conduct is irrational or perverse to a serious degree.[4]

1 *Imperial Group Pension Trust Ltd v Imperial Tobacco Ltd* [1991] 1 WLR 589, 596.
2 *Crossley v Faithful & Gould Holdings Ltd* [2004] EWCA Civ 293, [2004] ICR 1615 at [44] per Dyson LJ.
3 *Imperial Group Pension Trust Ltd v Imperial Tobacco Ltd* [1991] 1 WLR 589, 597.
4 *Prudential Staff Pensions Ltd v The Prudential Assurance Company Ltd* [2011] EWHC 960 (Ch), [2011] Pens LR 23 at [149] per Newey J.

13.27

In *IBM United Kingdom Holdings Ltd v Dalgleish*[1] an attempt by Warren J to widen the scope of the *Imperial* duty was decisively rejected by the Court of Appeal.[2]

1 [2014] EWHC 980 (Ch), [2014] Pens LR 335.
2 [2017] EWCA Civ 1212, [2018] ICR 1681.

13.28

The case concerned a series of changes by the employer to reduce the cost of its defined benefits (DB) pension schemes. In the course of communicating with members during the first two exercises, the employer indicated that there would be no further plans to change the pension arrangements and that the existing changes were viewed as long-term. A few years later, the employer put forward proposals to close the DB schemes and reduce existing benefits.

13.29

Warren J held that the employer's conduct, through its communications during the earlier exercises, had created 'reasonable expectations' for members in relation to future pension policy, which conflicted with the proposed further changes; the implementation of those proposals was held to constitute a breach of the *Imperial* duty.

13.30

The Court of Appeal allowed the employer's appeal, holding that, whilst the existence of members' expectations was a relevant factor to be taken into account by the employer when making its decision, the Judge was wrong to hold that the members' 'reasonable expectations' had an overriding significance and were to prevail unless there was no other way for the employer to achieve its business aims. The court held that the correct approach was to apply the public law *Wednesbury* test:[1] whether the relevant matters (and no irrelevant matters) had been taken into account; and whether the result was such that no reasonable decision-maker could have reached it. The employer had not breached the *Imperial* duty as it had taken account of member expectations as part of its decision-making process.[2]

1 *Associated Provincial Picture Houses Ltd v Wednesbury Corp* [1948] 1 KB 223.
2 [2018] ICR 1681 at [45]–[46]. The Court of Appeal was particularly influenced by the Supreme Court's decision in *Braganza v BP Shipping Ltd*: [2018] ICR 1681 at [37].

13.31

As well as reiterating the limited nature of the *Imperial* duty, the Court of Appeal in *IBM* confirmed that the duty requires the employer to take into account all the circumstances existing at the date of its decision. It therefore appears that Newey J's comment in *Prudential Staff Pensions Ltd v Prudential Assurance Co Ltd*[1] that the *Imperial* duty does not oblige the employer to have regard to particular matters, is not good law.

1 [2011] EWHC 960 (Ch), [2011] Pens LR 239 at [146]–[147].

13.32

The Court of Appeal in *IBM* also confirmed that the *Imperial* duty applied to constrain the exercise of the power by the principal employer under the scheme, even if the members affected by the decision were employed by a different employer.[1]

1 [2018] ICR 1681 at [232].

13.33

The exercise of a power in breach of the *Imperial* duty renders that exercise voidable.[1]

1 *IBM United Kingdom Holdings Ltd v Dalgleish* [2015] EWHC 389 (Ch), [2015] Pens LR 99 at [262] per Warren J. The judge went on to say that the court could not impose terms on setting aside the exercise of the power: [2015] Pens LR 99 at [294]–[297].

Limitation or exclusion of duties

13.34

Any attempt to include a term in the pension scheme to limit or exclude the duties imposed on trustees and employers in the making of judgments or the exercise of powers is likely to be unsuccessful. For example, a term of the scheme's rules providing that the decision-maker has the '*absolute*' or '*conclusive*' or '*final*' discretion in coming to the decision has been held not to preclude the application of those duties.[1] Moreover, an attempt to exclude the *Imperial* duty was held by the Pensions Ombudsman not to preclude a member from challenging an employer's decision not to consent to an ill-health pension, on the basis that the duty cannot be excluded by a document to which the member was not a party, and such exclusion would enable the employer to contract out of the Ombudsman's jurisdiction.[3]

1 See, for example, *Stephens v Michelin Pensions Trust Ltd* [2006] EWHC 1640 (Ch); *Harris v Lord Shuttleworth* [1994] ICR 991; *Trustees of the Saffil Pension Scheme v Curzon*, [2005] EWHC 293 (Ch), [2005] Pens LR 267.
2 Cf. *Armitage v Nurse* [1998] Ch 241.
3 *Mr B L Poole* (F00088, 16 May 1997) at [16].

The powers of the Pensions Ombudsman

13.35

Most challenges by members to decisions of trustees and employers will be made by way of complaint to the Pensions Ombudsman.

13.36

The Ombudsman's jurisdiction is wide enough to permit the setting aside of the exercise of judgments or powers by trustees or employers on the grounds discussed in this chapter.[1] The Ombudsman has no wider power than the court to set aside decisions on the grounds of unfairness or to substitute his own opinion for that of the decision-maker.[2]

1 Section 151(2) of PSA 1993: see *Wild v Smith* [1996] Pens LR 275 at [23] per Carnwath J.
2 *Edge v Pensions Ombudsman* [2000] Ch 602.

13.37

Moreover, the Ombudsman cannot set aside decisions where that would affect persons who were not parties to the determination. Thus, in *Edge v Pensions Ombudsman*,[1] the Court of Appeal said that a direction by the Ombudsman that the exercise by the trustees of a power to distribute surplus was invalid could not stand, because that would adversely affect the interests of the employers and other members of the scheme who were not parties to the determination.

1 [2000] Ch 602, 636–643 per Chadwick LJ (obiter), followed by Rimer J in *Marsh & McLennan Companies UK Ltd v Pensions Ombudsman* [2001] IRLR 505 and Hart J in *Alexander Forbes Ltd v Halliwell* [2003] EWHC 1685 (Ch), [2003] Pens LR 269 at [24].

Practice points: avoiding decision mistakes

13.38

Although the material considerations will vary according to the circumstances of each case, the following general points may be relevant when advising trustees and employers as to how they should exercise their pension scheme powers.

Advising the trustees

13.39

First, it is necessary to determine the purpose of the scheme and of the power in question. The governing provisions of the scheme may be of assistance here, as they may include an objects clause. Whilst such a clause will be the starting point,[1] it will not necessarily be decisive as, for example, there may have been changes in the organisation of an enterprise, through a process of natural development, making it necessary or expedient for the objects to be restated;[2] and for most powers it is unlikely that the general description of the object of the scheme will be of any practical assistance.[3]

1 *British Airways plc v Airways Pension Scheme Trustee Ltd* [2018] EWCA Civ 1533, [2018] Pens LR 506 at [62] per Patten LJ.
2 *Bank of New Zealand v Bank of New Zealand Officers Provident Association Management Board* [2003] UKPC 58, [2003] OPLR 281 at [21] per Lord Walker of Gestingthorpe.
3 See, further **7.35**.

13.40

Where the exercise of the power involves enquiries, the nature of the power and the circumstances of the case must be considered in order to assess what investigations must take place. This will often involve taking expert advice, such as medical advice in the case of ill-health benefits and actuarial advice in the case of a distribution of surplus. The decision then taken must logically follow from the information and expert advice.

13.41

Where the power in question is capable of being exercised regularly, trustees are entitled to adopt a general policy as to its future exercise, but they should be careful not to fetter its future exercise or to exercise it pre-emptively: the trustees should therefore continue to keep an open mind when occasions for exercise of the discretion arise, and they should not seek to bind themselves to exercise the discretion in a particular way in the future.[1]

1 *Entrust Pension Ltd v Prospect Hospice Ltd (No.2)* [2013] EWHC 3640 (Ch), [2013] Pens LR 73 at [36]–[37] per Henderson J.

13.42

The reasons for the exercise of the discretion should be clearly recorded in a formal document, such as the minute of the trustees' meeting at which the decision is made. Care should be taken to avoid unduly formulaic wording (such as 'the trustees took into account all relevant and no irrelevant factors') and the trustees should be prepared to provide those reasons to the person in respect of whom the decision was made.[1]

1 Whilst the common law position is that trustees are not required explain the reasons for their exercise of a pension scheme power (*Wilson v Law Debenture Trust Corp plc* [1995] 2 All ER 337), the Pensions Ombudsman has regularly held that a failure to give reasons constitutes maladministration: for example, *Mr C Allen* (L00370, 25 April 2002). Members may also be able to obtain the relevant minutes by making a subject access request under data protection legislation.

13.43

If the exercise of the power is particularly momentous, the trustees may consider applying to court for approval, under the principle identified by Hart J in *Public Trustee v Cooper*.[1] Approval will be given where the court is satisfied, after proper consideration of the evidence, that the trustees had in fact formed the opinion that they should act in the particular way relevant to that case; that the opinion of the trustees was one which a reasonable body of trustees properly instructed as to the meaning of the relevant clause could properly have arrived at; and that the opinion was not vitiated by any conflict of interest under which any of the trustees was labouring. This procedure is intended to be quick and accessible, and does not usually give rise to a conflict of facts, as the court is being asked to decide whether the trustees have presented sufficient evidence to permit approval to be given.[2]

1 [2001] WTLR 901, 922-923.
2 *Cotton v Brundenell-Bruce* [2014] EWCA Civ 1312, [2015] WTLR 39 at [78] per Vos LJ.

Advising the employer

13.44

The following points may be relevant when advising employers on how to avoid breaching the *Imperial* duty when exercising pension scheme powers:

(a) As with trustee powers, it is necessary to determine the purpose of the scheme and of the power in question, and to ensure that adequate investigations have been made and expert advice taken and that the decision is consistent with the information and advice obtained.

(b) The employer should consider how best to liaise with the trustees about the exercise of the power. Whilst, in the absence of any express requirement, there is no need formally to consult the trustees, informing them of the relevant factors prior to the exercise of the power will be of assistance, as openness and transparency encourages better decision-making and avoids the possibility of failing to take relevant factors into account.

(c) Where the exercise of the power affects employees who are members of a union, consultation with the union will also be helpful in avoiding future challenges.[1]

(d) The importance of good member communications cannot be overstated. Clear and consistent communication of the reasons for the decision will fortify any defence to a subsequent challenge, and great care must be taken to ensure that the communications process does not give rise to expectations in members which may later be relied upon by them to challenge any subsequent decision which conflicts with those expectations.

1 Certain changes to pension schemes also give rise to statutory consultation duties: see **3.38-3.39**.

14 Procedure

14.1

The correction of pensions mistakes may require legal proceedings to be instituted. Many of the remedies available to correct document errors discussed in this book can only be granted by the court; and members looking for redress following administration errors and decision errors will usually complain to the Pensions Ombudsman. This chapter describes the general procedure of these tribunals and highlights features of particular relevance to pensions errors.

The Pensions Ombudsman

14.2

The office of the Pensions Ombudsman was established in 1990 to investigate complaints and disputes about pension schemes. The Ombudsman's powers are set out in Part X of PSA 1993 and associated regulations.

14.3

An important part of the legislative purpose was to provide a quick, inexpensive and informal means of settling grievances relating to occupational pensions.[1] Unlike many other Ombudsmen, his determinations are legally binding on the parties.[2]

1 *Westminster City Council v Haywood* [1996] 3 WLR 563, 571 per Robert Walker J.
2 See **14.21**.

Jurisdiction in respect of pensions errors

14.4

The Ombudsman is authorised to investigate two broad types of issue: complaints alleging maladministration and disputes of fact or law.[1] Maladministration extends beyond the violation of legal rights, and encompasses the manner in which a decision is reached or a discretion is exercised.[2] However, for current purposes there is no material distinction between complaints or disputes, and what the Ombudsman must decide will not be affected by nomenclature. Accordingly, unless otherwise stated, all further references in this chapter to complaints include disputes.

1 Section 146(1) of PSA 1993.
2 *Arjo Wiggins Ltd v Ralph* [2009] EWHC 3198 (Ch), [2010] Pens LR 11 at [5] per Lewison J.

14.5

Where the Ombudsman makes a determination, he may direct any person responsible for the management of the scheme – i.e. the trustees or the employer or the administrator [1] – to take, or refrain from taking, such steps as he may specify in the determination.[2] This very wide power is qualified in two respects:

(a) the Ombudsman must decide disputes in accordance with established legal principles rather than by reference to what he himself considers to be fair and reasonable; and

(b) the Ombudsman does not have power to make an order that the court could not make or to direct remedial steps to be taken that are not steps that a court could properly have directed to be taken.[3]

1 Section 146(3), (4A) of PSA 1993.

2 Section 151(2) of PSA 1993.

3 *NHS Business Services Authority v Wheeler* [2014] EWHC 2155 (Ch), [2014] Pens LR 639 at [12] per Deputy Judge Gaunt QC, referring to the authorities collected in Lewison J's judgment in *Arjo Wiggins v Ralph* [2010] Pens LR 11 at [13]–[15]. See also *Wakelin v Read* [2000] Pens LR 319.

14.6

The Ombudsman can, however, fashion a suitable remedy for the case before him, even if the court would not have done so in that situation. Thus, in *Henderson v Stephenson Harwood*,[1] Park J endorsed a direction by the Ombudsman that required the member to be admitted to membership of a scheme in accordance with a contractual entitlement, even if a court in the same situation would have awarded damages instead.

1 [2005] EWHC 24 (Ch), [2005] Pens LR 209.

14.7

Provision for who can make a complaint, and who can be the subject matter of a complaint, is made in s 146 of PSA 1993. As regards administration errors and decision errors, a member can bring a complaint against the trustees or the employer; and if the administration error was caused by the scheme administrator, the member may also bring a complaint against them.[1] The Ombudsman accordingly may:

(a) correct underpayments by directing the trustees or administrator to provide the correct amount and to compensate the member for unpaid arrears, plus interest;[2]

(b) determine whether members can prevent the trustees from seeking the repayment of some or all of any overpayment of benefit;[3] and

(c) correct decision errors by directing that the exercise of judgments or powers by trustees or the employer be set aside.[4]

1 Regulation 2(1) of the Personal and Occupational Pension Schemes (Pensions Ombudsman) Regulations 1996 (SI 1996/2475); s 146(4A) of PSA 1993. No dispute of fact or law can be raised against an administrator.

2 See **Chapter 11**.

3 See **Chapter 10**.

4 See **Chapter 13**.

14.8

By contrast, the Ombudsman cannot provide the employer or trustees with a sufficiently comprehensive remedy to correct document errors. This is not because the Ombudsman is restricted in the remedies he can grant: as stated above, the Ombudsman can grant the same relief as the court, which can as a matter of principle extend to equitable remedies such as rectification.[1] The problem is that the Ombudsman is not entitled to investigate a complaint where a determination would affect persons who were not parties to the investigation and who did not have an opportunity to make representations on the matter; and the Ombudsman has no power to join any of the members as respondents.[2] For example, in a case where a member complained about an agreement involving the employer's overseas parent company which could not be made a party to the complaint, it was held that the Ombudsman was not entitled to investigate the complaint as, if it was successful, it would override the contractual rights of a non-party.[3] As the correction of a document error would affect other members of the scheme who were not parties, the Ombudsman will accordingly not investigate a complaint raising the correction of such an error.[4]

1 The relief granted in *Henderson v Stephenson Harwood* [2005] Pens LR 209 (referred to in **14.6**) was equivalent to an order for specific performance: see [46] per Park J. Although it should be noted that when he was Pensions Ombudsman, Dr Julian Farrand – who was no shrinking violet when it came to testing the boundaries of his jurisdiction – disclaimed the power to rectify scheme documents: *Peter Hancock* (J000351, 23 May 2000) at [14].
2 *Edge v Pensions Ombudsman* [2000] Ch 602; *Marsh & McLennan Companies UK Ltd v Pensions Ombudsman* [2001] IRLR 505; *Alexander Forbes Ltd v Halliwell* [2003] EWHC 1685 (Ch), [2003] Pens LR 269 at [24] per Hart J.
3 *Pensions Ombudsman v EMC Europe Ltd* [2012] EWHC 3508 (Ch), [2013] ICR 567.
4 See, for example, *Mr David Pusinelli* (PO-2591, 28 November 2014) at [59]. Whilst the Ombudsman would have had the power to make representation orders pursuant to s 54 of the Child Support, Pensions and Social Security Act 2000, that section was never brought into force, and was repealed by s 276(1) of PA 2004.

14.9

The remainder of this section will therefore focus on complaints brought by members against trustees and employers.

Limits to the Ombudsman's power to investigate

14.10

The Ombudsman cannot investigate a matter that is the subject of ongoing court or employment tribunal proceedings begun before the complaint was made;[1] if such proceedings are instituted after the complaint was made, the court has the power to stay those proceedings.[2]

1 Section 146(6)(a) of PSA 1993. In *Pell Frischmann Consultants Ltd v Prabhu* [2013] EWHC 2203 (Ch), [2014] ICR 153, the court rejected an attempt by a member to strike out proceedings commenced by an employer before the conclusion of the IDRP, which prevented him from making a complaint.
2 Section 148 of PSA 1993.

14.11

The Ombudsman may not investigate a complaint unless the member has gone through the scheme's internal dispute resolution procedure (IDRP), unless the Ombudsman is satisfied that there is no real prospect of a final determination under that procedure being received within a reasonable period under the scheme, or he decides that it is reasonable for him to investigate and determine the complaint.[1]

1 Regulation 3 of the Personal and Occupational Pension Schemes (Pensions Ombudsman) Regulations 1996 (SI 1996/2475). There is no need to go through the IDRP where the dispute is already the subject of court proceedings or an Ombudsman investigation: s 50(3)(c), (9) of PA 1995.

14.12

The time periods within which the complaint must be brought are as follows:[1]

(a) within three years of the act or omission which is the subject of the complaint;

(b) where the member was not aware of the act or omission within that period, within three years from the earliest date the member knew or ought reasonably to have known of the occurrence of the act or omission; or

(c) outside of those periods, where the Ombudsman considers that it was not reasonable for the complaint to be made in time.

1 Regulation 5 of the Personal and Occupational Pension Schemes (Pensions Ombudsman) Regulations 1996 (SI 1996/2475).

14.13

The Ombudsman is also required to apply any limitation defences which would have been available to the respondent had the matter been raised in court proceedings.[1]

1 *Arjo Wiggins Ltd v Ralph* [2009] EWHC 3198 (Ch), [2010] Pens LR 11.

Investigation and determination process

14.14

The procedure for investigating complaints is set out in the Personal and Occupational Pension Schemes (Pensions Ombudsman) (Procedure) Rules 1995[1] (the Procedure Rules). The process has been described as a mixture of the inquisitorial and the adversarial,[2] designed to deliver rapid, unlegalistic justice without cutting too many corners.[3]

1 SI 1995/1053.
2 *Wakelin v Read* [2000] Pens LR 319 at [33] per Mummery LJ. The Ombudsman accordingly does not expect the complainant to bear the burden of proof: *Mr Robert White* (PO-00925, 20 September 2005) at [31]–[32].
3 *Westminster City Council v Haywood* [1996] 3 WLR 563, 572 per Robert Walker J.

14.15

Whilst there is power for the Ombudsman to hold oral hearings,[1] the procedure is normally conducted in writing or online. It begins with the member making a written complaint.[2] There is a standard complaints form for members on the Ombudsman's website, which should be completed and submitted either through the Ombudsman's online system or by email.

1 Rule 10(1) of the Procedure Rules. The Ombudsman should hold an oral hearing where an allegation of dishonesty has been made: *Payne v Pensions Ombudsman* [2003] EWHC 3218 (Ch), [2004] OPLR 185.
2 Section 146(2) of PSA 1993.

14.16

The complaint will first be reviewed by a member of the Ombudsman's case team to determine whether it falls within his jurisdiction and, if so, whether the complaint is suitable for the Ombudsman's early resolution service. If the complaint is deemed suitable for investigation, an adjudicator will initiate an investigation by sending a copy of the complaint, together with any accompanying documents, to the respondent.[1] The respondent must then submit a written reply no later than 21 days after they receive details of the complaint from the Ombudsman,[2] although this period is often extended.[3]

1 Rule 5(2) of the Procedure Rules.
2 Rule 6 of the Procedure Rules.
3 Under r 16(1) of the Procedure Rules.

14.17

Both complainants and respondents must disclose to the Ombudsman all the documents on which they intend to rely.[1] The Ombudsman must receive all evidence which is admissible and relevant, but he may also receive evidence of any fact which appears to him to be relevant, notwithstanding that such evidence would be inadmissible in court proceedings.[2] The Ombudsman also has the same powers as the court in relation to directing the production of documents, but he cannot compel anyone to give any evidence or produce any document which they could not be compelled to give or produce in civil court proceedings.[3]

1 Rule 9(1) of the Procedure Rules.
2 Rule 15(5) of the Procedure Rules.
3 Section 150(3), (4) of PSA 1993.

14.18

The adjudicator or a resolution specialist in the Ombudsman's office may during this process also encourage the parties to seek to resolve the matter informally.

14.19

Whilst the scope of the investigation can be expanded by inviting the member to add to their complaint, and suggesting new matters of defence to the respondents, at the end of his investigation, only the matters then actually in dispute between the parties can be the subject of adjudication.[1]

1 *Hamar v French* [1998] Pens LR 321 at [73] per Millett LJ; *Wakelin v Read* [2000] Pens LR 319 at [12] per Mummery LJ. In *Grievson v Grievson* [2011] EWHC 1367 (Ch), [2011] Pens LR 283 at [28], Lewison J held that, where the complainant was not legally represented before the Ombudsman, the court will be generous in its assessment of the scope of the complaint. However, in *Sheffield v Kier Group Plc* [2019] EWHC 986 (Ch), [2019] 3 All ER 1086, HJJ Klein (sitting as a deputy High Court judge) confirmed that the Ombudsman had no inquisitorial function allowing him to investigate and determine questions which had not been referred to him by the complainant.

14.20

At the end of the investigation, the adjudicator will issue an opinion, which will set out the background facts and a recommendation of a course of action (if any). The parties then have an opportunity to accept the opinion or to provide further comments, which the adjudicator may review. If the matter is not resolved at this stage, the complaint is passed to the Ombudsman or his deputy, who may issue a preliminary determination on which the parties may comment, or else a final determination will be issued.

14.21

The final determination is binding on the parties, and is enforceable as if it were a judgment or order of the county court.[1] In addition to making any directions, the Ombudsman may award a modest level of compensation for the distress or inconvenience caused to the member by the maladministration and by the making of the complaint.[2] There are five categories of award, ranging from nominal (where no award is made) to exceptional (where the award is in excess of £2,000).[3] In practice, the Ombudsman's awards tend to range between £500 and £2,000.

1 Section 151(3), (5) of PSA 1993. Any enforcement action is required to be taken by the complainant, although the Ombudsman's office will supply a formally-certified copy of the determination for that purpose: Pensions Ombudsman Factsheet, 'Determination by the Ombudsman' (November 2021), p 2.
2 *Westminster City Council v Haywood* [1998] Ch 377, 410 per Millett LJ.
3 See the Pensions Ombudsman factsheet, 'Redress for non-financial injustice' (13 September 2018).

14.22

The Ombudsman will generally not make any order that members' legal costs be paid by the respondent, although he has occasionally made such an award on the basis that the complexity of the claim was such as to make it reasonable to incur such costs.[1] The Ombudsman has no power to make such an award in favour of the trustees, employer or administrator.

1 A practice endorsed by HHJ Klein (sitting as a deputy High Court judge) in *Sheffield v Kier Group plc* [2019] EWHC 986 (Ch), [2019] 3 All ER 1086.

Appeals

14.23

The appeal process only applies to final determinations: any preliminary decisions made by the Ombudsman, such as a decision not to investigate the complaint because of lack of jurisdiction or the expiry of a time limit, can only be challenged by way of judicial review.[1]

1 *Legal & General Assurance Society v Pensions Ombudsman* [2000] 1 WLR 1524.

14.24

The losing party may appeal the determination to the High Court on a point of law,[1] although they will require permission from the High Court to do so.[2] Such appeals are assigned to the Chancery Division.[3]

1 Section 151(4) of PSA 1993.
2 CPR 52.29(a).
3 CPR PD 52D, para 5.1(8).

14.25

No appeal lies on an issue of fact, but as a matter of law the court may interfere where the finding of fact contradicts the only true and reasonable findings which could be made based on the primary evidence before the Ombudsman, where the Ombudsman has not set out clearly what his finding of fact is or how he arrived at his conclusion, or where he has rejected without adequate reasons plainly credible evidence.[1]

1 *AF Blakemore & Son Ltd v Machin* [2007] EWHC 963 (Ch), [2007] Pens LR 189 at [3] per Lightman J. The appellate court cannot make a finding on an essential issue of primary fact if the Ombudsman has failed to do so: *Elliott v Pensions Ombudsman* [1998] OPLR 21.

14.26

Although the default time limit for filing an appellant's notice is 21 days from the date of the decision appealed against,[1] the Ombudsman may direct a longer period,[2] and he has given a general direction that the appellant must lodge their appeal within 28 days after the date of the determination.[3]

1 CPR 52.4(2)(b).
2 CPR 52.4(2)(a) and 52.1(3)(c).
3 Chancery Guide, para 29.108.

14.27

The parties to the appeal should ensure that all the points they wish to raise are included in the appellant's and respondent's notices, as the court may not permit any new points to be taken on appeal.[1] An appeal lies against findings made in the body of the determination as well as against the Ombudsman's directions.[2]

1 *Davies v Meadwestvaco Calmar Ltd* [2008] EWCA Civ 8, [2008] Pens LR 161.
2 *Davies v Meadwestvaco Calmar Ltd* [2008] EWCA Civ 8, [2008] Pens LR 161 at [10] per Arden LJ.

14.28

The appellant's notice must be served on the Ombudsman as well as on the other parties.[1] Although there is no obligation to do so, the Ombudsman's office often finds it helpful to be kept informed of the progress of the appeal and copied into relevant correspondence.[2]

Where the appellant member has no legal representation, the respondent should take it upon themselves to confirm both that the Ombudsman has been served with the appellant's notice and that the material put before the court includes all material that was before the Ombudsman and is potentially relevant to the appeal.[3]

1 CPR PD 52D, para 3.4(1).
2 Chancery Guide, para 29.109.
3 Chancery Guide, para 29.110.

Until recently, the Ombudsman did not appear at appeals, leaving it to the successful party to respond if they wished: this reluctance was presumably due to the fact that the Ombudsman may be liable to pay the costs of a successful appeal if he appears.[1] However, in 2016 the Ombudsman revised his practice, stating that he intended to participate more proactively to assist the court in appeals which had a wide impact on the industry or where there was a significant concern over access to justice.[2] The Ombudsman will only decide whether to participate in the appeal after receipt of the appellant's notice.[3]

1 *Moore's (Wallisdown) Ltd v Pensions Ombudsman* [2002] 1 WLR 1649.
2 Pensions Ombudsman press release, 'Our approach in appeals' (27 July 2016). This power has been sparingly exercised by the Ombudsman.
3 Pensions Ombudsman Factsheet, 'Determination by the Ombudsman' (November 2021), p 3.

14.30

The court has the power to limit the recovery of the costs of an appeal.[1] Any such application must be made as soon as practicable in relation to the progress of the appeal and will be determined without a hearing unless the court orders otherwise.[2]

1 CPR 52.19(1).
2 CPR 52.19(4).

14.31

It is desirable that the order made because of an appeal from an Ombudsman's determination is clear about which aspects of the determination are upheld, set aside, or remitted back to the Ombudsman for further determination. Therefore, where parties propose to compromise such an appeal, they should, where possible, liaise with the Ombudsman's office about the wording of the consent order.[1]

1 Chancery Guide, para 29.112.

Case studies

14.32

The Ombudsman's website contains a list of case studies, based on previous determinations. These are grouped thematically, and include studies on overpayments and decision error cases. If the trustees were minded not to uphold a dispute raised by a member in respect of an issue which is the subject of a case study, it may be useful to direct the member to the case study in question, to seek to dissuade them from taking the matter further.

Court proceedings

14.33

This section presents a high-level overview of the procedures involved in bringing court proceedings for the correction of pensions mistakes, and then considers ways in which the often very high costs of such proceedings may be controlled.

Where to start the proceedings

14.34

The appropriate venue will first be determined by reference to the value of the claim, as:

(a) claims for £100,000 or less must be commenced in the county court;[1] and

(b) where the proceedings are for relief from a mistake and the fund in respect of which the relief is sought exceeds £350,000, the claim must be commenced in the High Court.[2]

1 CPR PD 7A, para 2.1.
2 Section 23(g) of the County Courts Act 1984; art 3 of the County Court Jurisdiction Order 2014 (SI 2014/503).

14.35

Subject to that, the claim should be started in the High Court if by reason of:

(a) the financial value of the claim and the amount in dispute; and/or

(b) the complexity of the facts, legal issues, remedies, or procedures involved; and/or

(c) the importance of the outcome of the claim to the public in general,

the claimant believes that the claim ought to be dealt with by a High Court judge.[1]

1 CPR PD 7A, para 2.4.

14.36

In practice, most pensions claims are commenced in the High Court, and will generally be assigned to the Chancery Division Business List of the Business and Property Courts.[1] If it is considered that specialist knowledge of pensions is required, an application may be made to the Chief Master of the Chancery Division for the claim to be managed by the assigned pensions Master.[2]

1 Schedule 1 to the Senior Courts Act 1981 assigns to the Chancery Division cases relating to the execution of trusts and the rectification, setting aside or cancellation of deeds or other instruments in writing.
2 Chancery Guide, para 29.84.

The form of the claim

14.37

Proceedings may be commenced as either a Part 7 claim or a Part 8 claim, which are named after the provisions of the CPR which govern those claims.

14.38

The key determinant of which process is to be used is whether the claim is likely to involve a substantial dispute of fact: if it is, the Part 7 process must be used.[1] The Part 8 process provides a simpler mechanism for the resolution of disputes, as it does not require the determination of factual issues. The Part 8 process must also be used where required by the CPR or by legislation, such as an application under s 48 of AJA 1985.[2]

1 CPR 8.1(2)(a).
2 CPR 64.2(d). See **14.75–14.89**.

14.39

The use of the Part 8 process is normally suitable where a document error is sought to be corrected by construction, as that will not usually involve any disputed facts. Rectification claims, on the other hand, may well give rise to such disputes, and so should normally be commenced by use of the Part 7 process, unless it is known that there will be no significant factual dispute.[1]

1 Chancery Guide, para 29.91.

14.40

It is possible that, where a claim which was originally thought not to involve substantial disputes of fact is started as a Part 8 claim, it later transpires that substantial factual issues do arise. In such circumstances, the court may order the claim to continue as if commenced under Part 7 and/or may give such directions as are appropriate.[1]

1 CPR PD 8A, para 3.5.

14.41

Once a Part 7 claim has been started, the court will allocate it to one of three procedural 'tracks', depending on such matters as the complexity and financial value of the claims. Pensions cases will almost invariably be allocated to the highest track, known as the 'multi-track', which is suitable for claims worth more than £25,000.[1] All Part 8 claims are allocated to the multi-track.[2]

1 CPR 26.6.
2 CPR 8.9(c).

Representation orders

14.42

Where the claim relates to trust property, the court may make an order appointing a person to represent any other person or persons in the claim, where the represented persons are in a class with the same interest in the claim, where they cannot easily be ascertained, and where it would further the CPR overriding objective to appoint a representative.[1] Unless the court orders otherwise, any order made in a claim including a representative will bind all the persons so represented.[2]

1 CPR 19.7(2).
2 CPR 19.7(7)(a).

14.43

Representation orders are a feature of almost all pensions claims, because the large number of members (and possibly also employers) who the claimant will wish to be bound by the order makes it practically impossible for them all to be joined as individual parties to the claim.

14.44

For a full discussion of representation orders in the context of rectification claims, see **6.48–6.61**.

Part 7 procedure

Statements of case

14.45

The parties are required to provide a concise summary of the issues which are material to the cases they expect to prove at the trial in a series of documents which are together known as 'statements of case'. Statements of case enable the parties and the court to see the issues in dispute and the parties' position on those issues. The matters to be included in the statements of case are set out in CPR Part 16.

14.46

There are relatively short time limits for the service of statements of case, but extensions for a period of up to 28 days can be agreed between the parties.[1]

Otherwise, an application to court is required, although the court will usually, but not always, accept applications for an order made by consent.

1 CPR 3.8(3), (4); 15.5(1).

14.47

By the time a case comes to trial, the court will be provided with several documents prepared at a relatively late stage in the proceedings, such as skeleton arguments and lists of issues, which, at first sight, appear to supersede the statements of case. However, the courts have emphasised the critical role which statements of case play in enabling the parties to know the issues which need to be addressed in evidence and submissions, and the court to know what issues it is being asked to decide.[1]

1 *UK Learning Academy Ltd v Secretary of State for Education* [2020] EWCA Civ 370 at [47] per David Richards LJ; *Dhillon v Barclays Bank plc* [2020] EWCA Civ 619, [2021] 1 All ER 421 at [19] per Coulson LJ; *Satyam Enterprises Ltd v Burton* [2021] EWCA Civ 287, [2021] BCC 640 at [35] per Nugee LJ.

Case management

14.48

After statements of case have been filed and served, the court will convene a case management conference (CMC) before a Master. This gives the court the opportunity to understand the issues in dispute and how they may be narrowed, to manage the case and to give directions before trial. The court may also hear interim applications and will review the parties' cost estimates for the litigation and whether they are in proportion to the matters in issue.

14.49

Although the purpose of the CMC is to permit the court actively to manage the case, where there are no interim applications and the parties agree the directions for trial, it is not uncommon for the court to make the agreed directions without the need for a hearing. This is encouraged by CPR 29.4, which requires the parties to endeavour to agree appropriate directions and to submit them or their respective proposals to the court at least seven days before any CMC; if the court approves the agreed directions or issues its own directions, the parties will be notified and the CMC will be vacated.

14.50

Two issues which will usually be considered at the CMC relate to disclosure of documents and costs budgeting:

(a) Disclosure in Part 7 claims heard in the Business and Property Courts are currently the subject of a pilot scheme set out in CPR PD 51U. This scheme provides for limited 'Initial Disclosure' at the time of service of statements of case;[1] and if the parties want further documents, they must request 'Extended Disclosure' by sending a joint 'Disclosure Review

Document' to the court at least five days before the CMC. The court will consider the request at the CMC and will make an order only if it is satisfied that it is appropriate to do so in order fairly to resolve one or more of the key issues in dispute.

(b) Most Part 7 claims are subject to active costs management by the court, which is governed by CPR 3.12–3.18 and PD 3E. Normally no later than 21 days before the CMC, each party is required to prepare and file a costs budget on a prescribed basis, containing an estimate of their reasonable and proportionate costs of the litigation. The court will make a costs management order, which records what costs are agreed between the parties, and what other costs the court approves. At the end of the litigation, the costs awarded to the successful party will have regard to the approved budget which will not be departed from unless the court is satisfied that there is a good reason to do so.

1 See *Qatar v Banque Havilland* [2020] EWHC 1248 (Comm) at [16] and [18] per Cockerill J.

14.51

The directions made at the CMC will be based on the draft Chancery Case Management Directions (form CH1). Matters which are typically dealt with in CMC directions include:

(a) a stay to allow the parties to attempt to settle the dispute;

(b) the 'window' within which the trial will take place, and the estimated length of trial;

(c) disclosure and inspection of documents;

(d) witness statements and expert reports;

(e) trial bundle and skeleton arguments; and

(f) costs budgeting.

Steps to trial

14.52

The principal steps before trial concern:

(a) disclosure;

(b) witness statements; and

(c) expert evidence.

For a discussion of witness statements in the context of rectification claims, see **6.40–6.45**. For a discussion of expert evidence in the context of professional negligence claims, see **16.26–16.33**.

Disposal

14.53

The disposal by the court of a Part 7 claim may be effected by of a summary judgment application[1] or by trial.

1 See **16.64–16.66**.

Part 8 procedure

The claim form

14.54

The claim is initiated by the filing and service of a Part 8 claim form. This should not, in general, contain the same amount of detail as a Part 7 claim form, and should set out in summary form only the facts and the questions or issues the claimant wants the court to decide or the remedy that is sought.[1] Other matters to be included in the claim form are set out in CPR 8.2.

1 *Civil Procedure* (Sweet & Maxwell, 2021) vol 1, para 8.2.1.

14.55

The claimant must file and serve any written evidence on which they intend to rely when filing and serving the claim form.[1] Such evidence is usually in the form of a separate witness statement, although it can be set out in the claim form itself, provided that it is verified by a statement of truth.[2]

1 CPR 8.5(1), (2).
2 CPR 8.5(7).

Acknowledgment of service

14.56

The defendant must file an acknowledgment of service within 14 days after service of the claim form, and serve it on the claimant and any other party.[1] If the defendant fails to file an acknowledgment of service, they may attend the hearing of the claim but may not take part unless the court gives permission.[2]

1 CPR 8.3(1).
2 CPR 8.4(2).

Further evidence

14.57

The defendant must file and serve any written evidence on which they wish to rely at the same time as filing and serving the acknowledgment of service.[1] The claimant then has a short period to file and serve any further written evidence in reply.[2] In complex cases, it is common for the parties to seek extensions of the time periods for providing evidence. The parties can agree short extensions;[3] any longer extensions require permission of the court.[4] A party may also apply to the court for permission to file and serve evidence after the expiry of the time limit.[5]

1 CPR 8.5(3), (4).
2 CPR 8.5(5), (6).
3 PD 8A, para 7.5.
4 PD 8A, para 7.4.
5 CPR 8.6(1)(b).

Counterclaims

14.58

The defendant may make a counterclaim in the Part 8 process, although permission of the court is required.[1]

1 CPR 8.7.

Conversion to Part 7 claim

14.59

The court can at any time order a Part 8 claim to continue as if it were a Part 7 claim and give appropriate directions.[1] This will usually occur where the court considers there to be a substantial dispute of fact, although such disputes can be accommodated within the Part 8 process by the court making an order for cross-examination of a witness who has given evidence.[2]

1 CPR 8.1(3).
2 CPR 8.6(3). This occurred in *Merchant Navy Ratings Pension Fund Trustees Ltd v Stena Line Ltd* [2015] EWHC 448 (Ch), [2015] Pens LR 239.

List of issues

14.60

The absence of statements of case means that, in complex cases which raise a number of matters, it is not always possible to identify the issues in dispute in advance of the trial. The need for the parties to know of those issues in advance has led to the common practice of the parties agreeing at an early stage a list of the disputed issues, often accompanied by a short summary of the parties' positions on each issue. If provision for such a list is not agreed, the court may give directions to that effect.[1]

1 Chancery Guide, para 9.13. Alternatively, the parties can agree to exchange position papers on the list of issues.

Directions

14.61

Whilst it is possible for directions to be given immediately after the issue of the claim form,[1] it is more usual for directions to be considered later in the process, often after the evidence has been filed and served. This part of the process is overseen by a Master. As with a Part 7 claim, this gives the court the opportunity to take an active role in the management of the case. However, in most pensions cases, the directions will be uncontroversial and are likely to be agreed and approved by the court without the need for a hearing.

1 PD 8A, para 6.1.

14.62

As with a Part 7 CMC, two possible issues which may arise at a directions hearing relate to disclosure and costs budgeting:

(a) Because Part 8 claims are only to be used where there is no substantial dispute of fact, there is no provision for automatic disclosure: all relevant documents are expected to be exhibited to the parties' witness statements. However, the court has the power to order disclosure in appropriate cases, adapting as appropriate the pilot scheme referred to in **14.50**(a).[1]

(b) There is no requirement to file a costs budget under the Part 8 procedure until it is allocated to the multi-track.[2] In theory, the court may order the provision of a costs budget, with a view to a costs management order being made, in a Part 8 claim which involves a substantial dispute of fact and/or is likely to require oral evidence and/or extensive disclosure.[3] However, in practice, provision for costs budgets is rarely made in pensions cases, due to the existence of prospective costs orders[4] and agreements between the parties as to the legal advisers' charging rates and the provision of costs information.

1 *Practice Note: Disclosure Pilot and Part 8 Claims* (27 March 2019).
2 *Kershaw v Roberts* [2014] EWHC 1037 (Ch), [2014] 3 Costs LR 536.
3 PD 3E, para 2(e).
4 See **14.99–14.104**.

Disposal

14.63

The disposal of a Part 8 claim by the court may be effected:

(a) on paper without an oral hearing, if the parties agree or the court considers it to be appropriate;[1]

(b) by a summary disposal hearing;[2] or

(c) by trial.

1 CPR 23.8.
2 See **14.65**.

Summary judgment

14.64

Summary judgment may be granted where there is no real prospect of successfully defending the claim and there is no other reason why the case should be disposed of at trial.[1] In this context, real prospects of success means realistic and carrying some degree of conviction, as opposed to fanciful or merely arguable.[2]

1 CPR 24.2.
2 *Swain v Hillman* [2001] 1 All ER 91 at 92–94 per Lord Woolf MR; *ED&F Man Liquid Products Ltd v Patel* [2003] EWCA Civ 472, [2003] CP Rep 51 at [8] per Potter LJ.

14.65

The summary judgment procedure applies to both Part 7 and Part 8 claims, but in the latter case it is also possible for a 'disposal hearing' to be convened without the need for a summary judgment application.[1]

1 *Sovereign Trustees Ltd v Lewis* [2016] EWHC 2593 (Ch), [2016] Pens LR 345 at [3] per Chief Master Marsh.

14.66

Clear claims for rectification of document errors are often disposed of by summary judgment: the relevant principles are discussed in the context of such claims in **6.74–6.82**.

Trustee claims for directions

14.67

Claims to correct pensions mistakes which operate to increase the scheme's liabilities are usually brought by the employer, given its funding obligations to the scheme. However, such matters can also be resolved in the course of an application by the trustees seeking directions from the court as to how to administer the scheme. Such applications are governed by CPR Part 64.

14.68

An application for directions must be made by Part 8 claim.[1] If substantial factual issues need to be resolved, it is possible to seek an order that they continue as if commenced under Part 7,[2] but it is more normal for the resolution of those issues to be incorporated in the existing Part 8 process by way of directions.

1 CPR 64.3.
2 Chancery Guide, para 29.88.

14.69

The trustees should ensure that all those potentially interested in the question, such as the employer and the members, are made parties or are otherwise represented.[1] It may also be necessary to consider the potential impact of the litigation on the Pension Protection Fund.[2]

1 Chancery Guide, para 29.86. For representation orders, see **14.42–14.44**.
2 See *Capita ATL Pension Trustees Ltd v Zurkinskas* [2010] EWHC 3365 (Ch), [2011] 1 WLR 1274 at [22] per Sir Andrew Morritt C.

14.70

In some cases the court may be able to assess whether or not to give the directions sought, or what directions to give, without hearing from any party other than the trustees. If the trustees consider that their case is in that category they may apply to the court to issue the claim form without naming any defendants under CPR 8.2A. They must apply to the court before the claim form is issued and include a copy of the claim form that they propose to issue.[1]

1 PD 64B, para 4.2.

14.71

Unless there are very few of them, there is no requirement to consult with or notify members of a scheme.[1]

1 PD 64B, para 7.7(4).

14.72

The trustees' evidence should be given by witness statement. In order to ensure that, if directions are given, the trustees are properly protected by the order, they must ensure full disclosure of relevant matters, even if the case is to proceed with the participation of members as defendants.[1] In the case of a pension scheme the evidence should include the latest actuarial valuation, and should describe the membership profile and, if a deficit on a winding-up is likely, the priority provisions and their likely effect.[2]

1 PD 64B, para 7.1.
2 PD 64B, para 7.4.

Alternative dispute resolution (ADR)

14.73

The courts are keen to help the parties resolve their disputes other than by pursuing litigation through to trial. Thus, when exercising its duty actively to manage cases, the court will encourage the parties to use ADR and to facilitate its use where it considers that to be appropriate.[1] Thus, it is usual for directions made at the CMC to include time in the trial timetable for the parties to explore ADR before preparing for trial. Indeed, the Court of Appeal has gone further, and required parties to attend a form of ADR known as 'early neutral evaluation' without requiring their consent.[2]

1 CPR 1.4(2)(e).
2 *Lomax v Lomax* [2019] EWCA Civ 1467, [2019] 1 WLR 6527.

14.74

ADR, and mediation in particular, is a common method of settling pensions negligence disputes, and is discussed further in that context at **16.111–16.112**.

Section 48 of AJA 1985

14.75

This provision can be used where a question of construction has arisen out of the terms of a pension scheme established by trust: it permits the court to authorise trustees to administer the scheme in reliance on an opinion given on the construction issue by an advocate with a High Court qualification for at least 10 years. It is generally used to authorise the administration of private trusts and wills by trustees and personal representatives respectively. However, the procedure was successfully invoked in *Re BCA Pension Plan*[1] to enable the trustee of a pension scheme to administer the scheme as if the relevant rule had been corrected as a matter of construction.

1 [2015] EWHC 3492 (Ch), [2016] 4 WLR 5.Correction by construction is discussed in **Chapter 5**.

Procedure

14.76

The procedure for making an application under s 48 of AJA 1985 is as follows:[1]

(a) The trustee is the sole party to the claim, which should be made by Part 8 claim form without naming a defendant under CPR 8.2A. No separate application for permission under CPR 8.2A need be made.[2]

(b) The claim should be supported by a witness statement or affidavit to which are exhibited:

   (i) copies of all relevant documents;

   (ii) the instructions to the opinion-writer;

   (iii) the opinion-writer's opinion; and

   (iv) draft terms of the desired order.

(c) The application is for an order to authorise the trustees to act on a legal opinion, which may deal with construction issues: it should not seek a decision of the court itself on the construction of any instrument.

(d) The witness statement or affidavit (or exhibits thereto) should state:

   (i) the reason for the application;

   (ii) the names of all persons who are, or may be, affected by the order sought;[3]

   (iii) all surrounding circumstances admissible and relevant in construing the document;

(iv) the date of qualification of the opinion-writer and their experience in the construction of trust documents;

(v) the approximate value of the fund or property in question;

(vi) whether it is known to the applicant that a dispute exists and, if so, details of such dispute; and

(vii) what steps are proposed to be taken in reliance on the opinion.

(e) When the file is placed before the Master they will consider whether the evidence is complete and, if it is, whether it is appropriate for the Master to deal with the matter, or to send the file to the judge.

(f) The Master or judge will consider the papers and, if necessary, direct that non-parties be given the opportunity to participate under CPR 19.8A or request further information. If the court is satisfied that the order sought is appropriate, it will be made and sent to the claimant.

(g) If following service of notices under CPR 19.8A any acknowledgment of service is received, the claimant must apply to the Master (on notice to the parties who have acknowledged service) for directions. If the claimant desires to pursue the application to the court, the Master will ordinarily direct that the case proceeds as a Part 8 claim.

(h) If on the hearing of the claim the court is of the opinion that any party who entered an acknowledgment of service has no reasonably tenable argument contrary to the opinion-writer's opinion, in the exercise of the court's discretion it may order such party to pay all or part of any costs thrown away.

1 Chancery Guide, paras 29.29–29.35.
2 CPR PD 64A, para 5.
3 This is unlikely to be practically possible in the case of a pension scheme with a substantial number of members.

The limits on the scope of s 48

14.77

Whilst s 48 provides a relatively quick and inexpensive means of obtaining authority from the court to administer the scheme on the basis of the construed provision, the utility of this process for correcting mistakes in scheme documents is limited by three particular features of the process.

Existence of a dispute

14.78

Section 48(2) precludes an order being made where it appears to the court that a dispute exists which would make it inappropriate for the court to make the order without hearing argument. This clearly applies to construction issues which are the subject of challenges which have already been made by members, including references to the Pensions Ombudsman. However, not every dispute is caught by this provision, as a dispute which can be shown to have no merit will not be such as to make it inappropriate for the court to make the order without hearing argument.[1] Conversely, there may be sufficient evidence of a disqualifying dispute, even if that dispute has not been referred to a formal resolution process.

1 It has been suggested that a s 48 order can be made where, notwithstanding the existence of a dispute, the matter in issue is too insubstantial to justify more than a summary decision: *Lewin on Trusts* (20th edn, Sweet & Maxwell, 2020) (*Lewin*), para 39-081. Even if this is correct, it is unlikely to apply to pensions cases.

14.79

Where the court has any doubt as to the existence of a disqualifying dispute, it may direct the trustees to serve notice of the application to potentially affected persons.[1]

1 CPR 19.8A.

No substantial doubt

14.80

Secondly, even where no dispute exists for the purposes of s 48(2), the court will not grant the application where the opinion obtained by the trustees is open to substantial doubt. In *Greenwold v Pike*[1] the trustees of a settlement made a s 48 application based on advice from counsel as to the meaning of a term used in the settlement, in circumstances where they had obtained a prior opinion from a different counsel to the effect that it would be an uphill struggle to establish the construction being contended for. Briggs J refused to make the order sought, and directed that the application continue as a Part 8 claim.

1 [2007] EWHC 2202 (Ch).

14.81

This does not mean that the procedure can only be used where the question of construction is only open to one answer: in that situation, there should be no need to apply to court at all. The procedure exists to deal with difficult questions of construction which may give rise to different possible answers but on which the opinion-writer, despite that difficulty, is able to reach a clear view as to which of the answers is correct.

Non-binding

14.82

The final, and perhaps most significant, limitation on the scope of s 48 is that the order does not bind the members or employers of the scheme: they remain free to argue for a contrary construction in subsequent proceedings.[1]

This reflects the principal purpose of the s 48 jurisdiction, which is to protect trustees from any criticism by members for administering the trust on the basis of the order, should it subsequently prove to have been incorrectly made.

1 *Re BCA Pension Plan* [2015] EWHC 3492 (Ch), [2016] 4 WLR 5 at [36].

14.83

In these circumstances, if – as is the case in most pension schemes – the rules exclude the trustees from liability for any breach of trust save in the case of bad faith, does a s 48 order give the trustees any additional protection? The answer is, potentially, yes: if the trustees were simply to administer the scheme on a particular basis in reliance on an exclusion provision in the case of any subsequent challenge, there is a danger that that provision will be held not to apply. This is because such provisions protect trustees from past conduct, and cannot be relied upon to justify future conduct: in the leading case of *Armitage v Nurse*,[1] Millett LJ said that a trustee who relied on the presence of an exclusion provision to justify a proposed breach of trust would thereby lose its protection, as they would be acting recklessly and therefore in bad faith, which is beyond the protection of the provision.

1 [1998] Ch 241 at 254.

14.84

There may accordingly be a real advantage to trustees in having the protection of a s 48 order, where they would otherwise be exposed to potential liability if they administered the scheme on the basis of the construed provision.

Notification of members

14.85

The practice of notifying pension scheme members of proceedings before they are commenced is discussed in the context of rectification claims in **6.62–6.64**. In *Re BCA Pension Plan*,[1] Snowden J went further and directed that notice be given to the members after the order was made, explaining the terms of the order and the reasons for it being made.

1 [2015] EWHC 3492 (Ch), [2016] 4 WLR 5 at [41]–[43].

14.86

Initially, the judge was minded to make the order conditional on the trustees giving notice of it to the members, and granting liberty to any member of the scheme to apply to have the order varied or set aside within two months of receipt of the notification. Ultimately, the judge was persuaded not to attach conditions to the order, on the basis that s 48 does not bind members, and the order would maintain the increases to the pensions which the trustees had in practice being paying to individual members.

14.87

The judge was nevertheless convinced of the need to notify the members of the order and the reasons for it in the case before him. Although he said that there may be scope for dispensing with that requirement in certain cases, he thought that where the order directly related to the level of benefits payable to members, those members should be told of the order unless there were compelling reasons to the contrary.

14.88

The judge said that this requirement would be satisfied in the case before him by a notice being placed in a newsletter which was due to be sent to members shortly, and that:

(a) an appropriate form of wording should be used;

(b) any electronic communication should contain a link to the judgment and order, and any hard copy communication should provide hard copies of those documents; and

(c) both types of communication should offer to provide hard copies of the evidence filed in support of the application, excluding any confidential information concerning members.

14.89

Although they were not annexed to the judgment, the terms of the communication subsequently approved by the judge included a brief explanation of the issue, the fact of the making of the order and an explanation of the effect of the order, in particular its non-binding nature. The judge also approved a statement to the effect that any attempt by members to argue against the order would be at their own risk as to costs.

Costs

14.90

Costs are often a key consideration in the constitution of legal proceedings for the correction of pensions mistakes. Before considering the steps which may properly be taken to minimise costs in such cases, this section sets out the basic principles applied by the courts on costs issues.

14.91

For this purpose, it is necessary to consider separately trust claims and third-party claims.[1] Most claims to correct pensions mistakes will be trust claims, involving the employer, trustees and members. The primary example of a third party claim in this context is a claim by the trustees and/or the employer against negligent professionals.

1 See *Alsop Wilkinson v Neary* [1996] 1 WLR 1220, 1223–1224 per Lightman J.

Trust claims – costs of the trustees

14.92

Where the trustees are parties to any proceedings, the general rule is that they are entitled to be paid the costs of those proceedings, insofar as they are not recovered from or paid by any other person, out of the relevant trust fund or estate.[1] This applies to the trustees' own costs and to any costs they are ordered to pay to the other parties.[2]

1 CPR 46.3(2). This accords with the trustees' right of indemnity under s 31(1) of the Trustee Act 2000.
2 *Turner v Hancock* (1882) 20 ChD 303; *Blades v Isaac* [2016] EWHC 601 (Ch), [2016] WTLR 589 at [93]–[94] per Master Matthews.

14.93

This principle extends only to costs which were properly incurred, which will depend upon all the circumstances of the case including whether the trustees obtained directions from the court before bringing or defending the proceedings,[1] whether they acted in the interests of the scheme or in substance for a benefit other than that of the scheme including the trustees' own benefit, and whether they acted in some way unreasonably in bringing or defending, or in the conduct of, the proceedings; but the trustees are not to be taken to have acted for a benefit other than that of the scheme by reason only that they have defended a claim in which relief is sought against them personally.[2]

1 This is of particular relevance to third-party proceedings: see **14.107–14.109**.
2 CPR PD 46, paras 1.1–1.2, reflecting principles already established by case law: see *Lewin*, para 48-020.

14.94

In trust claims, the trustees are generally expected to remain neutral as to the outcome, and their right to an indemnity out of the scheme assets is conditional upon them so acting. If the trustees take the side of some members against others, thereby acting for a benefit other than that of the scheme, they are at risk of being held to have acted unreasonably and so being deprived of their right to an indemnity, and they may be ordered to pay the costs of the successful members personally.[1]

1 *Alsop Wilkinson v Neary* [1996] 1 WLR 1220, 1225 per Lightman J; *Breadner v Granville-Grossman* [2001] WTLR 377. This does not apply where the scheme rules give the trustees a right to an indemnity for its legal costs: *Granada Group Ltd v The Law Debenture Pension Trust Corp plc* [2015] EWHC 1499 (Ch), [2015] Bus LR 1119 at [91]–[97] per Andrews J.

14.95

The trustees should be entitled to take their costs of a construction application out of the scheme's assets, even where the claim arose because of a poorly-drafted document for which the trustees were responsible, unless the error was so inept as to amount to misconduct on their part.[1]

1 *Lewin*, para 48-038.

14.96

The trustees are entitled to have their costs assessed on the indemnity basis.[1] The differences between this basis and the standard basis of assessment are that:

(a) the standard basis places the onus on the claiming party to prove that the costs were reasonably incurred or reasonable in amount; the onus is reversed under the indemnity basis; and

(b) only the standard basis requires the costs to be proportionate to the matters in issue.[2]

1 CPR 46.3(3).
2 CPR 44.2(2), (3).

Trust claims – costs of the employer and members

14.97

The classic division of claims for costs purposes is the three categories identified in *Re Buckton*:[1]

(a) Category 1 is proceedings brought by the trustees to have the guidance of the court as to the construction of the trust or some other question of law arising in the administration of the trust. In such cases, the costs of all parties are, whatever the outcome, usually treated as necessarily incurred for the benefit of the trust fund and ordered to be paid out of it, to be assessed on the indemnity basis.

(b) Category 2 is proceedings where the same type of application as category 1 is made by someone other than the trustees, and would have justified an application by the trustees. An example in a pensions context would be where an employer brings a claim for the construction or rectification of a trust document which could properly have been brought by the trustees. In such cases, the same costs consequences as for category 1 cases apply.

(c) Category 3 is proceedings in which the application is made by someone other than the trustees, but have the character of a hostile claim founded on a point of construction or law. Such claims are bought for the benefit of the claimant rather than the fund as a whole, and the general principles applicable to the costs of hostile litigation apply.[2]

1 [1907] 2 Ch 406, 413–417 per Kekewich J.
2 See **14.107**.

14.98

These categories are not closed, as is demonstrated by *Singapore Airlines Ltd v Buck Consultants Ltd*,[1] in which a preliminary issue in a claim for negligence brought by a scheme employer raised a question of the construction of the document drafted by the defendant. The issue was raised by the defendant partly for the benefit of the members (in respect of whom a representation order was made) and partly for the defendant's own benefit. The Court of Appeal held that the case did not fall within either *Buckton* category 1 or 2, and the principled approach in that situation required a sharing of the costs between the parties: accordingly, the appropriate order was for half of the costs that would have been borne by the scheme had the case fallen within *Buckton* category 2 to be paid out of the scheme's assets.

1 [2011] EWCA Civ 1542, [2012] Pens LR 1.

14.99

Where a member is joined as a defendant to this type of claim in a representative capacity, they will want to be sure that their costs will be paid out of the scheme assets and not be borne by them personally. Whilst in some cases members may be satisfied that their costs are bound to be paid by the scheme on the basis that the case is a *Buckton* category 1 or 2 case, in practice that is likely not to be sufficient, as the representative will also want to pay the costs of their legal advisers on a regular basis throughout the course of the proceedings, rather than wait until after the disposal of the claim.

14.100

In such cases, the court may grant a prospective costs order, which means that the member's costs will be paid out of the scheme on the indemnity basis in any event, and payments will be made from the scheme from time to time so that the member's legal costs may be paid on an interim basis. A model form of order is annexed to CPR PD 64A; further guidance on such orders is set out in para 6 of that PD and paras 29.19–29.20 of the Chancery Guide.

14.101

The purpose of such orders is not to override the discretion of the trial judge to award costs: they will accordingly only be made where the court can be satisfied that the judge would inevitably, or almost inevitably, make an order for costs in favour of the member;[1] and the court will not make such an order where it is not clear whether the claim falls within *Buckton* category 1 or 2 or whether it might turn into a *Buckton* category 3 case.

1 *McDonald v Horn* [1995] 1 All ER 961, 971-972 per Hoffmann LJ; *Pell Frischmann Consultants Ltd v Prabhu* [2013] EWHC 2203 (Ch), [2014] ICR 153.

14.102

However, an exception has been made where members of a pension scheme seek a prospective costs order in respect of a hostile claim against the trustees brought for the benefit of the scheme as a whole, by analogy with costs orders made in favour of a minority shareholder bringing a derivative action on behalf of a company:[1] these are known as '*McDonald v Horn* orders'. When deciding whether to make such an order, the court will consider the strength of the case, the likely order as to costs at trial, the justice of the application, and any special circumstances.[2]

1 *McDonald v Horn* [1995] 1 All ER 961. The principal company law case is *Wallersteiner v Moir (No 2)* [1975] QB 373.
2 *Re National Grid Co plc Group of the Electricity Supply Pension Scheme* [1997] OPLR 161 at [18]–[19] per Rimer J.

14.103

If the members are bringing a claim in a representative capacity which falls within *Buckton* category 2, they can obtain a prospective costs order even before a representation order is made.[1]

1 *IBM UK Pensions Trust Ltd v Metcalfe* [2012] EWHC 125 (Ch), [2012] 3 Costs LO 420.

14.104

Where the trustees have power in the scheme rules to pay the costs of a member who is a party to the proceedings, and they properly exercise that power, a prospective costs order is not required and the trustees are entitled to recover out of the trust fund any costs which they pay pursuant to any agreement made in the exercise of that power.[1] In such circumstances, it is common for trustees to enter into contractual arrangements with the representative for the regular payment of their legal costs, together with (if considered appropriate) a nominal payment to the representative to recognise their personal service. Even without such a power, the trustees may well be permitted to pay from the assets of the scheme the (relatively modest) costs incurred by the member in preparing the application for a prospective costs order, on the basis that that power is ancillary to the trustees' power to bring the proceedings to which the member has been joined.

1 CPR 44.5: see CPR PD 64A, para 6.2. Of course, the employer could agree to indemnify the member in respect of their legal costs.

Trust claims – costs of appeals

14.105

Where the trustees have obtained directions from the court, they should generally not seek to appeal the decision: they will usually only be entitled to an indemnity in such circumstances where they were acting in the interests of the scheme as a whole, such as where the decision under appeal created significant uncertainty as to the interpretation or operation of the scheme.[1]

1 *Airways Pension Scheme Trustee Ltd v Fielder* [2019] EWHC 29 (Ch), [2019] 4 WLR 9 at [71]–[74] per Arnold J.

14.106

A member wishing to appeal will only obtain a prospective costs order in truly exceptional circumstances, where the application satisfies the *McDonald v Horn* test, which in this context may be relied upon in cases coming within *Buckton* categories 1 and 2.[1]

1 *Re IMG Pension Plan* [2010] EWHC 321 (Ch), [2010] Pens LR 131. A member who has been successful at first instance should be able to obtain a prospective costs order to resist an appeal brought by the losing party: see *Re National Grid Co plc Group of the Electricity Supply Pension Scheme* [1997] OPLR 161.

Third party claims

14.107

Claims involving third parties are generally hostile litigation, where the general rule is that the unsuccessful party will be ordered to pay the costs of the successful party.[1]

1 CPR 44.2(1), (2).

14.108

The trustees, when bringing or defending such a claim, need to be sure that any costs they are ordered to pay, together with their own costs, will be met out of the scheme assets come what may. However, unless there is express authority in the scheme rules, trustees in such a situation run the risk of losing their indemnity if they incur costs in such proceedings, and if their participation in the litigation is later found to have been unreasonable.[1] In such circumstances, the trustees should apply to court at an early stage of the litigation for directions as to whether or not to bring or defend proceedings: these are known as '*Beddoe* directions'.[2] Such applications fall within CPR Part 64, and guidance on them is provided by CPR PD 64B.

1 *Bonham v Blake Lapthorne Linell* [2006] EWHC 2513 (Ch), [2007] WTLR 189 at [123] per Kitchen J.
2 After the leading case of *Re Beddoe* [1893] 1 Ch 547.

14.109

In practice, most third party pensions claims will be brought by the employer and the trustees together, and it is usual in such situations for the employer to indemnify the trustees for their costs incurred in those claims, so as to avoid the need for potentially costly and time-consuming *Beddoe* applications.[1]

1 Chancery Guide, para 29.89.

Practice point: how to control the cost of pensions litigation

14.110

Because of the requirement for the trustees to remain neutral to preserve their right to an indemnity out of scheme assets for their legal costs, the classic pensions claim will involve at least three parties: the trustees, the employer and at least one defendant representing the members. However, the high cost of pensions litigation, combined with the poor funding state of many schemes, has caused trustees and employers to seek to control the costs of such claims by a number of methods.

Interest-based representation orders

14.111

In the early days of pensions litigation, when schemes were generally well-funded, it was not uncommon for several defendants to be joined to the claim to represent the interests of different categories of member. For example, in *LRT Pension Fund Trustee Co Ltd v Hatt,*[1] separate legal representation was provided for active members, for pensioners and deferred members, and for new entrants.

1 [1993] Pens LR 227.

14.112

However, when schemes began to fall into deficit and costs became more of an issue, employers and trustees sought to keep the number of representative defendants to a minimum. Accordingly, courts began to make 'interest-based' representation orders, whereby a party would represent all members in whose interests it was for the issue to be answered in one way, with another party representing all other members.[1]

1 In *Atos IT Services UK Ltd v Atos Pension Schemes Ltd* [2020] EWHC 145 (Ch), [2020] Pens LR 17 at [1], Nugee J said that interest-based representation orders dated back many years to one of the *Mettoy* cases in the early 2000s, which was heard before Jacob J.

14.113

Such orders are now well-established;[1] and claimants are now expected to ensure that the number of representatives and classes represented should be kept to the minimum necessary to enable the court to be satisfied that it has heard full argument on behalf of all those interested.[2]

1 *Atos IT Services UK Ltd v Atos Pension Schemes Ltd* [2020] EWHC 145 (Ch), [2020] Pens LR 17 at [1].
2 Chancery Guide, para 29.93.

The trustees represent the members

14.114

Even though the trustees should remain neutral in trust claims to preserve their right to an indemnity for their costs,[1] several pensions cases have seen the trustees representing members' interests and advancing arguments on their behalf.

1 See **14.94**.

14.115

One of the earliest of such cases was *BEC Pension Trustee Ltd v Sheppeck*.[1] That case involved two issues arising during the winding-up of an 'industry-wide' scheme. The only parties to the claim were the trustee and a representative defendant. The trustee had previously sought and obtained an order from the Master that it represent the employers of the scheme who had a particular interest on one issue and the members of the scheme who had a particular interest on the other issue, with the representative defendant representing all other employers and members. Etherton J went on to record the following:

> 'Although the trustee of a trust fund commonly takes a neutral position in proceedings for the interpretation of the trust's documents, joining representative beneficiaries to argue the opposing contentions, Master Moncaster was invited to make, and did make, the representation order in relation to the trustee in the present case, in the interests of efficiency and the saving of costs, bearing in mind particularly the substantial deficit in many sections of the scheme.'

1 [2002] EWHC 101 (Ch), [2002] ICR 1343 at [30].

14.116

Thereafter, pensions cases involving document errors and construction claims have gone further, and dispensed with a representative defendant altogether, so that the only parties were the employer and the trustees, with the trustees representing the members of the scheme whose interests were contrary to those of the employer. In some of those cases, the court made no comment on the active role taken by the trustees.[1] In others, the court explained that that role was justified because of the saving of costs, compliance with the overriding objective[2] and the fact that the trustees were in possession of all the relevant documentation.[3] Similarly, in a case where the approval of a compromise was sought, the court was satisfied that it was appropriate to appoint the trustees and the employer to represent members with different interests, for the sake of economy and good order.[4]

1 For example, *British Vita Unlimited v British Vita Pension Fund Trustees Ltd* [2007] EWHC 953 (Ch), [2008] ICR 1295; *Arcadia Group Ltd v Arcadia Group Pension Trust Ltd* [2014] EWHC 2683 (Ch), [2014] BTC 40.

2 See CPR 1.1.

3 *Premier Foods Group Services Ltd v RHM Pension Trust Ltd* [2012] EWHC 447 (Ch), [2012] Pens LR 151 at [4] per Warren J; *Royal Mail Group Ltd v Evans* [2013] EWHC 1572 (Ch), [2013] Pens LR 239 at [10]-[11] per Asplin J.

4 *Grolier International Ltd v Capital Cranfield Trustees Ltd* [2015] EWHC 1832 (Ch), [2015] Pens LR 485 at [15] per Mann J.

14.117

It now seems to be common practice for trustees to take an active role in pension claims without the need for prior approval, and without the court feeling it necessary to explain why the trustees were justified in acting in that way. Indeed, in *Ove Arup and Partners International Ltd v Arup*

UK Pension Scheme Trustees,[1] HHJ David Cooke, sitting as a deputy High Court judge, said that '*such orders are now routinely made*'.[2] However, this practice is by no means universal, and there are several recent pensions cases to which the employer, the trustees and at least one representative defendant have been separate parties.[3]

1 [2020] EWHC 1064 (Ch), [2020] Pens LR 21 at [3].

2 Other examples of recent cases where only the employer and trustees are parties include: *Atos IT Services UK Ltd v Atos Pension Schemes Ltd* [2020] EWHC 145 (Ch), [2020] Pens LR 17; *Burgess v BIC UK Ltd* [2018] EWHC 785 (Ch), [2018] Pens LR 280; *Engineering Construction Industry Training Board v Swift* (29 July 2016, unreported); *Dutton v FDR Ltd* [2015] EWHC 2946 (Ch), [2015] Pens LR 569. See also *Wedgwood Pension Trustees Ltd v Salt* [2018] EWHC 79 (Ch), [2018] Pens LR 283, where the trustees sought directions of the court on scheme issues which arose following the insolvency of the employer, taking an active role in putting forward arguments and joining a single representative defendant to argue to the contrary.

3 For example, *Britvic plc v Britvic Pensions Ltd* [2020] EWHC 118 (Ch), [2020] Pens LR 154; *G4S plc v G4S Trustees Ltd* [2018] EWHC 1749 (Ch), [2019] ICR 141; *Pollock v Reed* [2015] EWHC 3685 (Ch), [2016] Pens LR 129.

14.118

Has the requirement for the trustees to remain neutral been abrogated in pension scheme cases? The principle, after all, is not dead: it is still applied in private trust cases.[1] The practical reality is that no objection is made to the trustees taking an active role in pensions claims: it will be in the employer's financial interests for the trustees to represent the members; and the members will not be sufficiently closely involved with the mechanics of the claim for them to be aware of the issue. It is therefore likely that the nature of the trustees' involvement in the arguments will turn on their personal preferences, which may be affected by how controversial the issue is amongst the members, and how exposed the trustees feel to criticism from the members as a result.

1 See *Lines v Wilcox* [2019] EWHC 1451 (Ch), [2019] Costs LR 1215 at [21] and [46] per HHJ Matthews (sitting as a deputy High Court judge); *Granada Group Ltd v The Law Debenture Pension Trust Corporation plc* [2015] EWHC 1499 (Ch), [2015] Bus LR 1119 at [93] per Andrews J.

14.119

Finally, trustees have always been permitted to take an active role on behalf of the members, where an interest is discovered during the proceedings which cannot be represented by the existing parties, in circumstances where it is impractical to join another defendant.[1]

1 See, for example, *Lloyds Banking Group Pensions Trustees Ltd v Lloyds Bank plc* [2020] EWHC 3135 (Ch), [2021] Pens LR 295 at [17].

The trustees do not appear at the hearing

14.120

The neutrality of the trustees gives rise to the question of the extent to which they should be incurring legal costs in respect of the claim.

Obviously where the trustees have themselves brought an application for directions, they will be expected to appear; but what if they are joined as defendants to a claim instituted by the employer or the members, and have resolved to remain neutral?

14.121

The trustees may decide that it would not be appropriate for them to be legally represented at a hearing, where they do not consider that they will be of any further assistance to the court and are content to abide by the court's decision.[1] However, in pensions cases that tends to be the exception rather than the rule: in one case,[2] the trustees were represented by solicitors and leading counsel at first instance, in the Court of Appeal and in the Supreme Court, despite adopting a neutral stance and taking no active role in the arguments.

1 See, for example, *Carr v Thales Pension Trustees Ltd* [2020] EWHC 949 (Ch), [2020] Pens LR 19; *Girls Day School Trust v GDST Pension Trustees Ltd* [2016] EWHC 1254 (Ch), [2016] Pens LR 181.
2 *Barnardo's v Buckinghamshire* [2015] EWHC 2200 (Ch), [2015] Pens LR 501 (Warren J); [2016] EWCA Civ 1064, [2017] Pens LR 26 (CA); [2018] UKSC 55, [2019] ICR 495 (SC).

14.122

The proper approach for trustees in a commercial trust context has been set out by Lord Neuberger of Abbotsbury MR in *BNY Corporate Trustee Services Ltd v Eurosail-UK 2007–3BL plc*:[1]

> 'It appears to me that, unless a trustee has good reason to think that its actions will be subject to criticism or there is some other special reason, it should normally be unnecessary for it to make representations or to be represented at a hearing (save for instructing a note-taker), where, as here, its stance on the issues dividing the warring parties, is neutral. Directions can be sought at a relatively early stage to enable the trustee to make submissions (possibly in writing) if a point arises on which its assistance is required or on which it desires to have a say.'

There is no reason why this approach should not apply equally to pensions claims.

1 [2011] EWCA Civ 227, [2011] 1 WLR 2524 at [105].

The same law firm acts for more than one party

14.123

Of course, it is not the multiplicity of parties which leads to high legal costs: it is the need for each of those parties to have separate legal representation. Is there scope for two or more parties to be represented by the same legal advisers?

14.124

This situation occurs in other trust claims, such as applications under the Variation of Trusts Act 1958, where it is common for separate partners in the same firm of solicitors to act for the trustees and the different categories of beneficiary, although they must each be represented by separate counsel.[1]

1 *Lewin*, para 53-079.

14.125

There are several pensions cases in which more than one party has been represented by the same firm.[1] In *Alexander Forbes Trustees Ltd v Doe*,[2] a case involving a pure issue of law, the same firm of solicitors acted for the claimant trustees and the two defendants who argued each side of the issue: each of the defendants had separate leading counsel who shared a neutral junior counsel. No criticism was made of this arrangement by the court, although it considered that the use of fictitious defendants was unnecessary, and that the case could have been brought without defendants, with the trustees being directed to retain the two counsel to argue the case.

1 For example, *Manning v Drexel Burnham Lambert Holdings Ltd* [1995] 1 WLR 32; *Capital Cranfield Trustees Ltd v Beck* [2008] EWHC 3181 (Ch), [2009] Pens LR 71; *Misys Ltd v Misys Retirement Benefits Trustees Ltd* [2012] EWHC 4250 (Ch).
2 [2011] EWHC 3930 (Ch), [2012] Pens LR 231.

14.126

Occasionally, where the trustees are neutral, they have been represented by the same legal advisers as the employer: this occurred in *Sogefi Filtration Ltd v Havard*,[1] an application for the approval of a compromise, where the trustees and the employer shared the same solicitors and counsel.

1 (18 December 2017, unreported), Deputy Judge Tipples QC.

Costs capping and budgeting

14.127

The final way in which the costs of pensions claims might be limited is by using costs capping and costs management.

14.128

The general costs management power of the court has been referred to at **14.50**(b). There is also a general power for a party to apply to the court for an order limiting the amount of future costs which a party may recover pursuant to a subsequent costs order. This costs capping procedure is governed by CPR 3.19–3.21 and CPR PD 3F.

14.129

In the specific case of trust claims, any party who intends to apply for an order for the payment of costs out of the trust fund must file and serve on all other parties written notice of that intention, together with a budget of the costs likely to be incurred by that party.[1] The purpose of these documents is to enable the court, when the claim first comes before it for directions, to make a costs capping order of its own initiative, whether or not any party has applied for such an order.[2] However, in pensions cases, this requirement has been generally ignored in practice.

1 CPR PD 3F, para 5.4. Those documents must be filed and served either (in a Part 7 claim) with the first statement of case or (in a Part 8 claim) with the evidence (or, if a defendant does not intend to serve and file evidence, with the acknowledgement of service): CPR PD 3F, para 5.5.

2 CPR PD 3F, para.5.6. For examples of prospective costs orders and *Beddoe* orders where the court has imposed a limit on the costs which the members and trustees respectively can take out of the scheme assets, see *Re National Grid Co plc Group of the Electricity Supply Pension Scheme* [1997] OPLR 161 and *Airways Pension Scheme Trustee Ltd v Fielder* [2019] EWHC 29 (Ch), [2019] 4 WLR 9.

15 Compromises

15.1

Litigation is an uncertain process. The desire to achieve a definitive outcome in a situation where the law and facts are often unclear makes the compromise of a claim involving a pensions mistake particularly attractive, even before taking account of the expense and potential employee unrest which a protracted dispute can cause. The need for certainty requires the compromise to bind all the scheme members, which will usually only happen where the court formally approves the compromise.

15.2

This chapter considers the procedure involved in the settlement of claims relating to pensions mistakes, including the process for approval by the court, and concludes with an analysis of the matters which typically arise for consideration in the compromise of such a claim. The discussion takes place at a relatively high level of abstraction, as the issues which arise in each case will be fact-sensitive.

Preliminaries to a compromise

Parties to a compromise

15.3

The usual form of dispute relating to pensions mistakes features three parties: the employer, the trustees, and a representative of the members. Each will need to be involved in the settlement discussions.

15.4

The main parties to the negotiations will usually be the employer and the representative, as they have the principal financial interest in the outcome of the dispute, insofar as it involves an adjustment to the benefit structure of the scheme and its effect on the funding of scheme liabilities. If the proposed compromise will result in a change to the shape of the benefits, the scheme administrators should be consulted at an early stage to ensure that the pensions payment system is able to process the compromised benefits.

15.5

As regards the trustees, they have statutory power to settle any claim relating to the scheme,[1] and must exercise that power in accordance with their statutory duty to act with reasonable care and skill.[2] However, provided that they are satisfied that the representative is capable of properly acting on behalf of the members they are asked to represent, the trustees will not need to be overly concerned to ensure that the compromise is in the interests of the members, as the court will not otherwise grant its approval.[3] Accordingly, the trustees usually become involved later in the process, where discussions between the employer and representative have led to the realistic prospect of the claim being settled. However, there will be circumstances where it will be appropriate for the trustees to encourage and facilitate settlement, given that that would create certainty at an early stage and the saving of litigation costs for the scheme. Otherwise, the trustees' primary interest will be to ensure that the proposed settlement is administratively workable, and so their role will become more prominent when the structure of any settlement is being formulated. At that time, the trustees will also wish to consider the knock-on effects to other scheme provisions of any benefit changes occasioned by the proposed compromise.

1 Section 15(f) of the Trustee Act 1925.
2 See the closing words of s 15 of the Trustee Act 1925, introduced by s 40 of the Trustee Act 2000.
3 See **15.20**.

15.6

It is possible for a compromise to occur in a situation where there is no representative defendant: this could be because the issue and its proposed resolution have arisen prior to any proceedings being issued; or because it is proposed that the interests of the members will be represented by the trustees and/or the employer.[1] In either case, the court may be prepared to deal with the compromise on the basis that the trustees and employer formally represent the members. Thus, in *Grolier International Ltd v Capital Cranfield Trustees Ltd*,[2] Mann J approved the compromise of an issue as to whether a defined benefits (DB) scheme had been validly converted into a defined contribution (DC) scheme for future accrual, by ordering the trustee to represent the members who might want to argue that that conversion was invalid and the employer to represent all other members. The judge did so on the basis that the significant costs of adding another party to the claim for approval was unnecessary, and that it was extremely difficult to envisage what members would have fallen into the class of members to be represented by the employer.

1 In *Re Owens Corning Fibreglass (UK) Ltd* [2002] Pens LR 323, Neuberger J approved a compromise pursuant to an application made by the employer alone, because of the need to implement the settlement as quickly as possible.
2 [2015] EWHC 1832 (Ch), [2015] Pens LR 485.

15.7

However, there may be situations in which the trustees may be willing to depart from their usual neutral position to represent members for the purposes of advancing legal arguments at trial, but who do not feel comfortable in negotiating a settlement of the claim on behalf of those members because of the high-profile nature of the claim. It may therefore be necessary in that situation for a representative defendant to be joined to the claim for the purposes of negotiating a settlement and, if successful, supporting any subsequent application for its approval.

15.8

Where, in addition to the pensions dispute, there is an actual or contemplated claim against a professional adviser in respect of the error, consideration should be given to involving the professional in the settlement discussions, so as to remove or reduce the risk that, in such a claim, the professional will argue that the terms of the settlement do not constitute a reasonable mitigation of loss.[1] The scope of such involvement will vary according to the circumstances of each case, ranging from the adviser having a seat at the negotiation table to merely being given an opportunity to comment on the proposed terms of settlement.[2]

1 See **16.56–16.58**.
2 Consideration may also be given to settling the adviser claim at the same time as the pensions dispute, although that might prove too cumbersome in practice.

Negotiating a compromise

15.9

Discussions about a compromise may be more or less formal and structured, depending on the complexity of the issues involved. Most will involve meetings between the parties' legal teams, either on a face-to-face basis or with the assistance of a mediator.[1]

1 Mediations are more fully discussed at **16.111–16.112**.

15.10

All discussions should be on a 'without prejudice' basis, so that any statements made during the negotiation process which are adverse to a party's interests cannot subsequently be referred to in court. Whilst this principle only applies to statements made against those interests, the court will give a wide scope to the statements which are protected by this principle, as to dissect out such statements from the rest of without prejudice communications would create huge practical difficulties and undermine the underlying objective of enabling the parties to speak freely about all issues in the litigation.[1]

1 *Unilever plc v The Procter & Gamble Co* [2000] 1 WLR 2436, 2448-2449 per Walker LJ.

15.11

As with the compromise of any dispute, the parties need to be clear about the legal merits of the claim and the financial consequences of success, failure, or any terms of settlement which they intend to propose. They also need to be aware of their objectives in considering settlement: for the employers, are the costs of funding the scheme paramount? Or are there countervailing considerations, such as the need for certainty or to ensure that the claim does not affect relations with the workforce? For the members, the certainty of getting something from the claim now may outweigh the possibility of obtaining a much larger share through success at a later trial or following an appeal, particularly where the members were not expecting anything prior to the claim arising. The members may also not wish to put the solvency of the employer in jeopardy, where that may lead to a loss of jobs and/or a reduction in benefits following a transfer into the Pension Protection Fund (PPF). The benefit to elderly or ill members of a swift resolution to the claim may also be a relevant factor.

15.12

For this purpose, it is likely that the representative will want to have access to independent actuarial advice, to help assess the financial effect of any offers and counter-offers and the detailed impact of the proposed settlement on members' benefits. The other parties would generally be well advised not to refuse or place undue limitations on a request for such advice, as that will reduce the prospects of a compromise being reached or of any compromise being subsequently approved by the court.

15.13

It goes without saying that the parties need to be open-minded and flexible about each other's positions, maintaining a realistic attitude to any proposals by reference to the merits of their position. Generally, the need for the compromise to be approved by the court can be a strong bargaining tool for the representative defendant: their ability to negotiate a settlement is constrained by the need for them to be satisfied that the settlement is in the best interests of those they represent, in order that they can support an application for approval of the compromise. The representative accordingly has less flexibility than the employer to come to a commercial settlement, and the employer must be wary of putting too much pressure on the representative to negotiate a settlement which they cannot support wholeheartedly.

15.14

In cases where the mistake in question concerns a prior attempt to reduce members' benefits, the parties may consider settlement based on an evaluation of the strength of the members' case on a percentage basis.[1] If, for example, the parties agree to settle on the basis that the members have a 30 per cent prospect of success, the question becomes: in what form should that offer be put? Cash payments to the members outside of the auspices of the scheme is a possibility, although tax and cashflow considerations may make the enhancement of existing pension benefits a more attractive option.[2] In that situation, there is then the issue of how such an enhancement should be provided to the members, such as by way of a service credit, lump sum payment or a contribution to their DC pots or personal pension arrangements. In cases where the validity of changes to the normal retirement ages of members has been in issue, settlement has taken the form of applying the agreed percentage to produce a compromise retirement date for the relevant period of service.[3]

1 This method of settlement was approved by Sir Andrew Morritt C in *Capita ATL Pension Trustees Ltd v Zurkinskas* [2010] EWHC 3365 (Ch), [2011] 1 WLR 1274 at [25].
2 See **17.60–17.62**.
3 For example, *Thompson v Fresnius Kabi Ltd* [2013] Pens LR 157; *Sogefi Filtration Ltd v Havard* (18 December 2017, unreported), Deputy Judge Tipples QC.

15.15

The tax consequences of the compromise may require correspondence with HMRC:[1] as such issues can often take time to resolve, the parties must ensure that sufficient time is built into the settlement timetable to deal with any tax matters before the settlement is finalised. Where the provision of additional benefits on a compromise may have adverse tax consequences for members, such as those who are at or near their lifetime allowance, consideration should be given to informing them of those consequences, and whether they should be compensated in an alternative way or be removed from the application of the compromise.

1 See **17.51–17.64.**

15.16

Where the parties agree to settle a pensions claim which will require approval by the court, it will be necessary to enter into a comprehensive settlement agreement. Where a deal is done as a matter of principle, the parties should sign a 'heads of terms' document, pending the drafting of the complete agreement. Such a document can be made fully or partially binding, or not binding at all; and the parties should make sure that the extent to which the heads of terms are intended to be binding is clearly set out in the document. The court should then be prepared to stay the claim pending the settlement being fully negotiated, with a view to restoring the claim for approval of the final agreement.

Compromises affecting pension benefits

15.17

In *HR Trustees Ltd v German*,[1] the members of a scheme which had purported to convert DB rights into DC benefits entered into detailed compromise agreements in which they gave up any DB rights. At first instance,[2] Arnold J had to consider whether such agreements came within s 91 of PA 1995, which (amongst other things) rendered unenforceable any agreement by the members to surrender any entitlement or right to a future pension under the scheme. The judge held that s 91 encompassed entering into a compromise agreement the effect of which was that a member of a pension scheme waived rights which, but for the agreement, they would be entitled to, even if there was a bona fide dispute as the existence of those rights at the time of the agreement. However, the Court of Appeal overturned the judge's decision, holding that s 91 was directed at cases of the deliberate giving up of an actual existing entitlement or right, not one the existence of which was doubted or disputed so that it had to be established by legal determination, unless settled by agreement.[3]

1 [2010] EWHC 321 (Ch), [2010] Pens LR 23 (Arnold J); [2010] EWCA Civ 1349, [2011] ICR 329 (CA).
2 [2010] Pens LR 23 at [231].
3 [2011] ICR 329.

15.18

It is therefore now settled that, in a claim which brings into question the existence of pension rights, any settlement which involves the members accepting less than the full extent of those rights does not constitute a surrender of those benefits for the purposes of s 91, and will therefore be valid and enforceable.[1]

1 See also *Gleeds (Head Office) v Briggs* [2016] EWCA Civ 1284, [2017] Pens LR 67.

Procedure for court approval

15.19

Where a claim involves a potential increase in benefits under the scheme, the employer and the trustees will want the compromise of that claim to bind all members. As it will not usually be practical to join them all to the claim, the only realistic way to achieve this outcome is to seek the approval of the compromise by the court.

15.20

The court may make a representation order whereby all the beneficiaries of the trust who are so represented will be bound by the decision.[1] Where the claim involves a representative defendant under that rule, the court's approval is required to settle such a claim, which the court may do where it is satisfied that the settlement is for the benefit of all the represented persons.[2]

1 CPR 19.7(2), discussed at **14.42–14.44**.
2 CPR 19.7(5), (6).

15.21

An application for approval can be made either by Part 8 claim or, where there are already proceedings on foot in respect of the claim, by an application in those proceedings.

15.22

The court will almost invariably require an opinion on the merits of the proposed compromise from counsel instructed on behalf of the represented class. Such an opinion is normally confidential and not served on or shown to the other parties. The application for the court's approval should be in public, but discussion of the merits of the proposed compromise from the point of view of the represented class will usually take place in private and in the absence of the other parties.[1]

1 Chancery Guide, para 29.97.

15.23

In addition to the legal merits of the claim, the court will normally wish to have information about the funding state of the scheme and the solvency of the employers, to assess the potential effect on them of the compromise not being approved.[1]

1 See *Smithson v Hamilton* [2008] EWCA Civ 996, [2009] ICR 1 at [10] per Mummery LJ.

15.24

In *Punter Southall Governance Services Ltd v Hazlett*,[1] Morgan J approved a compromise on the grounds that:

(a) it represented a fair reflection of the perceived strengths of the rival arguments;

(b) it properly took into account the amounts at stake in relation to each of the issues;

(c) the certainty of outcome achieved by the compromise as compared with the uncertainty involved in continuing to litigate was highly desirable;

(d) it was of benefit to all parties that the compromise produced an immediate resolution of the issues, simplified the administration of the scheme, and avoided the delay involved in continued litigation; and

(e) it involved a saving of legal costs both in relation to the litigation and the future administration of the scheme.

1 [2021] EWHC 1652 (Ch), [2022] Pens LR 1 at [26].

15.25

Similar considerations persuaded Sir Andrew Morritt C in *Capita ATL Pension Trustees Ltd v Zurkinskas*[1] to approve a compromise despite his doubts as to whether the size of the increase in the employer's liabilities accurately reflected the merits of the issues in dispute. An additional consideration in favour of the compromise was the possibility that the scheme, in the absence of a sponsoring employer, might enter the PPF: if that occurred without a compromise in place, the costs would be payable out of the assets of the PPF to the detriment of all with an interest in it.

1 [2010] EWHC 3365 (Ch), [2011] 1 WLR 1274.

15.26

Although there is no requirement to consult with or notify members of a scheme where the court's approval to the settlement of a claim is proposed,[1] the members should ordinarily be notified (usually by the trustees) of the proposed application.[2] The scope of such notification may turn on the extent to which the issue has already been raised with the members. Where there has been no such notification by the time of the approval hearing, the court may decide to postpone the effective date of the order for a short period, to allow any person affected by it to apply to the court if they consider that, due to circumstances which are particular to them, they should not be bound.[3]

1 CPR PD 64B, para 7.7(4).
2 Chancery Guide, para 29.100. See also *Re Owens Corning Fibreglass (UK) Ltd* [2002] Pens LR 323 at [6] per Neuberger J.
3 See *Smithson v Hamilton* [2008] EWCA Civ 996, [2009] ICR 1 at [13]–[15] per Mummery LJ; *Archer v Travis Perkins plc* [2014] EWHC 1362 (Ch), [2014] Pens LR 311 at [26]–[28] per Rose J.

15.27

In *Airways Pension Scheme Trustee Ltd v Fielder*,[1] the trustees of a scheme had obtained a *Beddoe* order from the court[2] authorising the pursuit of an appeal by them; where the trustees had subsequently negotiated a settlement of the appeal, Zacaroli J held that an application by the trustees for approval of the settlement by the court need only be considered by reference to whether the trustees' decision was one that a reasonable body of trustees could arrive at: the court did not also have to consider whether the settlement was in the best interests of the members.

1 [2019] EWHC 3032 (Ch), [2020] Pens LR 7.
2 See **14.108**.

The terms and effect of court approval

15.28

The court order will cross-refer to the compromise agreement, or else include it as a schedule to the order; and the court will approve and authorise the implementation of the agreement by a provision along the following lines:[1]

> *AND THE COURT being satisfied that the Terms of Compromise are for the benefit of all the persons represented by the above representation orders HEREBY APPROVES the Terms of Compromise on behalf of all said represented persons pursuant to the powers conferred by CPR r. 19.7(6) and ORDERS that the Terms of Compromise shall be binding on those persons and the Defendants and that the Trustees shall administer the Scheme in accordance with the Terms of Compromise.*

The order will also provide for representation orders and the costs of the proceedings.

1 This is taken from the order made by Deputy Judge Tipples QC in *Sogefi Filtration Ltd v Havard* (18 December 2017, unreported).

15.29

As can be seen from the last part of the provision cited at **15.28**, the approved compromise operates as an order of the court which varies the beneficial interest under the trust,[1] not as a contractual arrangement. It derives its legal effect from the order that the compromise is binding on the represented persons and that the trustees are to administer the scheme in accordance with the compromise; it does not derive its legal effect from the agreement between the parties. This is presumably why a court-approved compromise is not regarded as a modification or amendment of a pension scheme for the purposes of s 67 of PA 1995 and/or s 37 of PSA 1993,[2] as those provisions do not operate to invalidate an order of the court. However, this issue has never been considered by the court. Similarly, it is an open question as to whether such a compromise might constitute:

(a) a legally enforceable agreement by the trustees which may prejudice the entry of the scheme into the PPF if it operates to reduce the amount of recoverable statutory debt from the employer;[3]

(b) conduct which gives rise to the issuing by the Pensions Regulator of a contribution notice;[4] or

(c) the commission of the offence of avoidance of an employer debt.[5]

1 *Chapman v Chapman* [1954] AC 429, 472 per Lord Cohen (cf. 457 per Lord Morton of Henryton).
2 See **3.34–3.37** and **3.40–3.46**.
3 Regulation 2(2) of The Pension Protection Fund (Entry Rules) Regulations 2005 (SI 2005/590).
4 Section 38 of PA 2004.
5 Section 58A of PA 2004.

15.30

Where the absence of scheme data makes it impossible to know the precise facts underlying the compromise, the court may make a *Benjamin* order[1] permitting the trustees to administer the scheme on the basis of a presumed state of affairs. For example, in *Punter Southall Governance Services Ltd v Hazlett*,[2] Morgan J ordered that the trustees could proceed on the basis that a rule which conferred a discretion on the trustees to restrict the benefits of certain beneficiaries had never been exercised. The effect of such an order is not to vary or remove a member's entitlement to benefits but to protect the trustees from any future claims; and in the *Punter Southall* case, the *Benjamin* order provided that, if any member could be shown to have been treated more or less favourably as a result of that order, they or the trustees could apply for directions as to the benefits to be paid to the member concerned.

1 Following *Re Benjamin* [1902] 1 Ch 723.
2 [2021] EWHC 1652 (Ch), [2022] Pens LR 1 at [38]–[39].

Practice point: the terms of the compromise

15.31

The following matters may be relevant to the drafting of the agreement to compromise a claim relating to a pensions mistake which results in members being compensated for loss of benefits.

Parties to the agreement

15.32

The employer, trustees and representative defendant should be parties to the agreement, together with any other non-representative person who is intended to be bound by the agreement, which might in some cases include the professional responsible for the mistake.

Court approval

15.33

The operation of the agreement should be made subject to the approval of the court, so that there is no danger of the agreement being perfected in the absence of such approval. The agreement should also require the parties to work together to ensure that approval is obtained.

Member communications

15.34

The proposed terms for notifying the members of the approval hearing and, if required, the outcome of the hearing, and the person responsible for sending those notices, should be identified in the agreement.

HMRC clearance

15.35

The terms of the compromise may well give rise to authorised payments issues which require discussions with, and possibly clearance from, HMRC:[1] in such circumstances, the agreement should also be made conditional on the resolution of such issues.

1 See **15.15**.

15.36

It may also be worth considering a provision which allows the trustees to provide any increase to benefits in a different form to that set out in the agreement, if that would avoid the increase being treated as an unauthorised payment.

The principal terms of the compromise

15.37

The substance of the agreement should be included in full and final settlement of the claims, which should be defined to include at least the claims which are the subject-matter of the proceedings, and might also extend to any issues which arise out of the claims, whether or not they are presently known to the parties.

15.38

If the substance of the agreement operates to apply either different benefit increases to different members, or such increases to only some members but not others, care must be taken to ensure compliance with preservation and equalisation requirements.

15.39

It will also be necessary to consider the application of any settlement terms to:

(a) members or their ex-spouses, in respect of whom pension sharing orders or earmarking orders have been made;

(b) beneficiaries entitled to pension or lump sum benefits on the death of the member;

(c) members whose benefits have been wholly commuted due to triviality or serious ill-health; and

(d) members who have transferred out of the scheme (whether by bulk or individual transfer) since the mistake was made.

The continuation of the existing regime

15.40

Where the compromise relates to document errors, the agreement should provide for whether, and if so to what extent, the scheme is to be treated as though those documents are valid and operative for the future.

Funding

15.41

Consideration may be given to how the employer is to fund any increased liabilities arising as a result of the compromise, including any necessary variations to the statutory funding documents.

Implementation

15.42

If the agreement involves a complex reorganisation of benefits, a term could be inserted which enables the trustees, if they reasonably believe that it is impractical or impossible to implement the agreement in accordance with its terms, to do so based on such revisions as they consider will, to the greatest extent reasonably possible, give effect to those terms.

Administration

15.43

In complex cases, the agreement should provide for how the compromise is to be administered. Such provisions may include:

(a) who is to be responsible for the administration of the compromise and for any monitoring or audit of that process;

(b) how individual current and former members and beneficiaries of the scheme affected by the agreement are to be contacted and informed about its terms;

(c) if any decisions have to be made regarding eligibility for payments, who is to make the decision, the evidence and expert advice upon which the decision-maker is entitled to rely, and any appeal process;

(d) if and to the extent that the compensation is based upon historical member or benefit data, what is to be done where such data is missing or incomplete, such as permitting payments to be calculated on the basis of reasonable actuarial assumptions;

(e) time limits for the provision of compensation payments, where it has proved difficult to contact the relevant person;

(f) how any compensation payments are to be made;

(g) whether interest is to be added to the compensation and, if so, at what rate and for what period;

(h) to what extent information relevant to the process is to be shared with any regulatory or adjudicatory bodies.

Confidentiality

15.44

If the parties wish to keep the settlement terms confidential, a provision to that effect should be included in the agreement.

Other terms

15.45

The agreement should provide:

(a) for the exclusion of the Contracts (Rights of Third Parties) Act 1999, to ensure that no non-parties can claim to enforce any of its provisions, although an express exception could be made for the members;

(b) for the agreement to supersede any heads of terms or other prior oral or written agreement, and that its terms constitute the entire agreement between the parties in relation to the subject-matter of the document; and

(c) that, in the case of any part of the agreement being held to be invalid or unenforceable, the remainder of the agreement shall continue to apply.

16 Negligence

16.1

Whenever a legal adviser discovers or is called upon to review a pensions mistake which results in an increase in the liabilities or costs of the scheme, it is necessary to consider whether there are grounds for a claim against the person who is responsible for the mistake.

16.2

Where the mistake is committed by an employee of the trustees or the employer, it is unlikely that a claim would be worth pursuing against them; and if trustees themselves are at fault, they are likely to be protected by a term in the scheme's governing provisions excluding liability for negligence or non-fraudulent breaches of trust. The principal targets for such a claim are therefore those persons providing professional advice and services in respect of the scheme, such as legal advisers, benefits consultants or actuaries.

16.3

The purpose of this chapter is to consider the components of a claim against the professional adviser responsible for the mistake, with particular reference to the features which may be relevant to a pensions claim, and to identify some points of practical importance for bringing such a claim. This chapter sets out general principles not related to any particular professional and is not intended to provide an exhaustive analysis of the subject.[1] Moreover, much of the discussion in this context is theoretical, as it is thought that no pensions professional negligence case has ever been tried to a conclusion in an English court: certainly, no such case has been reported.

1 For such an analysis, see *Jackson & Powell on Professional Liability* (8th edn, Sweet & Maxwell, 2017) (*Jackson & Powell*).

Structure of the claim

16.4

The elements of a negligence claim involve establishing the following:

(a) a legal duty of care owed by the professional to the person who has suffered the loss;

(b) a breach of that duty;

(c) causation;

(d) the quantum of loss; and

(e) that the professional is not able to rely on a defence to all or part of the claim.

Duty of care

16.5

To bring a claim against a professional, it is first necessary to establish that the professional owed a duty of care to the person who has suffered the loss.

Legal basis of the duty

16.6

The duty of care in question arises by way of either a contract or the tort of negligence.

Contract

16.7

It is likely that a contractual relationship will exist between the professional and the client to whom the professional's services are provided. The scope of the contractual duty will be either set out in one or more documents recording the terms of the professional's retainer, or, if there are no written terms,[1] derived from the services which were actually provided by the professional.[2] As the professional will be acting in the course of a business, a term will be implied into the contract requiring them to carry out their services with reasonable skill and care.[3]

1 Which was more common before professional advisers to occupational pension schemes were required to be appointed in writing, pursuant to s 47 of PA 1995 and reg 5 of The Occupational Pension Schemes (Scheme Administration) Regulations 1996 (SI 1996/1715).

2 Such an implied retainer only arises where, on an objective consideration of all the circumstances, an intention to enter into a contractual relationship ought fairly and properly to be imputed to the parties: *Dean v Allin & Watts* [2001] PNLR 39 at [22] per Lightman J.

3 Section 13 of the Supply of Goods and Services Act 1982.

16.8

Where the contract is in writing, it is necessary to consider its terms with care to determine the services which the professional has agreed to carry out, as the courts are reluctant to extend the professional's duty far beyond the retainer. Thus, in *Denning v Greenhalgh Financial Services Ltd*,[1] Green J held that a duty to advise outside of the terms of the retainer only arises in obvious cases, where there is a close and strong nexus between the retainer and the matter upon which it is alleged the professional should have advised, but omitted to do so. However, liability may well be established where a professional failed to consider a matter which fairly and reasonably arose while carrying out their instructions.[2]

1 [2017] EWHC 143 (QB), [2017] PNLR 19 at [53] and [55].
2 *Jackson & Powell*, para 11-169, citing *Gilbert v Shanahan* [1988] 3 NZLR 528.

16.9

It is also important to consider whether the contract seeks to limit the professional's liability to a particular sum or (more rarely) to exclude liability for negligence altogether, and whether any such limitation or exclusion is enforceable.[1]

1 For example, whether they comply with the requirements of the Consumer Rights Act 2015 (for consumer contracts) or the Unfair Contract Terms Act 1977 (for other contracts). Any term in a contentious business agreement with a solicitor which exempts the solicitor from liability is void: s 60(5) of the Solicitors Act 1974.

16.10

Where the contract is not in writing, it will often be more difficult to establish liability where the professional has omitted to do something which they were allegedly required to do, and where there is no evidence that they had undertaken that task in the past. However, where a service is provided which requires certain further services to be provided to make it effective, the professional is more likely to be liable for a failure to provide those services. For example, if a professional is responsible for drafting a trust deed for clients with no legal experience, the professional is likely to owe a duty to explain to the clients the requirements for the valid execution of the deed.

Tort of negligence

16.11

The issue of whether a person owes a duty of care in tort to another is not capable of being answered by reference to a universal formula or yardstick,[1] but the foundation of such a duty in the context of the provision of professional services is the assumption of responsibility by the professional to the client.[2] Thus, professionals who have provided services to clients owe a duty in tort to act with reasonable care and skill in the provision of those services.

1 *Michael v Chief Constable of South Wales Police* [2015] UKSC 2, [2015] AC 1732 at [103] per Lord Toulson JSC.
2 *NRAM Ltd v Steel* [2018] UKSC 13, [2018] 1 WLR 1190 at [24] per Lord Wilson JSC.

16.12

The issue of whether the service provided by the professional is sufficiently closely connected to the loss to establish liability has bedevilled the courts for many years since the *SAAMCO* decision,[1] which required a distinction to be drawn between the giving of advice and the provision of information. Two recent decisions of the Supreme Court[2] have signalled a move away from this distinction, with the focus instead being on the purpose of the advice or information and the risk the advice was intended to protect.

1 *South Australia Asset Management Corp v York Montague Ltd* [1997] AC 191.
2 *Manchester Building Society v Grant Thornton UK LLP* [2021] UKSC 20, [2021] 3 WLR 81; *Khan v Meadows* [2021] UKSC 21, [2021] 3 WLR 147.

16.13

This tortious duty is not affected by the fact that the parties are also in a contractual relationship: the professional will usually also owe the client a concurrent duty of care in tort.[1] In practice, where the mistake is only discovered many years after the event, it will be key to establish a duty of care in tort, because of the extended periods of limitation applicable to such claims.[2]

1 *Henderson v Merrett Syndicates Ltd* [1995] 2 AC 145.
2 See **16.68–16.73**.

To whom is the duty owed?

16.14

In a contract claim, the person to whom the professional owes the duty of care is clear: the client. No such duty is owed to third parties unless the contract expressly so provides or where a term confers a benefit on a third party in compliance with the Contracts (Rights of Third Parties) Act 1999; and most professional contracts will expressly exclude the effect of that Act.

16.15

However, in pensions cases where the contract was not reduced into writing, the identification of the professional's client may not be straightforward, as it used to be common for professionals involved in advising on pension benefits and providing documentation services to act for both the employer and the trustees, either at the same time or in respect of different pieces of advice, in circumstances where there was no conflict between those clients.

16.16

As for tort, the professional will owe the duty of care to the person to whom the advice was given, but often there is an issue as to whether the professional also owed a duty of care to a third party who also received the advice.

16.17

The following factors are relevant to determining whether a third party who received the advice (the advisee) is owed a duty of care by a professional adviser:[1]

(a) the purpose for which the advice was given;

(b) the purpose for which the advice was communicated;

(c) the relationship between the advisee and any relevant third party;

(d) the size of any class to which the advisee belongs;

(e) the state of knowledge of the advisee; and

(f) reliance by the advisee.

1 *James McNaughton Paper Group Ltd v Hicks Anderson & Co* [1991] 2 QB 113, 125 per Neill LJ. As the judge acknowledged, these factors involve a substantial measure of overlap.

16.18

In *Precis (521) plc v William M Mercer Ltd*,[1] the Court of Appeal rejected a claim by the claimant, which was considering the purchase of a company, against an actuary who had prepared for the company a valuation report on its pension scheme's liabilities, which the company sent to the claimant. The court relied on the following factors in finding that the actuary owed no duty to the claimant:

(a) the actuary had no pre-existing relationship with the claimant: its relationship was with the opposite party to the contemplated transaction;

(b) the actuary provided historic information, which could just as have easily been provided by the scheme trustee or the company;

(c) the claimant wanted to use the information in connection with the proposed purchase, whereas the purpose of the report was to advise the company on its contribution rate to the scheme;

(d) although the claimant asked for further information on the report, the claimant did not communicate with the actuary directly or inform it why the information was requested, and did not require the response to be given by the actuary;

(e) the actuary expected the claimant to have its own advisers, which indeed it did.

1 [2005] EWCA Civ 114, [2005] PNLR 511 at [31] per Arden LJ.

16.19

This issue is of particular relevance in cases involving defined benefits (DB) schemes, where tort is the only claim which is not statute-barred. The orthodox view in such cases[1] is that the loss caused by an increase in the liabilities of the scheme is suffered by the sponsoring employer rather than the trustees, because it is the obligation of the former to fund those liabilities. Thus, professionals who provide services for the trustees will often try to argue that they do not owe a tortious duty to the employer, so that their liability is limited to those who have not suffered any loss by reason of the negligent provision of those services.

1 But see the contrary views of Christopher Nugee QC (now Nugee LJ) in 'Suing for Losses to the Scheme – Some issues', a paper delivered to the Association of Pension Lawyers' Annual Conference in 2000.

16.20

Although the result will turn on the particular facts of each case, where the professional's services affect the liabilities of the scheme, and the employer has not retained its own professional in respect of the services, it will be difficult for the professional to resist owing a duty of care to the employer:

(a) As a general matter, where a professional gives advice to the trustees of a DB scheme, the professional will, or ought to, be aware that their advice will also have a material effect on the sponsoring employer of the scheme, as any mistake leading to losses is likely to have to be made good by the employer.

(b) Moreover, there is a general inclination in English law against depriving the claimant of a remedy in tort because the person to whom the defendant owed the direct duty did not suffer the loss. For example, in *Gorham v British Telecommunications plc*,[1] an insurance company advising a client in respect of pension and life cover was held to owe a duty of care to the client's dependents who suffered lost death benefits because of negligent advice.

(c) This analysis assumes that the subject-matter of the advice did not give rise to an actual or potential conflict between the interests of the trustees and the interests of the employer. In the case of document errors, where the negligence relates to the formal implementation of amendments which had already been agreed by the employer and trustees, it will be in the interests of both parties that the amendments were validly effected.

1 [2000] 1 WLR 2129, applying the House of Lords' decision in *White v Jones* [1995] 2 AC 207.

16.21

Another context in which this issue may be relevant is where the negligence affects a multi-employer scheme: will the duty be owed only to the principal employer,[1] or to all the participating employers? What if there are changes to the employer over time, so that the employer in situ at the time of the negligent conduct has since been replaced by another employer, who is required to meet the loss caused by the negligence? In such circumstances, it may be prudent to ensure that:

(a) on the appointment of a new principal employer, the departing employer assigns all its causes of action to its replacement; and

(b) when any proceedings are brought, as many of the past and present participating employers as possible assign their causes of action to the claimant employer.

1 Assuming that there is one: industry-wide schemes do not have a principal employer.

Breach of duty

Standard of duty

16.22

In tort claims, the duty is to act with reasonable care and skill: the professional is not under a strict obligation to ensure a particular result is achieved. The same is usually the case in contract claims: whilst it is theoretically possible for a contracting party to undertake an absolute obligation to perform a task, that must be clearly spelt out in the contract,[1] and it is highly unlikely that any pensions professional would agree to such a term.

1 *Platform Funding Ltd v Bank of Scotland plc* [2008] EWCA Civ 930, [2009] QB 426 at [30] per Moore-Bick LJ.

16.23

The standard that a professional defendant will be expected to exercise is that degree of skill and care which is ordinarily exercised by reasonably competent members of the profession, who have the same seniority and profess the same specialisation (if any) as the defendant.[1]

1 *Jackson & Powell*, para 2-135, cited with approval by Hamblen J in *Wright v Lewis Silkin LLP* [2015] EWHC 1897 (QB), [2015] PNLR 32 (overturned on appeal without reference to this point: [2016] EWCA Civ 1308, [2017] PNLR 16).

16.24

Professionals facing claims for document errors made before the 2000s often rely on the fact that the practice of implementing amendments by informal means such as announcements, rather than by reference to the terms of the amendment power, was widespread amongst a body of reasonably competent pensions practitioners at the time. However, it is doubtful whether this defence would be successful, as it is not enough that fellow professional genuinely held the opinion that the conduct was appropriate: it must also be shown that that opinion had a logical basis and in particular that the professional had directed their mind to the question of comparative risks and benefits and had reached a defensible conclusion on the matter.[1] Blindly following a practice which is not demonstrably reasonable and responsible will not protect the professional.[2] It is therefore likely that a reasonably competent pensions professional, with knowledge of the amendment power, should have foreseen that compliance with the general practice might result in loss, and that precautions could easily have been taken to guard against that risk by complying with the terms of the power.[3]

1 *Bolitho v City & Hackney Heath Authority* [1998] AC 232, 242 per Lord Browne-Wilkinson.
2 *Patel v Daybells* [2001] EWCA Civ 1229, [2002] PNLR 125 at [41] per Robert Walker LJ.
3 See *Edward Wong Finance Co Ltd v Johnson Stokes & Master* [1984] AC 296.

16.25

However, if the professional themselves had relied on specialist advice, it is likely that they will not be held to in breach of duty, if they had satisfied themselves that that advice was not obviously and glaringly wrong.[1]

1 See *Locke v Camberwell Health Authority* (1991) [2002] Lloyd's Rep PN 23 at [29] per Taylor LJ (solicitors' reliance on counsel).

The need for expert evidence

16.26

Where the court lacks the relevant specialist knowledge, it will require the assistance of evidence from expert witnesses. To establish that the duty of care has or has not been breached, it will usually be necessary to adduce expert evidence as to what a reasonably competent member of the profession in question would have done in the situation.

16.27

A distinction must be drawn between an expert adviser and an expert witness. The adviser provides advice to a party and may assist in formulating the claim and considering the other side's case. An expert witness, on the other hand, is instructed to give or prepare expert evidence for the purpose of legal proceedings. The key distinction is that the adviser acts on behalf of their client, whereas the expert's duty is to assist the court on matters within their expertise, which overrides any obligation to the person from whom the expert has received instructions or by whom they are paid.[1]

1 CPR 35.3.

16.28

Expert evidence should accordingly be independent and uninfluenced by the pressures of litigation, and the expert must not assume the role of an advocate, but should help the court by providing objective, unbiased opinions on matters within their expertise.[1]

1 CPR PD 35, paras 2.1 and 2.2.

16.29

Where the evidence in issue is likely to be uncontentious, it is possible for the parties to agree that the scheme actuary may perform that role, but that will not be appropriate where any of the relevant issues are contested. In disputed cases, the parties may consider agreeing to or seeking an order for the appointment of a single joint expert, where the issues are relatively uncontroversial.[1]

1 CPR 35.7.

16.30

There are two relevant situations in which expert evidence may not be necessary:

(a) The first situation is where the claim is against a solicitor, as the court will consider itself to possess the necessary professional expertise to decide whether they have discharged their duty of skill and care.[1] However, an exception may be made in claims involving advice provided in a highly specialist area of law,[2] which may well include pensions.

(b) The other situation is where the court applies the principle, identified at **16.24**, that there is no logical basis for the body of opinion in accordance with which the defendant acted; however, the court would normally only find that that principle had been established if there was expert evidence to undermine the body of opinion.[3]

1 *Bown v Gould & Swayne* [1996] PNLR 130.
2 *Bown v Gould & Swayne* [1996] PNLR 130, 135 per Simon Brown LJ, citing *Midland Bank Trust Co Ltd v Hett, Stubbs & Kemp* [1979] Ch 384, 402 per Oliver J.
3 *Williams v Cwm Taf Local Health Board* [2018] EWCA Civ 1745.

16.31

No party may call an expert without the court's permission.[1] If permission has been given to call an expert, objection may be made to its admissibility, but this should be done as soon as possible, and if there is real doubt as to whether the evidence should be admitted it should be allowed.[2]

1 CPR 35.4
2 *Liverpool Roman Catholic Archdiocese Trustees Inc v Goldberg (No 2)* [2001] Lloyd's Rep PN 518.

16.32

In determining whether the expert evidence sought to be adduced is admissible, the court will consider four questions:[1]

(a) whether the proposed expert evidence will assist the court in its task;

(b) whether the expert has the necessary knowledge and experience;

(c) whether the expert is impartial in their presentation and assessment of the evidence; and

(d) whether there is a reliable body of knowledge or experience to underpin the expert's evidence.

1 *Kennedy v Cordia (Services) LLP* [2016] UKSC 6, [2016] 1 WLR 597 at [44] per Lord Reed and Lord Hodge JJSC.

16.33

As to the first of those questions, in *British Airways plc v Spencer*[1] Warren J said that the correct approach to the admissibility of the evidence was to ask three questions:

(a) whether, looking at each pleaded issue, it was necessary for there to be expert evidence before that issue could be resolved; if it was necessary, rather than merely helpful, it must be admitted;

(b) if the evidence was not necessary, whether it would be of assistance to the court in resolving that issue; and

(c) if it would be of assistance, whether, in the context of the proceedings as a whole, expert evidence on that issue was reasonably required to resolve the proceedings.

The judge also said that it would not be sufficient that the evidence would help the court in its general understanding of the technical complexities of the case.[2]

1 [2015] EWHC 2477 (Ch), [2015] Pens LR 519 at [68].
2 [2015] EWHC 2477 (Ch), [2015] Pens LR 519 at [24].

Professional standards

16.34

In assessing whether the professional has breached their duty of care, the court will take particular account of guidance issued by the professional's regulatory body as to what is required to discharge the duty to exercise reasonable care and skill.[1] Thus, in *Nederlandse Reassurantie Groep Holding NV v Bacon & Woodrow*,[2] in determining a claim for breach of duty against an actuary for failing to state their assumptions about the range of accuracy of their advice, Colman J relied on guidance on that issue issued in a Guidance Note by the Institute and Faculty of Actuaries.

1 See *Lloyd Cheyham & Co Ltd v Eversheds* (1985) 2 Lloyds PN 154.
2 [1997] LRLR 678 at [567].

The preparation of deeds by non-lawyers

16.35

In the past, it was not unusual for pension scheme documents to be drafted by insurers or benefits consultants who did not employ solicitors to undertake that task. This would have been done in ignorance of s 22 of the Solicitors Act 1974,[1] which made it a criminal offence for a deed relating to real or personal property to be drawn or prepared by, or at the direction or under the supervision of, a person other than a qualified solicitor.

1 Now Part 3 of the Legal Services Act 2007.

16.36

Where the claim arises by reason of an error in such a document, contravention of this provision can be relied upon in support of the claim for breach of duty.

Causation

16.37

Whether the professional's acts or omissions caused the loss which is being claimed involves two elements: factual and legal causation.

Factual causation

16.38

This issue involves considering whether the loss would not have occurred but for the professional's conduct. This will generally not be difficult to establish in cases involving pension scheme professionals.

Legal causation

16.39

There are two elements to this question:

(a) whether the conduct was the effective cause of the harm, which involves considering whether an intervening act of the claimant or a third party has 'broken the chain of causation'; and

(b) whether the loss was too remote, ie whether there was a sufficiently close connection between the conduct and the loss to justify the imposition of liability. This test differs for contract and tort claims:

    (i) in contract, the loss must either arise according to the ordinary course of events or be as may reasonably be supposed to have been in the contemplation of the parties at the time they made the contract, as a probable result of the breach;[1]

    (ii) in tort, the type of loss must be a reasonably foreseeable consequence of the breach of duty, assessed at the time of breach.[2]

Where the professional owed both contractual and tortious duties, the relevant test for the recoverability of financial loss is the contractual one.[3]

1 *Hadley v Baxendale* (1854) 9 Ex 341, 355 per Alderson B.
2 *Overseas Tankship (UK) Ltd v Miller Steamship Co Pty Ltd (The Wagon Mound)* [1967] 1 AC 617.
3 *Wellesley Partners LLP v Withers LLP* [2015] EWCA Civ 1146, [2016] Ch 529.

16.40

In most cases involving pensions professionals, establishing the requisite connection will not be a problem for the claimant, as the professional is likely to have had particular knowledge of their client's intentions.

Loss of a chance

16.41

A claim may lie where the professional's conduct has led, not directly to a monetary loss, but to the claimant losing the chance to do something which would have been to their benefit.

16.42

This claim involves assessing what would have happened if the professional had not breached their duty. The court's approach to this will depend upon whether the question is what would the claimant have done or what would a third party have done:[1]

(a) what the claimant would have done had the defendant not been in breach of duty is determined by the court on the balance of probabilities; damages are then assessed on that hypothesis, without any discount to reflect the possibility that the claimant might have acted differently;

(b) where the question was what a third party would have done had the professional not been in breach of duty, the court will first determine what the chances were that the third party would have acted in a way which benefitted the claimant: if the court finds that the claimant has lost a real or substantial, rather than a speculative, chance,[2] it will award damages to reflect the value of the chance that has been lost.

1 *Perry v Raley's Solicitors* [2019] UKSC 5, [2020] AC 352 at [20] per Lord Briggs JSC.
2 *Allied Maples Group Ltd v Simmons & Simmons* [1995] 1 WLR 1602.

16.43

This principle is particularly relevant in pensions cases where the claimant argues that a negligent failure to spot an earlier mistake, which cannot be recovered because of limitation, caused them to lose the chance to make a claim for that mistake within the limitation period. This is considered at **16.78–16.83**.

Quantum

The general principles

16.44

Damages for breach of contract are intended to put the claimant into the position they would have been had the contract been performed; damages for breach of a tortious duty are intended to restore the claimant into the position they would have been had the breach not occurred.

Time of assessment

16.45

The general rule is that damages in contract and tort cases are assessed at the date of the breach, unless justice requires that some other date should be used.[1]

1 *Smith New Court Securities Ltd v Scrimgeour Vickers (Asset Management) Ltd* [1997] AC 254, 265–266 per Lord Browne-Wilkinson.

16.46

In pensions cases, where the loss caused is an increase in the liabilities of the scheme, the fact that those liabilities must be funded in the future, and the inherent fluidity in the valuation of assets and liabilities of the scheme, means that damages should usually be assessed at the date of trial, to take account of actual changes to assets and liabilities which would otherwise be a matter for actuarial estimation.

The valuation of the liabilities

16.47

Where the breach of duty has caused an increase in liabilities, there will usually be a dispute as to the correct basis for valuing the liabilities, given the various ways in which such liabilities are valued for different purposes.

16.48

A common starting point will be the circumstances of the scheme at the time for the assessment of loss, ie the valuation basis which best corresponds to the way in which the liabilities of the scheme are or have to be funded:[1]

(a) If the scheme has bought out benefits, or is in the process of buying out benefits, or will have to buy out benefits soon because, for example, it is in winding-up, the annuity valuation basis may be appropriate, as that matches the way in which the liabilities of the scheme will actually be funded.

(b) At the other end of the spectrum, if the trustees are simply paying benefits as they fall due from the scheme's assets, the technical provisions basis may be appropriate, as that reflects how those benefits will be funded.

1 Cf. *Wells v Wells* [1999] 1 AC 345, a personal injury case, in which it was held that the way in which any damages are invested by the claimant is irrelevant to how they are to be assessed.

16.49

Whether these, or any of the other valuation bases, are adopted, will involve striking the right balance between ensuring that the claimant is properly compensated, which will be affected by the future funding strategy for the scheme, and avoiding overcompensation, which will arise if (for example) the annuity purchase basis is adopted in circumstances where benefits are not intended to be bought out in the foreseeable future.

Expert evidence

16.50

Issues of quantum will require the assistance of an actuary. Initially, the claimant will need actuarial advice in assessing the loss caused by the negligence and to help in formulating the quantum aspect of the claim, and often the scheme actuary is used for this purpose. If the quantum claim is disputed by the professional, it will be necessary to instruct an actuary to act as an expert witness, whose overriding duty is to assist the court, not their client.[1] Whilst an actuarial adviser already instructed by the claimant can be appointed as an expert, this should not be the scheme actuary.[2]

1 CPR 35.3: see **16.27**.
2 See further, the Institute and Faculty of Actuaries' Actuarial Profession Standard X3: 'The Actuary as an Expert in Legal Proceedings'.

Defences

16.51

Several defences may be available to the professional: those most relevant to pensions cases are dealt with below. The defence of limitation is considered separately, as this will be a principal defence where, as is often the case, the error in question occurred many years before it was discovered.

Contributory negligence

16.52

Where a person suffers damage partly as the result of their own negligence, the damages recoverable will be reduced as the court thinks just and equitable, having regard to the claimant's share in the responsibility for the damage.[1]

1 Section 1(1) of the Law Reform (Contributory Negligence) Act 1945. This defence can be raised in a professional negligence claim irrespective of whether the claim arises in contract and tort, where the standard of care is the same: *Forsikringsaktieselskapet Vesta v Butcher* [1986] 2 All ER 488.

16.53

Whilst pensions professionals often seek to raise this defence in claims brought by trustees or employers on the basis that they should have spotted the mistake themselves, it is not thought that a court would usually have much sympathy with the defence, where the professional has been instructed to protect their clients from such mistakes.

Contribution

16.54

It is often the case that a pensions mistake has arisen in a situation where more than one professional has been instructed in the transaction in question. In such a situation, the defendant may seek an indemnity for their liability towards the claimant's loss or a contribution towards that liability, if another professional is also liable to the claimant for that same loss.[1] The amount of the contribution payable by each party is the amount the court considers just and equitable having regard to that party's responsibility for the damage in question.[2]

1 Section 1 of the Civil Liability (Contribution) Act 1978.
2 Section 2 of the Civil Liability (Contribution) Act 1978.

16.55

Contribution claims brought by the defendant professional against another professional will not usually be of particular concern to the claimant, where the liability of the professionals is joint and several: in such a case, the claimant can claim the entirety of the loss from the defendant and leave it to the professionals to determine the apportionment between themselves, whether that involves the defendant joining a professional as a third party to the main proceedings or by subsequently bringing separate proceedings.

Mitigation of loss

16.56

A claimant is obliged to take reasonable steps to minimise the loss caused by the professional and, if such steps are not taken, the damages claim will be reduced to the extent that those steps would have reduced the claimant's loss.

16.57

In cases involving document errors, the requirement for the claimant to mitigate the loss often manifests itself in two respects:

(a) If the increase in the liabilities of the scheme caused by the document error is ongoing, the claimant must act as quickly as is reasonably possible to stop the increases from continuing to accrue by entering into a 'capping deed', in order validly to effect the change which had not been properly implemented because of the error. A failure to act in this way may result in the claimant being denied recovery of any loss accruing after the date on which a capping deed ought reasonably to have been made.

(b) The professional may contend that the document error should be corrected in one or more of the ways described in earlier chapters, and may insist upon the claimant bringing legal proceedings to correct the error. Whilst the general principle is that a claimant does not have to embark upon difficult or uncertain litigation to mitigate their loss,[1] where the claimant is offered a full indemnity for the costs and the litigation involves no serious hardship for the claimant, it would probably be unreasonable for them to refuse.[2]

1 *Pilkington v Wood* [1953] Ch 770. In *Walker v Medlicott* [1999] 1 WLR 727, it was held that a disappointed beneficiary who sued a solicitor for negligently failing to include them in a will should have brought a claim for rectification of the will instead, as the two claims involved the same evidence; but that decision was subsequently distinguished in *Horsfall v Haywards* [1999] PNLR 583 in terms which casts doubt on the soundness of that decision.
2 *Jackson & Powell*, para 11-339.

16.58

Any legal costs incurred by the claimant as a result of taking reasonable steps to mitigate loss can be recovered from the professional as a head of damages, even if those steps were unsuccessful.[1] It was for this reason that, in *St Modwen Properties Plc v Herbert*,[2] the costs of a successful rectification claim were ordered to be met from the assets of the scheme rather than paid by the employer, as the trustee had a clearer relationship than the employer with the scheme's adviser who had drafted the erroneous deed, and therefore a better claim against the adviser.

1 *Lloyds and Scottish Finance Ltd v Modern Cars and Caravans (Kingston) Ltd* [1966] 1 QB 764, 782–783 per Edmund Davies J.
2 [2016] EWHC 428 (Ch), [2016] Pens LR 113 at [22] per Rose J.

Limitation

The primary limitation periods

16.59

The limitation period for claims in both tort and contract is six years from the accrual of the cause of action.[1] For this purpose, the cause of action in contract accrues when the contract is entered into, and the cause of action in tort accrues when real, as opposed to minimal, damage is first suffered.[2]

1 Sections 2 and 5 of LA 1980.
2 *Cartledge v E Jopling and Sons Ltd* [1963] AC 758, 774 per Lord Evershed.

16.60

In a claim relating to a document error where the drafting exercise continued for a long period of time, a claim for the loss caused by the error will not accrue in either contract or tort during the drafting process while the professional remains under instruction and has the opportunity to correct it; however, once the professional's role in the drafting process has ended, the limitation period will not be extended where there is any delay before the execution of the document caused by the conduct of the claimant.[1]

1 See *Bell v Peter Browne & Co* [1990] 2 QB 495, and in particular the ground on which Nicholls and Beldam LJJ (at 501 and 507 respectively) distinguished *Midland Bank Trust Co Ltd v Hett, Stubbs & Kemp* [1979] Ch 384.

16.61

Whilst the incurring of a contingent liability will not start time running for the purpose of a tort claim,[1] that will have limited application to pensions claims:

(a) It is immaterial that the affected members have yet to receive any payments from the scheme. A clear distinction has been drawn in the case law between transactions which give rise to pure contingent liabilities and transactions in respect of which the claimant had suffered a diminution in the value of an asset; the latter transactions have no relevance to a case in which a purely contingent obligation has been incurred.[2] Thus, in *Shore v Sedgwick Financial Services Ltd*,[3] the Court of Appeal held that a claimant had suffered loss as a result of advice to transfer his occupational pension scheme benefits to a personal pension scheme at the time of the transfer, as the investment was less advantageous to him at that time.

(b) It is also immaterial that the quantum of the loss is not yet capable of being determined. In *Integral Memory plc v Haines Watts*,[4] the claimant alleged that the defendant had failed in 2003 to advise on a change in the law regarding national insurance contributions, with the effect that the claimant had not paid enough to HMRC and interest began to accumulate on the unpaid contributions. Following the institution of proceedings by HMRC, the claimant reached a settlement in 2009 and claimed the settlement sum in damages from the defendant, contending that the defendant's liability was contingent on HMRC succeeding in the proceedings or on the claimant accepting liability. Deputy Judge Sheldon QC held that a contingent liability was a liability which, by reason of something done by the person bound, may or may not arise depending on the happening of a future event; by contrast, in the present case there was either an actual liability to pay the contributions or there was not; the existence of such liability was not contingent on HMRC succeeding or failing in its proceedings, and all the court would be deciding was whether or not there was an actual liability.

1 *Law Society v Sephton & Co* [2006] UKHL 22, [2006] 2 AC 543.
2 *Law Society v Sephton & Co* [2006] UKHL 22, [2006] 2 AC 543 at [22] per Lord Hoffmann.
3 [2008] EWCA Civ 863, [2008] PNLR 871.
4 [2012] EWHC 342 (Ch).

Preserving the limitation period

16.62

If the limitation period is close to expiry, the claimant will have to take steps to ensure that any subsequent claim is not statute-barred. A claim which is issued solely to preserve the limitation period, where there is no present intention to prosecute the claim, will be struck out as an abuse of process.[1] However, if the claimant believes that they have a claim, and the general nature of it can be stated even though full details cannot be finalised at the time of issue, it will not be an abuse where there is a genuine intention to pursue the claim, particularly where the claimant is actively engaged in preparations.[2]

1 *Nomura International Plc v Granada Group Ltd* [2007] EWHC 642 (Comm), [2008] Bus LR 1.
2 *USAF Nominee No 18 Ltd v Watkin Jones and Son Ltd* [2021] EWHC 3173 (TCC).

16.63

The preferable course of action for a claimant is to seek to agree the suspension or extension of time by entering into a standstill agreement with the professional. As such an agreement will not prevent time running unless the restriction is expressed in very clear terms,[1] it is important to ensure that the agreement is in writing, setting out the precise terms of the standstill. Sufficient time therefore needs to be left to negotiate and finalise the standstill agreement before the expiry of the limitation period.

1 *Fortisbank SA v Trenwick International Ltd* [2005] EWHC 399 (Comm), [2005] Lloyd's Rep IR 464 at [30] per Gloster J.

Extending the limitation period

16.64

Where the primary limitation periods have already expired, there are four potential options open to the claimant to extend the time within which they may bring an enforceable claim against the professional.

Continuing duty

16.65

It is theoretically possible to contend that the professional's duty of care to the claimant continues for the duration of the retainer, so that the cause of action does not accrue until the earlier of the discovery of the breach or the cessation of the retainer.

16.66

In the absence of special facts, courts are unwilling to impose a continuing duty on a professional to defeat a limitation claim.[1] An example in a pensions context is *Capita (Banstead 2011) Ltd v RFIB Group Ltd*,[2] where it was held that an adviser providing ongoing investment advice to trustees did not owe a continuing duty to correct an earlier negligent error, and that the obtaining and receiving of advice after the error did not mean that an obligation to correct that error continued to accrue and give a fresh cause of action every day after the error had been made.[3]

1 *Nouri v Marvi* [2010] EWCA Civ 1107, [2011] PNLR 100.
2 [2015] EWCA Civ 1310, [2016] QB 835. See also *Worthing v Lloyds Bank plc* [2015] EWHC 2836 (QB), [2016] WTLR 137.
3 See also *Shepherd Construction Ltd v Pinsent Masons LLP* [2012] EWHC 43 (TCC), [2012] PNLR 31 at [31] per Akenhead J: '*There is something commercially and professionally worrying if professional people are to be held responsible for reviewing all previous advice or indeed services provided.*'

16.67

However, where the transaction in question is ongoing and uncompleted, the professional may well remain under a continuing duty to complete the transaction, or to advise the client that the transaction has not been completed, up to and including the end of their retainer.

Extended limitation for negligence claims

16.68

The claimant can rely on the extended period of limitation provided by s 14A of LA 1980 where, at the time the cause of action accrued, they did not have knowledge of all material facts. This period is applicable to tort claims in negligence; it does not apply to negligent breach of contract claims.[1] Because document errors are often discovered many years after they were committed, trustees and employers regularly seek to rely on this extended period.

1 *Societe Commercial de Reassurance v ERAS (international) Ltd* [1992] 2 All ER 82.

16.69

The s 14A limitation period is three years from the date on which the claimant knew or ought to have known:

(a) of the material facts about the damage which is the subject of the claim;

(b) that the loss was attributable in whole or in part to the act or omission that is alleged to constitute negligence; and

(c) the identity of the professional.[1]

1 Section 14A(6)(a), (7) of LA 1980.

16.70

The legal principles applicable to ascertaining whether the claimant had the requisite knowledge have been summarised as follows:[1]

(a) knowledge for s 14A purposes is knowing facts with sufficient confidence to justify embarking on the preliminaries to the issue of a claim;

(b) knowledge that damage was attributable to the act or omission of the defendant alleged to constitute negligence means knowledge in broad terms of the facts on which the claimant's complaint is based and of the defendant's acts or omissions. It must also be known there is a real possibility that those acts or omissions were a cause of the damage;

(c) as to the degree of detail required, the claimant needs broad knowledge of the matters pointing to the defendant's acts or omissions, and appreciation in general terms and knowledge of the essence of the act or omission to which the injury was attributable;

(d) all that is required is sufficient knowledge to realise there is a real possibility of the damage having been caused by some flaw or inadequacy in the defendant's services: that is enough knowledge to start an investigation into that possibility;

(e) actual knowledge involves knowing enough to make it reasonable for the claimant to investigate whether or not there is a claim against a particular potential defendant;

(f) it is not necessary that the claimant should have all the detail of the knowledge required to bring an action or plead a case: the tipping point arises when a claimant has sufficient knowledge to make it reasonable to begin to investigate whether they have a case.

1 *Earnshaw v Prudential Assurance Co Ltd* [2017] EWHC 916 (Ch) at [46] per Master Marsh. The leading case on this issue in *Haward v Fawcetts* [2006] UKHL 9, [2006] 1 WLR 682.

16.71

In order to show knowledge in a corporate claimant for the purposes of s 14A, it is not enough to show that particular employees or officers of that corporation were in possession of different facts which, if aggregated, would lead to the relevant conclusion: at the very least it must be shown either that one responsible person had the relevant aggregated knowledge, or alternatively that it was reasonable to suppose that the relevant information would in fact have been aggregated within the organisation.[1]

1 *3M United Kingdom plc v Linklaters & Paines* [2005] EWHC 1382 (Ch), [2005] PNLR 46 at [29] per Hart J; this aspect of the decision was not challenged on appeal.

16.72

Constructive, as well as actual, knowledge will be sufficient to start time running. This is defined to mean knowledge which the claimant might reasonably have been expected to acquire from facts observable or ascertainable by them or from facts ascertainable by them with the help of appropriate expert advice which it is reasonable for them to seek, though in the latter case the claimant will not be fixed with knowledge where they have taken all reasonable steps to obtain (and, where appropriate to act on) that advice.[1]

1 Section 14A(10) of LA 1980.

16.73

However, this limitation period is subject to a 'longstop': it cannot be relied upon where 15 years have elapsed from the date (or, if more than one, the last of the dates) on which the act or omission in question occurred.[1]

1 Section 14B of LA 1980.

Deliberate concealment

16.74

If the professional deliberately concealed from the claimant any fact relevant to the right of action, the limitation period will not begin to run until the claimant has discovered the concealment or could, with reasonable diligence, have discovered it.[1]

1 Section 32(1)(b) of LA 1980.

16.75

For this purpose, deliberate commission of a breach of duty in circumstances in which it is unlikely to be discovered for some time will constitute deliberate concealment for the purpose of postponing the commencement of the limitation period.[1]

1 Section 32(2) of LA 1980.

16.76

To rely on deliberate concealment of earlier negligent advice, the claimant must establish that the professional was aware that the earlier advice was negligent.[1]

1 *Cave v Robinson Jarvis & Rolf* [2002] UKHL 18, [2003] 1 AC 384. Recklessness is sufficient to constitute the requisite awareness for this purpose: *Canada Square Operations Ltd v Potter* [2021] EWCA Civ 339, [2022] QB 1 at [137] per Rose LJ and [200] per Males LJ.

16.77

Where the professional took active steps to conceal earlier negligent advice, there will be little difficulty in establishing deliberate concealment, provided that the professional was aware that the earlier advice was negligent. Where the professional has taken no such active steps, they may still have deliberately concealed the earlier negligence where they were under a duty to disclose the information to the client. In the leading case of *Canada Square Operations Ltd v Potter*,[1] the Court of Appeal held that that duty need not amount to a freestanding contractual, tortious, or fiduciary duty, but would arise where common sense dictated that the defendant should disclose the information to the claimant.

1 [2021] EWCA Civ 339, [2022] QB 1.

'Piggyback' claims

16.78

Finally, the increasing prevalence of document errors being discovered more than 15 years after they were committed, so that not even s 14A of LA 1980 can be relied upon, has led trustees and employers to assert so-called 'piggyback' claims against professionals who failed to spot an earlier error, which led to the loss of the chance to claim for the original error within the 15-year longstop period.

16.79

As a general principle, a professional who has acted negligently is not under a continuing duty to remind themselves of the negligence of which, *ex hypothesi*, they are unaware: to do otherwise would take the professional's duty beyond their own specific instructions.[1] However, where a subsequent instruction was also negligently implemented, and this later negligence concealed the earlier negligence which, by the time it came to light, was outside the limitation period, the professional may be liable for the damage caused by the loss of the opportunity to claim for the earlier negligence.[2] This principle requires that the professional knew or ought to have known of the earlier breach of duty.[3]

1 *Midland Bank Trust Co Ltd v Hett Stubbs and Kemp* [1979] Ch 384, 403 per Oliver J.
2 *Gold v Mincoff Science & Gold* [2001] Lloyd's Rep PN 423.
3 *Ezekiel v Lehrer* [2002] EWCA Civ 16, [2002] Lloyd's Rep PN 260 at [24] per Ward J. Cf. *Mathiesen v Clintons* [2013] EWHC 3056 (Ch) at [182], where Asplin J suggested (obiter) that actual knowledge should be the touchstone.

16.80

Due to the lack of decided pensions negligence cases, the viability of such a claim has yet to be established in this context, and any such claim will need to overcome the court's reluctance to extend limitation periods by artificial means.[1] However, examples of when such claims might be brought are:

(a) where a solicitor or benefits consultant prepares a consolidating deed which includes a benefit which had been invalidly introduced by reason of an earlier document error, and the drafter fails to spot that error and inform the client accordingly; or

(b) where an actuary prepares a valuation based on an erroneous benefit structure, the accuracy of which they failed to take reasonable steps to investigate.

1 See *Steamship Mutual Underwriting Association Ltd v Trollope & Colls (City) Ltd* (1986) 2 Const LJ 224, 230 per May LJ.

16.81

The claim is based on the loss of the chance to recover substantial damages for the document error because of the expiry of the limitation period. It is therefore necessary to establish that:

(a) the defendant professional could and should have spotted the error and informed the claimant accordingly in time for them to bring a claim in respect of that error; and

(b) such a claim would have resulted in substantial recovery, either by way of settlement or judgment at trial, which involves proving:

    (i) that the claim had legal merit; and

    (ii) that the defendant to the claim would have had the means to meet the liability.

16.82

As to the merits of the claim, whilst the court is willing to discount for the uncertainties of litigation – even on a point of law – it recognises that it is unjust to discount where prospects of success in the original action are tolerably clear.[1] The burden of showing that the original action would not have succeeded is on the defendant.[2]

1 *Harrison v Bloom Camillin* [2001] PNLR 195 at [87] per Neuberger J.
2 *Mount v Barker Austin* [1998] PNLR 493, 510 per Simon Brown LJ.

16.83

The time for the assessment of damages for loss of the original claim may well be crucial in cases of document errors, as the increase in the scheme liabilities may be considerably greater when assessed at the time of the piggyback claim rather than the time of the original claim. The logically correct proposition is that the damages that would have been awarded in the original action fall to be assessed at the time when the original action would have been heard, or (if earlier) settled,[1] as opposed to the much later time that the piggyback claim is heard. This is because it is the chance of this outcome to the litigation that has been lost, and it is illogical for the defendant to be liable for more than the claimant would have recovered in the original action. However, whilst this position is supported by some first-instance cases,[2] a different approach has been taken in three personal injury cases decided the Court of Appeal, which allowed evidence of subsequent changes to the physical condition of the claimant to be considered, even though that would not have been available at the time of the notional original trial.[3]

1 Plus interest from the date the damages ought to have been awarded.
2 *Malyon v Lawrence Messer & Co* (1968) 112 Sol Jo 623. See also *Campbell v Imray* [2004] PNLR 1; *Johnson v Perez* (1988) 82 ALR 587; *Rose v Mitton* (1994) 111 DLR (4th) 217. See also James Edelman (ed), *McGregor on Damages* (21st edn, Sweet & Maxwell, 2021) paras 10-98 and 10-102.
3 *Charles v Hugh James Jones & Jenkins* [2000] 1 WLR 1278; *Dudarec v Andrews* [2006] EWCA Civ 256, [2006] 1 WLR 3002; *Whitehead v Searle* [2008] EWCA Civ 285, [2009] 1 WLR 549.

Practice point: key steps in negligence claims

16.84

When considering whether a claim for negligence arises following the discovery of a pensions mistake, the legal adviser should bear the following practical issues in mind.

Limitation periods

16.85

A preliminary investigation of the facts relating to the mistake should be undertaken as quickly as possible, to determine whether there are any limitation issues relating to the claim. If a limitation period is shortly to expire, a standstill agreement should be negotiated and entered into as a matter of priority.

The size of the issue

16.86

The claimant will need to understand the extent of the loss caused by the mistake at an early stage, to determine the most proportionate response, in terms of the time and money which should be expended in pursuing a claim. This will usually involve instructing an actuary, which at this early stage can, in an appropriate case, be the scheme actuary.

Where the legal adviser is responsible for the mistake

16.87

It is not unusual for a legal adviser to discover that their own firm was responsible for the mistake. In such a situation, even if the matter is still being investigated the adviser must grasp the nettle and inform the client as soon as is practicable and notify their insurers. Failure to do so may lead to the client being able to counter any subsequent limitation defence by an allegation of deliberate concealment, and may also cause the firm both reputational damage and difficulties in maintaining insurance coverage for the mistake.

Gathering documents

16.88

Documents relevant to the mistake must be obtained from the trustees, the employer and any professionals involved in the transaction to which the mistake relates, including the professional who was responsible for the mistake. Of particular relevance are documents which relate to:

(a) the terms of the professional's retainer;

(b) advice given and services rendered by the professional in relation to the transaction in question; and

(c) matters which brought, or should have brought, the error to the attention of the trustees or the employer, and which may affect any reliance on the extended limitation period in s 14A of LA 1980.

Consideration must also be given to the question of whether any of those documents are subject to legal professional privilege or without prejudice privilege.

Professional negligence pre-action protocol

16.89

A claimant wishing to pursue a claim against a professional should (save where limitation is an issue) not do so unless they have complied with the

CPR-mandated pre-action protocol for professional negligence claims:[1] a failure to comply with the substance of the protocol may lead the court to impose costs and other sanctions if proceedings are commenced.[2]

1 *Civil Procedure* (Sweet and Maxwell, 2021) vol 1, section C7.
2 See, for example, *Webb Resolutions Ltd v Waller Needham & Green* [2012] EWHC 3529 (Ch).

16.90

The purpose of the protocol is to encourage an early exchange of information, the narrowing of issues and a consideration of alternative methods of dispute resolution, with a view wherever possible to promoting the settlement of disputes without the need to issue court proceedings. Whilst this consequently involves a considerable element of 'front-end loading' of costs, the early resolution of a claim may still be in both parties' interests, especially if there is an ongoing relationship which they wish to maintain.

16.91

The following is a summary of the procedure set out in the protocol, together with the information which the parties must exchange and the timetable to which the parties must adhere.

Preliminary notice

16.92

As soon as the claimant decides that there is a reasonable chance they will bring a claim, they should send a preliminary notice giving a brief outline of the claim and, if possible, a general indication of its financial value. The notice should ask the professional to inform their insurers immediately. The professional has 21 days to acknowledge the preliminary notice, but need not take any other action.

Letter of claim

16.93

When the claimant decides that there are grounds for a claim, following the gathering and review of the evidence, they should issue a letter of claim setting out a chronology of the relevant facts, the allegations against the professional, an explanation of how the alleged error caused the loss and an estimate of the financial loss. The letter should be accompanied by the documents which support the claim and, if available, any expert reports. The letter can also include requests for documents and other information. As with the preliminary notice, the professional has 21 days to acknowledge the letter of claim.

Letter of response

16.94

The professional must provide a letter of response within three months of receiving the letter of claim. The letter of response should clearly state whether liability is admitted either in full or partially or whether it is denied completely. If liability is denied, the letter should provide the professional's detailed response to each section of the claim, providing their own version of events if these are disputed. The professional should also enclose any further relevant documents and any available expert evidence.

16.95

It is important that each party sets out their case in the letter of claim and letter of response, and that they do not hold anything back for later court proceedings: if their statements of case in proceedings differ materially from those letters without a reasonable excuse, the court may impose sanctions.

Letter of settlement

16.96

If the professional wishes to offer a settlement at this stage to avoid further proceedings, the offer should be issued at the same time as letter of response.

Alternative dispute resolution (ADR)

16.97

During the protocol period the parties will be expected to consider ADR and to treat court proceedings as a last resort. There are various forms of ADR, including mediation, arbitration, early neutral evaluation by a third party, and independent adjudication.

16.98

Mention in the protocol is also made of Ombudsman schemes, but this will not include the Pensions Ombudsman, who has no jurisdiction to deal with professional negligence disputes.

16.99

The most popular form of ADR for substantial pensions negligence disputes is mediation: this is considered in more detail at **16.111–16.112**.

Stocktake

16.100

Where the protocol procedure has not resolved the dispute, the parties should undertake a further review of their respective positions. The parties should consider the matter and the evidence on both sides to see if proceedings can be avoided and to attempt to narrow the issues between them.

Court proceedings

16.101

Court proceedings may be issued if there is no letter of settlement and the professional completely denies the claims against them in their letter of response. However, where there is a partial acknowledgement of a claim, the parties are encouraged to continue negotiations without using court proceedings to reach an agreement, with the aim of agreeing a resolution of the claim within six months of the acknowledgment of the preliminary notice.

Corrective proceedings

16.102

As discussed in **16.57**(b), the professional may require the claimant to apply to court to correct the error, reserving the right to contend that the claimant will not have reasonably mitigated their loss if they fail to do so. The claimant should, in such circumstances, demand that the professional indemnify them for the costs of such an application, perhaps in return for the professional being given an opportunity to see important documents and comment on key stages in the process. In turn, the defendant may seek to demand, as a condition for paying the costs of the corrective proceedings, that it has a say as to the legal team which prosecutes those proceedings.

16.103

If the claimant is in any event intending to bring a corrective application in parallel with negligence proceedings, they should seriously consider keeping the professional responsible for the mistake informed of its progress and allowing them some degree of involvement, to lessen the risk of a subsequent allegation of failure to mitigate if the application is unsuccessful or is compromised. An invitation to the professional to set out any arguments they would wish to advance in the application has the added advantage of giving the claimant a fresh perspective on the corrective process.

16.104

The risk of an allegation of failure to mitigate may be removed altogether by obtaining the agreement of the professional to be bound by the outcome of the corrective application. In extremis, the claimant may seek to have the professional formally bound, either by joining them to the proceedings[1] or by serving the proceedings on them pursuant to CPR 19.8A.[2] However the formal substantive role which the professional will have in the application may cause practical problems, such as if the professional wishes to play an active role in negotiations for the compromise of the corrective application.

1 This occurred in *Shannan v Viavi Solutions UK Ltd*: [2016] EWHC 1530 (Ch), [2016] Pens LR 193 at [3].
2 Chancery Guide, para 29.92.

Litigation

The venue

16.105

A claim for negligence will usually be commenced in the High Court, by way of Part 7 proceedings.

The claimants

16.106

Although the orthodox view is that the loss caused by an increase in liabilities is suffered by the employer,[1] it is usual for the claim to be brought by both the employer and the trustees. This ensures that the claim does not fail because either the person who has suffered the loss or the person to whom the duty is owed is not amongst the claimants.

1 See **16.19**.

16.107

If there is a risk that the costs of the proceedings may fall on the trustees, they should not commence proceedings unless they have obtained *Beddoe* directions from the court,[1] permitting them to take their costs, and any costs they are ordered to pay, out of the assets of the scheme. The need for such an order, which can be costly and time-consuming to obtain, can be avoided if the employer provides the trustees with an indemnity for those costs, although the trustees will need to be satisfied that the employer can meet any claim under the indemnity.

1 See **14.108**.

The defendant

16.108

Care must be taken to identify the correct defendant, as the professional who was responsible for the mistake may have since changed identity by reason of subsequent reorganisations or liability for its conduct may have transferred to another entity within the group. The pre-action protocol process should be used to ensure that there is no subsequent dispute as to the correct identity of the defendant.

Pleading the claim

16.109

It is important to ensure that the case against the professional is pleaded as clearly and as thoroughly as possible. In *Andrews v Messer Beg Ltd*,[1] a failure properly to plead an assumption of a duty of care against a professional led to the claim against them being struck out.

1 [2018] EWHC 2692 (Ch), [2019] PNLR 476.

Summary judgment

16.110

Because of the general requirement for expert evidence to establish the appropriate standard required of the profession in question, it is all but impossible to obtain summary judgment in professional negligence cases.[1] By contrast, summary judgment can be obtained in cases where the sole issue is the extension of the limitation period pursuant to s 14A of LA 1980 or by reason of deliberate concealment, if there is no dispute of primary fact. The court should, however, be wary of doing so where there were reasonable grounds for believing that a fuller investigation might produce a different outcome.[2]

1 *Sciortino v Beaumont* [2021] EWCA Civ 786, [2021] Ch 365.
2 *Davy v 01000654 Ltd* [2018] EWHC 353 (QB).

Mediation

16.111

Almost all pensions professional negligence cases are settled before getting to court – usually, where the loss is substantial, through mediation. The advantages of a relatively swift, confidential and non-adversarial approach to the resolution of such disputes, involving an area of law in which there is little decided authority, are obvious. Moreover, the court expects the parties to have seriously attempted to settle their dispute before proceeding to trial, and will regularly make space in the litigation timetable for ADR to take place.[1]

1 Indeed, the Court of Appeal has gone further, and required parties to attend early neutral evaluation without requiring their consent: *Lomax v Lomax* [2019] EWCA Civ 1467, [2019] 1 WLR 6527.

16.112

When preparing for a mediation of a pensions dispute, the following points should be borne in mind:

(a) There is little point to mediating in a factual or legal vacuum. It is therefore important to ensure that at least the relevant documents are disclosed in advance. Whilst it would also be preferable for crucial witness evidence to be provided, and for any liability and quantum issues requiring expert evidence to be either dealt with beforehand or be the subject of disclosed reports, those steps may need to be sacrificed if mediation at an early stage of the process is deemed to be more important.

(b) Carefully consider the identity of the mediator: whilst it may be helpful if the mediator has specialist pensions knowledge – particularly where the case involves technical issues – it is more important that they have experience of dealing with professional negligence disputes generally.[1]

(c) The persons within the organisations involved who have the authority to compromise the case must either be at the mediation or be available to be contacted during the mediation at short notice.

(d) The parties should exchange position statements in advance dealing with the relevant legal issues. It is often important that those statements recognise any weaknesses in the parties' own cases, taking advantage of the privileged nature of the mediation process. This is likely to earn the trust of the mediator and encourage all parties to adopt a realistic attitude to the mediation.

(e) If the parties are to meet at the beginning of the mediation (a so-called 'plenary session'), this meeting should focus on the issues which need to be dealt with to compromise the claim: it should not be used as an opportunity for the clients to vent their anger and frustration, or for the lawyers to display their oratorical skills.

(f) Do not give up hope of settlement just because the parties fail to reach agreement at the mediation itself. Often parties will reflect on the merits of their positions in the following days, and be receptive to further approaches: a good mediator will continue to be active during this period, and not let the parties simply dive straight back into the litigation.

(g) Even if the mediation does not achieve a settlement of the case, it will rarely prove to have been a waste of time: the parties' positions will have had the benefit of being scrutinised by an impartial but sophisticated mediator; and each party should emerge with a better understanding of the merits of their opponent's claims, and what non-legal considerations are driving their conduct of the litigation.

1 A list of members of the Association of Pension Layers who are willing to mediate pensions disputes is kept on the Association's website: http://www.apl.org.uk/mediators.

17 Tax

17.1

The correction of pensions mistakes will have potential tax consequences principally in four situations:

(a) overpayment of benefits;

(b) underpayment of benefits;

(c) mistakes in transfer payments; and

(d) the retrospective operation of orders in claims for rectification or setting aside the exercise of scheme powers.

Mistaken overpayments

17.2

Overpayments of pension instalments or lump sum benefits, even those made in error, are prima facie unauthorised member payments. However, there are circumstances in which overpayments will not be treated as such by HMRC, which are considered below. These apply to cases of overpayments due to genuine errors on the part of the trustees: they are not intended to cover payments which were deliberately intended to be made at a particular level, but where the trustees subsequently changed their minds because of unforeseen fiscal or other consequences of those payments.

Recovered overpayments

17.3

HMRC will not treat an inadvertent payment as an unauthorised payment where:

(a) the payment was made in genuine error, such that there was no intention to make a payment to that extent or at all;

(b) the erroneous payment was spotted by someone involved with the management of the scheme (or the recipient of the payment or the recipient's adviser might have brought the matter to the attention of the scheme managers); and

(c) the error is rectified and the overpaid sum repaid as soon as reasonably possible.[1]

The legal basis for this view is unclear, and probably constitutes a concession on the part of HMRC. To rely on it, the error in question must be of a type falling squarely within the scope of what HMRC identifies as a 'genuine error'.[2]

1 PTM146100. See also *Clark v HMRC* [2020] EWCA Civ 204, [2020] 1 WLR 3354 at [86] per Henderson LJ.

2 PTM146200. The examples given by HMRC are principally based on mechanical/administrative errors rather than legal or factual misunderstandings by the trustees.

17.4

Further consequences of recovering overpayments for the trustees may include the correction of the original lifetime allowance (LTA) calculation, the reclamation of excess withheld income tax payments and the recovery of any overpaid element of pension commencement lump sums.

Unrecovered overpayments

17.5

Overpayments will be exempt from being treated as unauthorised payments, even where they are not repaid, if they come within Parts 3 and 4 of the Registered Pension Schemes (Authorised Payments) Regulations 2009[1] (Authorised Payments Regulations):

(a) reg 13 exempts a pension payment made in error where it represented a payment which was permitted by the scheme and the trustees believed that the recipient was entitled to the payment;

(b) if, however, the error relates to the recipient having died, for example because the overpayment occurred due to the trustees not being aware of the death, reg 15 exempts that payment only if:

  (i) it is paid no later than six months after the member's death; and

  (ii) the trustees either did not know of the death before the payment was made, and could not reasonably have been expected to have known, or they did know of the death before the payment was made, and took all reasonable steps to prevent the payment being made;

(c) reg 14 exempts a pension payment made in error even after the error is discovered, provided that:

  (i) the trustees took reasonable steps to prevent the payment being made; or

  (ii) the payment was made while the trustees were considering whether the scheme rules should be amended to permit the payment, provided the trustees have not taken an unreasonable amount of time to decide; or

(iii) the payment was made while the trustees were in the process of amending the scheme rules to permit the payment, provided the trustees have not taken an unreasonable amount of time to amend the rules;

(d) regs 17 and 18 provide for similar exemptions for mistaken payments of pension commencement lump sums made in excess of the permitted maximum.[2]

1 SI 2017/397.
2 See PTM063260.

17.6

Even where the Authorised Payments Regulations do not apply, and the trustees are unwilling or unable to recover the mistaken overpayment, HMRC applies a *de minimis* threshold and will not seek to collect tax on any overpayments which do not exceed £250.[1]

1 PTM146300.

17.7

In the case of a member who was overpaid a pension due to the maladministration of the scheme's administrator, the Pensions Ombudsman has determined that any tax liability which arose because of the non-application of the Authorised Payments Regulations is to be met by the administrator.[1]

1 *Mr Alan John* (PO-351, 28 May 2013). See also *Mr M Williams* (PO-4814, 22 July 2015).

Overpayments of contributions

17.8

The mistaken overpayment of pension contributions by or in respect of a member may result in the member exceeding their LTA or losing their enhanced or fixed protection.[1] The member cannot avoid that consequence by arguing that the contribution did not constitute a 'payment' for the purposes of FA 2004.[2]

1 See **17.18**.
2 *Clark v HMRC* [2020] EWCA Civ 204, [2020] 1 WLR 3354.

17.9

However, in *Hymanson v HMRC*,[1] the First-Tier Tax Tribunal was prepared to ignore a mistaken overpayment of contributions for the purposes of the fixed protection legislation, where those payments would have been set aside by the court on the basis of mistake.[2] Even though the Tribunal did not have jurisdiction to grant that relief, it was prepared to regard it as having been granted, by applying the equitable maxim to treat 'that which ought to have been done as having been done'.[3]

1 *Hymanson v HMRC* [2018] UKFTT 667 (TC).
2 This remedy is discussed in **Chapter 7**.
3 See **8.2**.

17.10

When making such an application to the Tribunal, it is important that the member has evidence that the recipient of the overpayment is prepared to reimburse the overpaid contributions: in *Hymanson v HMRC*,[1] the recipient said that it would be prepared to do so, provided that HMRC would assure them that the repayment would not be treated as an unauthorised payment, which the judge considered to be well within HMRC's gift.

1 [2018] UKFTT 667 (TC) at [86].

Mistaken underpayments

Pensions tax consequences of correcting pension underpayments

Authorised payments

17.11

If an authorised scheme pension was underpaid, either at its inception or since it had come into payment, the provision of an increase to correct the underpayment can be treated as a late instalment of that authorised pension.

17.12

If, however, the underpayment relates to an element of pension which had not crystallised at the date it was required to be paid, the payment of the arrears relating to the period prior to crystallisation does not constitute an authorised payment. In that situation, the payment of arrears, insofar as it constitutes taxable pension income,[1] can be treated as an authorised payment pursuant to reg 2 of the Registered Pension Schemes (Authorised Payments – Arrears of Pension) Regulations 2006.[2]

1 Pursuant to s 579B of the Income Tax (Earnings and Pensions) Act 2003 (ITEPA 2003).
2 SI 2006/614.

17.13

To qualify, the payment must not exceed the amount accrued during the period ending with the date on which the member became entitled to the pension ('the actual start date') and beginning with the earliest date from which the member could, at the actual start date, have required the trustees, under the scheme rules, to make a payment of arrears of pension.[1]

1 Regulation 2(2) of the Registered Pension Schemes (Authorised Payments – Arrears of Pension) Regulations 2006. Where a member has died before those arrears are paid, the payment of those arrears will be authorised if they comply with reg 16 of the Authorised Payments Regulations: see PTM062800.

Calculation of LTA

17.14

The amount of the member's individual LTA is tested on each benefit crystallisation event (BCE) occurring in relation to the member. When an entitlement to benefit arises which is a BCE, the amount crystallised is measured against the individual's available LTA: if the former exceeds the latter, an LTA charge is due.

17.15

Where a pension has come into payment – classified as a BCE2 – an increase to make good an underpayment of that pension might be treated as:

(a) an upwards adjustment to the BCE2, which occurred when the member originally became entitled to the payment of the pension; or

(b) a new benefit, triggering a separate BCE2 when the underpayment is corrected.

17.16

Both approaches raise challenges in practice:

(a) under the former approach, the LTA calculation carried out at retirement will need to be re-run using the corrected pension amount: any resulting LTA charge will not result in a reduction to a pension in payment but will need to be paid out of post-tax income;

(b) the latter approach will require a new LTA calculation when the new pension is brought into payment, although it might (unlike the former approach) permit a second pension commencement lump sum to be paid. However, as the LTA has decreased since 2012, a member's LTA on the date of the second BCE2 might be lower than at retirement under this approach, resulting in a higher LTA charge than under the former approach.

17.17

In February 2020, HMRC issued guidance on the consequences for lifetime and annual allowances of the requirement to equalise guaranteed minimum pensions (GMPs) following the *Lloyds Bank* litigation.[1] That guidance states that increases solely referable to GMP equalisation are to be treated under the former approach identified in **17.16** but, where other adjustments are involved, that may give rise to a new BCE.[2]

1 GMP Equalisation Newsletter dated 20 February 2020.
2 GMP Equalisation Newsletter dated 20 February 2020, para 5.2.

Fixed and enhanced protection

17.18

A member with fixed or enhanced protection from the LTA charge will lose the benefit of that protection if, after the protection date, any contributions are made to a defined contribution (DC) scheme or further benefits accrue in a defined benefits (DB) scheme above a prescribed level of indexation.

17.19

If the increase in benefits caused by the correction of a past underpayment is treated as a pre-existing entitlement which should have been included in the calculation of the member's pre-protection date benefits all along, the member will not lose their protection, as the date of accrual was before the protection was obtained and so does not constitute a contribution or benefit accrual for these purposes. If, however, the increase is treated as a contribution or benefit accrual as at the date of the increase, the member will lose protection where the payment exceeds the permitted increase in accrual.

17.20

HMRC's February 2020 guidance comments on the effect of payments referable to GMP equalisation on fixed and enhanced protection as follows:

(a) a member who otherwise has fixed protection should retain that protection: any increase solely for GMP equalisation will not be benefit accrual and so should not result in loss of fixed protection, but if the reason for the increase is a mixture of GMP equalisation and other adjustments, then fixed protection could be lost;[1]

(b) for individuals who have been deferred members since before 6 April 2006 any GMP equalisation benefit adjustments should not be relevant benefit accrual for enhanced protection purposes; but other deferred members will have accrued benefits that with any GMP adjustments may result in relevant benefit accrual: when carrying out the relevant accrual calculations, the value of the member's rights under the scheme as at 5 April 2006 must include the adjustment for GMP equalisation valued at that date.[2]

It remains to be seen whether this guidance will apply to increases to make good underpaid benefits more generally.

1 GMP Equalisation Newsletter dated 20 February 2020, para 4.1.
2 GMP Equalisation Newsletter dated 20 February 2020, para 4.3.

Annual allowance

17.21

An annual allowance charge is payable where the amount of the member's contributions to a DC scheme or accruals in a DB scheme over the 'pension input period' (now aligned with the tax year) exceeds that year's annual allowance.

17.22

If the increases to benefits are properly treated as having accrued at the date in the past on which the legal entitlement arose, they will be taken into account in the past pension input period in which the entitlement to the increase arose; otherwise, the increases will be treated as having occurred in the pension input period in which the increase came into payment. The effect of those outcomes on the tax liability of the member will turn on the annual allowance available to the member for the input period in question and what other contributions or accrual had been made to the member's benefits during that period.

17.23

HMRC's February 2020 guidance states that, in relation to the effect on annual allowances of benefit increases following GMP equalisation, there is no need to revisit pension input amount calculations done in the past: calculations for the pension input amount in the tax year of implementing GMP equalisation and tax years thereafter will need to take into account the revised amount of the benefit entitlement in the relevant benefit calculations.[1] Again, it remains to be seen whether HMRC's concession in respect of past calculations will be applied to corrections of underpaid benefits more generally.

1 GMP Equalisation Newsletter dated 20 February 2020, para 3.3.

Ill-health pensions

17.24

Ill-health pensions are only authorised payments where the trustees have received evidence of the requisite incapacity from a registered medical practitioner immediately before the member became entitled to the benefit under the scheme.[1]

1 Section 165(1) (Pension rule 1) and para 1(a) of Sch 28 to FA 2004.

17.25

Where the right to ill-health benefits was terminated in error, their reinstatement long after the member in question has left service may cause practical difficulties, as the trustees will not have received evidence of incapacity at the material time, because the member would not at that time have been aware of their entitlement to such a benefit.

Interest payments

17.26

Any interest paid to members on the arrears of unpaid pensions will constitute an authorised scheme administration member payment,[1] if it is made on an arm's length, commercial basis.[2]

1 Section 171 of FA 2004. PTM143100 gives as an example of a scheme administration member payment, interest payable in respect of the late payment of a monthly instalment of benefit.

2 Section 171(2) of FA 2004.

Pensions tax consequences of underpaid lump sum benefits

17.27

Lump sums are potentially unauthorised payments where they are paid in such a way as not to conform to the applicable payment conditions. This section considers how those conditions are affected by the underpayment of the lump sum, and what constraints are imposed by those conditions on payments made to correct the error.

17.28

In July 2020, HMRC issued guidance on the tax treatment of additional lump sum payments payable in the light of the requirement to equalise GMPs:[1] again, whilst this guidance does not expressly apply beyond the specific context of GMPs, it may provide some indication of HMRC's approach to underpaid lump sums more generally.

1 GMP Equalisation Newsletter dated 16 July 2020.

Underpaid lump sums

The requirement to extinguish rights

17.29

The underpayment of a lump sum potentially infringes the requirement, applicable to a number of types of lump sum benefit, that the payment extinguishes the member's or dependant's rights under the scheme.[1] The underpaid lump sum does not prima facie comply with that requirement, as the member retains a right to payment by the scheme of the unpaid balance.

1 Namely, serious ill health lump sums, trivial commutation lump sums, small lump sums paid under either reg 11 or 12 of the Authorised Payments Regulations, winding-up lump sums, trivial commutation lump sum death benefits and winding-up lump sum death benefits.

17.30

HMRC's July 2020 guidance states that the requirement to extinguish the entitlement to benefits applies to all the benefits or rights that could reasonably have been known about at the time of the payment: the lump sum will accordingly not stop being an authorised payment purely because, due to GMP equalisation, further entitlement is later identified that the trustees could not reasonably have known about at the time of the lump sum payment. However, the guidance states that this analysis reflects the exceptional circumstances associated with GMPs: it is therefore unclear whether HMRC would apply the same analysis to underpaid lump sums generally.

Payment limits

17.31

Limits are imposed on the amount payable in respect of several lump sum payments.[1] For most of these payments, the limits apply to the amount of lump sum actually paid, so that any subsequent payment to make good an underpayment will not stop the lump sum from being authorised, provided that that payment would not cause the limit to be exceeded. The exception to this is the trivial commutation lump sum, as its limit is based on the value of the member's rights under all registered pension schemes on the day nominated by the member, which must be no more than three months before the first trivial commutation lump sum payment.[2] If, as a result of the subsequent payment, the value of the member's rights on the nominated date is more than the relevant limit, the original lump sum payment cannot be a trivial commutation lump sum, and it will be unauthorised unless the lump sum can meet the payment conditions for another type of authorised payment, such as a small lump sum.[3]

1 Namely, trivial commutation lump sums, small lump sums, winding-up lump sums, trivial commutation lump sum death benefits and winding-up lump sum death benefits.

2 Paragraph 7(1)(b) and (3) of Sch 29 to FA 2004: If the member does not make a nomination, the nominated date is the date of payment of the first trivial commutation lump sum from any registered pension scheme.

3 See **17.39**.

Correcting underpaid lump sums

17.32

Whether or not a lump sum payment is authorised depends on whether the payment conditions that applied at the time of the payment have been met. Thus, any future payments made to correct underpaid lump sums must satisfy the payment conditions in force at the time the payment is made, not at the date of the original payment. HMRC's July 2020 guidance confirms that any top-up payment is taxable in the tax year that the payment is made, not the date of the original payment.

17.33

For certain types of lump sum to be authorised payments, they must be paid to the member.[1] HMRC's July 2020 guidance confirms that any payment to top up those lump sums, made after the member's death to their estate or to any other person, will not be an authorised payment.

1 Namely, pension commencement lump sums, serious ill health lump sums, trivial commutation lump sums and winding-up lump sums.

Pension commencement lump sums

17.34

A payment only qualifies as a pension commencement lump sum if it is paid before the expiry of one year after the date the member becomes entitled to it.[1] It might therefore be argued that a payment made to a member to compensate for an underpaid lump sum after the expiry of that period will not be an authorised payment; and this argument is supported by HMRC's July 2020 guidance.

1 Paragraph 1(1)(c) of Sch 29 to FA 2004.

17.35

However, it may also be argued that payment of the full amount of lump sum is made where the payer intended the payee to receive the correct amount, even though part of that amount had been inadvertently retained by the payer, as the payee had an immediate right to the transfer of the balance. Whether a court will give an extended meaning to 'payment' in this way is uncertain: of some relevance in this respect is *Clark v HMRC*,[1] in which the Court of Appeal held that the question of whether a payment is made for FA 2004 purposes is to be answered by looking at the practical business reality of the transaction.

1 [2020] EWCA Civ 204, [2020] 1 WLR 3354 at [82] per Henderson LJ.

17.36

HMRC's July 2020 guidance states that, where the payment of a further pension commencement lump sum is possible, the relevant BCE (BCE6) will need to be recalculated, and a revised BCE statement given to the member.

Serious ill health lump sums

17.37

The top-up payment referable to this lump sum must satisfy the following conditions:[1]

(a) the payment must be to the member;

(b) it must be in respect of an uncrystallised arrangement; and

(c) it must extinguish the member's benefit entitlement under that arrangement.[2]

1 Paragraph 4 of Sch 29 to FA 2004.
2 A member may have a number of different arrangements under a scheme, as the scheme may use different arrangements to provide different types or tranches of benefit: this requirement relates to the arrangement in question, not to the scheme.

Trivial commutation lump sums

17.38

The top-up payment referable to this lump sum must satisfy the following conditions:[1]

(a) the payment must extinguish the member's rights under the scheme; and

(b) the payment must be made within a period of 12 months, beginning with the day the member is first paid a trivial commutation lump sum by any registered pension scheme.

Thus, no further payment can be made if any registered pension scheme paid a trivial commutation lump sum to a member more than 12 months previously.

1 Paragraph 7(1) and (2) of Sch 29 to FA 2004.

Small lump sums

17.39

Regulations 11 and 12 of the Authorised Payments Regulations authorise lump sum payments of up to £10,000. These payments do not have to be made to the member, and there is no period within which the payment must be made. Trustees may therefore consider using this to make good the underpayment of other lump sums which cannot otherwise satisfy the relevant payment conditions.

DB lump sum death benefit

17.40

Prior to 6 April 2016, where the member concerned was aged under 75 when they died, this lump sum was only authorised if it was paid within two years of the date the trustees either knew or could reasonably have been expected to know of the member's death.[1] However, that condition was removed for lump sum payments made on or after 6 April 2016.[2] There are no other relevant conditions for the payment of this benefit, and so it may be suitable for topping up an underpaid dependant's scheme pension.

1 Paragraph 13(1)(c) of Sch 29 to FA 2004 (as originally enacted); and see PTM073100.
2 Section 21(8)(a) and (10) of the Finance (No 2) Act 2015. HMRC's July 2020 guidance mistakenly refers to the two-year payment condition as still applicable.

Trivial commutation lump sum death benefit

17.41

There is no time limit for paying this type of lump sum. It may therefore also be suitable for topping up an underpaid dependant's scheme pension.[1]

1 See PTM073700 for the conditions for the payment of this lump sum benefit.

Income tax treatment of pension arrears

Basis of assessment

17.42

There are two bases on which a payment of arrears of pension can be assessed for income tax purposes:

(a) the cash basis, by which the member accounts for, and is taxed on, the payment in the tax period when it is actually received; and

(b) the accruals basis, by which the member accounts for, and is taxed on, the payment in the tax period in which it became payable, irrespective of whether it was actually paid in that period.

17.43

Typically, the member will receive the compensation payment in a single lump sum, even if that payment represents a number of years of underpayment. If the member had to account for that payment on the cash basis, it is possible that the level of payment would be such as to take their income into the higher or additional rate bands, which would not have happened had those payments been made at the correct time or times.[1] The member may therefore claim an increase in their compensation.

1 Damages payable by way of compensation are to be treated as the top slice of the claimant's income for tax purposes: *Lyndale Fashion Manufacturers v Rich* [1973] 1 WLR 73, 79 per Orr LJ; and see s 404A(1) of ITEPA 2003.

17.44

However, HMRC's position is that a member who has received a lump sum to make good an underpayment can account for it on the accruals basis, by supplying HMRC with a schedule showing the years to which underpayments are attributable; the members would then be taxed on those specified amounts only in each year to which the allocated amount relates, with underpayments in the earlier years being set off against the resulting overpayment in the year of the lump sum payment.[1] The member cannot in this situation claim the benefit of the four-year time limit for the issuing of an income tax assessment,[2] as where the payment is received in a tax year subsequent to that for which it is assessable, the time limit runs from when the payment was received rather than the notional year of assessment.[3]

1 HMRC Manual EIM74103. This position is consistent with both tax legislation and case law: see s 579B of ITEPA 2003 and *Re Houghton Main Colliery Co Ltd* [1956] 1 WLR 1219, 1225 per Wynn-Parry J.
2 Section 34 of the Taxes Management Act 1970.
3 Section 35 of the Taxes Management Act 1970.

17.45

In theory, the allocation of the overpayments to past tax years exposes the member to the imposition of interest and penalty charges for late payment of tax on the underpaid benefits,[1] but there is no evidence of HMRC attempting to impose any such charges in that situation.

1 Schedule 56 to the Finance Act 2009.

17.46

It has been suggested that the payment of interest on arrears of pension benefits will be subject to income tax in the year in which it is eventually paid.[1]

1 PASA GMP Equalisation Working Group's Guidance Note on Tax Issues, version 1.0 (February 2021), para 6.3(c).

Incidence of taxation on compensation payments

17.47

As explained in **11.4**, the underpaid member has a direct claim against the trustees for repayment of the sums due under the scheme, by way of equitable compensation. Payments made as a result of such a claim will give rise to a requirement to take account of the incidence of taxation in calculating the amount to be paid to the member, by analogy with the *Gourley* principle.[1] This principle requires the court, in assessing the correct level of damages payable to a claimant, to take account of the tax which would have been payable on the monies the claimant would have received or retained but for the matter giving rise to the damages award.[2]

1 Named after the leading case of *British Transport Commission v Gourley* [1956] AC 185.
2 Cf. *Bartlett v Barclays Bank Trust Co Ltd (No 2)* [1980] Ch 515, 545, where Brightman LJ declined to apply the *Gourley* principle to a claim by beneficiaries for the restoration of trust assets by a defaulting trustee, on the basis that the beneficiaries were not yet entitled to a distribution of capital or income out of the trust estate.

17.48

The basic intention of the *Gourley* principle is to ensure that the claimant is in no better or worse position than if the wrong for which they are being compensated had not occurred. In the tax context, it operates to reduce the compensation where the monies represented by the compensation would have been diminished in the hands of the claimant by the incidence of taxation. Thus, if the compensation award is not subject to tax, but the monies represented by the compensation would have been subject to tax in the hands of the claimant, the court will reduce the award to take account of that tax charge. However, if the compensation award is subject to tax, the compensation will not be reduced, leaving it to be taxed following its receipt by the claimant.

17.49

Pension underpayments are not payable by way of damages or compensation, but represent late payments of pension benefits to which members were entitled under the pension scheme:[1] they therefore fall to be taxed as pension income under ss 567 and 579B of ITEPA 2003. Thus, because such payments are taxed as pension income in the hands of the member, the amount of benefit will not be reduced under the *Gourley* principle. This also means that the member will not be assessed for capital gains tax, as no such liability arises on a payment which is assessed to income tax.[2]

1 See **17.11**.
2 Section 37 of the Taxation of Chargeable Gains Act 1992.

Payment of costs

17.50

Where a member receives their legal costs in respect of a compensation claim, whether those costs are agreed or are ordered, they are not taxable in the hands of the member as employment income.[1]

1 *Murphy v HMRC* [2021] UKUT 152 (TCC), [2021] STC 1404 at [77]–[78] per Michael Green J.

Correcting underpayments pursuant to a compromise

17.51

The tax treatment of lump sums paid under a compromise to members who had been wrongly deprived of benefits will depend on whether those sums are to be treated as a benefit which accrued to the member at the time it ought to have been paid, or as a new benefit which accrued at the time the compromise was agreed and approved.

17.52

Where the former argument is to the advantage of members, it will be easier to maintain if:

(a) the terms of the compromise are drafted so that both the arrears and future payments accurately reflect the lost benefits; and

(b) the court which approves the compromise declares that the compromise treats the entitlement to those benefits as if it arose in the past.

17.53

The first of those requirements will be satisfied where the compromise replicates the lost benefits. However, it is more likely that the compromise will give members only a percentage of those benefits, to reflect the parties' assessment of the merits of the claim. Such an outcome may make it more difficult to contend that the payments should be treated as having accrued prior to the agreement and approval of the compromise.

Unauthorised payments

17.54

The pensions tax consequences of the payment of a lump sum reflecting the arrears owing to the member as an authorised payment are dealt with at **17.27–17.41**.

17.55

The date on which the payment is treated as having been made is relevant where the payment relates to an element of pension which had not crystallised at the date it was required to be paid, so that reliance must be placed on the Registered Pension Schemes (Authorised Payments – Arrears of Pension) Regulations 2006.[1] If the right to the payment is treated as being first acquired at the date of the compromise, that payment will not be an authorised payment, because the 'actual start date' and the date on which the member could have required the arrears to be paid will be the same. However, if the proper legal effect of the compromise is to treat the member as having always been entitled to that benefit, the arrears payment will be authorised.

1 See **17.12–17.13**.

17.56

In any event, HMRC may theoretically argue that the effect of the compromise is that the members have surrendered the benefits to which they were entitled under the scheme, either wholly or to the extent not represented by the percentage of the benefit payable under the compromise: such a surrender would constitute an unauthorised payment to the member.[1]

1 Section 172A of FA 2004. However, a bona fide compromise of a pensions dispute was held in *HR Trustees Ltd v German* [2010] EWCA Civ 1349, [2011] ICR 329 not to constitute a surrender of benefits for the purposes of s 91 PA 1995: see **15.17**.

HMRC's position

17.57

HMRC will not be a party to the claim being compromised; nor will it be a party or privy to the compromise. Thus, even if the court approving the compromise declares that the entitlement to the new or increased benefits is to be treated as if it arose in the past, HMRC is not bound to accept the tax consequences of such a declaration, and may contend that the benefits are to be treated as if they took effect when the compromise was made and approved, should that result in higher tax charges.

17.58

Despite this, HMRC's past attitude to the treatment of benefits payable under a compromise has been that, if the compromise is genuine and results in the members being treated as a matter of law as having always been entitled to the benefits, HMRC will accept the tax consequences that flow as a result.

17.59

HMRC's stance is consistent with the principle that a compromise of factual issues involved in a claim is as binding as a decision of the court to that effect.[1] Thus, in *A-G v Trustees of the British Museum*,[2] a term in a compromise whereby the museum agreed that it had never been entitled to an artefact meant that it was to be treated as not having been the owner of the artefact for the purposes of legislation concerning treatment of the artefact.

1 See *Binder v Alachouzos* [1972] 2 QB 151.
2 [2005] EWHC 1089 (Ch), [2005] Ch 397.

Cash payments to members

17.60

Parties to a claim may consider structuring the compromise so that members are compensated for lost pension benefits by the payment of a lump sum, either by the trustees or the employer, in lieu of the benefits which are the subject of the claim. It is highly likely that, whatever the position is regarding other methods of compensation, the payment of cash to members will constitute unauthorised payments, irrespective of whether they are made from the assets of the scheme or by the employer.

17.61

To constitute an authorised payment, '*a payment by a registered pension scheme to or in respect of a person who is or has been a member of the pension scheme*' must be authorised by s 164 of FA 2004.[1] A cash payment by the trustees of the scheme which does not represent actual arrears of pension does not fall within any of the categories of payments authorised by that provision.

1 Section 160(2)(a) of FA 2004; s 160(2)(b) of FA 2004 also provides for payments to be treated as unauthorised payments where they fell within ss 172–174A of FA 2004, although these only apply where the member does something as a condition of receiving the compensation (but see **17.56**).

17.62

Cash payments made by the employer in the same circumstances may be treated in the same way as if made by the trustees, as the concept of '*payment by a registered pension scheme*' extends to a payment made by a third party '*in connection with an investment … acquired using sums or assets held for the purposes of a registered pension scheme*'.[1] There is arguably a sufficient connection between the cash payment by the employer and an investment held for the purposes of the scheme, where that payment represents lost pension benefits which would have been funded by payments made into the scheme by the employer.

1 Sections 279(2) and 161(3)(4) of FA 2004. See *Danvers v HMRC* [2016] UKUT 569 (TCC); [2017] STC 555.

Excluding affected members

17.63

One method of avoiding any adverse tax consequences for members because of the terms of the compromise is to include a term that any member whose receipt of compensation under the compromise would have adverse or disproportionate tax consequences is to be excluded from its terms.[1]

1 Such a provision may be necessary where it is not possible to tell at the time of the compromise whether members will lose out as a result of the payments, as (for example) the trustees and employer may not be aware of which members have obtained fixed or enhanced protection from the LTA charge.

17.64

Such a provision may call into question the ability of the court to conclude that the compromise is for the benefit of all the represented persons, which is a prerequisite for approval of the compromise of a claim in which a party is acting as a representative.[1] Where the scheme is in deficit, one way in which the court may be persuaded that the compromise is for the benefit of a member excluded from its terms, is to argue that the member benefits by avoiding any further detriment to the solvency of the scheme by requiring the claim to go all the way to trial.

1 CPR 19.7(6): see **15.20**.

Mistakes in transfer payments

Overpayments

17.65

A transfer payment will be authorised as a recognised transfer pursuant to s 169(1) of FA 2004 where the sums or assets being transferred are held prior to the transfer for the purposes of, or represent accrued rights under, a registered pension scheme and are transferred so as to become held for the purposes of, or to represent rights under, another scheme. The fact that the transfer is overpaid probably does not of itself give rise to any unauthorised payment charges, as the transfer payment still represents the member's entitlement under the scheme.

17.66

It is possible that an excessive transfer payment may cause the member to lose the benefit of any fixed protection where, if the transfer was otherwise permitted, the sums or assets transferred are not actuarially equivalent before and after the transfer.[1]

1 Paragraph 12(7)(c) of Sch 36 to FA 2004.

17.67

The tax treatment of the repayment of the overpaid element of the transfer to the transferring scheme depends upon whether the member has crystallised benefits in the receiving arrangement and how the reimbursement is to be paid:

(a) If the member has not crystallised any benefits in the receiving arrangement and reimbursement is made by a transfer back into the transferring scheme, there are not likely to be any tax implications, as that either does not contravene the requirements for a recognised transfer, or else is to be treated as a refund and so not a transfer at all.

(b) However, if the member has crystallised benefits in the receiving arrangement, reimbursement from the receiving arrangement's assets is made difficult by the requirement that the transfer must involve all the crystallised fund, held under a separate arrangement once it is received back into the transferring scheme,[1] and must be used to provide a pension with immediate effect.[2]

(c) If the member is able to reimburse the overpaid transfer in full from their own funds, there should be no tax implications for the member or the scheme, although the member may have had to make the payment from taxed income.

(d) However, if the member needs to draw sums from their pension to fund the reimbursement, that will give rise to income tax implications for the member. If this was done by way of an uncrystallised funds pension lump sum, 25 per cent of that sum would be tax free and 75 per cent subject to income tax.[3] However, if the funds are already crystallised, the entire payment would be subject to income tax.

1 Regulation 12(1) of the Registered Pension Schemes (Transfer of Sums and Assets) Regulations 2006 (SI 2006/499).
2 PTM053720, 062510, 072300, 072360, 104000, 107000.
3 Section 636A(1A) of ITEPA 2003.

Underpayments

17.68

An underpaid transfer payment satisfies the conditions for a recognised transfer set out in s 169(1) of FA 2004, as there is no requirement in that provision for the transfer to extinguish the member's entitlements under the transferring scheme.

17.69

HMRC has said that a partial transfer will be a recognised transfer '*if the scheme rules allow*',[1] which suggests that a mistaken transfer of less than the member's full rights will not be recognised where there is no express provision for a partial transfer. However, there is no requirement for such a provision in the legislative conditions for a recognised transfer.

1 PTM100010.

17.70

A partial transfer may in any event have certain tax consequences:[1]

(a) a partial transfer of a pension in payment will be an unauthorised payment; and

(b) a partial transfer may cause the member to lose (or have reduced) their LTA protection, scheme specific lump sum protection or pension age protection.

1 PTM100010.

Rectification and setting aside claims

17.71

An order of the court rectifying the provisions of a scheme will have retrospective effect.[1] In private trust cases, the motivation for rectification is often driven by tax considerations, where there is a concern that HMRC may tax the parties in accordance with the document as executed. Unless steps are taken to involve HMRC formally in the claim, it will not be bound by any order, and so could still seek to tax on the basis of the unrectified document.[2] In such situations, the practice has developed whereby the parties will ask HMRC whether it wishes to be joined to the rectification claim, and HMRC generally[3] agrees to be bound by the outcome of the claim, provided that the claimant agrees to draw the court's attention to certain authorities.[4]

1 See **6.1**.
2 *Yelkar Ltd v HMRC* [2016] UKFTT 663 (TC) at [64] per HHJ Clark.
3 But not always: see, for example, *Toronto Dominion Bank v Oberoi* [2002] EWHC 3216 (Ch), [2004] STC 1197.
4 The cases which HMRC wish to be cited are said anecdotally to be *Racal Group Services Ltd v Ashmore* [1995] STC 1151 and *Allnutt v Wilding* [2007] EWCA Civ 412, [2007] BTC 8003.

17.72

However, unlike in private trust cases, the principal purpose of pension scheme rectification claims is not to avoid tax, but to restore the benefit structure to how it had always been intended. Accordingly, no steps are ever taken to involve HMRC in a claim to rectify scheme documents. However, where rectification operates to reduce benefits which would have been payable to members under the unrectified document, HMRC has an interest in the outcome, as it will be deprived of tax payable on or following receipt of those benefits.[1] It is therefore theoretically open to HMRC to challenge a rectification order in the future if no approach is made to HMRC during the proceedings.

1 This assumes that at least some benefits which may be subject to a tax charge have accrued prior to the order being made: if that is not the case, the order will bind HMRC: *Re Sassoon* [1933] Ch 858, 893-894 per Romer LJ.

17.73

The same analysis applies where the exercise of a scheme power is set aside, on the grounds of equitable mistake or because of a decision error,[1] as the effect of such an order is that the transaction is treated as having never occurred.[2] In private trust cases, it is usual for HMRC to be notified of the claim to rescind the transaction, and for HMRC not to be joined as a party but to write to the claimant setting out its views and asking that those views be put before the court.[3] In such circumstances, the court is willing to take account of HMRC's views.[4] Again, in the pensions context no attempt is usually made to involve HMRC in the proceedings, so that HMRC is not bound by an order setting aside the transaction. However, in the limited situations in which inheritance tax charges apply to pension payments on the death of the recipient, no claim for tax can be made where the transfer has been set aside.[5]

1 See **Chapters 7** and **13**.
2 *Pitt v Holt* [2013] UKSC 26, [2013] 2 AC 108 at [130] per Lord Walker of Gestingthorpe.
3 *Wright v National Westminster Bank plc* [2014] EWHC 3158 (Ch), [2015] WTLR 547 at [9] per Norris J.
4 *Hartogs v Sequent (Schweiz) AG* [2019] EWHC 1915 (Ch), [2020] WTLR 505 at [4] per HHJ Hodge QC (sitting as a deputy High Court judge).
5 Section 150 of the Inheritance Tax Act 1984.

Practice point: liaising with HMRC

17.74

There is no statutory mechanism for HMRC to provide advance clearance or approval for any transaction which gives rise to potential pensions tax issues.

17.75

HMRC operates a non-statutory clearance service, but only where it considers that the transaction gives rise to genuine points of uncertainty and that the applicant is not asking for tax planning advice. Where the taxpayer is unsure which of two alternative analyses (one of which would result in less tax being paid) is correct – which is likely to be the case in an underpayment context when considering when the entitlement in question arose – it will be important to frame the application carefully so that HMRC does not conclude that the taxpayer is asking for tax planning advice.

17.76

Any application for non-statutory clearance requires the applicant to provide prescribed information about:

(a) the applicant and the application;

(b) the transaction to which the application relates; and

(c) information about legal points, including an explanation of why the applicant believes the application of the legislation is open to different possible interpretations, a summary of those different interpretations and an explanation of why the tax consequences are uncertain, including reference to HMRC published guidance and/or case law.[1]

Where an application is received, HMRC will provide a full response within 28 days, unless the application is very complex.[2]

1 Annex A to HMRC's Non-Statutory Clearance Service Guidance.
2 HMRC Internal Manual ONSCG2300.

17.77

The aim of the service is to give certainty, so that where the applicant's interpretation appears to be correct but is inconsistent with the policy intention underpinning the legislation, instead of providing clearance, HMRC will draw attention to the inherent risks in proceeding based on that interpretation.[1]

1 HMRC Internal Manual ONSCG5910, 5940, 6400.

17.78

In practice, HMRC does not consider that pensions tax issues arising on the compromise of a pensions claim give rise to genuine points of uncertainty, and its practice regarding the tax treatment of such compromises, referred to at **17.57–17.59**, is generally set out in a less formal way through correspondence with the parties to the claim.

Index

[all references are to paragraph number]